Wakefield Press

Dancing Before Storms

Robert (Bob) T. Harris is a well-known spokesperson for civil society and non-government organisations, and for many years represented them in a wide range of global institutions, including as former president of the Conferences of NGOs at the UN and UNESCO, secretary-general of the World Confederation of Organisations of the Teaching Profession (WCOTP), and chair of an OECD Working Group on education, training and employment policies.

In 1993, he co-founded Education International, which now represents more than 32 million educators in 178 countries.

A life member of the Australian Education Union, Bob regularly appears as an invited speaker on a range of education and public policy issues. He has edited and contributed to UNESCO, OECD and Education International Research Institute publications. In 2016, Bob and his wife, Yuko Matsuoka Harris, established the Swiss-based Magic Libraries Foundation to promote libraries for children in disadvantaged countries and regions, and to train translators in minority languages.

Dancing Before Storms

Five Revolutions
that Made Today's World

Robert T. Harris

Wakefield
Press

Wakefield Press
16 Rose Street
Mile End
South Australia 5031
www.wakefieldpress.com.au

First published 2022

Cover designed by Stacey Zass
Cover artwork by Jennifer Harris
Edited by Sheree Tirrell
Typeset by Michael Deves, Wakefield Press
Printed by Finsbury Green, Adelaide SA

ISBN 978 1 74305 868 8

NATIONAL
LIBRARY
OF AUSTRALIA

A catalogue record for this
book is available from the
National Library of Australia

CORIOLE
McLAREN VALE

Wakefield Press thanks
Coriole Vineyards for
continued support

Contents

Preface

The reader is invited to get ready for an express ride through modern history!

The story of five revolutions that shaped the modern world grew out of a simple question: Why do people in power and those who surround them so often ignore the signs of impending catastrophe? Hence the title – *Dancing Before Storms* – is both an assertion and a question.

I looked at the American and French revolutions of the late eighteenth century, then the revolutions that swept across Europe in the mid-nineteenth century, and the Chinese and Russian revolutions of the early twentieth century. Altogether, they spanned roughly 150 years.

Many accounts have been written about each of these events. I wanted to trace the links between them. By telling the personal stories of people who played key roles in these events, I have tried to give the reader a sense of the human factors behind the political decisions. I enjoyed including anecdotes in the story that show the human side of people. Hopefully, the reader will be intrigued by them, as I have been.

In this fast-paced narrative there will be names, places and events that may be familiar to the general reader. I have woven them into the broad sweep of history leading to the modern era. Notes are included on the social and economic conditions in each country, and I cross reference events occurring at the same time elsewhere in the world. A key point of this book is that the story is never about just one country's history. Inventions and ideas crossed land borders and oceans. Debates about governance and the participation of citizens accompanied major changes in rural communities, towns and cities as the industrial revolution proceeded. And, as literacy developed, people could read books, newspapers and pamphlets.

Finally, I felt deeply the relevance of the lessons of history for the world today. Jumping to the first twenty years of the current century was the most challenging part of writing this book. Events around the world keep highlighting the relevance of the simple question posed above. If ignoring the writing on the wall makes no rational sense, why does it still happen?

RTH

Acknowledgements

I am indebted to friends who took time to read parts of the text and responded with helpful comments. My motivation was maintained by those who found the concept of this book to be both ambitious and original. My thanks to John Bangs, Anthony Best, David Edwards, John Evans, Georges Malempré, Ron Pippett, Heather and John Riddell, Malcolm Skilbeck, Dennis Van Roekel and John West. A special word of gratitude to Laura Figazzolo, who helped me with research from the beginning of the project, and then with fact checking and illustrations, and to Sheree Tirrell, who brought her editing skills to bear with challenging and pertinent questions. Christine Chappuis, with her capacity to decipher my writing, typed many versions of the manuscript. My wife, Yuko, not only tolerated my frequent recounting of anecdotes about the lives of the main characters, but also offered critical and relevant commentary on the overall balance and structure of the narrative. I am grateful to them all. Any errors that remain are entirely my own.

Introduction

This is the story of five revolutions that changed the world over the period 1776 to 1918, and the multiple connections between them, prefiguring the course of events in this century.

The American and French revolutions of the late eighteenth century; the European Springtime of the Peoples of the mid-nineteenth century; and the Chinese and the Russian revolutions in the early twentieth century broadly shaped the contours of the world we know today. However, each of the nations that emerged from these tumultuous events tends to focus on its own history, with heroic portrayals of the main events and principal actors. The narratives of founding revolutions are taught in idealised and often nationalistic terms. The interactions between these great revolutions are often neglected or understated.

Key to a reframing of this narrative is an understanding of the influence of five active participants in the political struggles of the times, and of the women and men who were close to and supported, or opposed, them. These five individuals at the centre of the events leading up to the five revolutions – Benjamin Franklin, Jacques Necker, Alphonse de Lamartine, Kang You Wei, and Pyotr Stolypin – each exercised their considerable powers to try to change the course of events. Each saw the clouds on the horizon and tried, but failed, to prevent the storms of revolution.

Around these main characters there were many others. Like an epic novel or modern telenovela, the narratives twist and turn repeatedly, with interactions as dramatic as the events unfolding about them. But these were real people, not fictional characters, with complex personalities and eventful, and often complicated, personal lives.

Other uprisings and wars also changed the shape and fate of nations during this period. It is no coincidence that another type of revolution – the industrial – fundamentally altered the course of human affairs over the century-and-a-half between the American and Russian revolutions. The beginnings of the industrial revolution are generally set by historians around 1760 – which also happened to be the year when young George of Hanover became King George III of Britain. And none other than Benjamin Franklin, whose experiments with electricity made him one of the scientists who sparked the industrial revolution, was present at the coronation with his son.

With the unleashing of new technologies came dramatic expansion of trade across the oceans. Most of our main characters also travelled widely, as populations moved, both across borders and within countries, from the rural estates of feudal domains to crowded towns and cities. With new riches came new forms of exploitation. Yet education and literacy expanded across societies and the idea of liberty spread, as did the notion that the pursuit of happiness was a right for every person. The entire world was affected by these deep and fundamentally important changes, including the invention of the first telecommunications technology – the telegraph. The modern era was coming into being.

The story told here begins before the American Revolution of 1776, and continues through the French Revolution of 1789, just a few years later. These two events were closely linked through French intervention in the American War of Independence, which tipped the balance in favour of the rebels. The ideas that drove the American Revolution, in turn, inspired opposition to the absolute monarchy in France. These two revolutions overturned the established order – the global reach of the British Empire on the one hand and, on the other, the notion of rule by divine right on the continent of Europe.

The course of events was far from simple, however, as even after the Paris Peace Conference of 1783, the thirteen original American colonies struggled to agree on a constitution for their new nation. They finally adopted it, *in extremis*, in 1787, eleven years after their initial Declaration. The document left unsettled divisions that would erupt in the civil war of the next century, and new divisions emerge even as this book is being completed. In France, too, the revolution was followed by a decade of upheaval. Civil war, the Terror, the rise of a dictatorship, and later the Napoléonic wars, scarred and transformed Europe.

Half a century later, in 1848, these two earlier revolutions were the reference points for a new wave of revolutions that swept across Europe. For a time, they were called the Springtime of the Peoples. Feudal regimes fell, and some were replaced by constitutional monarchies. In France, a restored absolutist monarchy was replaced by a Citizen King, who was subsequently obliged to abdicate and make way for a Second Republic. Uprisings across Europe were then suppressed. The Second Republic was replaced by the Second Empire under Louis-Napoléon Bonaparte, the nephew of Napoléon. When later defeated by Prussia in 1870, France declared its Third Republic.

On the surface, the middle and late nineteenth century were times of growing prosperity. Victorian Britain expanded its empire anew. Immense fortunes were made on both sides of the Atlantic. Trade spread around the globe, as did colonial wars. Isolated Japan opened to the West, ended its shogunate and, from 1868, took the path to modernisation, just as the Suez Canal opened a more direct sea route between Europe and the Orient. Other events – notably the colonisation of Asia and Africa, and independence movements in Latin America – marked the rise and fall of worldwide empires, and geo-political changes altered maps and national boundaries.

In the western hemisphere, the United States of America also expanded and grew stronger, firstly with Jefferson's Louisiana Purchase from Napoléon, then after the discovery of gold in California in 1848. That same year, in London, in the very week of the uprising in France that sparked the revolutions across Europe, Karl Marx and Friedrich Engels published *The Communist Manifesto*. In 1889, a young student translated the *Manifesto* into Russian: he would become known to the world as Vladimir Ilyich Lenin.

In the Orient, the ancient civilization of China, once more advanced than Europe's, struggled to modernise. The Western powers imposed mercantile access under humiliating treaties. In 1898, attempts by China to reform as Japan had done, failed. By the turn of the century, uprisings across China became more frequent. Funds and agitators were sent in from Chinese emigrant communities around the world. The spark that finally lit the fuse of the Chinese Revolution of 1911 was a dispute over the ownership of railways. The dynasty that had inherited an empire dating back into the millennial mists of time was replaced by a republic.

At almost the same moment in 1911, the assassination of Russia's strongman reformer Pyotr Stolypin set the scene for a breakdown of the tsarist regime. Its fate was sealed by the grinding tragedy of the First World War and the accompanying massive loss of life. Early in 1917, the tsar abdicated and, after a brief interlude of reformist government, Lenin's revolutionary Bolsheviks prevailed.

The links described here between the five revolutions were multiple, forging the world as we know it today. To focus on these five revolutions helps us to trace the zig-zagging thread of history. Many people and events played key roles over this century-and-a-half, but in each of the countries at the centre of the five revolutions, there was a person of power and influence who saw the storms coming and tried to head them off by proposing reforms. Those five individuals, whose roles were particularly significant in the lead up to each of the revolutions, were:

Benjamin Franklin: Famous inventor and scientist, writer and publisher, civil servant and diplomat. He tried for years to persuade the government of King George III of Britain of the need to change its policies towards the American colonies. His warnings and proposals fell on deaf ears. In 1775, he returned to join the patriots of the American Revolution, befriended young Thomas Jefferson, and helped to draft the Declaration of Independence.

Franklin's personal drama was the relationship with his son, William. They were close for many years. Together they flew a kite into a storm over Philadelphia to draw lightning from the heavens, and demonstrated that it was static electricity. For years, the younger Franklin supported his father politically. But father and son eventually became bitter opponents in the epic struggle of the American Revolution.

Jacques Necker: Brilliant financier, successful business leader and prolific writer who, despite being a foreigner and a Protestant, rose to the top in the court of King Louis XVI of Catholic France. He took key decisions to ensure supply of cereals to the population of a nation in crisis. He sought consensus on finances with the nobles, the clergy and commoners when they met with the king at the General Estates, convened in Versailles in 1789. But he boycotted the king's speech, and his subsequent dismissal sparked the French Revolution of 1789.

His wife, Suzanne Curchod-Necker, founded the world's first hospital for children. Today the Necker hospital for children in Paris is world famous. Their only daughter, Germaine, later Madame de Staël, also played a major role in the events following the revolution, as a pan-European, an advocate for constitutional monarchy, and founder of the Romantic literary movement. The reach and influence of her salon was such that she became the nemesis of Napoléon Bonaparte.

Alphonse de Lamartine: Popular romantic poet, eminent historian and member of the Académie Française, independent politician. He became the key figure in the French Revolution of 1848, he wrote the declaration of the Second Republic and he proclaimed the tricolour flag which remains today. He was determined to avoid the excesses of the first revolution, but violence erupted once again in the streets of Paris. His dream of a peaceful revolution was shattered. The scene was set for the rise of Louis-Napoléon Bonaparte and the Second Empire.

Writing about the first French revolution, as well as his own experience of founding the Second Republic, Lamartine perceived earlier than most the tension between the liberal reform movement of the middle and upper classes and the grim opposition welling up among the labourers of the industrial revolution.

Kang You Wei: Confucian scholar and calligrapher, utopian philosopher open both to Buddhism and the modern technologies and ideas of the West. In 1898, he initiated the 100 Days Reform aiming to modernise China. But the return of the Dowager Empress, 'the Lady behind the screen', sent him into exile, fleeing the assassins of the regime. He became the most widely travelled Chinese personality of his time, writing extensively about the lessons to be drawn from other countries. His reform movement was overtaken by the revolutionaries of Sun Yat Sen. On New Year's Day in 1912, the republic was declared, putting an end to three millennia of Imperial rule in China.

Kang's daughter, Kang Tong Bi, the first Chinese woman to be educated in the United States, became a leading figure in the struggle for the emancipation of women in China.

Pyotr Stolypin: Aristocrat, agricultural reformer and authoritarian but effective provincial governor, tough anti-corruption fighter. He became prime minister of Russia and the most influential voice in the regime of Tsar Nicholas II. However, his political defeat in the Duma, followed by his assassination at the opera in Kiev, put an end to hopes for reform in Russia. Following the outbreak of the First World War, other reformers were swept aside, and the Bolsheviks of Vladimir Lenin took power in the revolution of October 1917.

The biography of Stolypin's daughter, Maria, provides an intimate insight into the life of a proud, yet tender, family man who tried to modernise a vast empire by the force of his will.

Around each of these *real* people, there were many others. The following narrative reveals their human side, and their many interactions. While the great novelists of the times brought history to life in their rich portrayals and accounts of *fictional* characters caught up in the events, some of these writers – Victor Hugo and Leo Tolstoy among them – were also active participants in contemporary political developments.

To help follow the stories of these historical characters who actually existed, we include a guide to all the people who figure in the narrative – the main actors, their partners and families, and many others. However, this book is not proposed as an academic work. The author has intentionally tried to make it accessible to a wider readership. At the same time, the narrative strives for accuracy, with fact checking and sources referenced wherever possible.

With today's interdependent world, it can only be helpful to understand more about how these five revolutions – these historical defining events – were linked. That is why we follow the thread of history. Each revolution had its own specifics, yet there were also remarkable parallels between them. We will explore whether those parallels can be found in today's global society.

History never precisely repeats itself, and history does not predict the future. Nevertheless, history provides lessons which may inform the present. One of those key lessons is to recognise that human beings have a great capacity for denial. Barbara Tuchman was one historian who influenced the author in developing the thread that runs through this narrative. Notably, Tuchman's *The March of Folly* highlighted how often, in human affairs, those in power have denied or ignored the warnings of impending catastrophe.

Much of this narrative is about denial, even in the face of ample warnings, and despite the efforts of people who were for a time in positions of great power and influence. In each of the stories of the five revolutions, the elites of the day refused to admit the prospect that their privileges and lifestyles could be swept away by the storms of revolution. How often, oblivious to their fate, have those elites continued dancing before storms. We may ask a key question: 'Are the elites of today also dancing before the storm?'

The final chapter leaps to the last decade of the twentieth and the beginning of the twenty-first century. It introduces a sixth key personality, **Kofi Annan** of Ghana, Secretary-General of the United Nations at the turn of the century. This chapter describes a spirit of hope that was widely felt at the dawn of the new millennium, then renewed anxiety arising from terrorist attacks and the Global Financial Crisis of 2008. The author was personally engaged during that time as an advocate and leader in organisations of civil society, and interacted with and observed the actions of political leaders and their advisors, and the leaders of the international community. As we complete this story, the entire world faces a dramatically disruptive pandemic, which has brought issues of equity and political competence into sharp focus.

Recalling the stories of the people who lived through the five revolutions described here, the question that naturally arises is: How much do the major actors in today's world understand what is happening? More fundamentally, have the processes of democracy that emerged from the enlightenment run their course? If so, what principles of governance might take their place in the multiple societies of today's interconnected world? And can people still hope that their aspirations will not be swept away by devastating new storms?

Part I:
America and France
1752 to 1815

Two men – Benjamin Franklin in America and Jacques Necker in France –
saw the storms of revolution looming over the horizon. Each for a
time exercised great influence in their respective kingdoms – those of
Great Britain and France; each made proposals for change, for reform.
Franklin decided to sail into the storm of the American Revolution and
try to channel it, as he had channelled lightning with his invention of
the lightning rod – the *paratonnerre*. Necker drove back by coach into
his storm – the revolution in Paris – and was hailed as the saviour of his
nation. But he retired from public office, defeated by events beyond his
control. These two men were key actors in the birth of two republics on
opposite sides of the Atlantic Ocean. Their destinies were linked by the
common thread of history.

Chapter 1

The American Revolution

Storm over Philadelphia

Early in the summer of 1752, on a day when black clouds filled the sky over Philadelphia, two figures walked onto an open field. One laid a mat on the wet ground beside a small wooden cabin. The other unfurled a kite that caught the wind and rose into the storm. Standing on the mat, touching a metal key at the end of the cord, the older of the two felt a tingle on his knuckle. He put the key into an earthen jar used to hold static electricity in a laboratory – a Leyden jar. And he trapped the electric charge drawn from the skies. Benjamin Franklin had just demonstrated that lightning flashing across stormy skies was the same as static electricity generated by friction in a laboratory. The younger man was his son, William Franklin.

Benjamin Franklin first published an account of the experiment in his newspaper without revealing that he and William had conducted it. But the truth was soon revealed, and his fame spread rapidly across the Atlantic and throughout Europe.

At the time of his lightning experiment, Benjamin Franklin's accomplishments were already considerable. He was mostly self-taught, having had just four years of formal schooling. Born into a large family in Boston, he was apprenticed at a young age to an older brother, James, who published the first independent newspaper in the American colonies, *The New-England Courant.* Benjamin spent his nights reading, including Plato's dialogues about the life of Socrates, and he quickly showed his talent for writing. When his brother was jailed for criticising the Royal Governor, Benjamin took responsibility for the paper at the age of seventeen.

The brothers fell out after James was released from prison, and Benjamin ran away, firstly to New York, then to Philadelphia, where he again found work as a printer. He was befriended by the Governor of Pennsylvania, who encouraged him to sail to London, with promises of help in setting up his own business. Although the governor failed to keep his promise, when Benjamin arrived in London, he earned a living in the printing trade, while attending tradesmen's clubs and building networks of friends. He showed his prowess as a swimmer in the River Thames and briefly considered a career as a swimming coach. Returning to the colonies at the age of twenty-three, Benjamin began publishing *The Pennsylvania Gazette*, which quickly became the leading newspaper in the American colonies. He was a prolific and witty writer but from an early age he often preferred to be anonymous. Yearly almanacks with collections of practical household hints, seasonal weather forecasts, puzzles, and proverbs, were popular in colonial America, and Franklin published the most successful one called *Poor Richard's Almanack*, under the pseudonym Richard Saunders.

His son William was born just before Benjamin married his former landlady's daughter, Deborah Read, in a common law marriage, without legal registration, in 1730. The identity of William's mother was never revealed, but the boy was recognised by Benjamin as his son and brought up by Deborah. They later had a son who died of smallpox at the age of four, and a daughter Sarah (known as Sally). By the time of the historic experiment in the storm, William had already fought for the British against French troops and Native Americans and had been promoted to the rank of captain while still a teenager.

When Benjamin was still a young man, he founded the first public library in the American colonies and the fire department in Philadelphia. In the early 1750s, he also founded the first public hospital in America, then a vocational college that later became the University of Pennsylvania. In 1753, he was named postmaster of Philadelphia, then the British Government named him as one of two deputy postmasters general for North America, making him responsible for mail services across the Atlantic to Britain and among the colonies north and east of Pennsylvania, as far as present-day Canada. In the years that followed, Benjamin Franklin was honoured with degrees from Harvard and Yale universities. He became active in Pennsylvania politics, joining with members of the provincial assembly who contested the proprietary rights of the Penn family and their exemption from taxes. The province had been given to William Penn as a massive land grant by King Charles II after the British civil war in the previous century. It had been founded with Quaker principles of religious tolerance and peace-making. But the heirs to William Penn ran the province as their private domain.

At the centre of the British Empire
Five years after the famous experiment in the storm, in the year 1757, father and son found themselves at the centre of events that would shape future relations between the empires of Europe and the new world of the north American colonies. In that year, the Pennsylvania Assembly voted to send Benjamin Franklin as its agent to London, the seat of power of the British Empire. William accompanied his father and entered law school.

Through friends, Benjamin found lodgings in Craven Street, close to the government offices at Whitehall and the River Thames, with a widow named Margaret Stevenson and her daughter, who was known as Polly. The Stevensons soon became used to a steady stream of visitors, and also to Benjamin's habits, including regular swims in the Thames, and his practice of taking what he called an 'air bath' each morning, which entailed opening all the windows and sitting naked in his room for an hour while reading his correspondence. Franklin was convinced that this practice was good for his health.[1]

In 1761, both Franklins attended the coronation of young King George III. Benjamin was admitted to the Royal Society and was awarded an honorary doctorate by the University of St Andrews in Scotland. He met and socialised with members of King George's new government and was considered a man of influence. In 1763, the prime minister, Lord Bute, a close friend of Benjamin, and the former tutor of King George, arranged for the appointment of William, freshly graduated from law school, as Royal Governor of the province of New Jersey in America.

During these years from 1756 to 1763, the Seven Years' War involved many of the powers of Europe. It had started with the Indian French wars in North America and had spread to the outposts of the British and French Empires in distant continents. In Europe, the British were allied with Prussia, Portugal, and Hanover, while the French were allied with their traditional rivals, the Austrians, and with Spain, Russia, and Sweden. By 1763, the war was over; the British prevailed and Britain became the leading power both in Europe and across the oceans. Prime Minister William Pitt, later called the Elder, was hailed for the victory and dominated British politics.

Philadelphia politics

In the same year, with William ready to take up his new position as Governor of New Jersey, he and his father sailed back to America. Benjamin returned to Philadelphia and built a new house – a complex for his extended family called Franklin Court in Market Street – next to the office and print shop of *The Pennsylvania Gazette*, run in Franklin's absence by his partner, David Hall, a Scotsman.

Again, Benjamin engaged in the rough and tumble of provincial politics. In December 1763, a group of frontiersmen known as the Paxton Boys massacred peaceful Native Americans. Then some 600 armed frontiersmen marched on the assembly in Philadelphia to demand better protection of their settlements to the west. Franklin met them and persuaded them to return home, while castigating their actions in his writings. The next year he was elected as speaker of the Pennsylvania Assembly, leading those opposed to the privileges of the Penn family. But six months later he was defeated. It was a dirty campaign. Benjamin's opponents spread rumours that he had buried William's unnamed mother in an unmarked grave. But he still had enough support in the assembly to win a majority vote to send him back to London as Pennsylvania's agent. Penn supporters feared that he would use his influence in Britain to pursue his opposition to the family's privileges and there were attempts to block his departure. With tensions high, several hundred horsemen escorted Franklin to the ship as it readied its sails for departure down the Delaware River and across the Atlantic Ocean in the winter of 1764. He took with him William's young son, his grandson, Temple Franklin. Along the way he began another scientific adventure – the discovery and charting of the Gulf Stream.

Access to power and English innovations

Back in London, Franklin returned to his lodgings with the Stevensons, mother and daughter, in Craven Street. Margaret Stevenson sent regular letters to Deborah Franklin, to keep her in touch with Benjamin's well-being. He was by then a father figure to Polly, and it was said 'almost a husband' to Margaret.[2]

Benjamin Franklin's early experience as a young man in London had taught him the importance of making connections. He was a natural organiser and networker, and upon his first return to America from abroad he had formed a club called Junto to encourage tradesmen to improve themselves through reading and conversation. From his early days in Philadelphia, Franklin had been a Freemason and, once back in London, he joined the Grand Lodge of England, as well as a gentlemen's club where the more liberal establishment figures gathered, giving him access to powerful figures in the British Government.

In the English heartland, changes were underway that were more momentous than any since medieval times, changes more fundamental even than the Renaissance. In 1764, James Hargreaves invented the spinning jenny, a device that revolutionised cotton spinning and weaving, and James Watt developed the steam engine for industrial use – going into business with Matthew Boulton. These innovations marked the beginning of the industrial revolution. Steam-powered textile factories in Manchester and Birmingham became the base for worldwide trade across the British Empire. Rural workers crowded into the cities.

Around this time, Franklin and his fellow scientist and friend, Joseph Priestley, joined a club that brought together the leading industrialists and scientists of the time in Birmingham, in the heart of the Midlands, and the cradle of the industrial revolution. Founding members included Matthew Boulton and Erasmus Darwin, grandfather of Charles, the botanist. They called it the Lunar Society because they met on nights of the full moon, so that after an evening of vigorous discussion over good food and wine, they could find their way home. Franklin was a corresponding member, attending in person only occasionally. The group was said to be second only to the Royal Society in influencing the age of discovery, but it was less formally organised. Its members were committed to scientific inquiry and invention, and they discussed social issues such as the abolition of slavery. Like Franklin, the participants were optimists. They firmly believed that together they would better the lot of humankind.³ It was like an early version of today's World Economic Forum.

It would be some time before the industrial revolution would reach continental Europe. Meanwhile, in 1764, a romantic triangle was playing out in Paris and Geneva. The protagonists had no idea that their destinies would one day be intertwined with that of the great American scientist and inventor Benjamin Franklin. Nor could they know that they would be key actors in two revolutions – the American and the French.

In the French town of Ferney, near Geneva, Suzanne Curchod, a pastor's daughter from nearby Crassier, was in love with Edward Gibbon, a hunched and brilliant young Englishman who had been removed by his father from Oxford and sent to Lausanne in Switzerland to study under a Protestant pastor. There he met Suzanne and proposed marriage to her, but their plans were vetoed by his father. Suzanne swore that she would wait for him, but in 1764, when they were both aged twenty-seven, she tearfully parted ways with Edward and went to Paris to begin a new life as the companion of a wealthy young widow. There, she soon married a rising star in the world of finance, a banker from Geneva named Jacques Necker, who until he met Suzanne, had been courting the widow. Edward Gibbon returned to England. Later he would become famous as the author of a monumental book of seven volumes, entitled *The History of the Decline and Fall of the Roman Empire*, still recognised today as one of the most influential history books in the English language.⁴

In London, Franklin joined other colonial agents to meet the new British Prime Minister, Lord George Grenville. The Seven Years' War was now over, but with the cost to England of the war still fresh in people's minds, Grenville argued that the colonies should in future pay for their own defence. He proposed the introduction of a Stamp Tax – a levy on every piece of printed paper used in the American colonies. Among other things, the tax would apply to legal documents, licenses, newspapers and other publications.

The colonists refused to accept that they should be taxed in order to pay for the stationing of British troops, whose presence was in any case not desired. Most of all, however, they did not accept that a new tax could be imposed on them without the consent of their colonial assemblies.

Their slogan of opposition became: 'no taxation without representation'.

Members of the British ruling class had difficulty in seeing the point, since in the home country they were wedded to the concept of 'virtual representation', which meant that they considered they alone represented the populations of their domains. In their minds they could see no reason to change a system that in practice denied electoral franchise to the great majority of eligible males – while the suffragette movement to demand voting for women was still a century away. As people moved from the country into the towns in search of work, distortions of the electorates became even greater. Rotten boroughs with populations of less than 200, passed on from father to son, were represented in the parliament equally with new industrial cities. So, they said, 'Why should the colonists complain?' Their mind-set was that 'virtual representation' was as valid for the colonies as it was at home. Of course, their rejection of the colonists' demand for a say over their own taxation was dressed up as a matter of principle, and there was much talk about exerting the authority of parliament. Grenville was determined to assert that only the British Parliament could legislate for taxes. The American colonial agents' entreaties that the tax was unjust were ignored. Benjamin Franklin, ever the optimist, believed nevertheless, as he wrote in his autobiography, that the British could eventually be won over. He was, if anything, overconfident of his powers of persuasion.

Trouble back home
The new tax was duly adopted by the British Parliament and the king signed the Act in March of 1765, to take effect on 1 November that year. There was a furious reaction from the colonists in America. The question of taxation without representation was debated raucously in taverns throughout the colonies of New England and along the eastern seaboard, and the new tax was decried in the columns of local newspapers. In the summer of 1765, tempers exploded in a riot in Boston. Franklin's paper, *The Pennsylvania Gazette*, reported on 24 August that the building to be used for the reception of stamps in Boston had been levelled to the ground, and the home of the designated stamp distributor invaded. This and other newspaper reports helped spark similar riots from New Hampshire in the north to Georgia in the south. In Philadelphia, however,

Franklin and his partner Hall took no position and simply published the official notice of the Stamp Act in the *Gazette,* without comment, while Franklin's already famous *Poor Richard's Almanack* merely advertised the same notice.[5] Moreover, in a community where gossip spread quickly, Franklin was said to have lobbied successfully to have one of his associates, named John Hughes, to be nominated as stamp distributor for Pennsylvania. So, Franklin's motives were questioned and he was accused by his critics of being complicit with the British rulers.

In mid-September, a mob gathered at a Philadelphia coffeehouse, and heard speeches accusing Franklin of supporting the Stamp Act. The mob set out to level Franklin's new home, along with the home of Hughes. After a warning from her cousin, Benjamin's wife Deborah Franklin sent word to her brother to bring guns, and an upstairs room was barricaded for their defence.[6] A group of Franklin supporters, called the White Oak Boys, joined the family to defend Franklin Court. Deborah confronted the mob and refused to leave the house. They held off the siege for nine days.

Once he heard the news, a few weeks later in London, Franklin quickly understood the need for him to take a more active role against the new tax. Writing letters to friends and neighbours, he asserted his firm support for the colonists' opposition. The Stamp Act was due to take effect on 1 November, but the protests and riots had been effective, making it virtually impossible to enforce the new law without causing major civil unrest.

Franklin turns the tables
With the Act still not enforced, Franklin was called before the British Parliament when it resumed in early 1766. In a brilliant performance, Franklin refuted the argument that the Stamp Tax was needed to pay for the defence of the colonies. When asked, 'What was the temper of America toward Great Britain before the year 1763?' Franklin replied, 'The best in the world ... They had not only a respect but an affection for Great Britain.' When asked, 'And what is their temper now?' he replied, 'Oh, very much altered.'[7] Franklin showed that the American colonies more than covered the costs of their own defence and were governed 'at the expense only of a little pen, ink and paper'.

Franklin argued that internal taxes like those planned in the Stamp Act should only be levied by local representative bodies. 'The colonies have assemblies of their own, which are their parliaments,' he said. None of the parliamentary supporters of the tax, including Grenville himself, succeeded in rebutting Franklin's case. As the parliamentarians' questions drew to a close, Franklin was asked, 'If the Stamp Act should be repealed, would it induce the assemblies to acknowledge the right of the [British] Parliament to tax them?' 'No, never!' he replied. 'No power, how great so ever, can force men to change their opinions.' The Irish parliamentarian, Edmund Burke said the hearing was 'an examination of a master, by a parcel of schoolboys'.[8] Franklin commented that those in favour of repeal 'were ready to hug me'.

Thanks to swelling popular revolt in the colonies and the skilful oration of Benjamin Franklin, the days of the Stamp Act were numbered. Grenville had lost the confidence of parliament and resigned as prime minister. William Pitt the Elder, hero of the British victory in the Seven Years' War returned to parliament briefly to denounce the Stamp Act. Drawing on his once immense authority, his voice rising above interjections, Pitt stated that the Stamp Act must be repealed 'absolutely, totally, immediately'.[9]

A pamphlet with the full transcript of Franklin's testimony was soon printed and distributed widely. Sent across the Atlantic, the transcript was reprinted throughout the colonies and Franklin became a hero. In addition to Pennsylvania, three other colonies – Georgia, New Jersey, and Massachusetts – asked him to become their agent in London. Already, since 1753, he had held a position on behalf of the British Government, being one of two deputy postmasters general for North America, and that had enabled him to be in regular contact with all thirteen colonies. Such mixing of roles was not unusual in colonial times.

A man of influence
Now in his sixtieth year, Benjamin Franklin was at the height of his fame and influence. Known throughout the world for his discoveries of the nature of electricity, he kept up his contacts with scientists such as Joseph Priestley, whom he visited in England, and the German scientist Otto von Guericke, with whom he maintained regular correspondence.[10] He visited Prussia after the parliamentary season to meet him and other German scientists. The following year, 1767, he went to Paris, where he was received by King Louis XV. He continued his scientific inquiries on

such subjects as Atlantic Ocean currents, while writing popular essays in support of the American colonists. With his sharp wit, he was a favourite of the salons of London. In those days he was dressed, as shown in portraits, wearing a velvet suit, like a proper English gentleman.

However, the tensions between the American colonists and the British Parliament did not go away. Although the Stamp Act was repealed, Pitt had accepted that the repeal should be accompanied by a statement of the British Parliament's 'sovereign authority over the colonies'.[11] Pitt himself left the House of Commons to sit in the House of Lords, as the king had awarded him the title of Earl of Chatham. The chancellor of the exchequer, Charles Townshend, introduced new revenue-raising measures in America, known as the Townshend Acts (1767).[12] Resentment against English high-handedness grew. From their experience with the Stamp Act, the colonists had learnt that they could successfully organise against official edicts. During the Stamp Act campaign, they had held the first congress of delegates from the colonial assemblies. More continental congresses followed, enabling the colonies to share their grievances and develop strategies. Although the actors of the day perceived but dimly the implications of the gathering protests, the scene was being set for the American Revolution.

In 1770, King George named his close friend, Lord Frederick North as prime minister of Britain and Ireland. North bore a strong physical resemblance to King George, and their contemporaries suggested that they were half-brothers. North's declared father was Lord of the Bedchamber to Prince Frederick, who was the father of George III, and godfather to the infant. Given Prince Frederick's reputation as a womaniser, who would not have hesitated to seduce his courtier's lady, it was widely said that he was young Frederick's real father. At any rate, George III made it obvious that he was comfortable with North as his prime minister, and North remained in that position for twelve years.

North was indolent, often dozing in cabinet meetings. He kept his position mainly because of his willingness to do the king's bidding. He moved quickly, undoubtedly with the king's support, to defuse the ongoing tension with the American colonists. As soon as he took office, North repealed most of the duties that remained in the American colonies. But as fate would have it, on the very day of the new prime minister's announcement in the parliament, and several weeks before the news of the repeal reached America, British troops fired on protesters in Boston, Franklin's birthplace. When the news reached him, Benjamin Franklin was deeply affected. The Massachusetts Assembly, seen by the British establishment to be the most provocative of the colonial assemblies, invited him to be the agent for them as well. Franklin accepted the invitation and called on the British Secretary of State for America, Lord Hillsborough, to present his letter of appointment, but Hillsborough angrily refused it. Hillsborough was a hardliner on colonial questions, and he remained a major obstacle to Franklin's attempts at reconciliation between the British Government and the colonists.

For a time there was a stalemate. Franklin was depressed by his inability to find a way to overcome Hillsborough's antagonism. The protests in the colonies gradually petered out. During this time of relative calm, British explorers reached across the globe. Far away in the antipodes, in April of 1770, Captain James Cook claimed land for Britain on the eastern seaboard of the vast southern continent known then as Terra Australis. In May of that same year, Louis XV's grandson and heir, Louis-Auguste, was married in Paris to Marie-Antoinette of Austria. It was a purely political marriage – an alliance of dynasties. The bride was fourteen and the groom not quite sixteen. These young people were blissfully unaware of the twists and turns of fate that awaited them, of the key role that Louis, as the future king of France, would play in support of the American Revolution, and the way in which their own lives would end two decades later in the turmoil of the French Revolution.

The heartland of the industrial revolution
In the following year, 1771, Franklin travelled through the English heartland, referring in his autobiography to his need to get away from London and his frustration with Hillsborough, for the sake of his health. Visiting the Midlands, Franklin saw with his own eyes the changes wrought by the industrial revolution, which was now well underway. With his acute sense of observation, he noted the intricacy of the new machines, but also the contrast between the wealth of the entrepreneurs and the appalling conditions of the workers, toiling for twelve to fourteen hours a day. The manager of a textile factory in Norwich boasted to

Franklin about his exports around the world. Looking at a ragged worker, Franklin asked, 'And what do you export to Norwich?'[13] He observed workers in cramped quarters in an underground mine[14] and saw children as young as five twisting silk in a Birmingham factory.[15]

After returning to London for the king's birthday, Franklin travelled to the village of Twyford near Southampton, where he stayed as the guest of Bishop Jonathan Shipley, a member of the House of Lords who firmly supported the American cause. At Shipley's suggestion, Franklin began to write his autobiography in the form of a letter to William, who he had not seen for seven years. Beginning with the words: 'Dear son …', he went on to write: 'Having emerg'd from the poverty and obscurity in which I was born and bred, to a state of affluence and some degree of reputation in the world …'[16] Those few words conveyed so much, for in an age dominated by aristocracies, Franklin had risen from humble beginnings to extraordinary fame and influence. His origins and his success may also explain the hostility towards him of some in the British establishment.

Visit to Ireland

In September, Franklin visited Ireland, where he was guest of honour at the parliament in Dublin. As he passed through the countryside, he was appalled by the poverty of the labourers toiling on the great estates of English lords. He equated the repression of the Irish by the English with the experience of the American colonists. One of those landowners was none other than Lord Hillsborough. To Franklin's great surprise, despite Hillsborough's aggressive criticism of the colonists and of Franklin personally, the British Lord invited the American to visit him at his feudal seat and received him with courtesy. Back in London, however, Hillsborough reverted to his old form and refused to receive Franklin. The conflict between them came to a head over a longstanding campaign by influential Americans and their British supporters to open up a new colony to the west of Pennsylvania in the Ohio River basin. After the king intervened, Hillsborough's opposition was overruled in the Privy Council and he resigned. Franklin then lobbied successfully for the appointment of a new secretary of state with a staunchly pro-American record, Lord Dartmouth. He wrote jubilantly to his son, William, that he could scarcely believe his victory.

Franklin still believed he could use his influence to persuade the British elite to change its ways in the American colonies, and his writings about the abuse of British rule became more forceful. Apart from his autobiography, Franklin kept up a private correspondence with his son in the governor's mansion in Perth Amboy, New Jersey. In these letters Benjamin lamented the weakness of Dartmouth, however well-intentioned, and the corruption of British politics. Even with Franklin's considerable influence, no rational argument could change policies at the centre of power. His reiteration of the American colonists' key demand of 'no taxation without representation' continued to fall on deaf ears.

Benjamin Franklin's satires

In May of 1773, the British Parliament passed the Tea Act in an attempt to bolster the finances of the East India Company, not expecting that the duties imposed on imports into the American colonies would arouse new protests. Although no longer secretary of state for America, Hillsborough remained close to Prime Minister North and continued to poison his mind against Franklin. As the historian Barbara Tuchman wrote, Hillsborough's expression of 'our inherent pre-eminence' over the colonists summed up the opinions of the British ruling class. Even America's friends like Lord Chatham thought of Britain as the parent and the colonies as the children.[17]

That year, Benjamin Franklin wrote two satirical essays highlighting the main issues in the colonists' growing revolt against British rule. In *Rules by which a Great Empire may be reduced to a Small One*,[18] Franklin stated that 'a great Empire, like a great Cake, is most easily diminished at the Edges'. The key grievances of the American colonists, which had been repeated often enough, were notably their lack of rights in the mother country, the denial of any say in the choice of legislators, and unfair taxation. Franklin pointed out that England's distrust of the colonists and the quartering of troops among them would 'convert your Suspicions into Realities'. He was severe in his criticism of the character and competence of governors and judges sent from the mother country under a system that favoured venality and bad administration. Taxes were arbitrary and odious, he said, financing the lifestyles of the collecting officers and representatives of the Crown. The system fostered resentment and resistance. Army generals were free from control by even the civil governors sent from London; they could act as laws unto themselves, and often did so capriciously and with scant regard for local public opinion.

Franklin drove his points home with a second essay, *An Edict by the King of Prussia*,[19] a hoax that became famous. In it, Franklin postulated that King Frederick II of Prussia had a claim to Britain because of settlements by German ancestors. This satirical royal edict purported to forbid the colony of Britain from smelting iron into steel and to restrict the manufacture of hats from locally procured wool and fur. Heavy taxes and duties were to be levied on the colonists in Britain, which would serve as a penal colony in order to empty the jails of Prussia.

Like all good hoaxes, Franklin's essay was at first taken seriously by some. Franklin later wrote to his son that when the *Edict* was first published, he was visiting a prominent friend, Lord le Despencer, who was at that time Postmaster General of Britain.[20] One of the guests, the poet Paul Whitehead, burst into the breakfast room, out of breath, with a newspaper in his hand, and cried out: 'Here's the King of Prussia claiming a right to this Kingdom.' Whitehead went on to read two or three paragraphs aloud. Another gentleman exclaimed: 'Damn his impudence. I dare say he will be upon the march with one hundred thousand men.' But, as the penny dropped, Whitehead looked at Franklin and said, 'I'll be hanged if this is not some of your American jokes upon us.' The reading went on and ended 'with an abundance of laughing'.[21]

Franklin used satire to draw public attention in Britain to the rising discontent in the colonies. But the ruling class remained unmoved. Benjamin Franklin, respected both in Britain and in the colonies as a man of reason and diplomacy, tried to sound the alarm but his repeated warnings were ignored. The British elite's refusal to heed Franklin's warnings was a classic example of the phenomenon described by historian Barbara Tuchmann as the 'pursuit by governments of policies contrary to their own interests'.[22]

Still hoping for a diplomatic solution to the rising problems in the colonies, Franklin urged his friends in the British Parliament to work towards an Atlantic alliance, in which the colonists would 'enrich the mother country and extend its empire round the whole globe and awe the world'.[23] In fact, he tried to warn the British establishment of the risks of ignoring the American colonists, and at the same time he put forward proposals in the hope of persuading the British to see the benefits of a genuine trans-Atlantic partnership.

All the time, there was a great deal of information gathering and spying going on, whether from the English side or among the colonists. Franklin proved to be a master at this game, building a network of contacts and informers to keep him abreast of the latest developments on both sides of the Atlantic.

Blamed for the Boston Tea Party

After he published his famous satires, Franklin obtained a package of confidential letters written some time earlier by Governor Hutchinson of Massachusetts and his deputy, in which they had urged the British Government to crack down on the people of Boston as agitators. Franklin sent these letters to the leaders of the Massachusetts Assembly in strict confidence, but they were leaked to the *Boston Gazette* and published. Tensions grew, as the letters revealed the governor's active push for repression.

As a result of the Tea Act passed earlier that year, the East India Company now had a monopoly on the trade of tea into the colonies. The company was exempt from export tax, but the Americans were required to pay a new duty when taking delivery of the tea. The enforcement of this new tax culminated in a showdown between the hardline governor, Hutchinson, and the colonists, that became known as the Boston Tea Party. A week before Christmas, protestors calling themselves the Sons of Liberty dumped two shiploads of a precious cargo of tea into the harbour, rather than pay what they considered was an unjust British tax.

Six weeks later, in early 1774, the news reached London. As the British parliamentary season resumed in the new year, Franklin bore the brunt of the scandal of the leaked letters. Their publication was blamed for inciting the colonists and sparking the protest that became the Tea Party. Franklin was called before the Privy Council, ostensibly to present a petition from the Massachusetts Assembly calling for the recall of Governor Hutchinson and his deputy. But a political trap was being set, and when Franklin returned for a second hearing on 29 January, the chamber was crowded with government notables, who had been alerted that something exceptional would happen. There was standing room only, and even Lord North could not find a seat. Instead of hearing the petition, the Privy Council listened as Franklin was subjected to an hour-long, mocking personal attack by the solicitor-general, Alexander Wedderburn, who blamed the leaking of the Hutchinson letters for the protest in Boston. Franklin stood silently and straight-backed as his name and character were ridiculed. For a man of his stature this was deep humiliation. Posturing with outrage, the government's representative failed to address the issues at stake, but chose instead to discredit the messenger. In so doing the ruling establishment persisted in ignoring the warning signs of impending revolt. Franklin declined to reply. But, leaving the chamber, he took Wedderburn gently by the arm, and whispered in his ear, 'I will make your master a little king for this.'[24] The British establishment had unknowingly taken a fatal step towards the loss of the empire's most prized colonial possession. Franklin described in *The Pennsylvania Gazette* how he had been abused 'to the great entertainment of thirty-five Lords of the Privy-Council, who had been purposely invited to a bull-baiting'.[25]

Franklin had been in London for a decade, representing four American provinces. For twenty years he had held one of the two positions of colonial postmaster general for North America, but he was dismissed within hours of the solicitor-general's attack on him. He stayed on in London for the remainder of 1774. Letters between Benjamin and William Franklin showed growing differences between them over the demand of the British Government for Massachusetts to repay the East India Company for the loss of the tea thrown into the harbour. William advised Benjamin to persuade the colonists to seek a settlement over the payments, but Benjamin disagreed. North dissolved the British Parliament and the country plunged into a new round of electioneering. At this time Benjamin Franklin met a young English official who shared his disgust with the rampant corruption of British politics. His name was Thomas Paine.

Last attempts at reconciliation

That winter, just before Christmas, Deborah Franklin died in Philadelphia. Governor William Franklin fought his way through the snow from New

Jersey to Philadelphia to pay his last respects to the woman he had always considered his mother. Then he sent the news to his father, who received it early in the new year. The news of Deborah's death came as a shock to Benjamin. There was no reason to stay longer. It was time for him to go home.

Before leaving London in March of 1775, Franklin met with Lord Chatham who tried to present a proposal for reconciliation with the colonial leaders to the British Parliament. But this last-ditch effort to bridge the growing rift between the British Government and the American colonists failed. Franklin's final meeting in London was with the Irish parliamentarian Edmund Burke. He sailed back to America as Burke made an eloquent plea in the parliament in support of the colonists. But eloquence was not enough. The die had been cast.

Across the Channel, in France, changes were underway. The previous year, in May of 1774, old King Louis XV of France had died and had been succeeded by his grandson, Louis-Auguste, who was crowned as King Louis XVI. With the change of monarch came changes in key positions in the royal court, and the financier Jacques Necker had political ambitions. But before pursuing them, he decided to make an extended visit to London. In an interesting twist of fate, at the very moment Franklin sailed from London, Necker arrived in the British capital with his wife, Suzanne, and their daughter, Louise. With introductions from Lord Stormont, Britain's Ambassador to France, they were received at the highest levels. They met King George at Kensington Palace and Prime Minister North at 10 Downing Street. They also met Suzanne Necker's former fiancé, Edward Gibbon, still a bachelor, who had just published the first volume of his epic book. The paths of Franklin and Necker did not cross this time. But these two men, who were to play key roles in revolutions on opposite sides of the Atlantic, would soon meet in France.

Franklin joins the revolution

On his way back to America with his grandson, Benjamin Franklin continued his soundings and records of the Gulf Stream. Then alone in his cabin at night, he wrote page after page of a letter to his son William, describing in extraordinary detail the history of his negotiations with the British Government. This most British of Americans, this man who had risen from humble beginnings in Boston to a position of great prestige and influence not only in Britain but across Europe, only to see his best endeavours derided and his reputation trashed, had taken the decision to join with the colonial advocates of independence. Now, his mind was made up, and he wanted his son and confidant to understand how he had come to that momentous decision. Undoubtedly, by writing in such detail, he was also consolidating his decision in his own mind. He kept the letter with the intention of giving it to William in person.

By the time Franklin reached Philadelphia in May of 1775, the fire of the American Revolution had been lit. Even as he sailed across the Atlantic, Paul Revere rode through the night to alert American militia that British Redcoat troops were on their way to Concord near Boston. By the evening of 19 April, the battles of Lexington and Concord had marked the beginning of the revolt.

Upon docking in Philadelphia, the elder Franklin sent no message to William to notify him of his return. Instead, after visiting his wife's grave, he travelled by coach to the governor's mansion in New Jersey to meet him in person. There, sharing a bottle or more of madeira wine, they talked about old times and their eleven years of separation.

Then Benjamin announced that he had decided to support independence from Britain. He read aloud parts of his ninety-seven-page letter. The two men argued all night, but neither changed their position. From that point on, father and son would be on opposing sides in the revolution for American independence. Benjamin Franklin – inventor, scientist, publisher, writer and diplomat – gave up his decades-long efforts to find an accommodation between the British ruling elite and the colonists, and threw his support to the colonial patriots. Governor William Franklin remained a loyalist to the British crown. There was one witness to the debate – Joseph Galloway, a close ally of Benjamin in the Pennsylvania Assembly, who had supported his opposition to the Stamp Act. Galloway had to decide which side to take. He eventually opted to support the loyalists.

Benjamin Franklin returned alone to Philadelphia. There he met a tall, red-headed plantation owner and gifted writer named Thomas Jefferson. In the new year Thomas Paine, the young Englishman recommended by Franklin, published a forty-seven-page pamphlet entitled *Common Sense,* arguing powerfully for American independence and the creation of a republic. He sent the first copy to Franklin. It was the first of 120,000 copies sold throughout the thirteen colonies, where it became a sensation.

By June, the Continental Congress of the colonies, initially established at the time of the Stamp Tax, tasked a committee with Jefferson as the principal scribe, to draft a Declaration of Independence from Great Britain. Benjamin Franklin was invited to join the committee, becoming a close friend and mentor to Jefferson. As they worked on the draft, in mid-June, Franklin's beloved son, Governor William Franklin, was renounced by the Provincial Congress of New Jersey, placed under arrest, and taken to Connecticut.

In Philadelphia, the Continental Congress met, debated and heavily edited Jefferson's draft, removing references to the abolition of slavery. Franklin consoled Jefferson with one of his anecdotes. On 4 July 1776, the Declaration of Independence of the United States of America was adopted. At Franklin's urging, all delegates signed the historic document. As Franklin said in response to a comment by the Congress chairman, John Hancock: 'We must, indeed, all hang together, or most assuredly we shall all hang separately.'[26]

George Washington, commanding the continental army, had taken Boston before the Declaration of Independence, but after the signing the British fleet launched an attack from the naval base in Nova Scotia and defeated the continental army in Brooklyn that August. Franklin had previous contacts in London with the Howe brothers, Admiral, Lord Richard Howe, and General, Sir William Howe. Their sister had tried to help Franklin negotiate an end to the conflict over payment for the East India Tea Company's tea. So, when the admiral proposed a peace conference, the Continental Congress sent a delegation including Franklin and John Adams to meet the British sea and land commanders in September on Staten Island. The British demanded withdrawal of the Declaration of Independence, a condition that the American delegation refused. The British Redcoats of General Howe then took New York City and nearly captured Washington's army, pushing the Americans back across New Jersey to Pennsylvania.

While all this was happening, across the Atlantic in London, Jacques Necker received news of the dismissal of the controller-general of finances in France. He and his wife, aspiring to the pinnacle of power, sensed that their time had come. They rushed back to France and, in October, King Louis XVI named Jacques Necker as director-general of the Royal Treasury in France.

At almost the same time, Benjamin Franklin was named by the Continental Congress of America as commissioner to France. Franklin headed back across the Atlantic in December of 1776, taking with him his two seventeen-year-old grandsons, Temple Franklin, son of William, who would serve as his secretary, and Benny Bache, eldest son of his daughter Sally. Temple had been with his grandfather in London and no doubt Benjamin wanted to keep him by his side, as he felt deeply the personal pain of his estrangement from William. In those days, it was normal for young men of seventeen to take responsibilities, and both grandsons were more than keen to join their illustrious grandfather in his latest adventure. Sally declined Benjamin's invitation to accompany them. The Franklin family group slipped out of Philadelphia in a small, fast ship – the *Reprisal* – into the winter squalls of the Atlantic Ocean. Forging through the storms, they avoided the British patrols commanded by Admiral Howe, and they reached France early in 1777.

An American in Paris
Franklin and his grandsons, with their valets, made their way to Paris by coach. The great man was acclaimed by crowds along the way, for the news of Franklin's decision to join the American revolutionaries had already reached France. Reinforcing this popular enthusiasm in France, there was a concordance of three interrelated factors. One was the recent memory of the Seven Years' War, which had begun with conflicts between British and French forces in North America before expanding to Europe and other regions, and had ended with the bitterness of defeat for France. The second was competition among European powers to open up trade in far away continents across the oceans. The third was the excitement of new scientific discoveries and inventions, which were drivers of the industrial revolution. Benjamin Franklin, the scientist, inventor, diplomat and man of letters, personified the times, and his decision to join the American rebels against France's old enemy and competitor captured the popular imagination in France.

Once in Paris, Franklin and his fellow delegate Silas Deane, an American trader, began negotiations with the French Foreign Minister, Charles Gravier, Comte de Vergennes. Very soon, Franklin met for the first time with Jacques Necker, now firmly in charge of the Royal Treasury. Franklin found Necker to be reserved and preoccupied with domestic matters, as France remained heavily indebted after the Seven Years' War. Franklin concentrated on official contacts with these and other representatives of the king. But, ever the networker, he also met Honoré Gabriel Riquet, Comte de Mirabeau, who had just published his *Essay on Despotism,* a key work setting out the case for opposition to the absolutism of the monarchy. During the decade that followed, Franklin would develop contacts with the main thinkers of the Enlightenment, whose ideas would underpin the future French Revolution.

Franklin joins forces with Lafayette

In August of that year, 1777, a young French aristocrat, the Marquis de Lafayette, sailed from France to meet George Washington. Lafayette came from a prominent family with a martial tradition, and had trained as a musketeer while attending the elite Collège du Plessis in Paris. His father was killed in a battle with the British before he was two, and the young marquis was brought up by his grandmother. He was commissioned as a second lieutenant before he turned fourteen, when his family arranged his marriage to a daughter of the Duc d'Ayen. At the age of eighteen he was a captain in the Dragoons. Visiting Metz, Lafayette met Charles-François de Broglie, commander of the French eastern armies, whose house guest was the British Duke of Gloucester, estranged younger brother of King George III. With animated discussions over dinner, peppering his host and his guest with questions, he became persuaded of the justice of the American cause. Lafayette's father-in-law was also his superior officer, and the older man was worried about his son-in-law's ideas. So the duke sent Lafayette to London with an introduction to the French Ambassador, the duke's brother. The ambassador arranged for Lafayette to be received by King George himself.

But Lafayette's mind was made up. Returning to France, he and other young French officers met with Silas Deane, and Lafayette made it clear that he had decided to support the Americans. Defying his father-in-law and a decree issued by the French King, he purchased a ship and crew with his own funds, and sailed to America, practising his English during the crossing. Benjamin Franklin sent a letter to the congress encouraging the American leaders to welcome the young French officer. On arrival, Lafayette soon met with George Washington, and was appointed a major general in the continental army, serving on Washington's staff. He saw battle and was wounded. After recuperating in a settlement, Washington gave him a field command. During this time, he sent numerous letters to France lobbying for support for the colonists.

Lafayette's letters provided Franklin with powerful support within French political and commercial circles. Networking as always, Franklin worked assiduously to influence leading figures in French society. One of the most significant centres for debate within French ruling circles was the literary salon held every Friday by Jacques Necker's wife, Suzanne. Franklin became a regular participant. It was said that he spoke French with an appalling accent, but with his natural wit and good humour he was able to get his message across. Necker himself was reluctant to give official support to the American cause because of the potential cost of France becoming involved, but he formed a respectful personal friendship with Franklin.

Meanwhile, Washington achieved a breakthrough at the Battle of Saratoga in New York. Franklin and Deane were joined in France by a third agent sent by the Continental Congress, Arthur Lee. Franklin continued to be the dominant figure in the delegation. He arranged for translations of the constitutions of the thirteen colonies and the Declaration of Independence into French, bound them in a document with the Great Seal of the United States, and presented them to the king and his ministers.

By February of 1778, their negotiations with Foreign Minister Vergennes succeeded. Louis XVI decided officially to support the American rebellion against Britain. France and the United States signed two agreements: the Treaty of Alliance, providing for mutual defence against Britain, and the Treaty of Amity and Commerce. For the signing ceremony, Franklin put on the same elegant velvet suit that he had worn when the British Solicitor General had humiliated him before the Privy Council. He had kept the suit for just such an occasion. The Continental Congress named him as Minister Plenipotentiary and sole representative of America in France.

Franklin had achieved the political goal set by the newly formed American Congress: he had gained the support of France for the American colonies in their fight for independence. At the royal court of Versailles, he was received by King Louis XVI and Queen Marie-Antoinette, now wearing his simple brown suit and fur hat. As he left the palace, he was acclaimed by a huge crowd of finely dressed nobles, all curious to see the famous American. King George III of Britain was furious. He recalled his ambassador to France, Lord Stormont, who had been outmanoeuvred by Franklin. Increasingly, George III saw the war as a contest between himself and Franklin.

But across the Atlantic, the War of Independence was not going well for Washington and his troops. New York was occupied by the British, and William Franklin – released from Connecticut in a prisoner exchange – had become the leader of American loyalists fighting with them. In 1779, with Washington's agreement, Lafayette returned to France to seek more support for the Americans, based on the treaties negotiated by Franklin. Upon his arrival he was briefly placed under house arrest for his defiance of the king, but this was a formality. He was hugely popular and Louis XVI soon invited Lafayette to join him hunting. The Continental Congress in America had cited the French officer for gallantry and voted to present him with a ceremonial sword. As Benjamin Franklin was ill, his grandson, Temple, presented the sword in Paris. Franklin and Lafayette then worked together to raise a force of 6,000 French troops who would give teeth to the new treaty in support of the Americans.

Dancing at Queen Charlotte's Ball

Early in 1780, King George opened the London Social Season with a great ball to celebrate the thirty-sixth birthday of his wife, Queen Charlotte. Each year, after Christmas and the New Year, 'The Season', as it was called, brought together the ladies and gentlemen of high society and their daughters and sons. This British elite of about 200 families effectively ruled the empire. The Season officially began when the king and queen returned to the capital from Windsor Castle west of London, prior to the opening of parliament, and ran through to June. Part of the tradition was the presentation at court of young ladies of an age to enter social life. Once these young women had made their curtsies to their majesties, they were considered to have made their débuts. This was their 'coming out'. These young ladies required a sponsor, a woman of rank either of her family or a close acquaintance, who had already made her début. Virginal white was the prescribed colour to wear, while hoops in their dresses and feathers in their elaborate headdresses were *de rigueur.*

Queen Charlotte's Birthday Ball made official a practice that had developed since the early eighteenth century. Rich English parents took their daughters to London during the round of social events (balls, concerts, afternoon teas and the Royal Ascot horse races) that took place when the aristocracy came for the parliamentary session. This was an exclusive marriage market that enabled parents to control their daughters' social lives, while meeting eligible suitors from a select group of aristocratic or rich men. The social season was an integral part of the lives of those who formed the governing class, and almost all members of the two Houses of Parliament were active participants. Along with the parliamentarians in attendance, there would be young officers from good families, many of whom had returned from service in the outposts of the empire, or those who were preparing to leave on missions. These ladies and gentlemen were to become the characters portrayed in romantic novels, set in the late eighteenth and early nineteenth centuries, notably Jane Austen's *Pride and Prejudice.*

By 1780 the American revolutionary war had been underway for five years, with support from France since 1778. There had been gains and losses in battles up and down the east coast of the American continent. The British believed that events were turning their way, and they were confident they could put down the American rebellion. The loyalists had recaptured Georgia, and that year they prevailed in South Carolina.

But even as the British elite danced at their society functions, Lafayette was sailing back across the Atlantic on the frigate *Hermione*, this time with the official blessing of the French King and Government. He arrived in Boston at the end of April and travelled south to rejoin Washington. The morale of the colonists was boosted by Lafayette's announcement of reinforcements on their way from France. The governing classes of Britain were, both literally and figuratively in this case, dancing before the storm. After parliament rose for the summer of 1780, violent tempests swept the colonies on the other side of the Atlantic – during the worst hurricane season on record. They were the harbingers of political storms to come.

'London in flames, a nation in ruins'[27]

As the social season came to an end in June of 1780, the threat of revolution came agonisingly close to home. For in that very month, the most destructive riots in English history broke out in the streets of London. Two years before, in 1778, the British Government sought to strengthen the manpower of its forces opposing the colonists in America. The government had introduced a new law which absolved Catholics, mainly Irishmen, from taking the religious oath when joining the armed forces, and granted some modest rights to them. The intent was to recruit more Catholics into the army to fight against the colonist rebels in America. Militant Protestants sought to get the bill repealed in parliament. Early in 1780, their leader, Lord George Gordon, had several audiences with King George, who became increasingly irritated and refused him further audiences. Gordon then organised a petition to parliament, calling for repeal of the law, which was presented at the beginning of June. As politicians assembled to debate the issue, a large crowd marched on the Houses of Parliament to present the petition. When parliament dismissed the petition, the crowd dispersed. But that night violence broke out. Catholic chapels of the embassies of Bavaria and Sardinia were attacked. The following night crowds gathered at Moorfields, an area with many Irish immigrant workers. They sacked and burnt the houses of Catholic merchants, then moved across London to burn houses belonging to politicians associated with the bill, and the home of the Lord Chief Justice in Leicester Square.[28]

When parliament resumed four days later, and refused to debate the bill, violence escalated across the city, and the rioting mobs turned their attention to symbols of the State. Newgate Prison was gutted and 300 prisoners set free. Most of the prisons in central London were also burnt. The Bank of England was attacked – unsuccessfully. A large Irish-owned distillery was set on fire. Paintings of the time portray dramatic images of flames and smoke across the London sky. The army was called in, and a force of 10,000 troops was sent to the capital, with orders to fire on groups of rioters who failed to disperse. Deaths were estimated at more than 280,[29] with hundreds wounded and many others arrested. Subsequently some twenty-five rioters were executed. Gordon was tried for high treason but was acquitted. The events were known thereafter as the Gordon Riots. They were immortalised later by Charles Dickens in his novel *Barnaby Rudge: A Tale of the Riots of Eighty*.[30]

The Gordon Riots of 1780 anticipated the French Revolution of 1789. There were remarkable similarities – political manoeuvres were overrun by the protests of the street; the attacks on key symbols of the State and in particular the prisons (Newgate Prison in London in 1780, the Bastille in Paris in 1789). In the years to follow, the British monarchy would survive and avoid the bloody fate of its French counterparts. Many historical treatises have been written about the survival of the British constitutional monarchy, which evolved through reform. But the lesson of that time is that history might very well have taken a different turn.

As it was, the riots of 1780 put paid to Britain's hopes for an alliance with Catholic Austria, and Spain broke off peace negotiations. There was another lesson to be drawn from the riots. After the initial attacks on Catholic chapels and businesses, the targets for violence extended to State institutions and 'persons of substance'. It has been suggested that, in fact, the breadth and intensity of the riots were driven by economic and political issues rather than religious ones.[31] The loss of trade during the war with the American colonists had led to falling wages, rising prices and unemployment. Voting for parliament was still restricted to property holders, so most Londoners were unable to vote. Parliament was dominated by the aristocracy and the landed gentry. These are among factors that we will look into as we seek to understand the underlying causes of the American Revolution and Britain's loss of its American colonies.

Defeat at Yorktown

In December of that year, Jacques Necker of France wrote a secret letter to Britain's prime minister, Lord North, proposing a negotiated settlement of the war. North passed Necker's letter to the king, who dismissed it as a sign of French weakness.[32] 'It shews [sic] France is certainly in greater difficulties than we imagined,' the king wrote.[33] The war in America dragged on into the next year.

In the summer of 1781, the British commander in the south, Lord Cornwallis, established a base at Yorktown in Virginia, at the mouth of Chesapeake Bay. Washington had joined forces with the French army of the Comte de Rochambeau and was stationed on the Hudson River, ready to attack the northern British forces in New York, commanded by General Clinton. Washington learnt, however, that French Admiral de Grasse could sail up the American coast from the West Indies and reach Chesapeake Bay by September. Washington decided with Rochambeau to march south to Virginia, where 9,000 Americans and 8,000 French besieged the British Army of about 7,500 at Yorktown. Escape by sea was blocked by Admiral de Grasse. On 17 October 1781, Cornwallis surrendered. As the British Army laid down its arms, the band played *The world turned upside down*.[34] General Clinton's relief force from New York arrived too late.

The news of the British defeat at Yorktown reached Benjamin Franklin in Paris by express mail from America (meaning in those days about four weeks after the event) just as he was about to meet Jacques Necker. He had scarcely read the letters about the surrender of Cornwallis, when Necker came into the room where Franklin was at his desk. Seeing tears in Franklin's eyes as he lifted his gaze from a letter and took off his reading glasses, Necker asked, 'What news?' 'Thank God,' replied Franklin, holding up the letter, 'the storm is past, the *paratonnerres* of divine justice have drawn off the lightnings of British violence, and here, Sir, is the rainbow of peace.'[35]

At almost the same time, on 25 November 1781, the news of the British defeat reached London. Lord North cried, 'Oh God, it is all over.' After holding the office of prime minister for twelve years, North resigned in March of 1782. The king drafted a notice of abdication but did not send it to the parliament. He finally accepted the defeat in North America and agreed to peace negotiations.

Negotiating the peace
Franklin was joined in Paris by other delegates from the Continental Congress of America: John Adams, later to be George Washington's vice-president and the second president; John Jay, future chief justice of the United States; and Henry Laurens, a wealthy merchant. Jay was a committed abolitionist while Laurens was a slave-trader, so while they had common cause in seeking recognition of the new country's independence, their very presence in the delegation represented the cleavage which had truncated Jefferson's draft of the Declaration of Independence. That

fundamental division between the southern and the northern colonies would reappear at the constitutional convention four years later, and decades later, it would lead to civil war.

As the negotiations dragged on, Franklin took time out, in August 1783, to observe the first-ever flight of a hydrogen balloon, invented by a young French scientist named Jacques Charles, later President of the French Academy of Sciences. Franklin was enthusiastic and helped to finance a manned flight a few months later. On that summer day on the Champ de Mars in Paris, neither of these two inventors could have imagined the revolutionary upheavals that France would experience before the end of the decade. Even less could they have imagined the thread of history that would one day link Jacques Charles through a love triangle to a young poet who would lead a new revolution in France in the middle of the next century. That story will be told in Chapter 3.

The Treaty of Paris was signed on 3 September 1783, some seven years after the American Declaration of Independence of 1776. It recognised the United States of America as a sovereign and independent nation, and it set the boundaries between the new nation and the territories retained by the British to the north, later to become the provinces of Canada. Separate peace treaties were signed concurrently with France, and with Spain and the Dutch republic, both of which had also supported the Americans. Franklin's political success was accompanied with personal pain, as he learnt that his son William, after being captured by the patriots and imprisoned in New York, had been exiled to London where he continued to represent the defeated loyalists. Father and son, once so close, had become, and would remain, bitter opponents.

Recognising a new nation

The British political establishment was in shock over the loss of America. Political alliances were disturbed and re-drawn. For a short time, North returned to power in a coalition that put forward a bill to reform the East India Company. But he no longer enjoyed the support of King George III, who had the bill defeated by the House of Lords. The king then named William Pitt the Younger, as prime minister. At twenty-four, the son of the hero of Britain's victory in the Seven Years' War, he became the youngest prime minister in British history. In March 1784, Pitt – acclaimed amidst a sea of political corruption as 'Honest Billy' – was confirmed in office with a massive election victory.

With the Treaty of Paris and the birth of a new nation, a great blow had been dealt not only to the British Empire but also to the old order of Europe and to the ideas and social mores that perpetuated it. Now representing a sovereign nation, Benjamin Franklin was named as the first Ambassador of the United States to France. The following year, he welcomed his friend Thomas Jefferson, who would later succeed John Adams to become the third President of the United States, and introduced him to French society and political circles. Foreign Minister Vergennes welcomed Jefferson with the words: 'You replace Monsieur Franklin, I hear.' Jefferson replied, 'I succeed. No man can replace him.'[36]

It was time for Benjamin Franklin to return home. Sailing across the channel from Le Havre in July of 1785, he stopped at the English port of Southampton, where he joyously met with Bishop Shipley and other old friends. Then he had an unannounced visitor – his estranged son, William, now in exile in London, where he was the spokesman for fellow loyalist exiles. The old man received his son coldly, produced a notice of debt from William's days as Governor of New Jersey, and demanded that he sign over his remaining properties in New York to Temple Franklin. Pensively, Benjamin Franklin sailed for the last time across the Atlantic to Philadelphia. Along the way, ever the inquiring scientist, he continued his study of the Gulf Stream and completed his report on the subject. He had previously avoided publishing information on how to shorten the time of the passage from America to Britain so as to keep it from the British navy. Now that information could be used for peaceful commerce.

A constitution for the United States of America

Back in Philadelphia, competing factions in the Pennsylvania Assembly rushed to seek Franklin's support. Within a month he was elected unanimously as President of the Council of Pennsylvania. He also became President of the Pennsylvania Abolition Society. Then came the work of preparing for the drafting of a constitution for the United States of America. In May of 1787, the thirteen colonies convened the Constitutional Convention of the new nation in the state house in Philadelphia. As President of the Council of Pennsylvania, Benjamin Franklin was the host for the conclave and nominated George Washington to preside over the proceedings, a nomination unanimously supported by the delegates.

As the convention got down to business, it almost broke down in fractious debates over slavery and the rights of the smaller states. Over four months that summer, compromises were hammered out on the structure of the future Senate and the Electoral College. Now 81, and increasingly frail, Franklin was too weak to take the floor himself, and had a speech read for him, calling for the adoption of an imperfect compromise in order to save the new nation. His speech began: 'Mr President, I confess that I do not entirely approve of this Constitution at present,' but then he continued: 'I consent to this Constitution because I expect no better ... I hope, therefore ... for the sake of our posterity, that we shall act heartily and unanimously in recommending ... this instrument.'[37] With that plea from the old statesman, the constitution was adopted in September 1787. Benjamin Franklin was the only founding father to sign all four of the principal documents that created the United States of America.

Franklin joined George Washington in the campaign for ratification of the constitution by the thirteen states, before Washington's election as the first president of the new country in February of 1789. Franklin followed with concern the outbreak of the French Revolution that July, then wrote a final letter to Washington early the next year, in 1790. In reply, George Washington wrote: 'If to be venerated for benevolence, if to be admired for talents, if to be esteemed for patriotism, if to be beloved for philanthropy, can gratify the human mind, you must have the pleasing consolation to know that you have not lived in vain ... so long as I retain my memory, you will be thought of with respect, veneration and affection by your sincere friend, George Washington.'[38]

These touching words of friendship from a man reputed to be taciturn were written in the wake of momentous events which, over more than a decade, gave rise to a new nation that would expand and grow in economic and political strength during the course of the next century, with consequences that would ripple around the globe. After 1783, the United States refused to accept convicts from Britain, so the government decided to establish a penal settlement on the land claimed in 1770 by the explorer James Cook for the British crown on the eastern coast of Terra

Australis in the southern hemisphere. A first fleet of about 700 convicts guarded by about 250 marines sailed across the Atlantic to Rio de Janeiro, then west to the Cape of Good Hope at the southern tip of Africa and traversed the Southern Indian Ocean to establish a new colony in 1788 in New South Wales on ancient land occupied for millennia by indigenous peoples.

And in the Orient, the seeds were being sown for another revolution, which in a later century would bring an end to the oldest empire of all – that of China. The East India Company, the same company whose tea had been dumped into Boston Harbor back in 1773, had found another way to generate revenue – by smuggling opium from India into China.

Why did the British lose America?

This narrative has moved rapidly over some thirty-five years to tell the story of people at the centre of events leading to the American Revolution and the independence of the United States. As Benjamin Franklin warned in his satires, the governing establishment at the heart of a great empire was so caught up in its own hubris that it failed to perceive that its prime asset could be lost. To understand why the British elite never imagined it could lose America, we should look into how it dominated political and economic affairs. In Britain of the early eighteenth century, wealth came essentially from the land, and ownership of property was the source of fortune. With it came power and influence. At the top of the social pyramid was the nobility, holding vast estates in the countryside and town houses in the capital. Below them was the gentry, with sufficient means to mimic the lifestyles of the aristocracy. Education and manners set these classes apart from the mass of the population. Birth determined social status and position, hence marriage was subject to rigorous social codes for those born into the upper classes. But from the early eighteenth century the strict divisions of social class began to break down. Though it must have seemed to those who lived in those times that the system was immutable, profound changes were under way. Gradually, a middle class was emerging, made up of smaller landholders in the countryside called yeomen, and of merchants and professional men in the towns. Below them in the social pyramid were the craftsmen and labourers. The majority of the population lived at the level of subsistence, scraping to survive.[39]

The British Empire appeared to be as strong as iron, but it had feet of clay. Its expansion was underpinned by a disequilibrium that was only dimly perceived by the ruling establishment, while gradually, ineluctably, creating the conditions for revolution. Colonial competition, wars and trade held the attention of the political elite, welded together by the notion of loyalty to king and empire. But the internal changes within the mother country, as well as its colonies, were of greater consequence than external affairs. And those changes were to give rise to new ideas that would form the justification for the American colonies to rebel.

Conditions in the mother country . . .
In the mid-eighteenth century the population of Britain was about 6.5 million and around 600,000 people lived in the capital, London. Life expectancy had been low in the first half of the century, with severe epidemics of a range of diseases – typhus, measles, influenza, dysentery, smallpox, chickenpox and whooping cough – which caused appalling death rates, especially among the poor and young children.[40] Towns and cities were especially unhealthy places to live. Nearly seventy-five per cent of children born in London died before they were five. In workhouses, the death rate for young children increased to more than ninety per cent.[41] From about the middle of the century, though, mortality rates began to improve, and the population grew rapidly to 9 million over the next five decades.[42] Infant and child mortality rates fell first among the professional and upper classes living outside London. They were the first to acquire new facilities, such as washbasins, bathtubs and early types of flush toilets, all of which dramatically improved hygiene.[43] A tiny minority of the population – those at the top of the social pyramid – lived in luxury. They built great country houses – usually in the neoclassical style. They hired landscape gardeners to create English country gardens. They ordered beautiful furniture, and master craftsmen like Thomas Chippendale made themselves names that remain known to this day.

Yet the majority of people lived in grinding poverty. Many went to the towns to find work, but even cheap housing was not to be found. Slums grew rapidly. Families often lived together in single rooms in tenements or in cellars. Water was often contaminated. Even graveyards became full. When grain harvests were poor, the price of bread rose, leaving families struggling to pay for their basic food needs. Many fell below the 'breadline'.

Charitable relief for the needy was provided through local parishes. Charity schools were founded in many towns.[44] Under the Poor Laws dating from Elizabethan times, local overseers examined claims and allocated money, clothing, or food, paid from rates levied on wealthier households. Parish workhouses were built to house the poor and provide work. By the 1770s there were some 2,000 workhouses in Britain, housing 100,000 people. Conditions varied greatly from one parish to another. Some provided clothing, healthcare and education. Others, especially in London, were overcrowded death traps. Disease was rife, and the dead were buried in unmarked paupers' graves.

The eighteenth century was also a time when private charity developed. Funds were collected from social events, such as balls or concerts. Charitable institutions were established, such as the Foundling Hospital in 1739. In 1756, at the beginning of the Seven Years' War, when the navy needed many more seamen, the Marine Society was formed to train poor boys for service at sea. Local infirmaries were built and offered free medical care. For the jobless poor in the rapidly growing towns and cities, the alternatives to the workhouses or living off charity were stark. Beggars were a familiar sight in towns and cities, despite the vagrancy laws. Prostitutes catered to rich and poor alike – and were to be found from the elegant Strand to the infamous bawdy-houses in the alleyways around the docks of London's vast seaport. This was the underside of the world's greatest empire.[45]

. . . and in the colonies

One path out of misery was to migrate to the colonies in America. In the mid-eighteenth century, population growth in the thirteen American colonies was dramatic. From 1.6 million in 1760, the numbers climbed rapidly in just twenty years to reach 2.8 million by 1780. Many of the immigrants from Britain were single men and women who went as indentured servants and labourers, contracted to work in order to pay their passage. Others were transported as convicts, often for minor offences, and generally from the poorest echelons of Britain and Ireland. There were also free settlers, artisans and traders. At the same time, as a result of the slave trade, the African population increased eight-fold over the half century from 1730 to 1780 – almost all in the four plantation states of the south.

The class-based nature of British society was replicated in the colonies, but with special characteristics. Plantation owners amassed fortunes from crops worked by slaves – tobacco in the upper colonies of Maryland, Virginia and North Carolina, and cotton in the lower colonies of Georgia and South Carolina. Others made fortunes from trading. Settlers struck out further to the west to farm and graze, and there were confrontations with Native Americans. Through all of this, there was continuous interaction between the leading colonisers and the British ruling families.[46] Young men from good families undertook military service in America as officers in the army. Trade and colonial expansion were the driving forces in almost continuous wars between the European powers, and colonial issues were at the heart of many debates in the British Parliament. There was an intersection between military conflicts, powerful mercantile interests, and the political manoeuvres of the ruling classes.

The disruptions of technological change

The era of colonisation was intricately bound up with major transformations in technology, production and commerce, which came to be described collectively as the industrial revolution. The consequences were far-reaching within Britain and beyond. Previously wealth had depended primarily on ownership of land. Now wealth could be generated by ownership of the means of production. Trade had been important from antiquity, but could now be conducted across an empire stretching around the globe, generating great wealth for merchants.

As we saw earlier in the chapter, in 1764 the invention of the spinning jenny revolutionised the production of cloth, in turn leading to the construction of factories in the English Midlands, accelerating the movement of rural workers to the towns, and opening up the prospects of wealth for a growing mercantile class trading in manufactured goods. This was the age of invention: machinery for agriculture and for the new factories, as machines replaced muscles, and also in the generation of energy, in the sciences of chemistry and metallurgy, and in medicine. In

1765, James Watt adapted an earlier steam engine for industrial use and opened the way for new steel technologies. Joseph Priestley pursued discoveries with electricity and gases. These discoveries and innovations transformed the bedrock of society. But the fundamental imbalances thus generated were only dimly perceived – if at all – by those in power at the time. As their wealth grew, the traditional elites made the best of their good fortune, while making sure that they maintained their status in the social hierarchy above the newly rich factory owners and merchants. They did not notice or did not think it important that the imbalances in society that they had taken for granted were changing under their feet. They did not see the risks emerging to their way of life, nor did they perceive the upheavals looming ahead.

The industrial revolution was not something that happened overnight. Innovations and discoveries during earlier decades, including Franklin's experiments with electricity, laid the groundwork for the transformations of 1760 onwards. Indeed, the term 'revolution' is not strictly appropriate, as it was more a series of evolutions. But the term 'Industrial Revolution' entered general usage from the early nineteenth century. We make a distinction here between the use of the term 'revolution' to describe social and economic transformations, occurring over several decades, and the political revolutions which were major upheavals that changed the fate of nations and their citizens – notably the five revolutions from the American and French revolutions of the eighteenth century to the Chinese and Russian revolutions of the twentieth century.

As we shall see, through each of these five revolutions, the course of history was changed suddenly and dramatically by political upheaval that was the consequence of fundamental transformations underway in society. The disruptions of industrialisation, which began in Britain around 1760, then reached other countries in Europe and their colonies in waves. Each wave of economic and social change had political consequences.

The expansion of international trade

Intimately linked with the industrial revolution was the expansion of international trade. For some two centuries, European expeditions of discovery across the oceans had been driven by the search for riches in distant lands. Historically, the Chinese had been more technologically advanced than the Europeans, with great ships that sailed throughout Asia and as far as Africa, but they had stopped their voyages of discovery early in the fifteenth century. From about that time, smaller European ships began to explore the world's oceans. Trade followed discovery, together with early colonisation. By the mid-eighteenth century, the prospects for generating wealth from sea-trade had increased dramatically. British seafarers established their pre-eminence over those of other European countries just as the first wave of the industrial revolution developed in the English Midlands, and new entrepreneurs made fortunes as trade expanded across the oceans.

What was traded? British merchant skippers could make fortunes out of triangular trading, down the coasts of Africa then across the Atlantic to the Caribbean and American colonies. They could barter goods for slaves in Africa, sell them in the plantation colonies, then carry raw sugar from the Caribbean to distilleries in America and tobacco or cotton from America back to Europe. Trading posts were established along the western and eastern coasts of Africa on the way to India and the Orient. Trade to and from India and the East Indies was also immensely profitable: tea and spices in one direction, manufactured goods, notably textiles, in the other. The European sea-faring nations – Britain, France, Spain, Portugal and Holland – jostled for trade and territory around the globe. Seafarers and traders were followed by settlers and troops. The age of colonisation and globalisation began with industrial transformation. And by the eighteenth century, the greatest of the global empires was that of Britain.

The cost of European colonial wars

Inevitably, the colonial powers clashed. In North America, the French and the British fought each other on and off, each with allies among the indigenous Native Americans. These skirmishes were precursors to the Seven Years' War, in which other European powers allied with either the British or the French also participated. The war extended throughout their empires from 1756 to 1763, and was played out in Asia, Africa, the Caribbean and, most of all, in North America. The preoccupation, if not obsession, of Britain's rulers was first and foremost the world-wide conflict between the British and French empires.

It was to be the irony of history that Britain's success in defeating France at the end of the Seven Years' War would sow the seeds for Britain's later loss of the American colonies. Even while private wealth grew in Britain, the coffers of the government were impoverished by the years of war. The empire had expanded but at a cost, and debates in the British Parliament – still dominated by the 200 families of the landed aristocracy – turned to financing the system put in place for preservation of the empire, and especially for the defence of the American colonies. So it was that the British Government of the 1760s under Lord Grenville conceived of the Stamp Tax for the colonies, with the argument that the colonies should contribute to their own defence – as we saw, an argument vehemently rebuffed by the colonists.

The force of ideas

Along with the huge changes underway in the structure of economies and societies, new thinking about the nature of power and governance was emerging. New ideas were debated, published and read by an increasingly literate population on both sides of the Atlantic. This era of new ideas came to be known as the Age of Enlightenment or the Age of Reason. Scientists and philosophers circulated their ideas through books and newspapers, literary salons, coffee houses and Masonic lodges. As society was transformed by discovery and innovation, fundamental questions were raised about the relations between rulers and populations. The notion that the social order was in the nature of things was challenged, as was the notion of divine right, which had sustained the established order from feudal times.

The prolific French writer known as Voltaire was outspoken through his essays, novels and plays advocating individual liberty, and he pursued his ideas with penetrating satires of intolerance, religious dogma and the institutions of the monarchy. Banned by Louis XV, he moved to Geneva in 1755. There, Jean-Jacques Rousseau had published *A Discourse on Inequality*. Although Rousseau was an admirer of Voltaire, the great author was dismissive of the naivete of the younger man's writings. Voltaire was a clever dilettante, but he was an advocate for personal liberty, not necessarily for democracy and he barely concealed his disdain for the masses. Just as the industrial revolution was getting underway in the English Midlands, in 1762 Rousseau published a work that would become the cornerstone of political thought: *The Social Contract*, which presented the then radical notion that the whole population, women included, constituted 'the sovereign', not a monarch who ruled by divine right. Under the Social Contract, the government should govern with the consent of the governed. The notion of the Social Contract underpinned the legitimacy of government. Legitimacy was a powerful idea, since it held that rulers could not rely on assertions of inherited or divine right but had to be legitimate in the eyes of the ruled. The Enlightenment also validated the idea that it was legitimate to contest the existing order, to rise up in protest and, if necessary, to overthrow that order.

In Britain, Edmund Burke, the Irish parliamentarian, and friend of Benjamin Franklin, developed these ideas into a rationale in support of the claims of the American colonists. Following the publication of the widely read Franklin satires in Britain, Thomas Paine went to America and distilled the case for a republic and independence in *Common Sense*. Thomas Jefferson and his friends in America drew upon other Enlightenment thinkers in France such as Montesquieu to develop the principle of separation of powers. Together, the thinkers of the Enlightenment laid the intellectual foundations for the American Revolution. But even as Benjamin Franklin negotiated the support of the French monarchy for the Americans rebelling against the British Empire, the force of ideas of the Enlightenment was also laying the groundwork for France's own revolution.

Hubris and nemesis

As the American Revolution began in 1775, the British elite remained confident that they could put the uprising down by force as they had before, both in the American colonies and elsewhere in the empire. They dismissed the colonial revolutionaries as undisciplined adventurers. The early clashes would later be immortalised in history courses taught to generations of American pupils. But on 4 July 1776, when the Declaration of Independence was read from a balcony in Boston, it was by no means certain that the revolution would succeed. As the battles wore on, the revolutionaries sought the support of Britain's traditional enemy, France, just as Lord Chatham, Pitt the Elder, predicted they would. As Franklin negotiated with the government of Louis XVI, republican revolutionaries and the French monarchy were united in mutual antipathy for the British. Even after the French formally agreed in 1778 to support the colonists and Lafayette sailed for America, the British believed that they would prevail. Certainly, they underestimated the fighting capacity of the revolutionaries and the critical importance of their alliance with France.

But something deeper was at work. Underlying the ebb and flow of the revolutionary war was a powerful tide of history that the British elite failed to perceive. In the tragedies of ancient Greece, *hubris,* or the arrogance of overwhelming pride and over-confidence, would inevitably be followed by the retribution of *nemesis.* The British elite was schooled in the classics but forgot this lesson. So, they continued to dance. In 1780 King George held the great ball in honour of his beloved Charlotte. The establishment families returned to London from their country homes for a new parliamentary season when yet again politics, business and courtship would be pursued and intertwined in a game of alliances. It was the year before it all changed.

Chapter 2

The French Revolution

A celebration and a catastrophe

In May 1770, two of Europe's monarchies were allied by marriage. The heir to the throne of France – the *dauphin* – was Louis-Auguste, grandson of King Louis XV, who had become heir to the throne when his father died in 1765. His bride was Marie-Antoinette of Austria, second youngest child of the redoubtable Empress Maria-Theresa of the Habsburg dynasty. The bride was fourteen, the groom not quite sixteen. Two weeks of celebration followed a ceremony in the Cathedral of Reims, culminating in a great fireworks display in the centre of Paris on 30 May, in the vast central square named for the groom's grandfather, King Louis XV. Suddenly, a rocket went astray, landing in the midst of the fireworks being readied for the grand finale. A huge explosion followed, causing panic in the crowd of thousands. As people tried to flee many were trampled to death. The official death toll was put at 131. The actual number of deaths was thought to be much higher – up to 400. The young couple were appalled and sent funds to the families of the victims. They could not have suspected that at this very same place, twenty-three years later, they would be executed by guillotine. Place Louis XV would become Place de la Révolution. Today, it is Place de la Concorde.

The game of alliances

In 1770, France was still recovering from the Seven Years' War (1756–1763), which involved, as we saw in Chapter 1, most of the great powers of Europe and their colonies. France was left heavily in debt, while Britain – whose king, George III, had been on the throne since 1760 – emerged with an expanded empire and became the dominant power. Prussia was rising as a force on the European continent. In the game of alliances among the competing monarchies of Europe, the marriage joining the ruling dynasties of France and Austria was above all a political calculation.[1]

This was the year, as we also saw in Chapter 1, when King George appointed a new prime minister, Lord Frederick North. Shortly after the marriage of the French *dauphin*, North faced a crisis when the Spanish governor in Buenos Aires sent ships and troops to threaten the British base in the Falkland Islands in the southern Atlantic Ocean. The Spanish called for France to support them, invoking the family pact between the related Bourbon monarchies of the two kingdoms. But when Louis XV of France declined, the Spanish had to back down and leave the Falklands to the British. This incident heightened North's reputation and also reinforced a belief in British ruling circles that the French would not confront them again in colonial matters. That belief would later prove to be misguided when Benjamin Franklin succeeded in negotiating French support for the Americans. In the meantime, North would remain in office for the next twelve years – including the whole period of the American Revolution.

A new king

Upon the death of Louis XV in 1774, Louis-Auguste became King Louis XVI, a month before reaching the age of twenty. The new French king took the decision to inoculate himself and his brothers against smallpox, which had caused the death of his grandfather. Taking more doses than his brothers, Louis-Auguste suffered fever and other symptoms, but he recovered in time for his coronation. With the French economy in recession since 1770, Louis XVI took early steps to reduce expenses, for example cutting the number of horses in the royal stables by more than two-thirds, from 6,000 to 1,800. Louis aspired to be a good king, and showed in his edicts his desire to be loved by the people,[2] beginning with an early decision to exempt his subjects from the tax usually levied for the coronation of a new monarch. At the beginning of his reign, these measures were part of a modest attempt to curb the excesses of the royal court, following the grandiose eras of his forebears, Louis XV and especially that of Louis XIV, the builder of Versailles.

Louis XVI's young wife, Marie-Antoinette, was now Queen of France at the age of eighteen. By the time of the coronation, the marriage of the young couple had produced no heir. Rumours spread around the court of Versailles about the incapacity of the king to fulfil his conjugal duties. Doctors were consulted, but by most accounts they could find nothing physically wrong with him. Louis simply preferred to go hunting! In April 1777, the queen's brother, Emperor Joseph II of Austria, the last Holy Roman Emperor, visited Paris, travelling incognito under the name of the Count of Falkenstein. His young sister confided in him that her husband never joined her in bed. Joseph talked frankly with his brother-in-law about the need for him to give attention to his wife. Finally, seven years after their marriage, Marie-Antoinette wrote to her mother in Vienna: 'At last!' to announce that the marriage had been consummated. Their first child was born the following year.

Jacques Necker

During the later years of the long reign of Louis XV, a young banker from Geneva in Switzerland had made his fortune in Paris. Jacques Necker had moved to Paris at the age of fifteen as a clerk in a bank owned by a friend of his father. Within a few years he became a partner, before founding his own bank with another Genevois named Peter Thellusson. The two Swiss bankers, operating in London and Paris, became very wealthy by speculating on the trade in grains and by making loans to the French Treasury.

In his early thirties, Necker courted Madame de Vermenoux, the young widow of a French officer from a leading family. When visiting Necker in Paris, Madame de Vermenoux took along her companion, the impoverished but well-educated daughter of a pastor from Crassier in Switzerland. Her name was Suzanne Curchod and, as we heard in Chapter 1, she was recovering from the break-up of her engagement to the young British scholar, Edward Gibbon, later a famous historian, whose father had vehemently opposed the match. Back in 1758, as his romance with Suzanne was thwarted by his father's veto, Gibbon wrote: 'I sighed as a lover, I obeyed as a son.'[3] In May 1764, Suzanne and Edward had a final emotional parting in Ferney, near Geneva. Returning to Paris, Suzanne turned her attention to the ambitious young banker who was courting her benefactor. By the end of the year, she and Jacques Necker were married. Suzanne's lively intellect attracted Necker, but perhaps he also saw in her a partner for his ambitions. In any case, he turned away from the wealthy young widow for the girl from the Swiss countryside.

Necker and his new wife quickly became the eighteenth-century equivalent of a power couple. Suzanne encouraged Jacques to take a public position, and he became Syndic (director-general) of the French East India Company, which was owned by the State. He was also appointed as Representative of the Republic of Geneva, which introduced him into political circles. Necker demonstrated both his financial knowledge and his skill as a writer, with a memoir defending the autonomy of the East India Company from the French Treasury. By 1772 he had left the affairs of his bank in the hands of his partner, Thellusson. With a considerable fortune at his disposal, he confided the management of the family's personal finances to his wife, Suzanne, so as to concentrate on writing.[4] In 1773, he won the prize of the Académie Française for a book entitled *Eulogy to Colbert*, referring to the minister of finance under Louis XIV, who had managed the nation's budget for nearly two decades. This was the era when France expanded its trade and possessions across the seas, and Colbert was the founder of the French merchant marine. Necker's book on Colbert was essentially a defence of State corporatism, but he also devoted much of it to a description of the qualities required to be a great minister. In it, he outlined the main themes that would guide his own role later when he was in charge of the finances of the French State.

Meanwhile, Suzanne Necker established a Friday salon, where she entertained the leaders of the political, financial and literary circles of Paris. They included, for example, Denis Diderot, co-compiler of the monumental work *L'Encyclopédie*, and Baron von Grimm, friend of the philosopher Jean-Jacques Rousseau from Geneva. There was Jean-Baptiste Greuze, the portrait artist most in vogue at the time; there were writers, poets, and philosophers, renowned in their day, even if their names have since disappeared into the mists of time. Suzanne also maintained an extensive correspondence with various men of letters as they travelled across Europe.

Benjamin Franklin arrived in Paris in December of 1776 to represent the second Continental Congress as the Commissioner of the thirteen

American colonies fighting for their independence from the British. Preceded by his fame, as we saw in Chapter 1, Franklin was received by Louis XVI at Versailles, and soon proved adept at influencing the French opinion-leaders who met in salons like that of Suzanne Necker. As a sign that Franklin was accepted in the circles of French power, Greuze painted his portrait.[5]

The *acquis* of privilege

During his years as a banker, Necker had established close relations with the controller-general (or minister) of finances, Abbé Terray.[6] When Louis XVI succeeded his grandfather in 1774, he appointed a new minister for finance, Anne-Robert Turgot, together with a new minister in charge of the royal household and the police, Chrétien de Malesherbes. Turgot and Malesherbes tried to levy new taxes on the nobles, but were blocked in the regional parliaments, which were non-elected bodies dominated by landowners and local dignitaries. The aristocrats argued that it was their legal right to live off their vast properties without paying taxation to the State.

The notion of 'acquired rights' or '*acquis*' of the privileged was a continual and powerful thread that can be found running through all the resistances to reform that preceded each of the five revolutions described in this book. This notion of inherent rights to privilege has always been intangible yet immensely powerful. It helps to explain why elites have so often ignored the writing on the wall, the signs of danger ahead[7] and have continued to 'dance before storms'. It is a theme to which we will return.

Turgot was in favour of free trade and issued an edict to deregulate the trade in grain, against opposition within the Ministerial Council. Many leading figures of the day, including members of the nobility, had made large profits from the grain trade. Necker published a voluminous work on the subject, which had even more success than his award-winning *Eulogy to Colbert*. He took issue with Turgot by arguing against free trade and in favour of regulation. The poor grain harvest of 1774 reinforced popular sentiment against Turgot's edict.

Mirabeau's personal rebellion

In the year of the American Declaration of Independence, 1776, Count Honoré Mirabeau published his *Essay on Despotism*, which denounced arbitrary royal power. Mirabeau had been born into provincial nobility. Ugly and deformed at birth, with an enormous head, he was scarred by smallpox at the age of three. His childhood was marked by the severity of his father, while as a young man in the military, he gained a reputation for *libertinage* and accumulated gambling debts. His father had him sent to prison several times in an endeavour to control his dissolute son. Mirabeau's father arranged a marriage for him with the daughter of a powerful marquis. But then, to escape his debtors, he was exiled to the Château de Joux in Franche-Comté, in the Jura mountains. Using his charm, he persuaded the governor of the prison to allow him to visit the nearby town of Pontarlier on the Swiss border. In 1775, on the occasion of a celebration in the local town as Louis XVI was crowned in Reims, he met the young wife of the Marquis de Monnier, who was also almost fifty years older than her. A powerful noble, the marquis was President of the Court of Accounts in Dole, the regional capital. Mirabeau began a passionate affair with the young woman. The two lovers fled across France and Belgium all the way to Holland. During their flight Mirabeau wrote his *Essay on Despotism*. Forged by the severity of his childhood, his essay was derived from his personal rebellion against the protocols of society, and when published it became a powerful protest against the monarchy of the *ancien régime*. Later it would be cited to establish his revolutionary credentials.

The fugitive lovers were captured in Amsterdam. Sophie de Monnier was condemned for adultery and sentenced to seclusion for life in a convent. Mirabeau was sentenced to death for kidnapping and seduction. Sophie gave birth to a daughter, who was taken from her and given to a wet nurse. Through family influence, combined with his charm and eloquence, Mirabeau managed to escape the death sentence, but was imprisoned in the dungeon of Vincennes from 1777 to 1780. There, Mirabeau met the infamous Marquis de Sade who was also imprisoned; it is said that the two even fought physically over some difference.

Mirabeau's daughter with Sophie died in 1780. He never saw her. While in prison he wrote profusely, ranging from philosophy to crude eroticism. His book entitled *Letters of the Signet and the Prisons of the State*,[8] again based on his personal experience, was published in 1782. His passionate collection called *Letters to Sophie* was published much later, in 1792, after his death, and was widely acclaimed for its literary merit. This was the story of the early life of a man who would later play a key role in the French Revolution, who would recklessly undermine Necker's calls for peace and then his reforms, and who would after his death be exposed as having played a shameless double game.

Necker's rise to power

In April and May 1776, just as the American Revolution began near Boston, and knowing nothing of Mirabeau, Jacques and Suzanne Necker visited London, where they were received by King Georges III. They also met with the prime minister, Lord North, and Edward Gibbon, Suzanne's former fiancé, who was by now a famous author and member of parliament. Conveniently, they were away from Paris when Turgot's dismissal was announced on 12 May,[9] followed by the resignation of Malesherbes, so Necker was able to keep his distance from the plots at the royal court, while positioning himself for high office. At his wife's suggestion, Necker transferred his bank shares to his older brother Louis, clearing the way for government service.

Returning to Paris, Necker was appointed by the king as director of the Royal Treasury. In June 1777, he was promoted to the post of director-general of finances. Drawing on his experience as a banker, Necker initially sidestepped the thorny taxation issue, which had led to the downfall of Turgot, by taking out large international loans. As he had foreshadowed in his book on Colbert, once in office Necker was an assertive reformer. He set about tightening the administration of finances, limiting arbitrary decisions by officials, advocating transparency in government, proposing devolution of taxation and other powers to provincial assemblies, and establishing commissions for the reform of hospitals and prisons.

When, in May 1778, the royal court announced the joyful news that the queen was pregnant, Suzanne Necker seized the opportunity to obtain from the king a personal commitment to open a hospital for children in a Benedictine convent. The finesse of her strategy and extent of her influence are evident: here was the daughter of a Protestant pastor taking this initiative in a Catholic convent at a time when the king and queen were expecting their first child. While her husband exercised effective control of the monarchy's finances, he was excluded from the council of ministers because of his Protestant faith. But his wife's initiative conveyed a message that they as Protestants could integrate themselves into a Catholic society that still bore the scars of the religious wars of past centuries. Madame Necker's initiative also demonstrated the social conscience of the couple. Some years later the revolutionary council named the hospital in her honour. The Necker Hospital for Sick Children, the first paediatric hospital in the world, is still operating today and is known worldwide as one of France's leading medical institutions.

Benjamin Franklin conducted his negotiations on behalf of the American colonies officially with the French Foreign Minister, Vergennes. But, ever the networker, he made sure that he maintained regular contact with other key officials, in particular Necker as the powerful new director-general of finances. Turgot had opposed France's engagement in the American uprisings on financial grounds. His reticence was shared by Necker, who made it clear to Franklin that he was cautious about the financial implications.[10] Far from being deterred, Franklin set about cultivating, in his usual affable way, a personal friendship with Necker while encouraging the lobbying efforts of French traders. As we saw in Chapter 1, the Marquis de Lafayette also mounted an effective campaign, sending letters to influential French political and business figures from George Washington's winter encampment in Valley Forge, near Philadelphia.

A burgeoning national debt

France's public finances were already in a parlous state when France signed the Franco-American Treaties in 1778, committing support to the American Revolution and thus increasing the nation's debt considerably. Necker turned his financial expertise to finding a way to fund French participation in the American war. He continued to negotiate loans with high interest rates to fund the national debt. These loans were based on *rentes viagères* (life annuities), which enabled him to raise capital against the promise of annuities with a guaranteed interest rate of ten per cent, regardless of the age of the subscriber. Well-to-do families of the nobility and bourgeoisie hastened to lend capital to the State, subscribed in the names of their youngest children, so as to get the high interest annuities for as many years as possible. Necker was widely applauded as a financial genius, although discordant voices pointed to the flaws in the system, not only the high interest rate, but also the scope for speculation. Necker's system was based on an eighteenth-century version of what would be called 'financial engineering' in the late twentieth century.

Necker's aura of financial genius was enhanced by his wife's continued hosting of the premier literary salon of France, and her ability to attract the participation of leading thinkers of the day. For a time, the prevailing consensus of opinion-leaders was strongly in his favour. But even as he was lauded for his financial acumen, Necker was engaged in constant battles with the ministers for the marine and the army. Both refused to provide accounting for their expenditures, notably for the rebuilding of the French marine fleet and the army. They relied on their political influence with Vergennes to resist the demands of the Finance Directorate. The Ministry for Marine issued bonds without the Finance Ministry's approval, which could not be reimbursed when they reached their due dates. For Necker, it was a nightmare.[11] The minister for the marine, Antoine de Sartine, wielded influence with the king, having previously served as his chief of police. Sartine had developed a secret police considered to be the most efficient in Europe, which he used to provide the king with reports of political manoeuvres as well as titillating sexual scandals. Finally, in late 1780, Necker protested to the king, who angrily dismissed Sartine.[12] The king told his wife, 'We have to sacrifice Sartine, as we cannot do without Necker.' The minister for war, an ally of Sartine, resigned shortly thereafter. Necker's political star was in the ascendant. But from the American rebels came more requests for financial support, astutely presented to Foreign Minister Vergennes by Franklin, and supported politically by Lafayette, who had returned to America with the official support of the king and government. Some private French suppliers to the Americans were unpaid, and Necker released State funds to bail them out. While supporting the war effort, Necker also looked for a way of ending it before the burden on the French economy became too great. It was during this time, in December 1780, that Necker wrote his secret letter to England's prime minister, Lord North, proposing a peaceful settlement between France and Britain.[13]

By January 1781, France was approaching bankruptcy. In February 1781, with the Council's approval, Necker ordered the issue of two new loans, with high interest rates, which made them attractive to investors such as the Bank Pictet et Cie in Geneva. But they would prove to be ruinous for the State.[14]

Report to the King

Then, still in February 1781, Necker took the unprecedented step of making public a document in three volumes entitled *Report to the King*, which detailed the finances of the kingdom and of the royal household itself. Necker announced that the proceeds of the sale of the document would be allocated to programmes to aid the poor. Within weeks, after several reprints, more than 100,000 copies were sold, breaking all previous records for book sales in France.[15] However, Necker omitted any mention in his voluminous report of the loans[16] used to finance support for the American war of independence, and this drew much criticism, both from his contemporaries and, later, from historians. The need to service the loans with their high interest rates had a major impact on expenditures, yet Necker chose not to mention them. Rather, he laid out the excesses of the royal court – a legitimate criticism in itself, but one that did not tell the full story. The *Report to the King* gave a rosy picture of state finances, so as to maintain the confidence of lenders, but it remained silent about the loans used to cover the cost of support for the Americans. Necker's exposure of the extravagance of the royal court won him great popularity with the people but earned him the enmity of the king's brothers[17] and the circles around them, and of all those who benefited from royal patronage. Most of all, Necker committed the cardinal sin, in the eyes of the elite, of making his report public. Criticism against Necker developed.

Suzanne Necker took the unusual step of going directly to Jean-Frédéric Maurepas, the king's chief adviser, to ask him to stop the campaign of criticism against her husband.[18] Maurepas had previously influenced the king to appoint Turgot and Malesherbes as well as Vergennes, before turning against Turgot and proposing Necker in his place. But Necker's political support crumbled, and he sensed that he no longer had the king's support. After meeting with Maurepas, Necker wrote a brief and laconic letter of resignation. As the king made himself unavailable, he gave it in person to Queen Marie-Antoinette. She tried for a moment to dissuade him, but she then took it to Louis XVI who, offended by the peremptory tone of Necker's letter, declared, 'I will never employ him again anywhere.'[19]

By all accounts, Necker had become more and more frustrated by the infighting at the royal court and the refusal of the aristocratic elite, including members of the royal family, to face the realities of the impact of their excesses on the nation's finances. He had risen to power as an outsider, a Protestant from Calvinist Geneva, where Swiss tradition held that the people were sovereign. With that background, he tried to change the ways of an entrenched Catholic aristocracy under an absolutist monarchy. He introduced significant administrative reforms and, together with his wife, he demonstrated a keen social conscience. Moreover, he was well aware of his popularity with the general public. This combination of factors would have played into his unprecedented decision to release his report to the public, announcing at the same time that the proceeds of the sale of the report would be donated to charitable causes. There was an element of political calculation – or miscalculation – but also a sense of martyrdom, or at least a belief that he could appeal to the people over the heads of the elite, hence the unrepentant and laconic tone of his letter of resignation to Louis XVI.

Upon hearing the news of his resignation, crowds of Parisians went to Necker's home outside the capital to express their support – a precursor to events that would lead to the French Revolution eight years later. Necker's depiction of the royal court as extravagant gained him widespread support among ordinary people, and street demonstrations protesting his departure continued for several weeks. Artists and engravers produced drawings and stamps in Necker's honour, and pamphlets in support of Necker, often with caricatures of the royal family, were distributed throughout Paris and in the provinces. At the Paris Bourse, the values of royal bonds and shares in the Compagnie des Indes fell dramatically. Necker himself fell ill, but by September he was able to attend a public event at the Louvre, where he was applauded by the crowd.

The education of a prodigy

For a time, the Neckers rented an apartment in Paris so that Suzanne could continue holding her weekly literary salons. They had only one child, their daughter Anne-Louise. Suzanne Necker's intelligence was directed to support for her husband in his career and to her charity work, but most of all to the education of her capable daughter. That Suzanne excelled in all three tasks was evident. But as she wrote later, her daughter's education was her greatest achievement, the education of a young girl who would become a leading thinker and writer in her own right and would show that a woman could exercise immense political influence in a world dominated by men.

Suzanne Necker's approach to education was strict. Young Anne-Louise was given a traditional and rigorous education, learning Latin and English, as well as dance and music. Suzanne employed teachers for this variety of disciplines, while supervising her daughter's general upbringing with the perfectionism that she applied to everything she did. In later years, Suzanne wrote: 'For thirteen years I cultivated her memory and her mind. These were the best years of my life.'[20] Suzanne also passed on her own passion for literature. As a ten-year-old, during her mother's Friday salons, Anne-Louise sat on a little stool, listening to the conversation of the adults. Around this time, her parents began to call her by her second name, Germaine.

By the age of fourteen, when her father was at the height of his career as the king's financial maestro, Germaine Necker opened her own literary circle. More luminaries were attracted to the family home in Paris. In the very same year (1780), across the Channel in England, young girls of her social status and not much older than her, were presented at the first Queen Charlotte's Ball. As debutantes, these young ladies entered the social round of 'the Season', preparing for courtship and marriage, while still in their teens. But this kind of frivolous social whirl was not for Germaine Necker. Instead, in Paris, she was engaging in thought provoking discussions with the leading intellectuals of the day.

Necker was inclined to be pompous, but his daughter could make him loosen up. One anecdote described the Necker family at table, dining with dignity under the severe regard of Madame, when a servant entered to tell her mistress that a visitor had arrived to see her. The instant her mother left the room, Germaine threw her napkin at her father, who caught it and made it into a turban for his head. Laughing together, father and daughter danced around the table, then as they heard Madame Necker returning, quickly regained their places, looking like naughty school children.[21]

Necker in exile; Mirabeau out of prison

Such innocent diversions were soon overtaken by political upheaval. By the time Germaine turned fifteen, her famous father was out of office. Following his resignation, Necker travelled around Europe, then returned to the region of Geneva. Along the shores of Lac Léman, in the town of Coppet, he purchased a medium-sized chateau from the family of his former banking associate, Peter Thellusson. There, he wrote a treatise on the administration of finances. Like his earlier books, this new three-volume publication had great success in France.

Meanwhile, Mirabeau was released from prison in 1782 under the tutorship of his father. He rushed to see Sophie de Monnier at the convent of Gien. But he soon returned to Paris and never saw her again. Released from the convent after the death of her husband in 1783, Sophie lingered for several years, before committing suicide at the age of thirty-five in September 1789, just as her former lover rose to power in the year of the Revolution.

Overcoming a congenital speech defect, Mirabeau showed his powers of oratory in a trial for divorce brought by his wife in 1783, the year of Sophie's release. The case and the eloquence of Mirabeau and of the opposing lawyer, Jean-Étienne-Marie Portalis, captured the headlines of the newspapers of the day, overshadowing even the reporting of the Paris peace negotiations culminating in recognition of the United States of America. Mirabeau lost the case, which was decided in favour of his wife. But later, when Mirabeau was rejected by his own class of nobles at the General Estates, he would gain the political support of Portalis in winning election to the Third Estate of the common people. As for Portalis, he would later be commissioned with other jurists by Napoléon Bonaparte to draft the Civil Code, notably the sections on marriage, property and contracts, which remains the basis for law in France and throughout continental Europe to this day.

The marriage of Germaine

Jacques and Suzanne Necker were preoccupied with Germaine's marriage prospects, as she reached the age of eighteen. Among the pretenders was William Pitt, who at the age of twenty-four, had become prime minister of Britain. He was the son of William Pitt the Elder, later the Earl of Chatham who, we recall from Chapter 1, had steered Britain to victory in the Seven Years' War with France and had worked with Benjamin Franklin in support of the demands of the American colonists. Pitt the Younger came to power at the end of 1783, after a succession of British governments had failed following the loss of the American colonies and the collapse of the North government, and after the Paris Peace Treaty was signed. He was the youngest prime minister in British history. About the time of his landslide victory in the 1784 elections, Pitt expressed his interest to the Neckers in marrying their daughter. But Germaine refused. That Necker was prepared to consider marrying his only daughter to the British Prime Minister is intriguing, as it showed once again his affinity for France's traditional adversary. Remember that he attended an English-speaking school in Geneva, that during his banking career his partner operated in London while he managed affairs in Paris, that he was received at the highest levels in British society just before he rose to power in France, and that he had tried secretly to negotiate an agreement to end the war with Britain over American independence. But the idea of an alliance with Britain through the marriage of his daughter came to nought, and Pitt remained a bachelor until he died in office years later, in 1806.

The marriage of Anne-Louise Germaine Necker became an affair of state. She attracted the interest of Erik Magnus de Staël, seventeen years older, a member of the diplomatic legation of Sweden in Paris, who had seen her for the first time when she was twelve years old. De Staël was a protegé of Swedish King Gustav III. The Neckers made it known that to be eligible, de Staël would have to hold the rank of ambassador. De Staël successfully negotiated for the island of Saint Barthélemy in the Antilles to be ceded by France to Sweden in exchange for trading access to the port of Göteborg,[22] and a grateful Gustav III then named him Ambassador to France, with the title of Baron Staël-Holstein. Suzanne and Jacques Necker now considered him to be worthy of their daughter. Detailed negotiations followed, as the Neckers sought guarantees that Germaine would never have to leave France against her will, that she would be guaranteed an income for the rest of her life and that Queen Marie-Antoinette would approve the marriage. Finally, the matter was settled when King Gustav, returning from a visit to Italy, spent three days privately at Versailles, and reached an agreement with Marie-Antoinette. This level of negotiation for the marriage of Anne-Louise Germaine Necker showed that, even out of office, Jacques Necker remained close to the royal family and wielded great influence. In 1786, at the age of twenty, Germaine married the ambassador. As Madame de Staël she would become famous as a leading intellectual and writer of the Romantic period in Europe, and she would be closely involved with the twists and turns of the Napoléonic wars and related events in France and throughout Europe.

Financial crisis

Meanwhile, the succession of financial and political crises continued in France. Necker's successor, Charles Alexandre de Calonne, tried other methods for balancing the national accounts, but failed. Bad weather exacerbated the situation, with failures of cereal crops leading to shortages of bread, while the movement of labourers and their families from the countryside to the towns increased. Necker was an expert on the cereal trade, and his writings on finance and commerce continued to win him popularity. But already he was attacked in writings by Mirabeau, who was ferociously opposed to the world of financiers, bankers and traders. In 1787, while back in London, Necker published his own defence, referring to himself in the third person and writing: 'Necker and Mirabeau; two men diametrically opposed, by their character, their morals, their manners, their intelligence, their minds, their talents and their different kinds of occupation.'[23]

By 1788, the monarchy of France was effectively bankrupt. The cost of support for the American Revolution had been enormous. The minister for finance, Calonne, accused Jacques Necker of having used false figures in his famous *Report to the King*. Necker replied publicly through the press. Calonne lost the support of the royal court. Under pressure from Maric-Antoinette and the king's principal advisor, Maurepas, Calonne resigned and was succeeded by the Archbishop de Brienne, a member of the Assembly of Notables who had specialised in financial matters.

France at that time had regional parliaments, composed not of elected deputies but of appointed judges, who mostly defended the interests of the nobility and the Church, but were also the only counterweights to the absolute monarchy. Under pressure from these parliaments and especially the Parliament of Paris, the king announced that he would convene the General Estates, an institution dating from the fourteenth century, which had in earlier days brought representatives of the nobility, the Church and the common people together to address national crises. The General Estates had last been convened by Louis XIII in 1614–15, but they had never been held during the long reign of Louis XIV nor that of Louis XV. So, the announcement by Louis XVI conveyed a recognition by the king and his court of the state of crisis facing the nation. But the announcement did little to improve the situation. The Church announced donations to help the State finances, but these were drops in the ocean. The payment of capital invested in bonds was delayed for a year and interest payments were halved. These measures were tantamount to admitting the bankruptcy of the State. They were followed by panic on the stock market.

Marie-Antoinette believed that Necker's recall would help to re-establish confidence. Louis XVI had not forgiven Necker for his cavalier attitude when he resigned after the publication of his *Report to the King*, so the queen arranged for Necker to be approached indirectly by an Austrian diplomat. Necker made it clear to the diplomat that he would not accept a technical position as deputy to the finance minister. His reinstatement was negotiated and occurred in a series of steps orchestrated by Marie-Antoinette, involving even the Vatican. The Pope agreed to make the Archbishop de Brienne a cardinal. The minister resigned in return for an indemnity and the cardinal's hat, and he left for Italy. By the end of August 1788, Necker was appointed a minister of the king. He was the only non-noble and non-Catholic minister. When the news became public, the stock market bounced back. But this demonstration of Necker's popularity was not enough to solve the State's financial problems, as Necker himself knew only too well.[24]

Necker's return to power

Now the leading political figure in France, Necker had the political authority to act, and he did so quickly. There was a grave shortage of wheat, and thus of bread, the staple food of the French population. Necker banned the export of cereals, imported wheat, and instructed the police to ensure that the grain reached local markets. He recalled the Parliament of Paris, whose members were in exile.

Necker then took the initiative in negotiations for the convening of the General Estates, which had been announced previously by the king. He gave particular attention to the Third Estate, which was supposed to represent ninety-seven per cent of the population. Necker persuaded the Assembly of Notables, representing the aristocracy, to accept that the representation of the Third Estates should be doubled so as to equal the representation of the Nobility and the Church combined. He also proposed that the date for this national crisis meeting be advanced to May 1789. He obtained loans of 70 million livres to keep State finances going until that date, noting that 100 million livres would be required to fund a full twelve months. He personally lent two million livres to the State.[25] All his actions from September 1788 to the following May were those of a man who recognised the acute danger facing the royal regime, and who sought to reform that regime in order to save it. Meanwhile, his policies on taxation and budget reform continued to win him widespread popularity among the broad public.

Even so, an alliance was forming between two men, an alliance that would later harass Necker. These men were Mirabeau and his neighbour in Paris, a young priest named Charles-Maurice de Talleyrand-Périgord, who was already showing his capacity for political influence. In 1786, Talleyrand had arranged for Vergennes to send Mirabeau on two missions to Berlin. The following year, Mirabeau published his *Secret Chronicles of the Court of Berlin*.[26] The book was an embarrassment for the French Government because of its revelations of behind-the-scenes political deals, and it was censored, but copies were circulated and helped to boost Mirabeau's notoriety. When the General Estates were convened in 1789, Mirabeau was refused a seat in the First Estate of nobles, and he was elected instead, with the support of his former adversary in his divorce trial, Portalis, to a seat in the Third Estate of commoners. Talleyrand took a seat in the Second Estate, that of the clergy.

The General Estates

On 4 May 1789 there was an air of anticipation. More than a thousand participants in the General Estates from all parts of France gathered in Versailles. They marched in procession through the streets to the chapel of the palace for a solemn mass. On the next day they took their places in the Great Hall before the king. The clergymen – a total of 219 bishops, priests and monks – sat to the right of the throne. On the king's left were 270 nobles. Seated directly in front of him were 578 deputies of the Third Estate, elected by districts, known as *baillies*, throughout the kingdom. King Louis opened the proceedings, followed by the Garde des Sceaux, the keeper of official seals. The main speaker was Jacques Necker, the minister of finance. His speech on the finances of the State was long, detailed and tedious. As he suffered from a cold, much of it was read for him by an official. He concluded with an appeal for representatives to leave aside their factional interests and to consider instead the interests of the nation, setting aside personal rivalries and radical claims, in a pragmatic spirit of moderation and conciliation. Necker's last sentence had echoes of his friend Benjamin Franklin's final appeal to the Constitutional Congress of the United States just eighteen months earlier, as he said: 'Finally, gentlemen, you will not be envious of what only time can achieve, and you will leave something for it to do. For if you attempt to reform everything that seems imperfect, your work will lead to poor results.'[27]

The deputies of the Third Estate paid little attention. They were furious about the king's announcement, on the advice of his councillors, that the votes of each of the three Estates – clergy, nobles, and elected deputies, would be counted as three equal blocks. The announcement of this decision nullified the effect of the November agreement negotiated by Necker to double the representation of the Third Estate. It was perceived as betrayal.

Necker, supported by his daughter, favoured a constitutional monarchy like that of Britain, with a bicameral parliament, and he saw the Third Estate becoming the equivalent of the House of Commons. A meeting was arranged between Necker and Mirabeau, who had similar ideas, although as we have seen, the two men had nothing but disdain for each other. When Mirabeau was ushered into Necker's presence, the minister assumed his chilliest air: 'Well, Sir, Monsieur Malouet tells me you have some propositions for me. What are they?' Mirabeau looked Necker up and down, and replied: 'My proposition, Sir, is to wish you a good day,' turned on his heel and stalked out of the room. He then returned to the meeting where he told his fellow deputy Pierre-Victor

Malouet, leader of the Constitutional Party: 'Your man is a fool. He'll have news from me.'[28]

With Mirabeau in the lead, the deputies of the Third Estate ramped up their demands for political representation and an end to autocracy. Meeting separately at the palace *racquet* court, the Jeu de Paume, they took a solemn vow not to leave Versailles until the Third Estate was recognised as the National Assembly. The short-sighted manoeuvre of the royal court to deny the Third Estate proper representation, and the refusal of the nobility and the Church to relinquish even a modicum of their power doomed the General Estates to failure. The manoeuvre was the fatal flaw that prevented Necker from focusing the General Estates' attention on the need to address the bankruptcy of the State.

In every one of the five revolutions described in this work, there was an opportunity to forestall disaster. These opportunities were missed because of petty calculations which, with the benefit of hindsight, can be seen to have caused the players to lose sight of the larger picture. The British Parliament lost the Americas when the elite acquiesced in the humiliation of Benjamin Franklin before the Privy Council. The monarchists of France lost their opportunity to reform when they reneged on Necker's agreement to increase the representation and thus the votes of the Third Estate. We will find similar moments in each of the other revolutions of the nineteenth and early twentieth centuries. Each time, the miscalculations of those hanging on to power amounted to political failure.

On 28 June, Louis XVI decided to address the General Estates again, and to set out the limits of his concessions. With the support of the nobles and most of the clergy, he sought to re-affirm his authority by refusing to relinquish royal prerogatives, thus rejecting the main demands of the Third Estate. Necker, the reformist, hesitated. He was the king's minister, but he was neither of the nobility nor of the Church, and he knew that something had to change. He was immensely popular with the people. He faced a dilemma, for his presence next to the king would be taken as an endorsement for the hard-line position of the royal court. Germaine pressed her father to assert his position as the advocate of reform. Her views undoubtedly swayed her father, and Jacques Necker decided to boycott the king's speech. Neither Necker nor his daughter foresaw the consequences of this decision. On 11 July, Jacques Necker was dismissed by the king for what he described as Necker's 'extreme condescension towards the General Estates'. This statement was no more than 'spin', for Necker's decision to stay away was clearly intended to show his disapproval of the king's refusal to recognise the demands of the Third Estate for a greater say in the affairs of the nation.

Revolution

The news of Necker's dismissal reached the population of Paris early the next day. Crowds gathered in the streets, as they had after Necker's resignation eight years before. This time the mood was angrier, darker. Demonstrations were held across Paris. In the gardens of the Palais Royal, home of the king's cousin, the Duc d'Orléans – who would later support the revolution – a young journalist named Camille Desmoulins mounted a table before a cafe, a pistol in each hand, and harangued the crowd: 'The dismissal of Monsieur Necker sounds the alarm that the royal guards will come out to massacre us,' he cried. 'Our only recourse is to take up arms.' The crowd marched through the streets holding aloft a wax bust of Necker. The marches and demonstrations continued the next day. More armed bands roamed the streets as the situation became increasingly ominous. On 14 July, thousands of Parisians marched towards the Tuileries Palace in the centre of the city. Groups invaded the military base of Les Invalides, ransacked the arsenal where arms were stored, then crossed the river Seine to the prison of the Bastille. The prison governor at first negotiated with the crowd, then ordered guards to open fire. Troops mutinied. The Bastille fell, and the few prisoners held there were released. The governor was beheaded, and his head carried on a spike. Throughout the city there were scenes of pillage, particularly of grain stores, and tax offices were attacked and burnt. The prévôt des marchands, equivalent of the mayor, suffered the same fate as the prison governor. Other summary executions of officials followed. The French Revolution had begun.

A long fermentation of discontent

When Jacques Necker was dismissed by King Louis XVI on 11 July 1789, the scene was set for the storming of the Bastille three days later, on 14 July. Yet none of the protagonists, neither the protestors who poured into the streets of Paris, nor Jacques Necker, nor certainly the king, could have imagined that they were setting in motion events that would bring down one of the most illustrious monarchies of Europe. Even less could they imagine the terror that would follow.

Just as the American Revolution followed years of growing frustration, so the explosion of revolutionary fervour that erupted after the storming of the Bastille was the consequence of a long fermentation of discontent. As director of the Royal Treasury under Louis XVI, then director-general of finances of France, Necker had sensed the disaffection of the population. Necker's analysis and his intuitions were well-placed. His quest for reform was rational, but it failed. The convening of the General Estates, which Necker believed would oblige the political forces of the nation to confront the realities of the desperate financial situation, in reality provided a forum for the political crisis to come to a head. Necker and his wife Suzanne played the game of influence in Parisian high society better than most. Few doubted the sincerity of the social conscience they displayed, particularly that of Madame Necker. Yet Jacques Necker, brilliant banker and financier, mixed his keen sense of the need for change with a strong dose of political calculation.

Already, in 1781, Necker had been dismissed after the publication of his *Report to the King*, spelling out in detail the excessive spending of the royal court. The report won him popularity with the masses but the antagonism of the elites and the royal court itself. They demanded, and obtained, his resignation. The popular demonstrations of support at that time were a precursor to the protests that would culminate in the storming of the Bastille eight years later. But these earlier demonstrations in 1781 had been peaceful. Thousands of Parisians had marched to Necker's home to express their support for him, but they were certainly more peaceful than the Gordon Riots in Britain in 1780, when the city of London was set ablaze. Yet nine years later, France would plunge into a revolution that changed the course of history in Europe and the world.

The struggle of ideas
We recall from Chapter 1 that during the eighteenth century there was a great deal of interaction across Europe among writers and thinkers in the movement broadly described as the Enlightenment, or the Age of Reason,

which traced its roots back to Isaac Newton's *Principia Mathematica* (1687). Thinkers included the Scots – Adam Smith and John Hume; Montesquieu and Voltaire from France; and Jean-Jacques Rousseau from Switzerland. As a young man, Voltaire (his real name was François-Marie Arouet) had been imprisoned at the Bastille for his criticism of French institutions and he had gone into exile in Britain. There he developed his ideas on individual liberty, freedom of speech, religious tolerance, and opposition to absolutism. After time in France and Prussia, he was banned from Paris by Louis XV and moved to Geneva, finally settling in the nearby village of Ferney. As the industrial revolution got underway in Britain, Rousseau published *The Social Contract* (1762), presenting the case for the consent of the governed and the legitimacy of government.

The writings of Voltaire, Rousseau and Montesquieu – the latter noted for promoting the concept of the separation of powers – strongly influenced Thomas Paine as he wrote *Common Sense* in the American colonies in late 1775 and Thomas Jefferson as he drafted the American Declaration of Independence for its adoption in July 1776. The ideas of the American Revolution in turn strongly influenced the reformists whose writings set the scene for the French Revolution in 1789, and notably the Declaration of the Rights of Man and the Citizen, adopted soon after the storming of the Bastille. Necker, bilingual and able to function like Benjamin Franklin in both French and English, was at the centre of these exchanges. The ideas of the Enlightenment were brought together in Diderot's monumental work, *L'Encyclopédie*, to which many thinkers of the movement contributed, and Diderot was one of the regular participants in Suzanne Necker's literary salon. After Jacques Necker's earlier withdrawal from French politics, he and Suzanne maintained a voluminous correspondence with political figures, intellectuals and reformers across Europe, many of whom visited them at Coppet along the lake near Geneva. By the time Necker was recalled to power in Paris in 1788, this rich exchange of ideas across Europe and the Atlantic gave him a basis for proposing not only economic and administrative reforms, but also reform of the system of absolutist monarchy.

Underlying these intellectual exchanges was the harsh reality of life for the majority of the population of France, and indeed most of Europe. Faced with repeated famines, many people decided to move from the countryside to the cities, but they were still unable to escape grinding poverty. In widely circulated tracts they read about the excesses of the nobility, and those accounts contributed to the long fermentation of discontent. By the time of the General Estates at Versailles, Necker's attempts to adjust the system with stronger representation and more powers to the Third Estate were too little, too late. When even those adjustments were resisted and rejected by the nobility and the Church hierarchy, when Necker boycotted the king's speech and when he was then dismissed, the spark of revolution was lit.

The vigorous, intense and continuous exchange of ideas in salons and in many different meetings, backed by prolific correspondence and pamphleteering, reflected a growing awareness of deep changes underway in the structure of society. The absolute monarchy had reached its pinnacle in France a century earlier under Louis XIV. Thoughtful people close to the elite understood that the political system had to respond to change. These thinkers knew that the old order could no longer be maintained. Necker's role was critical, for he had already held high office, while being by nature a reformer, open to change of the system, and willing to modify political processes.

Necker knew that the notables would not give up their opposition to increased taxation, so he tried to get around the problem by covering the national debt through financial engineering. In so doing, he left himself open to criticism that he continued to avoid the underlying problems of the State. His aim was to bring together reformers and the establishment to seek a consensus on a path to financial stability. So, he moved quickly to recall the Parliament of Paris, most of whose members were in exile, while advancing the convocation of the General Estates. Necker understood the need to reform the system in order to save it. Yet, like many reformers before and after him, Necker's political moves for reform failed to prevent the forces for violent revolution welling up from within a deeply divided society. Indeed, the king's convening of the General Estates in order to seek consensus on how to confront the crisis only revealed the deep divisions in French society and exacerbated them politically. When the king addressed the General Estates and refused to recognise the Third Estate as a National Assembly, Necker showed his disapproval of the king's position by refusing to attend. His subsequent dismissal, for the second time, on 11 July, marked the beginning of the revolution, and of events that were to spin out of anyone's control.

Necker's departure and return into the storm

In his letter of dismissal on 11 July 1789, the king requested that Necker leave Paris immediately. Within hours, Jacques and Suzanne Necker gathered a few belongings and set out by coach for Brussels. They were accompanied by Germaine's husband, Baron de Staël.

The day after the fall of the Bastille, crowds marched to Versailles and demanded that the king and queen go to Paris. The king bent to the crowd's demands. On 16 July he and the queen were driven in a coach escorted by horse-guards into the city. Beyond the royal complex of the Tuileries and the Louvre, they went with their entourage to the City Hall, where the deputies of the Third Estate, joined by some clerics and a few nobles, had moved from Versailles to join the Parliament of Paris, and had declared the formation of a National Constituent Assembly. Lafayette, hero of the American Revolution, was there, having participated in the General Estates as a member of the nobility. A National Guard was rapidly formed with 48,000 citizens and Lafayette was elected as its commander. He immediately ordered the demolition of the Bastille. From the hands of Lafayette, the king accepted the red and blue colours of Paris and joined them to the white ribbon of royalty to form a tricolour *cocarde* fixed to his hat. This became the symbol of the revolution. Seeking to restore calm the king ordered the recall of the royal troops surrounding the city.

That night in the Tuileries Palace, the king wrote to Necker asking him to return to his post as quickly as possible. The king's letter was not an order but a plea for help. A Finance Ministry official named Saint-Léon carried the king's letter and rushed on horseback to Brussels. But the Neckers had already left, taking the route of the Rhine for Basel. Changing horses along the way, Saint-Léon rode to Basel. Coming from Paris by coach, Germaine met her parents there. As Saint-Léon arrived with the letter written personally by Louis XVI, several nobles fleeing Paris gave vivid accounts of the rioting in the capital. Suzanne Necker, in tears, implored her husband to stay away from such a dangerous situation. Their daughter, at first furious at the king's treatment of her father, was now exalted at the idea that Necker could return as the saviour of the nation.

As they gathered for dinner, Necker kept an olympian calm. After dinner, he wrote his reply to the king, insisting that he would agree to return only out of a sense of duty. To his brother he wrote that he returned to Paris reluctantly. 'I am going to regret Coppet,' he wrote, 'for it seems that I will be going into the abyss.'[29]

The next morning, Necker's coach and horses were waiting to take him back to Paris – to his destiny, or to his fate. With his wife and daughter, the man whose dismissal had set off a revolution turned away from the road leading through Switzerland to the calm of Coppet on Lac Léman near Geneva, and he took the direction of the French capital and the revolution. Along the way, peasants lined the country roads, throwing flowers and cheering the great man. The triumphant voyage took five days. In each town, at the end of the day, the horses were released, and men pulled the coach to an *auberge* where Necker and his family rested for the night. Until then, only kings had received such a welcome when they traversed the country.

Reaching the gates to the city, Necker learnt that the former commander of the king's Swiss Guard, Baron Besenval, was being held prisoner in a local *auberge*, and was threatened with transfer to the centre of Paris for execution. Getting down on his knees so as to use the seat of the coach as a writing table, Necker hastily composed a note giving his personal guarantee for the Baron, and sent it to the local municipal authority. As night fell, Jacques and Suzanne Necker, with Germaine de Staël, reached Versailles, welcomed by fireworks and salves of artillery. The next morning, he met the king and queen, who had returned to Versailles, in private. After bending to kiss Marie-Antoinette's hand, Necker made it clear that his approval would be required for ministerial appointments. In the afternoon he appeared to acclamation before the royal court and the king's advisors urged him to go into the capital to restore order and confidence.

On the road from Versailles to Paris, with a cavalry detachment protecting the coach, crowds again called out the name of Necker and threw flowers in his path. Some managed to reach the coach and kiss Necker's hand. His wife, so at ease in her literary salon, was confronted now with the popular enthusiasm of the crowds. Her discomfort was palpable. The coach and cavalry drew up before the grand Hôtel de Ville of Paris. On the steps, waiting to welcome Jacques and Suzanne Necker was Lafayette, the immensely popular commander of the newly formed National Guard. Lafayette led Necker into the municipal hall where the Constituent Assembly was waiting. Acclaimed by the delegates with a standing ovation, Necker accepted, as the king had done just days earlier, the red, white and blue *cocarde* ribbon as the 'colours of liberty'. Then he spoke. Necker appealed: 'With humility, I ask the citizens of Paris' to spare Baron Besenval and thereby signal a general amnesty which will restore calm to France. Moving to the Parliament of Paris, meeting in another room, he made the same appeal. His call for amnesty was enthusiastically endorsed in both assemblies. Then Necker's coach took him back to Versailles, acclaimed again by crowds along the route.

On this day, 30 July, just sixteen days after the storming of the Bastille, Necker's popularity was at its zenith. Mirabeau complained: 'Necker is the new King of France.' But the general amnesty was short-lived. As the news reached the sixty districts of the capital, the legality of the proclaimed amnesty was challenged on the grounds that the delegates had no mandate to adopt it. In the district of l'Oratoire, Mirabeau successfully called for the amnesty to be denounced and called on other districts to do the same. Bands roamed the streets, ripping down posters announcing the amnesty. Within twenty-four hours, by 31 July, the Paris Assemblies revoked their decision of the previous day. 'This defeat would be followed by many others,' wrote Madame de Staël later.[30]

Mirabeau and Necker: the confrontation

By August 1789, in the heady days of the month following the storming of the Bastille, feudalism was abolished, most of the prerogatives of the monarchy were taken away, and with them the privileges of the nobility and the clergy. The assembly adopted the *Declaration on the Rights of Man and of the Citizen*. It was introduced by Lafayette and was directly influenced by his friend, United States Ambassador Thomas Jefferson. The preamble was written by Mirabeau.

Necker's title was now First Minister of Finances. He reported no longer to the king but directly to the Constituent Assembly. But the deputies refused his financial proposals to seek more loans, as 'more of the same'. Talleyrand, the priest who had been a clerical delegate to the

General Estates with the title of Bishop of Autun in Burgundy, had joined the Constituent Assembly. He proposed the sale of Church property, amounting to some ten per cent of all the land in France, for the benefit of the nation. As these sales would take time, the assembly authorised the issuing of notes, called 'assignations', based on the anticipated value of the properties, in return for cash. These notes brought badly needed funds into the national treasury, but they were soon being traded as a form of 'paper money'. Records were poorly kept, and the notes were often not destroyed as the underwritten Church properties were sold. Talleyrand's idea was vigorously promoted by his neighbour and friend Mirabeau, who poured scorn on Necker's proposals for traditional loans. Necker was in turn resolutely opposed to the system of assignations.

Outside the assembly, Necker was the object of especially virulent attacks in Jean-Paul Marat's newspaper *L'Ami du peuple*, which had been published since September 1784. Marat accused Necker of counselling the king to demand the restoration of his powers and privileges, an accusation that seemed ill-founded in view of Necker's history of public advocacy for reform. While Necker's focus was on finance, his political positions were consistent with the notion of a constitutional monarchy responding to the will of a representative assembly. Meanwhile, Mirabeau was engaged in secret negotiations with the king and the queen, for which he was paid, even while supporting the revolution. He advised the king to let the revolution run its course, scheming secretly for the royal powers to be restored with himself as first minister. He tried unsuccessfully to form a political alliance with Lafayette. As Mirabeau pursued his manoeuvres, he showed he had lost nothing of his capacity for oratory and he was elected president of the assembly.

The women's march on Versailles

Meanwhile, economic conditions were harsher than ever, with worsening shortages of bread, a French staple. In October, all it took was a rumour that the king's troops had trampled the new tricolour flag, for the women of the marketplaces of Paris to decide to confront the king and queen at the Palace of Versailles. Seven thousand women took part in what became known as the Women's March on Versailles. The women demanded that the king relocate to Paris to demonstrate his commitment to address the deepening poverty of the people. Lafayette still had 20,000 national guardsmen under his command to keep order, and he persuaded the king to accept their demands. The next morning the king and the royal family moved from Versailles to the Tuileries in Paris, under the escort of Lafayette and the National Guard.

Over the next months, and into the next year, debates continued in the assembly over the financial situation. The royalist democrats or *monarchiens* were allied with Necker, but the majority of deputies opposed his proposals, supporting instead the positions of Talleyrand and Mirabeau. On 11 June 1790, the news reached Paris that Benjamin Franklin had died in Philadelphia. Mirabeau asked for the floor at the Constituent Assembly, pronounced an eloquent eulogy, and proposed three days of mourning in France. Lafayette supported him and the assembly agreed unanimously. The next week, the assembly voted to abolish hereditary titles.

A month later, on 14 July 1790, came the first anniversary of the fall of the Bastille. To mark it, a national festival was proposed by Talleyrand and convened by Lafayette. Still a bishop, Talleyrand celebrated mass before 300,000 people. Lafayette, followed by the deputies of the Constituent Assembly, swore fidelity to the king, the nation and the law, while Louis XVI swore allegiance to the new constitution which abolished his absolute powers and the notion of divine right. Louis XVI recognised that France had become a constitutional monarchy. He and the queen were acclaimed by the crowd.

On 3 September, the Constituent Assembly adopted a new constitution for France. Faced with the constant opposition of the delegates, and notably of Mirabeau, Jacques Necker resigned the next day, on 4 September. With his wife, he left the city of Paris, where he had once enjoyed such great popular acclaim, and he returned to the calm of the Swiss lakeside at the Château de Coppet. Necker, the honourable family man and reformist, was brought down by men like Mirabeau and Talleyrand, of lesser scruples and without moral compass.

Madame de Staël

As Jacques and Suzanne Necker faded quietly from the scene, their daughter, Germaine de Staël was close to many of the events of that tortured time. Germaine remained with her husband at the Swedish embassy in Paris. There, she had established a new literary salon, which quickly became the meeting place for rising politicians. She was the inspiration for the constitutionalists, who supported a monarchy responding to the will of the assembly.

After the adoption of the new constitution, elections were held for a Legislative Assembly, with the right to vote accorded to all male citizens having paid a designated level of taxation. All the deputies were new. While the debates wore on at the National Assembly, Germaine de Staël's salon was the place where ideas and political tactics could be freely and vigorously argued. Rising politicians mingled with writers such as Montesquieu, Edward Gibbon, once her mother's fiancé, or Grimm and Diderot, as well as military leaders such as Lafayette and Comte Louis Marie de Narbonne.

The figure whose personal trajectory epitomised the twists and turns and the contradictions of those years was Talleyrand. His designation at a young age as a bishop, as a result of the political influence of an uncle, perfectly illustrated the corruption of the elites, including the upper levels of the clergy, under the *ancien régime*. Initially appointed as a representative of the Second Estate, the clergy, Talleyrand became a deputy in the National Constituent Assembly, and joined forces with Mirabeau. A notorious womaniser, Talleyrand had a brief affair with Germaine, but of greater significance was the life-long friendship they maintained through an extensive correspondence. At the end of 1790 Talleyrand resigned as a bishop, defying the Pope's threat of excommunication.

The marriage between Germaine and Erik Magnus de Staël, seventeen years her senior, was not a happy one. Tragically, they lost their first child. A son was born in 1790. But after early motherhood, Germaine grew apart from the Baron. A romantic, and a woman asserting her independence, she took a succession of lovers, several of whom played significant roles in the events of revolutionary France. As her father returned to Coppet, twenty-four-year-old Germaine began an affair with Comte de Narbonne, an illegitimate son of Louis XV, and one of her earlier suitors. Narbonne was a colonel in the army and secretary to Vergennes, with whom Franklin negotiated support for the American revolutionaries. Narbonne and Germaine were open about their relationship, and Baron de Staël was humiliated. There were tempestuous scenes, but he and Germaine did not divorce. They continued to see each other and, especially, to correspond. Germaine's letters to and from her husband, lovers, friends, children, politicians and intellectuals across Europe left an amazingly detailed record of her life and of these turbulent times.

Revolutionary France, still with Louis XVI as its constitutional monarch, was buffeted both from within and outside its borders. The Austrian Empire, now ruled by Marie-Antoinette's brother Leopold who had succeeded their older brother Joseph, sought to mobilise support among European monarchies for the French king and queen, but these efforts were perceived by the revolutionary leaders as a military threat. Turmoil continued in Paris and in the provinces. In April 1791, Mirabeau died. As a mark of respect, the assembly ordered that his body be entered in the Panthéon. Shortly afterwards, in June, as the political situation continued to degenerate, the king took the fatal decision to flee France with his family, aiming to reach the eastern border. But he was recognised and caught in Varennes, then taken back to Paris under armed escort. As he returned to the Tuileries Palace and descended from the coach, Lafayette welcomed him with a show of deference, a last attempt to save the king's honour. But from that point on, public opinion turned against the monarchy.

Insurrection and the Terror

France declared war on Austria in April of 1792. Lafayette was given command of the army of the centre based in Metz. In June, he went to Paris and delivered a fiery speech against the growing influence of the radicals, but he was then sent to command the army of the north. A declaration by the Austrians and Prussians threatening the civilian population if they harmed the king only played into the hands of the radicals. In August, the *sans-culottes* – the ordinary people of Paris dressed in simple work clothes – invaded the Tuileries in Paris. Narbonne, by then designated minister for war and promoted to general, was by the king's side as he and the queen took refuge in the Legislative Assembly. Several hundred Swiss Guards were killed while trying to protect the Tuileries Palace. With the aid of Germaine, Narbonne escaped to England.

In October, Germaine de Staël gave birth to Narbonne's son. Lafayette took refuge across the northern border in the Austrian Netherlands – today's Belgium – where he was arrested by the Austrians then handed to the Prussians.

Power in the capital of France passed from the 'legal' Parliament of Paris to the 'Commune of the Insurrection' which became the voice of the *sans-culottes*.[31] After new national elections, to form a National Convention, power struggles intensified between the radical Jacobins (also called the Montagnards, as they sat on the upper levels of the Convention) and the moderate Girondins. The National Convention replaced the Legislative Assembly as the government of France. One of its first acts was to proclaim the abolition of the monarchy. France became de facto a republic. Louis and Marie-Antoinette were imprisoned with their children and stripped of their titles. The dark time of summary trials and execution by guillotine began and would become known as the Terror. Prisoners accused of crimes against the revolution were massacred by mobs. As France descended into the Terror, the nobility lost more than their privileges, properties and possessions. Many paid with their lives. They had failed to see the coming of the storm.

A leading member of the Jacobins, which had earlier supported Mirabeau's political ascent, was Maximilien Robespierre, who led the Committee for General Security. As civil war broke out and opponents of the Republic were massacred in Vendée, in the west of France, Robespierre exercised the powers of a despot. Germaine de Staël fled Paris for exile in England. Talleyrand was already there, with papers stating he was in England on official business, so he was able to stay away from Paris and avoid the Terror. In January 1793, the Convention voted by a majority of a single vote for the execution of Louis XVI, now called Citizen Clapet, defended in vain by Malesherbes, who had the task of announcing the condemnation to Louis. Without appeal, the former king was guillotined four days later on the Place Louis XV, on 21 January 1793, in front of the magnificent building where the Treaties of Paris had been signed between the United States and Britain, ten years earlier, in 1783.[32] It was the very place where the fireworks tragedy had occurred when his marriage to Marie-Antoinette had been celebrated just over two decades earlier in 1770.

Robespierre was elected President of the Convention in August. Two months later the deposed queen was accused of high treason, as well as incest, condemned and executed at the same place, now renamed Place de la Révolution, ten months after her husband. Revolutionary France was torn by civil war and threatened on its borders. The Terror continued, with summary executions ordered by the National Convention's revolutionary tribunal. Malesherbes was guillotined with all his family. The same fate befell the Duc d'Orléans, who had changed his name to Philippe Egalité, and had supported the Republic, even voting for the execution of his cousin, the king. His son, the future King Louis-Philippe, joined his father in early support for the revolution and commanded revolutionary troops, but he broke with the Republic and his father over the execution of the king, and he went into exile in Switzerland. Later he moved to America.

Talleyrand left London, expelled by Prime Minister Pitt. He, too, crossed the Atlantic and went to New York, where he was the house guest of Aaron Burr, at that time a US Senator. Talleyrand became the friend of Alexander Hamilton, the first US Treasury Secretary under President George Washington. This was all before the presidential election of 1800 when Thomas Jefferson and Aaron Burr tied with equal votes in the Electoral College, ahead of incumbent John Adams, and Jefferson was elected to the presidency by the state delegations to Congress, with Burr as vice-president, and it was a decade before the fatal duel when Burr killed Hamilton. Back in 1794, Talleyrand dined frequently with both.

With the execution of Robespierre in July 1794, the Terror in France came to an end. Talleyrand moved to Philadelphia then to Boston, speculating in real estate and commodity trading with the East Indies. He stayed for two years in America before returning to France in 1796.

Conditions in France

As in Britain and other European nations in the late eighteenth-century, wealth in France came from the land. With a population of around 26 million in the 1780s, three times that of Britain and second only to that of Imperial Russia, the sheer size of the French economy gave it the strongest GDP[33] in Europe. France followed Britain with the industrial revolution but at a much slower pace, and without a rapid 'take-off' of industrialisation like that experienced in the English Midlands in the 1760s. There was slower mechanisation of artisanal factories and agriculture. Trading with North America and other parts of the world was increasingly important, and although the majority of the population lived in the rural areas, France was also one of the most urbanised countries in Europe.[34] Paris was second in population only to London, and the nation had several other large cities. Per capita wealth figures put France near the top of the scale.

Yet these raw figures failed to reveal the underlying weaknesses of the French economy and, more particularly, of its political structures. First and foremost was the long-running problem of debt. Louis XV, who reigned from 1715 to 1774, ran up huge debts in the course of the Seven Years' War against Britain (1756–1763), which France ultimately lost. The extravagant spending of his predecessor, Louis XIV, was maintained at Versailles and throughout the nation. His grandson and successor, Louis XVI, after some early attempts to reign in expenditure, aggravated the debt through French support for the American War of Independence, as well as renewed extravagance at the royal court, notably by the entourage of Queen Marie-Antoinette and the king's brothers.

Inevitably, political debates and manoeuvres were centred on a succession of financial crises. The dominant question throughout was that of taxation – just as it had been in Britain and the American colonies in the series of crises leading to the American Declaration of Independence. And the question of taxation led invariably to debates about equity and about representation. Twenty-one million people out of a total population of 26 million relied on agriculture for their subsistence, often owning small plots of land while working as poorly paid labourers on larger farms. Peasants had to pay taxes to the State as well as feudal dues to local lords and tithes to their churches. Vast tracts of land were owned by the nobility, while one tenth of the national territory was owned by the Church,[35] whose higher echelons came from the nobility and wealthy families. Neither the nobility nor the Church paid taxes.

As in Britain, the movements of peasants to towns and cities, and the beginning of industrialisation, had the effect of transferring poverty from rural to urban areas. There was little change in traditional farming methods. Crop rotation, for example, had been introduced around Paris, but poor harvests in most of the country meant hunger for peasants and urban labourers alike. The agricultural and climatic problems of these years increased poverty. Criminality increased; groups of bandits or beggars roved the countryside and the dark streets of cities.

Another great social change was underway. In the seventeenth century, groups of teachers in the Catholic churches had set up 'little schools' where they taught children from all social classes in French rather than Latin.[36] This was a major innovation for the time. By the late eighteenth century, a significant proportion of the population could read. Artisans could conduct their affairs in writing. Domestic servants, who came mostly from the countryside, could read their contracts of employment.[37] Printing was by then a well-established activity, so pamphlets and news bulletins could be written, distributed, and widely read among the populace. Newspapers that were once reserved for the elite developed into a medium for the masses.[38] It is interesting to note that Talleyrand promoted public education in the early days of the revolution.

Aftermath of the revolution

The French Revolution is generally considered to have lasted for ten years after the storming of the Bastille. From 1792 on there was burning and destruction across the land. It was a dangerous time. Germaine de Staël left England and returned to the Château de Coppet to be with her parents. In 1793, Germaine published an essay in defence of Marie-Antoinette: *Reflections on the trial of the Queen*, in which she described the executed queen as a prisoner of her gender. Suzanne Necker died in 1794 in Lausanne after a long illness. Jacques Necker devoted his time to editing the writings of his late wife, including her *Reflections on Divorce*, published later that year. Dismayed by the very public affair of his daughter with Narbonne, Necker was just as disturbed when Germaine began a new liaison with a rising politician from Lausanne, Benjamin Constant. De Staël and Constant would be intricately involved in the political manoeuvres of the time.

In September 1794, after the end of the Terror, the National Convention took two decisions of symbolic importance. After a scandal of letters hidden in an iron safe had revealed the extent of Mirabeau's double game of dealing in secret with the royal family while being a prominent revolutionary, the Convention ordered that his body be removed from the Panthéon. This disavowal of Necker's former nemesis gave scant comfort to the old man writing his memoirs in Coppet. The following month, the ashes of Jean-Jacques Rousseau of Geneva, Germaine's inspiration and one of the original 'Luminaries' whose ideas underpinned the revolution, were moved into the Panthéon.

One year later, in September 1795, a new constitution was adopted for France, with a lower and upper council to replace the National Convention. The councils combined to elect a government composed of a Directory of five. Germaine de Staël and Benjamin Constant were by now in Paris, where they plunged into the ongoing political manoeuvres.

The rise of Napoléon

Now expecting another child, this time with Constant, Germaine successfully lobbied Paul Barras, the Directory's leader, to appoint Talleyrand as minister for foreign affairs. On the night of 3 October 1795, royalists organised a rebellion against the Directory. Barras called on a young general, Napoléon Bonaparte, to help defend the Tuileries Palace. Bonaparte had witnessed the massacre of the Swiss Guards when they tried to defend the palace three years earlier. Determined to avoid the same fate for the members of the Directory, he called in heavy artillery. Fourteen hundred royalists were killed, and the rest fled. Bonaparte's bloody success earned him sudden fame among the revolutionary anti-royalists and, with it, the patronage of the new government. Upon his return to Paris (20 September 1796), Talleyrand joined those supporting the rise of the young general. To begin with, like many others in her circle, Germaine saw in Bonaparte the person who would save France from civil war. For a time, her romantic desire to find a hero seemed to prevail over her belief in constitutional monarchy.

The republic continued to face both internal and external threats. Bonaparte won acclaim with his military campaign in Italy in 1796, followed by a succession of victories over Austrian forces in 1797. The terms of victory included the release of Lafayette, with his wife and two daughters, from Austrian custody. The Prussians had handed Lafayette and other French prisoners back to the Austrians, and he had suffered harsh solitary confinement after an escape attempt. Thomas Jefferson, by then US Secretary of State, rushed a resolution through Congress, duly signed by President Washington, awarding Lafayette payment in recognition of his years as Major General in the American War of Independence. His son, Georges Washington Lafayette, had been smuggled out of Europe to America, and his wife and daughters were then allowed by Emperor Franz II to join him in Vienna. Napoléon ordered the Lafayette family to be placed under the protection of the US consul in Hamburg.

In January 1798, Talleyrand arranged for Germaine de Staël to meet the brilliant young general. She was fascinated by him, bringing to bear her legendary charm, but Napoléon remained cool. They met several more times. Germaine assailed Napoléon with questions, most famously: 'General, what woman, dead or alive, do you consider to be the greatest?' To which Napoléon replied: 'The one who has had the most children, Madame.'[39]

That year Napoléon had moved with his army through the Swiss region overlooking Lac Léman, where the Château de Coppet was located, and announced that the French-speaking canton of Vaud would be liberated from the domination of its powerful German-speaking neighbour, the canton of Bern. He called to pay his respects to Jacques Necker at the Château de Coppet. But he was disappointed by Necker, commenting that he found him uninteresting.

Bonaparte then led an expedition to Egypt and defeated the Egyptian army. Scientists accompanying the expedition discovered the Rosetta Stone, and Bonaparte was admitted to the French Academy of Sciences. But the French forces were defeated in the Battle of the Nile by the British fleet of Admiral Horatio Nelson. In 1799, Napoléon returned to Paris, where his brother, Lucien Bonaparte, presided over the Lower Chamber, called the Council of Five Hundred. With the support of Talleyrand, Napoléon Bonaparte launched a coup d'état on 9 November. A new constitution naming him 'first consul' for ten years was approved by a popular plebiscite, rigged in his favour by Lucien to show support from 3 million voters, or ninety-nine per cent of the electorate.

Benjamin Constant was still a supporter of Napoléon, but Germaine de Staël was already disillusioned. She perceived that the young general, for a time her romantic hero, was in reality preparing a dictatorship that would betray the ideals of the revolution. Her father, Jacques Necker, wrote to her warning that France had everything to fear from her new master. He even recommended that she burn his letter as a precaution.

A clash of egos

By the turn of the century, in 1800, Benjamin Constant decided to speak out against Napoléon. Just after New Year's Day, attending Germaine's salon were Talleyrand, Napoléon's two brothers, Lucien and Joseph, and others. Constant said to Germaine: 'If I give a speech which places me in the opposition, tomorrow your salon will be deserted.' 'Just follow your conviction,' replied Germaine. The next day, Constant rose at the first meeting of the Tribunate, a body of 100 notables, to speak powerfully against 'servitude and silence', underlining that 'such a silence will be heard throughout all of Europe'. Napoléon was furious, and blamed Germaine for the speech. His brother, Joseph, tried to intercede on Germaine's behalf. 'What does she want?' asked Napoléon. 'The repayment of her father's loan? I will order it. The right to stay in Paris? I will permit it.'[40] When Joseph returned to Germaine, she cried: 'My God, it is not what I want but what I think!' In this clash of two egos, Germaine's biographer summed it up: 'Madame de Staël wanted to speak and be heard; Bonaparte wanted to speak and be obeyed.'[41]

A published essay by Germaine de Staël on literature and social institutions highlighting the ideals of the Enlightenment further annoyed Napoléon. Then, when Talleyrand convened a great ball, Germaine thought she would have a chance to meet again with the first consul on neutral territory. Ignoring Talleyrand's friendly advice to stay away, she arrived early, but as she entered the ballroom, all conversation stopped, faces turned away, and she was confronted with the reality of her social ostracism. A young officer's widow named Delphine felt sorry for her and sat next to her. When Germaine began writing her first novel, she named it for her.[42]

In the spring, Napoléon took his troops across the Swiss Alps into Italy and again defeated the Austrians. Talleyrand negotiated peace treaties with Austria in 1801, then with the British in 1802. In May of that year, Baron de Staël died. His diplomatic status had until then provided

Germaine with protection. The very next day the results were announced of a new plebiscite to endorse Napoléon as first consul for life, with a majority of more than ninety-nine per cent in favour. One prominent figure who publicly declared that he had voted against the new constitution and Napoléon was the French hero of the American revolution, Lafayette.

France and the United States of America: intertwined destinies

Napoléon was also engaged in decisions beyond Europe. There had long been French settlements along the Mississippi River, but the territory then known as Louisiana was ceded to Spain at the end of the Seven Years' War in 1762. In 1800, Napoléon secretly forced Spain to cede it back to France. When Thomas Jefferson took office as the third President of the United States in 1801, and discovered the cession, which he took to indicate renewed French ambitions in America, he decided to confront Napoléon, and he sent envoys to Paris. As he did so, Napoléon faced another crisis to the south of the United States, in the Caribbean.

On the prosperous island of Saint-Domingue, slaves had been freed after the French Revolution and some had joined the military. In 1799, the military leader, Toussaint l'Ouverture, declared himself to be governor-general. Refugee plantation owners lobbied Napoléon to restore French authority, and he sent 20,000 troops to the island. A tropical storm approached; Toussaint's men took it as an auspicious sign and launched a revolt. A civil war followed with terrible massacres on both sides, until the freed slaves prevailed and proclaimed the independent republic of Haiti in November 1803.

French losses in the war in Saint-Domingue fed into Napoléon's loss of interest in the Americas. and he became open to a negotiation with Jefferson's emissaries. Before the Haitian declaration of independence, he agreed to sell all the land ceded to France by the Spanish to the United States for 15 million US dollars. The land surface of the United States was doubled with the stroke of a pen, for the Louisiana Purchase included all land west of the Mississippi as far as the Rocky Mountains, covering fifteen of the present-day states. It is stupendous to think that Napoléon Bonaparte simply sold a vast land mass that would dramatically expand the territory of the new power emerging across the Atlantic. Jefferson, once ambassador to France, now President of the

United States, was more far-seeing than Bonaparte, who kept his sights set on his ambitions in Europe.

Napoléon had restored Lafayette's citizenship of France in 1800 and proposed to him the post of Minister to the United States, but Lafayette refused, as he did Napoléon's offer of a seat in the Senate and the Legion of Honour. After the Louisiana Purchase, Jefferson asked Lafayette if he would agree to become governor of the new territory, but Lafayette declined, stating his desire to work for democracy in France.

De Staël in Germany
As such strategic matters were negotiated, Napoléon continued his feud with Germaine de Staël, for it had become personal. Germaine's novel *Delphine,* inspired partially by Jean-Jacques Rousseau's 1761 novel *Julie or the New Heloise,* had been published the previous year. An assertively feminist work, *Delphine* attracted both acclaim and criticism, and especially the ire of the first consul for its political commentary. In 1803, Napoléon ordered Germaine to leave France with Benjamin Constant, who was by now his main political critic. De Staël and Constant journeyed across the Rhine to Weimar, where Germaine met Johann Wolfgang von Goethe, Friedrich Schiller and other prominent writers. She found herself inspired by romantic German literature. In the same year, Napoléon gave the canton of Vaud its first constitution at the same time as it joined the Swiss Confederation.

In April 1804, while still in Germany, Germaine learnt of the death of her father of respiratory and cardiac failure at the age of seventy-two, in Coppet. She rushed back with Constant. For months she was inconsolable. Much later, the full extent of Necker's disillusion with the revolution would become known, when his grandson published the complete works of his writings, including his reflections on equality. The once enlightened reformer was embittered by the course taken by the revolution in the name of *Liberté, Egalité, Fraternité*. He found common ground with Edmund Burke, Irish Member of the British Parliament and an intellectual who wrote an influential treatise on the excesses of the revolution, as a warning to his own countrymen and to Europe.

That same year, Jacques Charles, eminent physician, President of the French Academy of Sciences and friend of the late Benjamin Franklin, married a beautiful young refugee woman named Julie, of creole origin from Saint-Domingue, fifty-seven years his junior. We will see in the next chapter that Julie would inspire a young devotee of Madame de Staël, a romantic poet who would write a hugely popular account of the first French Revolution, before leading a new revolution more than four decades later.

The emperor

In November 1804, Napoléon won a plebiscite of 3.6 million voters to declare himself emperor. The coronation, in the presence of the Pope, took place on 2 December. With Bonaparte's proclamation of himself as emperor, Madame de Staël became one of his fiercest critics. Back in Coppet in June of 1805, she hosted the Group of Coppet, with leading thinkers from Europe, invariably opposed to Napoléon. Her visitors included the British romantic poet, Lord Byron, and the man who would ultimately defeat Napoléon, the Duke of Wellington. Every day, the table was set for some thirty people – leading writers and political figures – who debated the future of Europe. The Coppet of the early nineteenth century anticipated the 'think tanks' of the twentieth century, an embryo of Davos in the Swiss Alps. In Paris, friends tried to persuade the emperor to allow Germaine de Staël to return, but Napoléon remained inflexible, aware of her influence, and expressing indifference about her claim to the 2 million livres that her father had loaned to the State back in 1778 before the General Estates and the revolution.

Germaine de Staël then decided to travel again and left Coppet for Italy, where she collected material for one of her most famous works, *Corinne, or Italy*, which told the story of a woman's search for liberty, while highlighting Italian nationalism. She visited the Vatican in Rome and the wonders of Florence. Wherever she went, Napoléon sent instructions that her security was to be assured. Why was this? Napoléon made no secret of his view that she was a thorn in his side. Yet, he evidently made the calculation that any harm to her would be even more dangerous for him. Although an obvious misogynist, did he also have a secret respect for this woman who dared to challenge him?

By November 1805, Napoléon's Grande Armée marched across Europe, captured Vienna, and defeated the Austrian and Russian armies at Austerlitz. Napoléon went on to defeat the Prussians, then turned south, invaded Spain and deposed the Bourbons, cousins of the former French dynasty. He turned his attention to France's traditional enemy, Britain, and moved to invade the British Isles. But a combined French and Spanish fleet was defeated by Nelson's British fleet off Cape Trafalgar, and Napoléon gave up the idea of invading Britain.

Benjamin Constant finally broke off his long relationship with Germaine de Staël. She began work on her book *On Germany*, praising German culture, and foreshadowing the creation of the German nation. Wherever she went, she engaged with writers and thinkers on literature and politics across Europe.

War and peace

In 1810, Napoléon divorced his empress, Joséphine, who had not borne him a child and heir. Like the Bourbon kings before him, he married a young Austrian aristocrat, the Archduchess Marie-Louise. In the same year Germaine de Staël published her monumental *On Germany*, introducing the concept of romanticism into French literature. Derived from the Germanic *Sturm und drang* (storm and drive) school of an earlier time, it was, somewhat paradoxically, a reaction to the rationalism of the Enlightenment, with an emphasis on emotion, individualism, and heroism, with roots in legends of medieval chivalry. Ten thousand copies of the first edition were printed in Paris. Napoléon ordered all copies to be seized and burnt. Germaine returned to Paris but Napoléon ordered her to leave within three days. The book was later published in London and had great success.

Across the Atlantic, with Spain weakened by Napoléon's domination, the Spanish American wars of independence had begun with the creation of Juntas, starting under Simón Bolívar in Caracas. In 1812, Napoléon took the fatal decision to invade Russia, marching the Grande Armée across Germany and Poland. Madame de Staël, exiled from Paris and uncertain of her safety in Coppet, travelled north ahead of the Grande Armée. In Moscow, her host was the governor, Count Fyodor Rostopchin. She left just before the Grande Armée took the city. The Russian troops withdrew to the forests, and the governor ordered that Moscow be burnt. Germaine moved to St Petersburg, where she met with Tsar Alexander, and shared detailed conversations with him about Napoléon, his personality, and his strategies. With the onset of winter, Napoléon was forced to retreat, harassed by Russian attacks. The tsar's commanding general, Mikhail Kutuzov, sent Germaine letters as he chased the French Grande Armée out of Russia. She moved to Sweden, where she still benefited from her name as the widow of the late Swedish Ambassador to France. From there, she moved to England, where she met with Lord Byron and addressed meetings of both main British political parties. She also met Stanislas, younger brother of the executed Louis XVI and wrote to Talleyrand favouring him as a future constitutional monarch of France. Like her father, she believed that the British political system provided a model for France. Finally arriving back in Coppet, Germaine met and married a young Geneva-born officer of the French army, named Albert Jean Michel de Rocca. Their son was born in April 1812.

By early in 1814, the Russians had pushed the French all the way to the gates of Paris. On 31 March, Talleyrand, Napoléon's former foreign minister, gave the key of the city of Paris to Tsar Alexander of Russia. Lafayette called for Napoléon's abdication. The tsar addressed the French Senate, which voted to depose the emperor. Napoléon abdicated and was exiled to the island of Elba. Talleyrand was elected by the Senate to lead a provisional government. He convinced the victorious allied powers to agree to the restoration of the Bourbon dynasty under Stanislas, as proposed by Germaine de Staël. Stanislas was crowned as Louis XVIII, King of France, in a constitutional monarchy with two houses of parliament, similar to the British model. The signs of Germaine de Staël's influence were to be seen everywhere in these events.

Waterloo – defeat and capture

At the end of February 1815, Napoléon escaped from Elba and marched north to Paris. The king fled to Belgium, accompanied by a young officer and admirer of Germaine de Staël, whose story will be told in the next chapter. Germaine herself went once more into exile in Coppet. After 100 days, Napoléon was defeated at Waterloo. He tried to escape to America, but he was captured by the British and sent to his final exile on St Helena. Germaine de Staël, reunited with de Rocca, travelled to Italy for the marriage of her nineteen-year-old daughter, Albertine, to the Duc Victor de Broglie, from an eminent aristocratic family. She returned with her family to Coppet that summer, in time for a visit from Lord Byron. Then de Staël returned to Paris and showed once again her capacity to influence, by persuading the victorious Duke of Wellington to reduce the size of his army of occupation.

Sent to represent France at the Congress of Vienna, from late 1814 until June 1815, Talleyrand negotiated brilliantly, even though he had a weak hand following the successive defeats of Napoléon. Upon his return from Vienna, he was named Grand Chamberlain of France, an honorary post, and for the first time in many decades, he no longer occupied a position of power. Talleyrand, the arch-manoeuvrer of the time, served the revolution, the Napoléonic Empire, then the restored monarchy. He personified the vagaries of a revolution that overturned an old order, only to be overturned itself by a dictator, who was in turn defeated.

The death of Madame de Staël

The return of Louis XVIII as monarch of France was approved by the Congress of Vienna. Germaine de Staël's son-in-law, the Duc de Broglie, was appointed minister for police. That winter, Germaine de Staël returned for the last time to Paris. As in the past she met with kings, ministers and generals. She also met with Joséphine, who had retained the title of empress after her divorce from Napoléon, and was by then quite ill. Germaine asked her about her life with Napoléon. In February 1817, however, Madame de Staël's own health took a turn for the worse. Suffering from insomnia and exhaustion, she had a stroke. She had developed the habit of taking opium to help her sleep. At the end of May, she learnt that Empress Joséphine had died after walking in her garden in Paris with the Tsar of Russia. On Sunday 13 July, at the home of her daughter and son in law, Germaine de Staël was unwell again. Nevertheless, later that day she received the Duc d'Orléans, who had returned to France after the abdication of Napoléon and the restoration of the Bourbon monarchy under his cousin, Louis XVIII. Without her knowing it, the last official guest Germaine received would later succeed his cousins as a constitutional monarch. She went into the garden to choose some roses for her friends. That evening, she took opium again and fell asleep. In the early morning of 14 July, the anniversary of the

French Revolution, the Duc de Broglie found her. She had passed away peacefully at the age of fifty-one.

Madame de Staël was described as Napoléon's nemesis. In the wake of his conquests Napoléon left a reformed legal system, the Napoléonic Code, which remains the basis for civil law across Europe. But it was Germaine de Staël, more than any other person of the time, who fostered the flow of pan-European ideas. In doing so, she helped to prepare the way for a new wave of revolutions that would shake the entire continent three decades after her death.

Part II:
France and Europe
1815 to 1870

A famous poet rose to speak to a great crowd as storm clouds gathered over the River Saône, north of its conjunction with the mighty Rhône. Ignoring the thunder and lightning, Alphonse de Lamartine's voice carried across the valley to predict the fall of the constitutional monarchy in France. Six months later, in January 1848, leaders of the liberal opposition approached him to lead the formation of a new republic. Lamartine hesitated, then plunged into the fray, proclaiming a second republic, reinstating the tricolour flag, and drafting a new constitution. A wave of revolutions swept across the European continent, ending the autocratic regimes of many nations, in what was called for a time the 'Springtime of the Peoples'. In those same days, a manifesto written by two German exiles signalled that a new storm was building across Europe. Lamartine, a man wishing peace for France and for Europe, sensed it, but could not prevent new massacres. By the end of 1848, he retired from the political scene, defeated by a man who would establish a new dictatorship and a second empire.

Chapter 3

The European revolutions of 1848

Lamartine: A romantic young man

As Napoléon Bonaparte was stripped of his title of emperor and exiled on the island of Elba, the man who had helped his rise to power, the former bishop and consummate negotiator Talleyrand, now engineered the restoration of the Bourbon dynasty under the younger brother of the executed Louis XVI. The new king, whose birth name was Stanislas, was called Louis XVIII.[1] Alphonse de Lamartine, from Mâcon on the River Saône north of Lyon, went to Paris to serve as an officer in the king's guard. For a young man of the landed gentry, it was considered to be a duty and an honour to serve the monarchy in the royal guard. But Lamartine, as he would later be known to the nation, found military life to be oppressive. A dreamer and a poet, his mind was elsewhere.

In March 1815, the Bourbon restoration was thrown into turmoil when Napoléon escaped from Elba, and marched north to Paris, calling troops again to his side. As Napoléon reached the gates of Paris, the new king left Paris to seek shelter in Belgium. Lamartine and other guards accompanied him as far as the Belgian border. Then Louis XVIII and his court continued to the city of Ghent with just a few guards. Lamartine and the others were dismissed and told to remove their uniforms.[2] As Napoléon returned, Germaine de Staël also fled Paris, again in the direction of Switzerland and the family chateau in Coppet.

Once the king was across the border, Lamartine – freed from his military obligations but with just a musket and a few gold 'Louis' coins in his pocket – made his way across France. After several weeks, he crossed the Jura mountains to the Swiss border. Arriving at Saint-Cergue in the canton of Vaud, just over the border from France on the 'smugglers' road', he was advised by a guide to continue down the mountain trail and to seek refuge with the Baron de Vasserot, at the Château de Vincy. When he knocked on the door, he had no letter of recommendation. Yet the baron invited him in, then questioned the young gentleman at length. Finding Lamartine's responses to his many questions to be convincing, the baron offered his hospitality. Lamartine stayed on, and spent pleasant weeks writing and walking, engaging in discussions with the Vasserot family, and lingering for evenings on the chateau's terrace with splendid views of Lac Léman; Geneva being just visible at its western extremity. In the near distance, over the treetops, he could make out the roof of the Château de Coppet, knowing that Germaine de Staël was there, living like him in exile as Napoléon took back power in Paris.

An aspiring poet, Lamartine was a devotee of the romantic literary movement founded by Madame de Staël, describing her later in his autobiography as 'the genius who most dazzled my youth'. He resolved to try to see the woman whom he admired from afar. So, day after day, this tall, slim young man, dressed in the well-worn clothes of a gentleman without means, waited beside the Route de Lausanne in the hope of transport to Coppet. On a day in late spring, he was about to give up, when a cloud of dust appeared from the direction of Coppet. Two open carriages drawn by magnificent horses raced past him. He raised his hand, as if to stop the horses, but they were gone like lightning, and he could only stand and watch the carriages disappear into the distance. He had glimpsed Germaine de Staël. But how, he asked himself, could this luminary of European romantic literature, have even been aware of the passionate admiration rising toward her from a dusty ditch beside the road? The young man was left with but a fleeting image of his heroine.[3] On that day, he was far from imagining that three decades later he would be as well-known as Madame de Staël, that his poetry would be taught in schools and that he would play a leading role in a new French revolution – the revolution of 1848 – that would spark upheavals across Europe and feudal regimes across the old continent. Nor that he, a young royalist, would one day officially proclaim the Second Republic of France.

When Napoléon's army was defeated later that year at Waterloo,[4] and the Duke of Wellington led his victorious allied troops into Paris, Louis

XVIII and his retinue accompanied the occupying army, while Germaine de Staël returned to Paris as a friend of the victorious duke. But young Lamartine did not go to Paris, lingering instead along the Swiss shore of Lac Léman. His thoughts were far from the great political issues of the day, as Talleyrand and his peers negotiated the fate of Europe at the Congress of Vienna in 1815.[5]

1816 was a year of gloom, literally, as the skies of Europe were darkened by ash from a huge volcanic eruption the previous year on the other side of the world, on the island of Sumbawa in Indonesia. Temperatures dropped, crops failed, and it was called the year without summer. Lamartine was not well, and in the autumn he went to the spa town of Aix-les-Bains for a health cure. There he met a young woman called Julie Charles, a meeting that would mark a turning point in his life. Julie was married to the famous physicist Jacques Charles, president of the French Academy of Sciences, and inventor of the hydrogen balloon. Back in 1783 Benjamin Franklin had been one of the special VIP guests at a crowd of 400,000 who watched Jacques Charles lift off from the Jardin des Tuileries in Paris in the first-ever manned hydrogen-balloon flight.[6]

Julie was a beautiful yet fragile young woman of creole origin from Saint-Domingue who had lost her mother at sea as the family fled a massacre in 1791. Her father, originally from Nantes in the west of France, was violent and erratic. When the eminent scientist showed his interest, her uncle argued with her father to accept the marriage. After many disputes between the father and the uncle, which further affected Julie's health, the marriage took place in 1804. This was the year when the freed slaves of Saint-Domingue won their independence and recognition in France for the republic of Haiti. Jacques Charles wrote to a friend: 'I found her state of health to be degraded to a worrisome degree, but she has now quickly recovered from all the storms that she had been through.'[7] Charles was thirty-seven years her senior, and treated her benevolently, perhaps more as a daughter than a wife. There were no children.

In 1816, as Julie's health deteriorated, her doctor sent her to take a cure at Aix-les-Bains, along the shores of Lac du Bourget at the foot of the Alps. Alphonse de Lamartine came to the same pension. He soon heard about a beautiful woman who stayed mostly in her room, apart from the required daily visits to the baths. Deeply unsure about the direction of his life, plagued by melancholy, Lamartine took lonely walks along the lake. Then, returning to the pension one day, suddenly in an alley of the garden, he saw a solitary woman sitting on a bench to catch the pale autumn sun. She wore a thick dress and a white shawl around her shoulders, partially forming a hood over her head. He was entranced. Their first words were exchanged. Back in his room, Alphonse wrote a poem, which he slipped under her door.[8]

From the next morning the two were inseparable. Their passion found expression in their writing, and they spent long hours together, either in Julie's salon or walking together by the lake. When separated for just a few hours Julie wrote with operatic drama: 'Is it you, Alphonse, is it really you whom I have just held in my arms and who escapes me as happiness escapes me?'[9] – this to tell him that she would be free by noon after settling some formalities for her husband. After two weeks, Alphonse had to return to his hometown of Mâcon. Julie accompanied him as far as the Lamartine family property, then returned to her husband and her literary salon in Paris. From then on, the two exchanged passionate letters. After several months, in the spring of 1817, Lamartine went to Paris where he joined Julie's literary salon and she presented him to her friends. The lovers managed to escape the city to the hills of Saint-Cloud or the prairies of Vincennes, meeting for trysts in the hills and woods around the city. Jacques Charles could not have been unaware of their escapades, but he accepted Julie's absences for the sake of her happiness.

That summer, on the twenty-eighth anniversary of the French Revolution, Lamartine learnt in the press of the death of Germaine de Staël, his distant heroine and inspiration. At the end of summer, he consulted Julie's doctor who advised him to return to Aix-les-Bains. The lovers promised to meet again by the lake. They wrote to each other daily. But when Lamartine returned to Aix-les-Bains and the Lac du Bourget, Julie was not there, for she was too weak to travel.[10] She died of tuberculosis in Paris on a wintry night that December. Their passionate love affair had ended in tragedy. Grief-stricken, Lamartine composed the poem that would make him famous: *The Lake*. The lyrics describe how this place of beauty, shared with his great love, was altered forever by his loss.

Lamartine went on to write a series of poems with the flamboyance but also the melancholy and tragedy of the Romantic movement. He published them in 1820, collected in a book entitled *Poetic Meditations*, which included *The Lake*. The book was immensely successful, and propelled him to fame as a lyrical poet of the Romantic era. His new renown brought him into contact with the political leaders of the day, including the famous Talleyrand. After obtaining a diplomatic appointment Lamartine married a noble English woman, Marianne Elisa Birch. He was posted firstly to Naples, then to the embassy in Rome. But he continued to live with personal tragedies. A son, Alphonse, was born, then a daughter, Julia. But little Alphonse died at the age of twenty months. Two years later, in 1824, Lamartine lost both his sisters.

While Lamartine was in Italy, political turbulence continued in Paris, with the assassination of the Duc de Berry, nephew of the king and second in the line of succession to the throne. King Louis XVIII, a long-time sufferer of gout, was increasingly handicapped by arteriosclerosis, and appeared in public on crutches. In 1824, with his body putrefied by gangrene, he died atrociously. His younger brother, the last of the brothers of the executed Louis XVI, was crowned as King Charles X of France and Navarro. Back at the time of the General Estates in 1789 he had been the most conservative member of the family and, on becoming king, he soon showed himself to favour the authoritarianism of the former *ancien régime*.

That year, President James Monroe and the US Congress invited Lafayette to make an official visit to the nation, so they could pay tribute to his role in the birth of the United States of America. As we saw in Chapters 1 and 2, Lafayette remained a principled defender of democracy all his life. Accompanied by his son, named after George Washington, Lafayette had planned to visit only the original thirteen states, but ended up staying for sixteen months, visiting all twenty-four states. He paid his respects at Washington's grave in Mount Vernon, was in Yorktown for the anniversary of the surrender of General Cornwallis, and visited his old friend Thomas Jefferson in Monticello, where they were joined by James Madison, another founding father, who was Jefferson's successor and Monroe's predecessor as US President. In February 1825, when the Electoral College had failed (for the second time) to decide the outcome of a presidential election, a contingent election was held by the House of Representatives and John Quincy Adams was declared elected. That evening, Lafayette looked on as General Andrew Jackson, defeated in the House election, shook Quincy Adam's hand at the White House.[11] In Massachusetts that June he laid the cornerstone for the Bunker Hill monument, and collected soil from the site to take back to France. His last stop in October was a reception with President Quincy Adams at the White House, before leaving the next day for France, more determined than ever to promote democracy.

In this same year, Lamartine was awarded the Legion of Honour in recognition of his literary achievements together with Victor Hugo, who would become a friend. Later he was transferred to Florence as *chargé d'affaires*. In 1828, he returned to France and, in a state of depression, wrote a new poem *Novissima Verba*, a poem of despair. In 1829, his literary status was recognised by his election to the Académie Française.

Constitutional monarchy

In July 1830, France was again in the throes of revolution. The liberal opposition led by Germaine de Staël's son-in-law, the Duc de Broglie, and François Guizot, won parliamentary elections, but Charles X refused to recognise the result, issued an edict to disenfranchise middle-class voters and dissolved the assembly. In the space of three days of revolt in the streets of Paris – *Les Trois Glorieuses* (three glorious days) – the government fell, and both the king and his son, the *dauphin* or heir, abdicated. Charles X was the last monarch of the senior branch of the Bourbons.

To succeed him, the National Assembly named Louis-Philippe, Duc d'Orléans, from the branch of the Bourbon family usually described as the cadet or junior branch. Louis-Philippe was known for his liberal views. Once again, Lafayette, hero of both the American and the French Revolutions and now elder statesman of France, intervened to tip the balance of power in favour of a liberal alternative to autocracy. Fearful of a return to the excesses of 1789, the assembly had named Lafayette as commander of a restored National Guard. Lafayette obtained Louis-Philippe's commitment to reforms, then appeared with him, as Louis-Phillippe held aloft the tricolour flag, and accepted the role of constitutional monarch.

As a young man, Louis-Philippe had supported the revolution. He had helped to demolish the iron doors of the prison holding political prisoners at Mont-Saint-Michel and had joined the Jacobins. He served as an officer in the revolutionary army, where his personal courage was recognised. But when his father, known as Philippe Égalité, voted in the national convention for the execution of his cousin, Louis XVI, he became alienated from his father and from the radical turn of the revolution. A close friend was implicated in a plot to restore the monarchy with Austrian support, and suspicion fell on Louis-Philippe as well. So, he went into exile at the age of nineteen, moving around Swiss villages under an assumed name, never staying in the same place more than forty-eight hours. Crossing the upper Rhine, he obtained work teaching mathematics at a boys' boarding school in the German town of Reichenau. There, under the name of Monsieur Chabaud, he learnt that his father had been sentenced to death by the revolutionary tribunal in Paris and had been guillotined.

Thereafter, Louis-Philippe travelled to the Nordic countries and then spent four years in the United States, in Philadelphia, with his two exiled brothers, then in Boston and New York. He later wrote that these years in America had a profound impact on his thinking. From America, the three brothers went to Cuba for a year, then sailed to Nova Scotia, where they were welcomed by Prince Edward, Duke of Kent, who was commander of the British maritime provinces described as Upper and Lower Canada. The duke – who was the fourth son of King George III and would later have a daughter named Victoria, the future queen – arranged for them to stay in England. They remained there in exile for the next fifteen years. Louis-Philippe married a Princess of Naples. By 1830 they had ten children. After the defeat of Napoléon and the restoration of the senior Bourbons in 1815, Louis-Philippe was at last able to return to France at the age of forty.

Louis-Philippe had been strongly influenced politically by the experience of his long exile, especially in America, and he shared his views with Lafayette. When he was designated by the National Assembly as king, after the uprising of *Les Trois Glorieuses* of July 1830, Louis-Philippe renounced the absolute powers of the Bourbons and agreed to a constitutional monarchy. To mark his difference from the absolutism of the *ancien régime*, he called himself 'King of the French' rather than of France. He became known as the 'Citizen King'. His rise to power reflected the changing times, for the industrial revolution had shifted economic power away from the aristocratic landholders, who were inclined to support the 'legitimists' of the Bourbon dynasty. Instead, entrepreneurs and bankers formed the power base of this new, more liberal monarchy.

Conditions in Europe

By 1830 the movement from the countryside to towns and cities was well engaged in the cradle of the industrial revolution across the Channel, in England. Greater London already had a population of 1.5 million inhabitants, which made it the largest city up to that time in history, with a tenth of the entire population of England. Over the next two decades London grew by another million people. As the industrial revolution progressed across continental Europe, notably in France and Germany, the same movement from countryside to towns and cities took hold.

These major changes were accompanied by mobility, not only within nations but also through emigration across borders and oceans. It all had massive social consequences. Basic features of daily life changed. This was the beginning of the machine age. Early textile and metal-working factories employed workers for up to fourteen hours a day. Women and children were widely used for less skilled operations, with little attention to their health or safety. The middle-class people who employed them, the factory managers, and the merchants, held to a work ethic similar to that of the new settlers in North America, which they contrasted with the relaxed lifestyles of the landed gentry. Stories read by adults and to children were full of uplifting messages praising hard work and self-improvement. But this new class of employer was hardly more attentive to the working and living conditions of the urban labourers than the rural landholders had been.

The growth of cities and industry had a major impact on family life. At least in rural villages, poor families could stay together, but that was often not the case as they moved to towns and cities. The majority of women workers in the cities went into domestic service in wealthier households or laboured in factories. Another social consequence of mobility and precarity, as workers moved from job to job, was a steep rise in illegitimate births among young rural and urban workers.[12]

- There was political pressure for governments to intervene against the worst abuses. Middle-class women, while unable to vote, were literate, read widely, and exerted influence on their husbands, fathers, and brothers. Protestant and nonconformist denominations of Christianity, which emphasised study of the written word of the Bible, provided opportunities for social movements to develop in opposition to slavery and child labour. Laws were introduced in Britain, France, and Prussia during the 1830s to restrict child labour in the factories and to open schools. Workers began to organise themselves. Shortly after the revolution of 1830 which brought Louis-Philippe to power in France, major strikes took place in the silk industry around Lyon, calling for a minimum living wage for workers. In Britain, textile industry workers joined with blacksmiths and mechanics to form a National Association for the Protection of Labour, marking the beginning of attempts by working people to organise themselves as they left the countryside and crowded into the new industrial cities. In 1833, a small group in Tolpuddle, England, founded the Friendly Society of Agricultural Labourers to protest against the reduction of their wages. They were tried in court, charged under a law forbidding the swearing of secret oaths, and sentenced to penal transportation to Australia. Becoming popular heroes, 800,000 signatures were collected calling for their release. The petitioners marched on London, and the story of the 'Tolpuddle Martyrs' entered into the legend of the emerging labour movement. Tradesmen also organised themselves through craft guilds, which began to demand better conditions and arranged mutual aid in case of sickness. While unskilled urban workers toiled twelve or more hours a day and lived in squalid slums, the skilled craftsmen had better living conditions but also became increasingly dissatisfied.

In 1832 François Guizot, a Protestant like Jacques Necker before him, and also educated in Geneva, became minister for public instruction in France and instituted major reforms to ensure primary education for all children, whether in local Catholic schools or in secular State schools. He introduced teacher-training academies and a national manual setting out guidelines on standards, while leaving the sensitive questions of moral and religious education to be determined at the local level by the mayors and the local priests. By the 1840s, large numbers of people had achieved basic literacy. A popular press extended political awareness. The scene was set for the spread of disruptive ideas and protests against the conditions faced by the majority of the population across the nations of Europe. While literacy was more widespread, civil rights were denied, since their recognition was linked to the owning of property. The denial of rights, combined with the growing and keenly felt inequalities in society, provided all the ingredients for a revolutionary explosion.

Lamartine enters the political fray

It was in this context that Lamartine, well-known poet and member of the prestigious Académie Française, became engaged in politics and stood for election to the French Parliament. Unsuccessful with his first attempt, he left Paris again to travel abroad, writing of his travels to Greece, Lebanon, and the holy sites in Palestine in 1832. His only daughter, Julia, accompanied him, but Lamartine's life was again marked by tragedy. Julia fell ill of tuberculosis. The young girl died in Beirut at the age of ten.

Returning to France in 1833, Lamartine was elected as a deputy in the parliament. The following year, he was among the founders of a French society for the abolition of slavery. His speeches attracted attention. He turned away from the royalists, of which there were two camps: the dynastic royalists or 'legitimists' who supported the return of the senior Bourbons, and the constitutional monarchists or 'Orléanists' who supported the Citizen King. Lamartine sought to steer an independent course between the different factions: the two camps of monarchists, the reformists who wanted a republic and the emerging socialists.[13] On the monarchist side, the Orléanists led by the Duc de Broglie and François Guizot, had the upper hand during these years. On the reformist side, Lamartine was closest to the liberals of the bourgeoisie, but he also perceived with a certain clairvoyance the rise of a working-class revolutionary movement. The historian François Furet wrote that he detested Orléanism and socialism equally, so that he gravitated towards the reformist republicans. The *nouveaux riches* of the rising bourgeoisie, who supported the constitutional monarchy of the Orléanists, included more than a few 'wheelers and dealers' who made fortunes less than honestly and did not hesitate to buy political influence with bribes. Corruption became increasingly obvious. Lamartine's own *History of the Revolution of 1848*[14] provided a detailed account of his perceptions and thinking at this time. Describing himself as a 'liberal and Christian republican', he called for moderation and social progress.[15] So it was that he came to play a role in the events leading up to the revolution of 1848 and, importantly, in efforts to steer the revolution onto a moderate course.

In 1834, Lafayette, the figure of national unity, died at the age of seventy-six. The following year, an attempted assassination of Louis-Philippe had a dramatic impact on the ongoing political struggles between the two factions of royalists and the republicans. On 28 July 1835, Louis-Philippe reviewed the National Guard in a parade to celebrate the fifth anniversary of *Les Trois Glorieuses*. From a first-floor window of a nearby building, a volley of bullets and buckshot was fired at the king and his party, from an 'infernal machine', consisting of twenty-five gun barrels strapped together.[16] Bending down from his horse to receive a petition from someone in the crowd, the king was only lightly grazed on the forehead, but Édouard Mortier, who had headed the government earlier that year, was killed, along with eighteen others. The king's sons escaped injury, along with the new head of government, the Duc de Broglie, who was the son-in-law of the late Germaine de Staël.[17] The assassin, Guiseppe Fieschi, a Corsican ex-soldier and follower of the former King of Naples, Joachim Murat, brother-in-law to Napoléon I, was arrested, tried, and executed. Before his death Fieschi revealed the existence of several revolutionary groups, leading to more arrests and trials. The episode severely discredited the anti-monarchists and the republican movement in general. The de Broglie government had 'the laws of September' passed by the parliament, restricting, inter alia, the right of the press, or theatre performances, or public gatherings, to criticise the king in person, or to criticise the constitutional monarchy. For the next twelve years, the voices of the republican opposition were muzzled.

In the same year, a young French academic named Alexis de Tocqueville published the first volume of a monumental work entitled *Democracy in America*. This book, written in French and translated into English, initially had greater impact in America than in France. But its influence grew, as it provided a detailed account of the new republican nation across the Atlantic, whose independence had been supported so decisively by France through such leaders as Lafayette. De Tocqueville's second volume, published in 1840, influenced a growing movement in

French intellectual circles in favour of republican institutions. Louis-Philippe and de Tocqueville had both spent years in America, and when de Tocqueville became director of the prestigious Académie Française, the king sought him out. De Tocqueville recounted later how Louis-Philippe had engaged him in a long and intense recollection of his time in America and had spoken to him of 'men he met forty years ago, as if it were yesterday'.[18] Lamartine, now a deputy in the national parliament, was an active participant in the debates among intellectuals about the nature of democracy. Although he was a Romantic literary figure, elevating sentiment above reason in his poetry, Lamartine's transformation from royalist to republican seemed to be the fruit of careful reasoning.

In June 1840, the first world convention against slavery was held in London, with the initiative coming especially from Quakers in Europe and North America. Some 500 abolitionists attended the convention as delegates and up to 1,000 spectators came each day to observe the proceedings. Women had strongly influenced the movement but at this first convention they were only allowed to observe from behind a curtain! In October of the same year, Guizot became foreign minister of France, and from that time on, he was the dominant figure in the government of Louis-Philippe.

Steamships and the electrical telegraph

Industrialisation and expansion across the oceans went hand in hand. In 1837, shipyards in Bristol in England and Leith in Scotland began building side-paddle steamers able to cross the Atlantic. In April 1838, the small Scottish-built steamship *Sirius* became the first ship to cross the Atlantic entirely under steam, crossing from Cork in Ireland to New York. It arrived a day ahead of the larger English ship, the *Great Western*, which made the crossing from Bristol in three fewer days, and from then on established the Blue Riband service. The average time for the crossing with steamships was around sixteen days, compared with the forty or so days of the fastest sailing ships, so strengthening the already well-established commerce between Europe and America. Within a short time British and other European steamships began to ply the routes down the coast of Africa and across the Indian Ocean to India and the Orient, and it was not long before the Americans built their own steamships, crossing the Atlantic to the east and the Pacific to the west. The national powers whose trading prowess had been built on sail already encircled the globe. Now the industrial revolution and the technology of steam enhanced their reach and power enormously. As we shall see in the next chapter, the ancient civilisations of the Orient, China and Japan, as well as South East Asia, were soon to be confronted by the military consequences of European and American advances with the new technology of steam power.

But there was another breakthrough of great importance: the electric telegraph provided a means of communicating over distance. In 1838, Samuel Morse sent the first telegram over two miles of wire in New Jersey in America.

As steam began to take the place of sail, the British continued for a time to dominate their rivals on the high seas. In Asia, the lucrative trade in opium became more commercially important than earlier European trade in tea and spices. The first Opium War began in China in September 1839, when a British fleet of steamships destroyed Chinese junks in Kowloon. In 1841, the British took the port of Hong Kong. In the same year, an act of union in the British Parliament established the United Provinces of Canada, incorporating the French speaking province of Quebec.

Tragedy strikes the royal family

In 1842, King Louis-Philippe suffered a personal tragedy, which had consequences for his succession. His oldest son and heir was killed in a coach accident at the age of thirty-two. Increasingly, the king left the affairs of State to François Guizot. They shared personal histories, as both their fathers had been executed during the Terror of the French Revolution. Guizot spent six years in exile with his mother in Geneva and earned his first degree there. Returning to Paris he studied law, spent time with writers opposed to Napoléon I, who were close to Madame de Staël's Group of Coppet, then became a professor of history, and published major works on the history of Europe and France. Under Louis-Philippe, he was appointed minister of education, then ambassador to London, before becoming foreign minister. He was a strong defender of the constitutional monarchy, but he was a ferocious opponent of the ideas of universal franchise espoused by the reformists and republicans.[19] He argued consistently that the preservation of the constitutional monarchy was essential for the prevention of disaster. In foreign policy, Guizot cooperated closely with Prince von Metternich of Austria, but was often at loggerheads with the British, notably Lord Henry Palmerston. Increasingly, the decisions of colonial European powers, their explorations and their trade, had a major impact across the globe. The main European powers increased their activities in the Orient, all seeking openings for trade.

Contests for influence in the Orient

After taking Hong Kong, Britain imposed a treaty on the Imperial Chinese Government to open up trade and access for Christian missionaries across China – the first of several one-sided treaties that humiliated the imperial court. The seeds were sown for upheavals across the vast empire of the Orient that, decades later, would culminate in revolution and civil war. Our next chapter will trace those upheavals and show how the political movements behind them interacted with the West. Meanwhile, in early 1842, on the other side of Asia, where the Indian subcontinent linked to the Middle East across the legendary Khyber Pass, the British Army was forced by Afghan fighters to retreat from Kabul. Only a few of the British troops survived the massacre. It was Britain's worst military defeat since the beginning of the colonial era. When the news reached London, it sent shockwaves through the Victorian political establishment.

In these early decades of the nineteenth century, after the trauma of the Napoléonic wars, the contests between European monarchies were increasingly projected around the world and were driven above all by trade. In most European governments the ministers responsible for foreign policy were generally the most powerful. That was certainly the case in the France of King Louis-Philippe and his loyal foreign minister, Guizot. Louis-Philippe fully supported Guizot's desire to compete with the British in the Orient. French ships visited the Ryukyu kingdom south of Japan, now called Okinawa, but the big prize was China. France moved to prevent the British from having that vast land to itself, and sent officials to negotiate its own trade treaties with China.

The Chartists push for reform

The constitutional monarchies of Britain and France allowed for vigorous debate in their parliaments on both home and foreign policy, and men like Lamartine could make their mark. To the east and north, however, the Habsburg Kaisers of the Austro-Hungarian Empire and the Romanov tsars of Russia were absolute rulers. Tsar Alexander II decided that the Russian Empire should expand to the east and, in 1843, decreed the first great migration towards the empty spaces of Siberia.

The industrial revolution's impact was increasingly felt in Europe and abroad. Immense fortunes were being made as new means of production opened up opportunities for trade far beyond the shores of Europe. But the working and living conditions of those who produced this wealth continued to be deplorable. In 1843, the British Parliament rejected a petition organised by the Chartists, a working-class reform movement based on a People's Charter, that had obtained 3 million signatures. For the first time a general strike was held and industry in England ground to a halt. In that same year, a young German journalist named Karl Marx moved to Paris and became co-editor of a newspaper aimed at bringing together German and French leftist radicals. The following year, he met a fellow German emigrant, Friedrich Engels, at the Café de la Régence, beginning a life-long collaboration.

In 1845, Guizot expelled Marx from France. The French strongman was astute enough to see the danger posed by the ideas of Marx and his radical friends, who rejected reform and advocated a complete change of the political and economic system through revolution. Marx moved to Brussels where he was joined by Engels, and the two travelled to England, where they met the Chartists.

Crop failures and calls for reform

That year, 1845, the United States expanded, as Florida was admitted as a state of the union, following the removal of Seminole Native Americans in a forced exodus to the west. At the end of the year the Republic of Texas was annexed, leading to a three-year war with Mexico. The harvests were poor throughout Europe. Then, a potato blight appeared in Ireland, most likely brought by transatlantic clippers from the eastern seaboard of America. Over the next four years, the blight caused a devastating famine in Ireland, with an estimated 1 million deaths from starvation among poor tenants. Waves of migrants left for the new world – the United States, Canada and Australia.

In Europe, droughts continued, and Britain repealed corn laws, which had kept grain prices high for the benefit of landowners; the repeal enabled the importation of staple cereals. As before the first French revolution, France was in an economic crisis; food prices had doubled and its population was hungry. France's industrial revolution was well underway, but so was financial speculation, leading to the bankruptcy of many enterprises in the new technologies of metallurgy and railroad construction. Fortunes were made by some, while others were ruined. Workers in many towns found themselves unemployed and, like the rural poor, they had to struggle for their very survival. Scandals of corruption involving businessmen, bankers, politicians and government officials, were reported in a variety of newspapers, which were widely read by an increasingly literate population.[20]

In 1846, after another year of poor harvests, the government in France was re-elected, but as land-holders were still the only ones with the right to vote, the government remained in power with a mandate from a limited electorate of only 240,000 voters. The great majority of people were wage-earners who rented basic housing and owned no property, so could not vote. Guizot continued to refuse electoral reform to expand the right to vote. Lamartine wrote at the time that 'only these electors were legal men. The masses were only the masses carrying the government, without participating in it.' He described the system as 'a parliamentary oligarchy'. This system perfectly suited the Citizen King, who sought to emulate the British parliamentary system of the Victorian era.

In foreign policy, despite Guizot's differences with Palmerston, the government's alliance with Britain was popular, and seen as a source of stability and peace. But this stability was upset by a move from Louis-Philippe to forge an ill-considered alliance with his Bourbon royal cousins in Spain – a move contested by Lamartine and others as a threat to stability. Since the Napoléonic wars, the French middle class, with its focus on entrepreneurship and trading, had favoured peace with its traditional British adversary. Queen Victoria and Prince Albert had visited France, and Louis-Philippe himself, with memories of his welcome to Canada by the Duke of Kent, Victoria's father, crossed the Channel and was hosted by the queen at Windsor. He was the first French monarch to visit Britain in 500 years. So, his move in 1846 to seek an alliance with Spain through the marriage of one of his sons caught both the British and his French supporters by surprise. Lamartine commented that 'the nation was calm on the surface, but anxious underneath'. This underlying unease was expressed increasingly by the journalists of the day. The predominant theme was a call for the right to vote for all men, for universal male franchise, a reform that would inevitably weaken the power of those who held the levers of industry and finance, and whose right to participate in political affairs was defined by their ownership of property. This call was to develop into a nationwide campaign for 'la réforme'.[21]

Across the Channel in London, Marx and Engels organised the first communist congress. The British Parliament responded to liberal reformers by limiting work for women and children to ten hours a day. In the Orient, France mounted an expedition in Indochina, and Jesuit priests established a mission in Shanghai.

The Campaign of Banquets
In these conditions, republicans and reformists conceived the idea of holding great street banquets in cities around France. The banquets were designed to get around the prohibition of political meetings, instituted after the attack on Louis-Philippe at the time of the de Broglie government. They were open to everyone, but the cost of participation excluded poorer people. Some of the banquets were joined by monarchists who favoured reform. The banquets had the support of most of the newspapers of the day, which reflected a diversity of political opinion – from the moderate centre right to the left. Lamartine wrote that a tacit coalition against Guizot emerged among all these newspapers and the parties they represented, including several papers that were independent of parties.[22] The nationwide protest movement known as the Campaign of Banquets began in mid-1847. The first banquet, at Château-Rouge in Paris, on 10 July 1847, was attended by 1,200 people.

Storm over France
Earlier in 1847, Lamartine had published eight volumes, two per month, of his *History of the Girondins*. An analysis of the first revolution, this publication developed his ideas of moderate republicanism, advocating

non-violent reform and a new peaceful republic. To celebrate the success of this new historical work, not only in France but throughout Europe, a banquet was convened in Lamartine's home city of Mâcon. It was held on 18 July, one week after the first great banquet at Château-Rouge in Paris. Unlike most of the banquets that followed in other cities, this one was attended by many women, readers of Lamartine's literary and historical works. The Mâcon banquet was presented as a literary event, but it took a political turn, notably with the speech of Lamartine as the guest of honour.

Lamartine spoke before 300 banquet participants, surrounded by a crowd estimated at 6,000 to 7,000 people, all straining to hear his words. As he rose to speak, a violent summer thunderstorm broke out over the valley of the river Saône. Unperturbed, Lamartine continued, using his experienced orator's voice, 'like a virtuoso playing a bass violin', to rise above the noise of the storm and the crowd.[23] Paying tribute to the crowd's resistance to the stormy conditions, as the banquet tents collapsed and were torn asunder, Lamartine harked back to the violence of the first French Revolution and all that had followed, and cried to the crowd: 'Do not leave for a second time France and Europe in the obscurity of the age of darkness.' Pleading for the ideals of peace and progress, Lamartine called for 'the sovereignty of ideas, the royalty of the mind … the true republic. The republic of intelligences! In a word … public opinion!' He continued: 'This modern power … [was] born on the day when Gutenberg invented with his printing press the multiplication of ideas, thoughts and human reason.' Then Lamartine launched a warning: 'If royalty turns a nation of citizens into a pack of traffickers … after the revolution of liberty and the counter-revolution of glory, you will have the revolution of public conscience.'[24]

With the storm clouds lit by flashes of lightning, and his oration punctuated by thunder, the voice of the political man of reason and the lyricism of the Romantic poet were one. One woman who attended that day, the Countess Marie d'Agoult, wrote later: 'The severe voice of a poet predicted the fall of the throne and the overthrow of the monarchy.'[25]

After the drama of his speech in the storm, Lamartine thought it prudent to withdraw temporarily from the campaign, and he declined further invitations to speak at banquets.[26] In the months that followed, some seventy more banquets were held across France. They all followed a similar format: Participants had to pay, so workers and the poor were unlikely to take part; the participants were bourgeois reformers; women were absent or marginalised[27] and each banquet usually lasted a full day. While presented as festive occasions, they really had a political purpose. During the course of each banquet, toasts followed one after the other – toasts to electoral reform, to the end of corruption, even to the honour of King Louis-Philippe. Their common cry was: *Vive la réforme*. These were occasions for orators to show their eloquence. De Tocqueville wrote: 'A wind of revolution blows, the storm is on the horizon.'

Guizot had dominated the government for a decade, and he was finally named prime minister in September 1847. By then, the Campaign of Banquets was well underway. At about the same time the minister for public works, Jean-Baptiste Testé, was dismissed and tried in court, by order of the king, for taking bribes from a former minister engaged in mining, a scandal that was widely covered in the press.

As the Campaign of Banquets spread across France, Friedrich Engels attended the banquets in important cities like Lille and Dijon. He wrote articles about them, several of which were published in the Chartist newspaper *The Northern Star* in Britain. Workers' movements were developing across the cities of Europe but had not yet become as prominent as they would later. The reform movement was essentially pursued by politically active liberal elites.

Revolution in the rain

As 1847 drew to a close, on 28 December, the king convened the two chambers of parliament. The session began with the announcement of a military success – the end of opposition to French colonial rule in Algeria. With strong majorities in both chambers, Guizot was confident that the government's response to the Campaign of Banquets, which conceded the right of assembly subject to government regulation and approval, would be endorsed. But the king's speech included a phrase calling those associated with the reformist banquets 'hostile or blind'.[28] Since many of the deputies in the assembly had participated actively in the banquets, along with several of the nobles, this phrase provoked angry responses in the parliament. Lamartine had not participated personally in the banquets after his speech in the storm in Mâcon six months earlier but he, too, rose to speak. The prime minister could regulate the right of assembly, said Lamartine, but not brutally suppress it. Far from being an artificial protest, he continued, the movement grew from a deep-seated refusal of the oligarchy to countenance differing views, such that a new authoritarianism had taken the place of the great democracy promised in 1830. Corruption had risen like a tide until it had reached the feet of those in power. Moreover, he said, the foreign policy of peace and stability pursued by Guizot since 1830, had been undermined by the recent dynastic calculation of the king, seeking an alliance with Spain, which had threatened the entente with Britain and thus stability in Europe. Recalling the oath of the Jeu de Paume just prior to the first revolution, and all that followed, Lamartine concluded by stating that refusal of the right of assembly created a great peril to the nation.

Alexis de Tocqueville, now a conservative deputy, wrote: 'We are sleeping together in a volcano … A wind of revolution blows, the storm is on the horizon.'[29] De Tocqueville had avoided involvement in the Campaign of Banquets. On 29 January, he warned of the coming revolution in a speech to the National Assembly. 'Look at what is happening within the working classes,' he said. 'Do you think it an accident? … *Non, messieurs*, there was another cause: that the class which governed had become, by its indifference, by its egoism, by its vices, incapable and unworthy to govern … Can you not feel,' he concluded, 'that the land trembles again in Europe … a wind of revolution … is in the air?'[30]

On the very eve of the revolution, the dancing continued. As elites generally do, those with power and money loved to party, flaunting their affluence and their connections. De Toqueville wrote later: 'I remember, two days before the revolution of February, finding myself at a great ball, at the residence of the ambassador of Turkey …' and there he warned an opposition politician, whom he knew well, 'My dear friend, you are playing a dangerous game.'[31]

The final great banquet, which would be the culmination of the campaign of some seventy political street banquets, was planned for Paris in the New Year, at the Place de la Madeleine. This is when the government of Guizot made its mistake. It banned the banquet. Not to be deterred, the organisers changed the date to several weeks later,

22 February, to celebrate George Washington's birthday. The new date was charged with symbolism, as it marked the common ideals of the American and French revolutions. The banquet was to be held in the 12th district of the capital, near the Place de la Bastille, in the rue du Faubourg Saint-Antoine. By Lamartine's account, the main leaders of the banquet protest movement negotiated an agreement with the government to test the legality of the banquet in court.[32] However, the more radical members of the movement rejected this legal solution. So, the government instead prohibited the banquet by decree. The constitutional opposition met under a leading liberal monarchist deputy named Odilon Barrot. Republican deputies also met and were joined by Lamartine, who until then had maintained his independence. After listening to other speakers, Lamartine rose to support a revolt against the decree. The man who had written so studiously about the violent outcomes of the first French revolution, this time threw caution to the wind, declaring that providence would determine the consequences. Later, when he took the full measure of the consequences, he would write that this had been a serious mistake.[33]

In the streets of Paris, an angry crowd marched past the prime minister's residence chanting 'Down with Guizot.' Barricades were put up in the streets and fighting broke out between the protesters and police. To Lamartine, the movement seemed more like a riot than a revolution.[34] The king remained calm, saying 'The Parisians never make a revolution in the winter, and they won't overthrow the monarchy for a banquet.'[35] But the pressure from the streets increased and the next day, 23 February, Guizot resigned.

As the news of the resignation spread, a large crowd formed in front of Guizot's ministry office, in freezing rain. Lamartine vividly described the scene. Firstly, elegantly dressed marchers from the liberal reform movement moved towards the ministry building. Joining the protest, but in a separate formation, were the workers, marching in their work clothes, many carrying tools and with grime on their faces and hands.[36] Lamartine's description was prescient, for these same divisions would bring down the provisional government within a few short months. The crowd grew in front of the Ministry of Foreign Affairs, the official seat of Guizot. Their way forward was barred by a battalion armed with loaded weapons. The commander's horse, frightened perhaps by the flags of the marchers, reared. A nervous soldier discharged his gun. The crowd surged forward. The soldiers panicked and fired more shots, now directly into the crowd. There were fifty-two deaths. The word spread like wildfire. Protests broke out across the city. Lamartine wrote: 'Nobody knows [whether] by crime or hazard, this [first] shot lit the revolution.'

As fighting spread across the capital, the king called on an opposition leader, Adolphe Thiers, who like Lamartine and Guizot was an historian and member of the Académie Française. When he responded to the king's call in the middle of the night, Thiers found Guizot leaving the king's office while the army commander, Marshal Thomas Bugeaud, remained. Although Thiers had been an early supporter of Louis-Philippe and had joined Lafayette in persuading him to accept the throne in 1830, he had left the king's government. Critical of the hardline politics of Guizot and the Party of Order, he had nevertheless served briefly as prime minister in 1836. After that, he was considered to be part of the opposition. Comparing the political situation with that of 1789, Lamartine commented that Thiers did not wish to be the Necker of the dynasty of Orléans, nor an apologist for the king's imprudence. So, Thiers agreed to form a new government on condition that he would hold effective power. The announcement of a new government under Thiers, including the historical opposition leader Barrot, did nothing to calm the protests. On the contrary, students from the university forged links with the workers' movements. A young socialist pamphleteer named Louis Blanc, who like Lamartine and Thiers had published a history of the first French revolution, began to emerge as a leader of the revolutionaries.

Abdication
The king had always believed in having direct contact with the people and had often appeared in public and been acclaimed. So, at this critical juncture, he and his sons mounted their horses and rode out of the palace to salute the army and the volunteers of the National Guard, with the queen and the princesses watching from the balcony. But from the crowd the king heard for himself the cries of 'Down with the ministers' and 'Vive la réforme.' He returned with dejection written across his grizzled features. In an atmosphere of consternation and hesitation,

meetings followed within the palace with political and military leaders, and within the royal family. The queen held out against abdication until the end. But the king took his decision. As he did so, she went to a window, looking back to her husband with indignation and tears in her eyes. With the king's letter of abdication in his hands, Marshal Bugeaud observed respectfully that nobody had the legal authority to take over the government. 'I know, Marshal,' replied the king, 'but I do not want blood to run any longer for my cause.'[37]

In his letter of abdication, on 24 February, Louis-Philippe named his grandson, Philippe, aged nine, as heir to the throne, as he had lost the boy's father, his eldest son, in the carriage accident several years earlier. Now, as he discussed the terms of abdication with Thiers, Marshal Bugeaud and his family, it was proposed firstly that the boy's uncle, the Duc de Nemours, be the regent, which would give him effective regal power. But the mood conveyed from the assembly was unfavourable to this proposal because of the duke's reputation for conservatism, and the boy's mother, the widowed Duchess of Orléans, was proposed instead.

The king took off the jacket of his uniform with its medals, placed his sword on the table, and put on a simple black coat. He took the queen's arm. The white-haired couple, who had been together through so much, walked slowly out to exile. Even the republican supporters among the gathered troops shed a tear, for nobody doubted Louis-Philippe's basic decency as a man. Victor Hugo wrote in *Les Misérables*: 'He had been prescribed a wanderer, poor. He had lived by his own labor. In Switzerland, this heir to the richest princely domains in France had sold an old horse in order to obtain bread. At Reichenau, he gave lessons in mathematics, while his sister Adelaide did knitting and sewed. He had, with his own hands, demolished the iron cage of Mont-Saint-Michel, built by Louis XI, and used by Louis XV to hold prisoners of the state. He was the companion of Dumouriez, he was the friend of Lafayette; he had belonged to the Jacobins' club; Mirabeau had slapped him on the shoulder; Danton had said to him: "Young man!" What is there against him? That throne. Take away Louis-Philippe the King, there remains the man. And the man is good. He is good at times even to the point of being admirable.'[38]

Louis-Philippe d'Orléans and the queen went out into the night where a coach was waiting for them. They were driven from Paris to the coast where, as Mr and Mrs Smith, they boarded a ship and crossed the Channel to England and exile.

A political vacuum

The king's abdication created a political vacuum. The situation was chaotic and fighting continued in the streets. The assembly was in continuous session, but without clear direction. Lamartine was invited into a room by the leading republicans. There, they proposed that he lead a provisional government. By Lamartine's own account, he sat with his two elbows on the table, his head in his hands. Hardly breathing, he plunged into deep thought for several minutes, as the republican leaders stood around him, waiting for his response. Finally, he took his hands from his face, raised his head, and agreed. A child with his mother as regent could not solve the problems and create a legitimate government, he said. The risk of anarchy was real. Only the declaration of a republic could win popular support.

With that agreement from Lamartine, the republicans moved together to the assembly, presided over by the respected but aged Jacques-Charles Dupont de l'Eure. The Duchess of Orléans entered, holding the hands of her two sons, Prince Philippe, formally called the Count of Paris, and Prince Robert, accompanied by her brother-in-law, the Duc de Nemours, other family members and officers. But as the debate over succession of the monarchy began, the doors to the assembly broke open and a crowd of protestors broke in. In the chaos, Lamartine called for the assembly to be suspended. A young butcher advanced, knife in hand, with blood stains on his apron. The deputies closed around the duchess and the young princes to protect them. Lamartine continued speaking. Troops of the volunteer National Guard entered. In the general melee, the Duc de Nemours decided to move the duchess and the boys out, protecting them with his body. But the princes were separated from their mother. A man of colossal size grabbed Prince Philippe by the throat and lifted him up. A national guardsman knocked the man to the ground with the butt of his gun, and returned the boy to his mother, who burst into tears, kissing him. She searched for her other son, Robert, now lost in the crowd, left the assembly chamber, and found him later in the care of a baker's wife. Lamartine remained standing at the tribune of the assembly. A young worker raised his gun and aimed it at him. Deputies shouted: 'Don't fire. It is Lamartine,' and the young man was disarmed.

A provisional government

As calm was restored, Lamartine read the names of the ten members proposed to form a provisional republican government. There were calls to add the name of Louis Blanc, the socialist activist. Lamartine accepted, and the names were approved by acclamation. As the assembly adjourned, a young man turned his gun on the portrait of Louis-Philippe behind the podium, fired and tore it apart with bullets. Lamartine and the other newly named members of the government decided to leave the assembly and march together to the Hôtel de Ville of Paris. The president of the assembly, Dupont de l'Eure, was driven by carriage. As Lamartine marched at the head of the crowd with Alexandre Ledru-Rollin, François Arago, and the other members of the government, he could see another column marching along the other side of the Seine river. At the caserne du quai d'Orsay military barracks, he asked for a glass of wine. Then the marchers crossed the river and converged with the others at the vast square in front of the Hôtel de Ville.

Entering the building, the new government met for the first time. De l'Eure delegated Lamartine to take his place in case of his absence or infirmity and *de facto* ceded his powers. Recognised as the real leader of the government, Lamartine was named minister of foreign affairs, like Guizot before him. Ledru-Rollin was assigned the key post of minister of the interior. Blanc was named as a secretary of state. Lamartine wrote the first proclamations to the people and to the army. They were taken to be printed and distributed. The members of the provisional government were acutely aware that their legitimacy could be challenged by the competing factions and by the street. Returning to the meeting room, Lamartine said ironically to Arago, a mathematician: 'Have you calculated by how much our heads remain less on our shoulders compared with this morning?'[39] To his colleagues he said: 'To proclaim nothing is to proclaim anarchy, sedition, civil war. The only solution is to proclaim the republic subject to ... ratification by the National Assembly.' The proclamation of the Second French Republic, written by the hand of

Lamartine, was adopted unanimously by the provisional government and sent to the national printer.

Rapidly, the word passed through the crowd before the Hôtel de Ville that 'The republic has been proclaimed, the republic has been proclaimed.'[40] Blanc circulated among his radical friends, convincing them to support the proclamation. A young officer named Chateaurenard, athletic and blond, raised his sabre and called for allegiance to the republic. But still, the matter was far from settled. Lamartine descended the stairs from the meeting room to address the crowd, estimated at 10,000. As he descended, some of the more heated revolutionaries called for his head. But as he spoke, the crowd responded '*Vive la République, Vive Lamartine*' and, as he walked back up the stairs, those who had harangued him a few minutes earlier now applauded.[41]

But the case for the new republic was not yet won in the streets. Again, Lamartine descended the stairs to speak to the crowd. Finally, he and the other members of the government left the Hôtel de Ville for the night. For the next three days, groups without leaders roamed the streets. There were more riots, more deaths. The next day, Lamartine went out to address the crowd five times more. The symbol of the ongoing disputes became the flag. The monarchists no longer dared to show the blue and gold flag of the Bourbons – the Fleur de Lys. The socialists waved their red flag. Before the crowd, Lamartine waved the tricolour, red, white and blue flag of the first revolution and of the empire. The tricolour flag prevailed. Lamartine called for a republic of reason and justice, rejecting vengeance and violence. The death sentence for political crimes was abolished, so as to mark clearly the difference with the first revolution. The royal family was offered protection as its members followed the former king and queen into exile.

The Second Republic

Finally, calm returned to the city. Lamartine and Arago marched at the head of a procession that took four hours to pass – 120,000 people marching together, of all professions and opinions. The proclamation of the republic was read at the Place de la Bastille, which was so full of historical significance. Lamartine was again acclaimed by the huge gathering. But once people moved away from the Place de la Bastille,

Lamartine, ever the man of reflection, slipped to the back of the procession, taking off his insignia of office, so as to melt into the crowd. After a time, he was recognised and acclaimed enthusiastically. At the rue St Antoine, he took refuge in a house owned by Victor Hugo. A carriage was arranged to take him away. Lamartine discovered to his astonishment that the coach driver was the one who had taken Louis-Philippe and the queen to Calais and their exile.

Throughout the nation, in all the departments, the announcement of the republic was accepted. Lamartine mused, and wrote in his history: 'Thirty-six million souls changed sovereignty without loss of life. Blood was spilt in Paris for or against *la réforme*. But not a drop of blood was spilt in France for or against the Republic.'[42]

De Toqueville presented a quite different account of these times. Although he was an early admirer of Lamartine's poetry, de Toqueville detested him as a politician. De Toqueville's own account, published much later, in 1893, portrayed Lamartine as being driven entirely by self-interest. A conservative and member of the Party of Order, de Toqueville complained that Lamartine ignored him. But there was indirect contact between the two academics, as Lamartine's wife would often visit Madame de Tocqueville, and de Toqueville himself wrote that he listened attentively and with respect to her comments on political affairs.

Louis Napoléon Bonaparte, nephew of the late emperor, had been exiled in London and now visited Paris. He wrote to Lamartine, stating that he 'was without any other ambition than that of serving my country'. Not trusting a Bonaparte for an instant, Lamartine replied to Louis Napoléon asking him to leave Paris, and he returned to London.

Progressive steps
An early decision of the provisional government was to implement the Campaign of Banquet's call for *la réforme*, which meant, first and foremost, the introduction of universal suffrage for men. In 1793, under the First Republic, France was the first country to declare universal male suffrage in 1793, but it was not implemented because of the upheavals at the end of the Terror. Another important decision was the abolition of slavery, also decreed under the First Republic in 1794, then reversed by Napoléon. Britain and the United States had outlawed the international

slave trade in 1807, but slavery was maintained in the southern American states. Years later, in 1861, the civil war over slavery and secession would divide the nation born of the American Revolution. As we have seen so often, the destinies of the United States and France would be intertwined. Philippe d'Orléans, the young boy named briefly as king in 1848, and his brother, Prince Robert, would go to America to fight with the Unionists of Abraham Lincoln, and Philippe would write about the history of the Civil War.[43] His book, widely regarded as one of the definitive histories of the American Civil War, highlighted, yet again, not only the fertile exchanges of concepts of democracy between the two nations born of revolution, but also the way in which citizens of both nations were active participants in each other's great historical events. The struggle for civil rights would continue into the twentieth century. For the remainder of the nineteenth century, as the concept of universal suffrage was pursued across Europe, the focus was on male suffrage. The right of women to vote would be won much later, beginning at the end of the century in the distant colonies of New Zealand and South Australia. Voting rights for women would be achieved decades later in Europe and North America.

The provisional government of Lamartine was determined never to return to the abuses of the monarchy, and just as determined to avoid the descent into violence and terror that had followed the first revolution. Hence the decision of the new government to abolish the death penalty for political crimes. As foreign minister, Lamartine also sought to reassure France's neighbours, knowing that European powers were on their guard against any resurgence of Bonapartism.

The year of revolutions

1848 stands out as a moment in history. We have seen in our first two chapters how the American and French revolutions of the late eighteenth century were inter-linked. By the mid-nineteenth century, after the Napoléonic wars and a time of relative peace, events in one country reverberated more than ever across Europe and beyond. 1848 would become the year of revolutions across Europe. The year began with an uprising in Sicily, but the big event was the new revolution in France, which followed the turbulence of the Napoléonic Empire, the restoration of the Bourbon monarchy, and the constitutional monarchy of Louis-Philippe. The upheavals of 1848 were centred in France and its capital. However, unlike the first French revolution, this time the interaction with the rest of Europe was ongoing and intense. The industrial revolution had dramatically shortened travel times. In the era of steam, travel on land by railway was much quicker than it had been on horseback or carriage.[44] On the oceans, steam replaced sail. There was more international mobility than ever. Both middle-class and working people could travel across the seas to the new Eldorado of America, or to the far-flung colonies of Asia or Latin America and, increasingly, to Africa.

As rebellions spread across Europe following the events in Paris, the autocracies of the German states and the Austrian Empire were shaken. Huge demonstrations were held in Vienna on 12 March. The Holy Roman Empire had ended with the defeat of the Austrians by Napoléon at Austerlitz in 1805, and it had been replaced by the Austrian Empire, still ruled by the Habsburg dynasty. The conservative Prince von Metternich emerged after Napoléon's final defeat as the master diplomat of the Treaty of Westphalia of 1815. As chancellor of Austria from 1821, he had been the architect of the Concert of Europe, a series of congresses that kept peace among the ruling dynasties. The uprising of March 1848 in Vienna forced Metternich to resign, and he went into exile in Britain.

There were also uprisings in the Prussian capital, Berlin. People took to the streets in Denmark, Sweden, the low countries of Holland and Belgium, in Ireland, and even in the republican cantons of Switzerland. More marches followed in Poland calling for independence from Prussia, and a short-lived military uprising was put down. In the weeks and months that followed the fall of Metternich there were nationalist uprisings across the Austrian Empire, in Venice and Milan in Italy, in Bohemia, in the Czech and Slovak lands, in Serbia, and especially in Hungary. Only the tsarist empire of Russia to the north remained unaffected, although the tsar sent troops to support the Habsburg emperor in Hungary. One after the other, the autocracies of Europe fell. The revolutions of 1848 across Europe marked the end of the feudal regimes in these countries. Tensions were felt across the Channel in Britain, and as a precaution Queen Victoria moved out of London with Prince Albert and their family. The rebellions became known in various countries as the Springtime of the Peoples, or as the Spring of Nations.

As the 1848 revolutions rippled across the continent of Europe, the consequences were felt in other parts of the world. European powers were competing across the globe to extend their trade and colonial empires. One consequence of the revolutions, and of the social conditions of labourers in Europe, which were underlying drivers of the uprisings, was a dramatic increase in European migration to North America. As fate would have it, the great California gold rush also began in January 1848. Migration from the American east coast, from Europe, and also across the Pacific Ocean from China, transformed the tiny settlement in the port of San Francisco into a boomtown. With the end of the Mexican American war, which had been sparked by the annexation of Texas three years earlier, control of California was ceded to the United States under the Treaty of Guadalupe Hidalgo signed in February.

As we shall see in the next chapter, the Orient was also drawn into the disruptions of the industrial revolution, and there were remarkable coincidences of seemingly unrelated events. In that same year – 1848 – a printing press arrived for the first time in Japan, helping to pave the way for the Meiji restoration just twenty years later, when Japan would open itself to the West and embark on modernisation and its own industrial revolution.

The Communist Manifesto
Before the 1848 revolution broke out in France, Karl Marx had been working with his friend Friedrich Engels on the text that would come to be known around the world as *The Communist Manifesto*. Published in London on 21 February 1848, it was written in German and was soon distributed throughout the states of the German Confederation and across the Austrian Empire. As power shifted from autocratic dynasties to diets or parliaments in these German-speaking lands of central Europe, political divergences emerged that were similar to those in France. Middle-class activists in those coalitions were committed to liberal principles such as universal suffrage. But workers wanted more; they wanted radical improvements in their working and living conditions.

This was the age of steam and steel. Railways spread across the continents of Europe and North America; steamships crossed the Atlantic. Workers laboured in factories and forges making steel. They built the trains and the ships. They toiled underground to mine the coal that fuelled the factories, the locomotives, and the steamships. Entrepreneurs and traders made fortunes, but there was also a great deal of speculation, corruption and scandal. The workers were becoming literate, and they could read all about the latest scandals in newspapers and pamphlets. They could also read the ideas of radical intellectuals who challenged the system. *The Communist Manifesto* was one of several pamphlets being circulated. It was disseminated first throughout the German heartland, then across the European continent. Karl Marx was living in Belgium, but he was accused by the government of arming Belgian workers, and with just a few hours' notice he was expelled with his family. He and Engels returned to Paris.[45]

The main idea of the manifesto was that of class struggle. It argued against the reform movements, stated that the bourgeoisie would become 'its own grave diggers', and held that the working class would inevitably overthrow the bourgeoisie through revolution. The manifesto had no immediate impact on events in France when it was published at the beginning of 1848. But its appearance at almost the same time as the revolution was not just a coincidence. For the declaration of the Second French Republic by liberal reformers and the publication of *The Communist Manifesto* by advocates of revolution, were both consequences of the immense social change underway as the industrial revolution rolled on. From then on there would be a struggle of ideas about the shape of the future – about change through reform, or change through revolution.

The struggle of ideas

Underlying all these movements and upheavals was a great struggle of ideas. The organisers of the Campaign of Banquets held across France from July 1847 to February 1848 were upper or middle-class liberals advocating electoral reform and opposing endemic corruption. Some, like Ledru-Rollin were republicans, while others, such as the main opposition leader Odilon Barrot, favoured the continuation of a constitutional monarchy. Reformers, not revolutionaries, they were members of the elites of the day. *The Communist Manifesto* articulated a much deeper discontent welling up from the disenfranchised working class whose labour propelled the spreading industrial revolution. As we shall see, the liberal reformist protests of the Campaign of Banquets in France paved the way for an uprising of the dispossessed, and then the resulting repression.

Again, history did not follow a linear path. The protests and uprisings faded away. It seemed for a time that the contests between great powers and their empires would simply continue as in the pre-1848 era. Events in the Old World and in the New World interacted across three oceans – the Atlantic, the Indian and the Pacific. European powers continued their skirmishes in colonial outposts and trading stations, in Asia and the Caribbean, and later, in the infamous 'race for Africa'.

Yet, something fundamental had changed. The struggle of ideas that had erupted in these revolutions across the old continent would not be laid to rest. The feudal regimes which had governed the peoples of Europe and had extended their colonial outreach around the world either fell or altered their autocratic natures. The scene was set for the momentous changes of the next century. Seventy years later, *The Communist Manifesto* would form the basis for Lenin's Bolshevik revolution, overthrowing the last European dynasty to escape the aftermath of 1848 – the dynasty of the Russian tsars.

The romance of the railways

By the mid-nineteenth century France had wholeheartedly joined the industrial revolution. Lamartine was a leading advocate for the railways as a means of modernising the rural regions of the country. This poet turned politician took quite the opposite position to his fellow poet in England, William Wordsworth, who wrote: 'Motions and Means, on land and sea at war. With old poetic feeling, not for this, Shall ye, by Poets even, be judged amiss!'[46] Lamartine, on the other hand, called the railways: 'One of the most urgent necessities ... to place [France] at the level of industry and civilisation of neighbouring peoples,' and he continued by predicting that the companies 'will be masters of the government and the parliament within ten years'.[47]

As in the United States, the financial stakes were enormous. The Rothschild banking family continued to build its fortune by investing in railway bonds, as well as lending funds for wars and colonial expansion. One of the sons, James Mayer de Rothschild, had arrived in Paris from

Frankfurt in 1812, and in 1817 he set up the Paris-based bank Rothschild Frères. Another bank funded Napoléon's return from Elba in 1815. James de Rothschild quickly aligned himself with the Bourbons after the Restoration that same year, then in 1830 with Louis-Philippe the Citizen King, who brought in his new modernising government. The rails and locomotives for the new French railway networks were forged in Le Creusot in the Saône Valley, and the new coal-powered economy was supplied by the mines north of Paris around Lille – the setting for Victor Hugo's classic novel *Les Misérables*. Rapid change created the conditions for great fortunes to be made, while also provided a breeding ground for speculation, corruption, and scandal. And people could read about all of this in the many newspapers and pamphlets distributed throughout the country.

Factions in France

During the years of the constitutional monarchy in France leading up to the revolt of 1848, the parliament elected by property holders was described by Lamartine as an oligarchy. But this elite was riven with deep divisions. Factionalism was rife, hence the multiplicity of parties and interests. These divisions had been present through the Campaign of Banquets from mid-1847 onwards. When Guizot banned the final banquet in February, the divisions were put aside, but only momentarily. As a politician who had remained independent of the competing factions, Lamartine emerged as the leader of the new republic. His own account described vividly how he navigated through the turbulence of the storm, carried by his oratory, and his instinctive feel for a middle course between the abuses of the old elitist system and the excesses of the mob. But he also perceived the risks welling up from the deep changes underway in a society now experiencing the full impact of the industrial revolution. These forces would bring about his political downfall and thrust France back into populism. Lamartine's ideal of non-violent revolution was soon shown to be an illusion. As a poet he dreamed, as a politician he calculated, but neither could prevent the impending storm.

The provisional government of the new republic – composed of middle-class liberals, and a couple of socialists – was soon confronted by the clash of parties in the National Assembly. Alexis de Toqueville, famous for his books on democracy in America, was a leading light in the conservative opposition of Guizot's Party of Order. Lamartine subsequently recounted in his memoirs how the new government worked day and night to tackle an array of challenges: restoring food supply in Paris, winning acceptance of the new authorities in the local departments, the navy and the army. There was also the challenge of Algeria, declared just before the revolution to be an integral part of France. Funds had to be raised for the national treasury. The list went on and on …[48] At the end of the first week, Lamartine moved to the ministry of foreign affairs, where he felt 'the shadow of M. Guizot still there'.[49] Guizot had left behind papers, and Lamartine was intrigued to see his own name in Guizot's handwriting. A note said: 'The more I listen to M. de Lamartine, the more I feel that we will never agree.'[50]

The new republican foreign minister quickly plunged into the ongoing game of alliances among the powers of Europe – most of them at this stage still governed by monarchies. He wrote a letter, which he described himself as being 'short and vague', to all French diplomats, stating 'the republic has not changed the place of France in Europe'.[51] He then recalled all ambassadors to Paris and replaced them with confidential agents, with instructions to convey a message that the new republic wanted peace in Europe.[52] In a somewhat whimsical passage of his written account, Lamartine summed up his foreign policy as follows: 'Wait upon England with dignity, seek out Prussia, observe Russia, calm Poland, caress Germany, avoid Austria, smile to Italy without exciting it, reassure Turkey, and leave Spain to herself.'[53]

As he met the ambassadors of the powers of Europe, Lamartine's first task was to remove the fear of a resurgent France and the all-too-recent spectre of Bonapartism. Britain's Duke of Wellington, now advanced in years and still commander-in-chief of the British armed forces, wrote personally to Lamartine expressing Britain's desire for peace. Within two weeks of the revolution, on 6 March, Lamartine convened the provisional government of seven men and wrote: 'Seven men coming several days earlier out of a storm held in their hands peace or war.' Unanimously they adopted Lamartine's declaration of peace, entitled the Manifesto to Europe,[54] stating 'the French Republic will not go to war against anyone'. The manifesto concluded: 'The republic was born pronouncing three words: Liberty, Equality, Fraternity. Not one of these words signifies war.' Then he added, 'If Europe is prudent and fair, there is not one of these words which does not signify peace.'[55]

Nevertheless, the government immediately formed an army of 62,000 men along the Alps, from the Var to Grenoble, both to defend against any attack from Italy, and to keep domestic peace in a region still favourable to the restoration of the monarchy. Another army of 100,000 men was sent to defend the border along the Rhine river, and 30,000 to defend the northern border towards Belgium. They also decided to reduce the active forces in Algeria, a decision opposed by the generals there, which would soon have political consequences.

Meanwhile, the treasury was virtually empty, and interest had to be paid on bonds. Lamartine wrote that failure to do so would set off a crisis of confidence. He complained bitterly that the republic would be charged with the responsibility of taking unpopular measures to redress a situation left by the monarchy and its ministers.[56] The Bank of France was strengthened. A levy was added to property taxes. But this measure weakened support from the property owners who had been the main participants in the Campaign of Banquets.

Lamartine's independence from political factions had been a key factor in the liberal republicans' approach to him on the eve of the revolution when they had asked him to join the provisional government. Lamartine had demonstrated careful judgement, determination, and oratorical skills to navigate the tumultuous birth of the new republic. But now, as the effective leader of the government, his decisions were contested from all sides. On one side were radical groups that articulated the rebellion of the emerging working class, and essentially sought to overthrow the parliamentary system dominated by the bourgeois elite. Engel's disdainful dismissal of Lamartine's 'pompous ideas' resonated with these groups. Lamartine later wrote in his book about the various clubs that were organising against the government. He counted on the socialist Louis Blanc to carry his message of moderation to them, which Blanc did as long as he could pursue the policy of establishing national workshops for the unemployed. On the other side were the conservatives, opposed to universal male suffrage, many supporting a return to monarchy, constitutional or otherwise. Guizot's Party of Order, now led by de

Toqueville, was the leading group on this side. In the struggle between conservatives and radicals, Lamartine's stance as an independent moderate and a pacifist was increasingly a lonely one.

By April 1848, national workshops employed more than 100,000 men. But the workshops were financed by increases in property taxes, which were vehemently opposed by landholders. Tensions increased. Once again, as in the revolution of 1789, and as in the American Revolution before that, taxation became the flash point. Funds had to be found to reduce the deficit, and to finance new expenditure, especially for the national workshops. As the landed gentry resisted the proposed land taxes they were joined by the small farmers – millions of them across rural France – whose families had owned their plots only since the first revolution, just a generation earlier. Working hard, trying to make ends meet, farmers resisted paying for unemployed people in the cities and their 'right to work' in national workshops. En masse, they disobeyed the collection of land taxes.

Elections and insurrections

Two months after the abdication of Louis-Philippe and the declaration of the Second Republic, elections for the new National Assembly were held in April throughout the nation, with universal male suffrage. For the first time, all men could vote, and ownership of land was no longer a requirement to be able to go to the polls. Lamartine described how columns of men formed in villages, each waiting for their turn to vote. 'It was the same in the cities,' he wrote. 'One saw citizens rich and poor, soldiers or workers, owners or employees ... taking their voting papers ... placing them in the urn, and returning with satisfaction on their faces as with a pious ceremony.'[57] Eighty-four per cent of the electorate voted.[58] They elected 880 deputies to the National Assembly, with a majority composed of middle-class conservative republicans, and minorities of monarchists on the right and socialists on the left.

Lamartine emerged personally triumphant from this first national election. A total of 2 million French men voted for him – ten times the number of votes received by any other candidate.[59] Of the seventeen departments in which he was elected, he opted to represent the department of the Seine. Reinforced by the election results, the government sought to establish its legitimacy. On 27 April, it signed a decree definitively abolishing slavery.[60] On 4 May, as proposed by Lamartine, the National Assembly again formally proclaimed the republic, this time with the authority of an electoral mandate. The following week, on 9 May, the assembly adopted a new structure of government, with a five-member body called the Executive Commission, which was mandated to fulfill collegially the functions of head of state and designate ministers. The moderate republican majority appointed five members from the earlier provisional government, including Lamartine, to the commission. But Louis Blanc and the socialists were excluded. Ledru-Rollin, a key organiser of the Campaign of Banquets, was included only at the insistence of Lamartine, as a condition for his own participation. A number of ministers were named. Lamartine invited Victor Hugo to take the post of minister of public instruction, but Hugo refused. Aurore Dupin, an early feminist better known as the writer Georges Sand, lover of the famous composer Frederick Chopin, accepted a post in the ministry of the interior. But the proposal of Blanc to name a minister of progress, for the improvement of conditions for the popular classes, was refused.

The radicals had lost out badly in the elections and were now excluded from government. Protests returned to the streets. As revolutions swept across Europe, events in one country quickly had repercussions elsewhere. On 15 May, a demonstration was held in Paris in support of the independence demands of Poland. Many of the demonstrators and their radical leaders then forced their way into the National Assembly. Repulsed by the National Guard, the incursion failed in its attempt to replace the government. The conservative majority blamed the Executive Commission for the upheaval, and the collegial body was weakened politically. Two days later, the Party of Order imposed the nomination of a new minister for war, Louis-Eugène Cavaignac.

General Cavaignac was the recent commander in Algeria, who was credited with putting down the rebellions there. Back in December 1847, Louis-Philippe had opened the old assembly by announcing this victory for the Guizot government. In the wake of the February revolution, the provisional government ended Algeria's status as a colony and declared it to be an integral part of France. Cavaignac was appointed governor-general of the province. In April he had been elected to the National

Assembly, and he prepared to return to Paris. When he arrived on 17 May, he immediately accepted his nomination as minister of war.

Debates in the assembly intensified around the budget and the national workshops. The commission proposed credits for farmers and a reduction in an unpopular salt tax. Lamartine came up with a proposal that would address the issue of unemployed workers in Paris, and the need to overcome the divide between the capital and the provinces. He proposed that the railways be nationalised, and the unemployed workers engaged on the extension of the railway network. The conservatives, who now dominated the assembly, considered this proposal to be an assault on private ownership. For them it was the final straw and they voted that the national workshops should end.

On 21 June, the National Assembly voted no-confidence in the Executive Commission, forcing its resignation. A decree was adopted obliging all men under twenty-five years of age to join the army, and other workers to return to their home regions. The national workshops were dissolved. The workers rebelled. On 23 June, 70,000 citizens came out into the streets of Paris to build barricades, firstly near the Porte Saint-Denis, then across the city. Paving stones were ripped out of the streets to build hundreds of barricades. At the beginning of the rue du Faubourg Saint-Antoine, a high barricade was built, described vividly by Victor Hugo as 'monstrous', with nineteen other barricades along the street behind it. Leaders of the insurrection, who had been meeting since February in various clubs, decried at the time by Lamartine, moved from house to house recruiting supporters and collecting arms and ammunition. Pitched battles broke out across Paris.

The assembly then decreed a state of siege. On 24 June, Cavaignac was appointed to head a new government with full powers, making him France's de facto head of state, and effectively the country's dictator. Cavaignac immediately took personal command of the army's Paris garrison, and ordered his troops to attack the barricades and their defenders. Calling in reinforcement from the cavalry and the National Guard, he mobilised some 120,000 soldiers to carry out a systematic assault on the workers' barricades, with artillery and cavalry charges. Pitched battles broke out. The insurgents had raided armouries to seize weapons.

The Archbishop of Paris, Monseigneur Denis-Auguste Affre, tried to stop the bloodshed. This normally reserved man interposed himself between the insurgents and the troops at one of the biggest barricades, at the entrance to the Faubourg Saint-Antoine, over which flew an immense red flag. The founder of the Society of Saint Vincent de Paul, in the service of the poor, had begged him to intervene. Although Cavaignac warned him of the personal risk, Monseigneur Affre mounted the barricade, holding high his archbishop's cross. For an instant, there was silence. Then the sound of drumbeats began again, giving the signal for the battle to continue. Shots were exchanged between the rebels and the soldiers. The archbishop fell, fatally cut down by a bullet.

By 26 June, Cavaignac forced his way to the Place de la Bastille, headquarters of the insurrection. The June Days uprising was the bloodiest ever seen in the streets of Paris. In three days, more than 4,000 insurgents and 1,600 soldiers were killed.[61] Thousands more were injured. More than 10,000 insurgents were arrested, and 4,000 were deported to Algeria.

Crisis of governance

Three months after Lamartine had read the Declaration of the Second Republic, and just four weeks after his triumph in the National Assembly elections, he was discredited by conservatives and radicals alike. The dismissal of the Executive Commission by the assembly had effectively ended his political career. The idealistic republic imagined by Lamartine, a republic born without bloodshed and committed to the ideals of the first revolution of 1789, had instead descended into a terrible massacre and the defeat of the aspirations of the new working class. Lamartine's perceptions of the political struggle between conservatives and radicals were conveyed in his incisive writings and his lyrical speeches. He tried to navigate a path for peace at home and abroad through the turbulence of competing factions, but his aspirations were overwhelmed by cynical manoeuvres, and confrontation between the fears of the bourgeoisie and the bitterness of the proletariat.

Victor Hugo, elected as a conservative to the assembly in the complementary elections of 4 June and as mayor of the 8th district of Paris, commanded the troops in that district. But he later wrote a scathing critique of the bloody repression. In his greatest work *Les Misérables*, published in 1861, he wrote: 'Who stopped the revolution halfway? The bourgeoisie. Why? ... Only because they were afraid for their petty coins.'[62] Friedrich Engels wrote from Germany: 'The revolution of June is the revolution of despair,' noting that: 'The cry from the insurrection of Lyon in 1834 – "live working or die fighting" – suddenly appeared, after fourteen years, written on the flags.'[63]

Several radical leaders were arrested and held for trial. Louis Blanc was threatened by the National Guard and was given refuge by the president of the assembly in the Palais Bourbon, house of the assembly. Cavaignac called for the lifting of Blanc's parliamentary immunity, and the vote was adopted at six in the morning. Blanc left immediately for Belgium, where he was arrested and expelled to London. He would remain there in exile for the next twenty years.

Aftermath in France

In the elections of 4 June, Louis-Napoléon Bonaparte's name was put forward in several departments and he had been elected in four of them. Lamartine had tried in vain to have a law adopted to prevent members of a former ruling family, including the Bonapartes, from entering French territory. Louis-Napoléon astutely announced that he would renounce a seat in the assembly. Thus, he was absent from France and not implicated on either side of the bloody fighting of the June Days. Finally, he was elected in yet another intermediate election in September. He returned from exile and took his seat in the assembly.

Louis-Napoléon had been brought up to believe in his destiny as a Bonaparte. His father, the youngest brother of Napoléon, was named King of Holland under the empire. His mother was the only daughter of Joséphine, Napoléon's great love and empress, from her first marriage. Napoléon and Joséphine were, respectively, his godfather and godmother. Raised in exile in Switzerland, his tutor – from a revolutionary family closely linked with Robespierre – taught him French history and radical politics. After a stint in Rome as a teenager, he moved incognito to Paris with his mother, using the name 'Hamilton', where his mother met secretly with the new king, Louis-Philippe. But when their presence in Paris became known, Louis-Philippe ordered them to go back to exile in Switzerland. There, Louis-Napoléon joined the Swiss army and became an officer. At the age of twenty-five he published a book: *Political Dreams*, followed by two others in which he outlined his ideas for a benign monarchy 'which procures the advantages of the Republic without the inconveniences'.[64] During Louis-Philippe's reign he tried twice to mount coups, both of which were fiascos, and he was imprisoned. He escaped from prison to London, where he renewed a friendship with the prime minister, Benjamin Disraeli, and with the writer Charles Dickens.

As calm returned to France, the National Assembly adopted the constitution drafted largely by Lamartine. The assembly decided on an election based on the American model: a president with executive powers to be elected as head of State by universal male suffrage. The constitution was adopted by the assembly in early November.

The presidential election was held under the new constitution in December. Louis-Napoléon's campaign, based on his ideas of combining the destiny of the Bonapartes with progressive policies, was financed by his wealthy English mistress, Harriet Howard, and supported by political figures like Adolphe Thiers. His campaign was essentially populist and could have been summed up in a slogan such as 'Make France Great Again'. Louis-Napoléon Bonaparte was elected in December with more than 5 million votes, seventy-four per cent of the electorate. His nearest rival was General Cavaignac, with under twenty per cent; two other candidates had much smaller scores and Lamartine received just under 18,000 votes, a minuscule 0.3 per cent of the national total. A tired and fractured nation turned away from idealism and embraced populism.

Aftermath in Europe

In most countries across Europe the uprisings of 1848 came to an end and stability seemed to be restored. But this appearance of a return to normality was only on the surface. Deep changes were underway, rooted in the industrial revolution, and the manifestation of competing interests, which Karl Marx described as the conflict of classes.

This conflict interacted with nationalist movements for independence. In Poland, divided between the empires of Russia, Prussia and Austria, the desire for nationhood could not be extinguished. In Hungary, a rebellion was crushed when the Russian Tsar Nicholas I marched in with 300,000 troops to support the Austrians. Brutal martial law followed, with Austrian dominance restored. But conditions were laid for the Austro-Hungarian compromise of 1867, which marked the birth of the Austro-Hungarian Empire under the Habsburg dynasty. In Denmark and the Netherlands, absolute monarchies, albeit benign, gave way to constitutional ones with enhanced parliamentary powers. A rebellion in South Tipperary, Ireland, was put down by the British. Peaceful Switzerland, after a brief civil war in 1847, adopted a new constitution in 1848, becoming a federal state of autonomous republican cantons.

The revolutions of 1848 had begun in Sicily, and they had spread to other Italian states. Back in 1833, a young Italian sea captain, Giuseppe Garibaldi, joined a secret society of exiles in Geneva dedicated to the liberation of Italian states from Austrian occupation. He had then travelled to Italy, but was sentenced to death in Genoa, and fled across the border to Marseille. From there, he sailed first to North Africa, then to South America. He married a young revolutionary, Anita Ribeiro da Silva, and fought with her for the independence of the states with populations of Italian emigres from the empire of Brazil. In 1841, Garibaldi took command of the Uruguayan fleet, and raised an Italian legion known as the Red Shirts, which defended Montevideo against rival factions. As news of the revolutions in Europe reached him in 1848, he left South America, and returned to his homeland. There he supported the provisional government of Milan in Piedmont against Austrian occupation. That uprising was unsuccessful and, after its defeat, he moved to Rome to support the republic proclaimed in the Papal states.

Louis-Napoléon was by now President of France and, like his uncle, Napoléon I, he gave special attention to the situation on the Italian peninsula, sending an army to defend the Holy See against the republicans. Initially defeated by Garibaldi's smaller republican army, the French mounted a siege of Rome. By July 1849, Garibaldi was forced to retreat, ending the first war of Italian independence, and restoring the Pope's temporal powers. The irony of a French republican president crushing a republican rebellion was explained by French domestic politics, as the role of the Church had become an issue in new legislative elections. But it was also a precursor to Louis-Napoléon's own imperial ambitions. In the years that followed, the republican Garibaldi, in his quest for Italian unification, became the key military supporter of Victor

Emmanuel II of Savoy. Garibaldi used the instrument of the plebiscite to gain popular support for declaring Sicily and Naples to be part of the Italian nation, and in 1861 a new parliament proclaimed Victor Emmanuel King of Italy. By that time, calm had returned across the European continent. But the feudal regimes of absolute monarchs had come to an end. In the new era, it was increasingly accepted that all men – but not yet women – should have the right to vote in elections, regardless of property.

From republic to empire

The constitution of the Second French Republic stipulated that the president be elected for a single mandate of four years. But after three years of continual confrontations with the National Assembly, on the night of 1 December 1851, Louis-Napoléon staged a coup d'état. He sent troops to occupy the capital, taking possession not only of the Palais Bourbon where the assembly met, but also the printing presses of newspapers, so as to prevent opposition papers from appearing. For him, popular opinion was the key, and that meant getting control of the media. The writer and politician Victor Hugo, who had initially supported Louis-Napoléon in 1848, tried in vain to organise resistance, but left France for exile.

Within a week, Louis-Napoléon and his supporters organised a plebiscite to replace the constitution and to name him as Prince-President. All opposition newspapers were banned. The result of the plebiscite was overwhelmingly in support of Louis-Napoléon, with 7.5 million in favour, and 640,000 against. A new plebiscite was held eleven months later, and by an even bigger margin proclaimed Louis-Napoléon as Emperor Napoléon III. The Second Republic was replaced by the Second Empire.

Europe and the world

We have seen that the revolutions of 1848 were strongly influenced by the two major political revolutions of the end of the eighteenth century: the American and the French revolutions. In the intervening years, the industrial revolution had swept across Europe and North America, bringing about a major shift in economies and populations that set the conditions for the so-called Springtime of the Peoples.

One by one, the uprisings across Europe were put down, and Europe settled back into a semblance of social and political stability. Yet the seeds had been sown for the revolutions of the early twentieth century. In a world where trade, often backed by military force, reached every continent, the waves of the revolutions of 1848 would travel across the oceans. They would reach China, in the declining days of a dynasty governing a civilisation far older than any in Europe. Then, in the decades that followed, those waves would resonate back to Europe. A war of the imperial powers of Europe, which began with a gunshot in a corner of the Austro-Hungarian Empire in the Balkans, would become a World War. And a revolution would change the face of the world in the only European empire to have escaped the upheavals of 1848 – that of tsarist Russia.

In the year 1864, the International Workingmen's Association was founded in London, bringing together socialist, communist and anarchist groups engaged in what they described as 'class struggle'. Karl Marx was an active participant in this new organisation – soon renamed the International – and hosted meetings in his home. In 1866, another financial panic spread across the world from the city of London. The International met again in Geneva. The following year, 1867, Marx published volume one of his massive work *Das Kapital*. The British Parliament, perceiving, albeit dimly, the threat to the established order, convened a Royal Commission on Trade Unions, which stated that the establishment of such organisations would be to the advantage of both employers and employees. In France, the government of Napoléon III recognised the right of workers to organise trade unions, and engaged in other social reforms, including the expansion of women's education, while extending the French railway system and expanding the merchant marine with steamships. The new technology of the telegraph carried news across the continents and the International Telegraph Union was founded in Paris in 1865.

Meanwhile, the colonial powers pursued their interventions in the Orient and in the Americas. The second Franco-Mexican War (1862–1866) had the effect of weakening France's Second Empire. After the American Civil War and the assassination of Abraham Lincoln in 1865, the United States renewed its expansion, notably with the purchase of Alaska from a weakened Russia in 1867. That same year, in central Europe, the Habsburg dynasty declared the creation of the Austro-Hungarian Empire.

In 1868, the British Trade Union Congress brought together earlier tradesmen's groups, and in the next year workers in the US established the first nationwide labour organisation: the Knights of Labor. This was also the year when Leo Tolstoy published *War and Peace* in its entirety. A unified Germany emerged under Prussia's Chancellor, Otto von Bismarck, and the Second Empire of Napoléon III was defeated.

Alphonse de Lamartine, the idealist, the romantic, the poet, the politician, the historian and the modernist would not live to see the tectonic shifts that would change not only Europe but the entire world in the following decades of the nineteenth century. He died in Mâcon in 1869. A year later, his nemesis, Louis-Napoléon, was captured by the Prussian armies of Bismarck, and sent into exile in Britain, where he died shortly after. In 1871, following the defeat of France, the German nation-state foreseen by Germaine de Staël took shape, as Bismarck engineered an agreement among historic German states to establish the German Empire, or Reich, with the King of Prussia, Wilhelm I, being named as the first emperor, or kaiser. With the defeat of Louis-Napoléon and the end of the Second Empire, France declared its Third Republic, with Adolphe Thiers as president. Alsace-Lorraine was ceded to the new German Reich. The occupying troops returned home, and peace was restored in Europe, until the next century.

Part III:
China and Russia
1858 to 1920

By the mid-nineteenth century, the ancient empire of China and the Eurasian empire of Russia were still largely unaffected by the industrial revolution that had so dramatically changed life in the countries of the West. Both these vast empires were mainly agrarian societies. In China, a philosopher, Kang You Wei, convinced a young emperor and a new generation of scholars that the time had come to modernise and reform. But the old guard of the imperial court put a brutal end to the effort. The scene was set for the first Chinese revolution and the end of the Manchu dynasty. In Russia, an autocratic governor, Pyotr Stolypin, became the most powerful man in the tsarist regime, but his attempts at agrarian reform ended with his assassination. Several years later the Romanov dynasty was swept away by two revolutions, culminating in the takeover of the Russian State by the Bolsheviks. The tsar perished with all his family.

Chapter 4

The Chinese Revolution

Two bright boys

In the years that followed the revolutions of 1848 across Europe, two boys were born on the other side of the world along the estuary of the Pearl River in China. They would change the destiny of the Empire of the East. In 1858, Kang You Wei was born into a scholar's family, upriver from Guangzhou (Canton).[1] Eight years later, Sun Yat Sen was born near the Portuguese colony of Macau. Both were bright students. During the remainder of the nineteenth century, and at the beginning of the twentieth, their destinies would be intertwined. Kang would become the leading advocate for reform and modernisation of the imperial regime. Sun would become a revolutionary and would succeed the last emperor as first president of the Chinese Republic.

When Kang You Wei was ten, his father died, and the boy's education was from then on supervised by his grandfather. An uncle noted his bright inquisitiveness, so his family sent him to study the Confucian classics as preparation for the civil service exams. These exams in China were known as the 'eight-legged' exams, because of the rigorous eight-part structure of the essays that students had to prepare. The format had been unchanged for some 400 years. They required detailed knowledge of the four books and five classics of Confucian sages.[2]

When Kang You Wei was eighteen, he was tutored by an old family friend and eminent Confucian scholar named Chu Tz'u Chi. But Kang failed in his first attempt at the provincial examination in 1876. Two years later, at the age of twenty, he underwent an emotional crisis. He had begun to engage in Buddhist meditation as a form of relaxation. This was unusual for a Chinese scholar of the time. Then, in late 1878, he abandoned his studies, withdrew from his friends, and closed himself in his room to meditate and contemplate. As he sat in solitary meditation, his friends thought he had gone mad. After a time, he felt that he had experienced mystical enlightenment. 'I perceived suddenly that I was in an all-pervasive unity with heaven, earth, and all things. I beheld myself as a sage and laughed for joy. But thinking of the sufferings of mankind I wept in sorrow,' he wrote later.[3] Out of this experience came the idea of unifying Confucian thought with both Buddhism and the ideas of the West.[4] And the West was to be found at the mouth of the Pearl River in the British port of Hong Kong.

Sun Yat Sen did not start life with Kang's advantages. His family were peasants, born to hard work in the rice fields. His father had a small plot of land but also worked as a porter and tailor in Macau. At the age of ten Sun went to a local school and learnt quickly. In 1879, just as Kang made his first direct contact with the West in Hong Kong, young Sun, aged only thirteen, embarked on a ship bound for Hawaii. His older brother, Sun Mei, had emigrated there as a labourer before becoming a successful merchant. He enrolled his brother in the prestigious Iolan school in Honolulu, where young Sun rapidly learnt English, receiving a prize for outstanding achievement from the King of Hawaii.

The personal sagas of these two young men from the banks of the Pearl River would set the scene for a struggle between reform and revolution in the empire of the Qing dynasty. That struggle of ideas and influence would later be pursued within China and also across the world, with support in Chinese emigrant communities, and engagement with foreign governments, writers and the media. It would continue for three decades.

China and the West
To understand how the first Chinese revolution, which ended 2,000 years of imperial rule, was linked to revolutions in the West, we must go back in time. For centuries, traders had travelled along the complex of routes stretching across Eurasia known as the Silk Road. In the thirteenth century, the Venetian adventurer Marco Polo travelled the entire distance between Europe and the Orient, returning to his homeland with stories of

the fabulous wealth of the court of Kublai Khan and the civilisation that lay in the East. By the fifteenth century, Chinese shipbuilding technology was far more advanced than in Europe. Some eighty years before the European voyages of discovery that began with Christopher Columbus and Vasco de Gama, China had sent a fleet of more than 300 great ships seven times across the seas. They followed ancient maritime routes south to Java and west to Sri Lanka, the Arabian Gulf, and the Horn of Africa. But the ships were destroyed as the Chinese imperial court turned inwards and stopped exploration. Direct maritime trade with Europe began in the sixteenth century when Portuguese sailors arrived and were permitted to establish a trading post in the south, at Macau on the delta of the Pearl River. By the mid-nineteenth century, the Qing dynasty of northern Manchus had ruled China for some 200 years, reigning over an empire stretching across the vast eastern landmass of Asia that traced its origins back more than 2,000 years.

At the beginning of the nineteenth century, China's economy was the biggest in the world. But the Chinese Empire had been weakened by European incursions and internal rebellions. There was great demand in Europe for Chinese silk, porcelain, and tea, which was mainly transported by sea through the southern port of Guangzhou, called Canton by the Europeans. The Chinese insisted their goods be paid for with silver, bolstering trade in the precious metal across the Pacific from mines in South America, via the Spanish colony in the Philippines. By the early nineteenth century, there was a huge trade imbalance between the Chinese and British empires, in favour of China. The British East India Company, whose duties on tea had helped to provoke the American Revolution, continued to wield immense power and influence in Britain. When the company began sending illicit opium from India to China, essentially to replace silver when paying for the trade in Chinese goods, the Chinese authorities appealed to Queen Victoria to stop the trade on moral grounds. Failing to receive a reply, in 1839 the Chinese confiscated opium from East India Company ships. In response, the British sent gunboats, inflicting a series of decisive defeats on Chinese junks, in what became known as the first of the Opium Wars. The British warships included several side-paddle steamers used as transports, and the *Nemesis*, the first iron steam-powered gunboat – one of six commissioned by a secret committee of the East India Company after the successful crossing of the Atlantic by the *Great Western*, described in the previous chapter. The Chinese called the *Nemesis* 'the devil ship'.

After two years of skirmishes around the mouth of the Pearl River and further north where the Yangtze River flowed to the ocean at Shanghai, the Chinese were defeated. As a result, in 1842, the Qing government was forced to sign the Treaty of Nanjing, in one of the ancient capitals of China on the Yangtze delta upstream from Shanghai. The treaty, later described by successive Chinese governments as the first of several 'unequal treaties', ceded the island of Hong Kong, across from Macau on the delta of the Pearl River, to the British, and opened five other ports to trade. The United States and France followed with trade treaties of their own – the Americans with the Wangxia Treaty and the French with the Treaty of Whampoa, both signed in 1844. France under King Louis-Philippe and his foreign minister François Guizot added a clause to their treaty protecting Catholic Christian missionaries. China was fertile territory not only for commercial competition between Western traders, but also for the competing zeal of missionaries carrying the religious conflicts of Europe and the Americas to the Orient.

In 1850, as Europe settled into a tenuous calm after the Springtime of the Peoples, a major uprising began in the south of China, in the province of Guangdong, with Guangzhou as its capital. American Protestant Christian missionaries had started a cult-like movement there called the God Worshipping Society, which combined elements of Christianity with traditional Chinese Taoism and folklore. Thousands of local Chinese joined, but they had to move north to flee repression by the Imperial Army. Forming their own army, they became stronger militarily and, after a series of battles, succeeded in taking the ancient capital of Nanjing, where they established the Taiping Heavenly Kingdom. All Manchus in Nanjing were massacred. The Taiping rebellion became a civil war of opposition to the ruling dynasty of the northern Manchus and lasted fourteen years, with massive loss of life.

At this midpoint of the nineteenth century, the British Empire spanned the globe. It had recovered from the loss of its American colonies seven decades earlier and continued to dominate world trade. In 1851, just three years after the revolutionary events of 1848 in Europe, Queen Victoria and

Prince Albert convened The Great Exhibition of the Works of Industry of all Nations in London's Hyde Park. Its huge success was a sign of renewed confidence in progress – in Britain and beyond. As already noted, in that same year a new phase of the industrial revolution began, with the laying of the first telegraph cable under the Channel, connecting England to the continent. Two years later, in 1853, in the Far East, Commodore Matthew Perry of the United States, commanding four steamships – labelled the 'black ships' for their ominous dark colour – forced open the port of Edo in Japan, today's Tokyo. The empires of Europe and those of the East had for centuries been based on feudalism. But as the industrial revolution advanced, feudalism had come to an end across much of Europe, and the revolutions of 1848 spelt the end of several absolutist regimes. Shortly thereafter, the opening of Japan to trade from 1853 would lead to the fall of the feudal system of the shoguns and the modernisation of Japan – an island nation like Britain, which had similarly carved a destiny separate from the dynastic struggles of the adjacent continent.

End of the East India Company

1856 and 1857 were critical years for the British and the French in the East. For 100 years, since the Battle of Plassey against the Nawab of Bengal and his French allies in 1757, the East India Company had effectively ruled India with its own private armies of local troops and British officers. At the height of its power, the company's armies in India had more than 260,000 troops, twice the size of the British Army. In 1857, a series of mutinies broke out across the country. The catalyst for the rebellion was the propagation of rumours that animal fat was used to grease bullets used in a new type of rifle; beef fat was unacceptable for Hindus, as was pork fat for Muslims. The Moghul capital of Delhi was overrun; there were terrible massacres of both Indian and British civilians.

At almost the same time, an incident involving a British registered ship, the *Arrow,* in Hong Kong harbour, and the killing of a French missionary in the adjacent province of Guangxi near the border with the Kingdom of Vietnam, led to a joint intervention by British and French forces in China. On New Year's Day 1858, the year of Kang You Wei's birth, these forces captured Guangzhou (Canton), with a population at that time of more than a million people. This was the beginning of the second Opium War.

Again, the Chinese forces were overwhelmed by the superior British and French military technology. The British sent the Chinese Viceroy into exile in India. By June of the same year, Britain and France were joined by Russia and the United States in forcing the Chinese to agree to a new set of treaties in the northern port city of Tientsin (Tianjin), opening eleven more ports to Western trade, enabling Westerners to travel throughout China, and removing restrictions on Christian missionaries – Protestant, Catholic or Russian Orthodox. Although the delegates of the imperial court agreed to these terms, Chinese resistance continued, and Emperor Xian Feng refused to ratify the treaties. He was the ninth emperor of the Qing dynasty, and his reign name meant 'universal prosperity'. He held to the belief that the Chinese Empire was the centre of civilisation and was superior to the barbarians from the West.

The British were preoccupied with the aftermath of the Indian mutiny. The handling of the mutiny and the news of terrible massacres were the subject of vehement debates in the British Parliament in London, and the crisis marked the end of the East India Company. Founded by Royal Charter as far back as the year 1600 under Queen Elizabeth I, the company had wielded increasing power through the wealth it generated for many of the ruling families of Britain and Ireland. By the eighteenth century, as we saw in Chapter 1, the protests of American colonists against levies on the company's imported tea culminated in the Boston Tea Party, and in retaliation, Benjamin Franklin had been humiliated before the British Privy Council – probably the key event in his decision to support the American patriots. Then, in the nineteenth century, the company actively promoted the opium trade between India and China, leading to the Opium Wars and the unequal treaties. Finally, after the Indian mutiny, the company was nationalised, and its property, assets, armies and functions in India were transferred to the British Crown.

Competition in trade and colonial expansion between the Victorian empire of Britain and the Second Empire of France under Napoléon III was stronger than ever. These two powers would cooperate when they found it useful, as in the taking of Guangzhou, and they no longer fought each other as they had in centuries past, but they remained competitors all the same. In 1859, the year after the liquidation of the East India Company, an ascendant France began work on the construction of the Suez Canal, a hugely ambitious project driven by her political, military and trading interest in bringing Asia closer to Europe.

Chinese resistance and defeat

That same year, 1859, the British turned their attention again to the Orient and sent more troops to China. The emperor still refused to recognise the Treaty of Tianjin, thereby preventing the opening of Chinese ports to trade. The British and French again joined forces with the aim of imposing ratification of the treaty. Overcoming resistance at the forts of Taku to the north, they took Tianjin and marched inland to the imperial capital of Peking (Beijing). A British delegation went ahead of the army to negotiate for Chinese surrender. But the talks broke down when word reached Beijing that the British had imprisoned the Chinese Prefect of Tianjin. The Chinese arrested and tortured the British emissary and his delegation in Beijing. Several members of the delegation and a journalist from *The Times* of London, were executed in atrocious fashion by 'slow-slicing',[5] or 'death by a thousand cuts'.

When the news reached European capitals there was public outrage, with scathing press coverage and fierce condemnation in national parliaments. Orders from London and Paris were sent to move on the Chinese capital. The Anglo-French forces overcame the imperial Mongol cavalry protecting Beijing. The emperor fled to the mountains and the surviving British diplomats were freed. The British commander, Lord James Elgin, ordered that the Summer Palace be destroyed in retaliation for Chinese 'perfidy'. The Summer Palace was a collection of temples and gardens of great beauty, with priceless treasures of silk, porcelain, and art, many of which were looted. Empress Eugénie of France opened a special section of the Palace of Fontainebleau, south of Paris, to house many of the looted treasures. Others would find their way into the collections of the great houses of the British and European nobility. Not everyone supported this retribution. 'We Europeans are the civilised ones, and for us the Chinese are the barbarians. This is what civilisation has done to barbarism,' wrote Victor Hugo to a British friend.[6]

The second Opium War came to an end when the emperor's brother agreed to the Convention of Peking (Beijing) in October 1860, which not only ratified the Treaty of Tianjin but also ceded Kowloon to Britain, reaffirmed the right of Christian missionaries to evangelise, paid reparations to Britain and France, allowed British ships to carry indentured Chinese labourers to the Americas, and legalised the opium trade. Seen from the perspective of history, the inclusion of all these elements in the one treaty – particularly the right to evangelise and the legalisation of opium trading – underlines the moral hypocrisy of the colonial era. Two weeks later, the Russians forced the Qing government to sign a supplementary treaty that ceded part of outer Manchuria to the Russians, who then founded the port of Vladivostok. The ancient civilisation of China was defeated and humiliated. Emperor Xian Feng fell into depression. He died the following year, aged only thirty, in August 1861.

During this time, other hugely significant events occurred in Europe and the United States. In November 1860, Abraham Lincoln was elected President of the United States. Before his inauguration in March 1861, seven states depending on slavery for their tobacco and cotton-based plantation economies declared secession, marking the beginning of the American Civil War. In the same month, Tsar Alexander II of Russia signed the emancipation law, freeing serfs throughout the Russian Empire across the north of Europe and Asia. The freed serfs were accorded the full rights of citizens, including the right to own property. And in that same month, in the south of Europe, the new parliament of Italy, with the support of Guiseppe Garibaldi, proclaimed Victor Emmanuel the first king of a unified nation.

It was also an eventful year in the literary world. In 1861, Victor Hugo in France arranged to publish *Les Misérables* and Leo Tolstoy in Russia began writing *War and Peace*. Both authors, towering figures of Western literature, who had met in Brussels the previous year, closely followed and wrote about events in China. West and East were becoming inescapably linked, certainly through trade and military incursions, but also through the interest of the intellectuals of the time. We will see how Kang You Wei, in turn, developed his intellectual interest in the West, and the influence his studies would have on attempts to reform and modernise China.

Two women take control in China
When Emperor Xian Feng died in 1861, he was survived by his five-year-old son, Zaichun. On his deathbed the emperor gave orders for a

council of eight regents to be formed to run the affairs of the empire on behalf of his son. The boy's mother was given the title of Dowager Empress Cixi, while the late emperor's first consort, who was childless, was called Dowager Empress Ci'an. Cixi had entered the imperial court as a concubine, but unlike most Manchu aristocratic women, she could read and write, had often advised the emperor on replies to memoranda addressed to the throne, and had risen up the ranks of the court with the birth of the emperor's only surviving son. She formed an alliance with Empress Ci'an and two of the Xian Feng Emperor's brothers – Prince Gong and Prince Chun (Yixuan) – and seized the occasion of the emperor's funeral to accuse the regents of causing his early death by failing to protect China from the barbarians. In what became known as the Xinyou Coup, Prince Gong was designated as prince-regent, but all decisions were subject to the consent of the two dowager empresses 'without interference', thus handing them effective power. They ruled, according to an old Chinese tradition, from 'behind the curtain'. The reign name of the boy emperor was changed from Qixiang, meaning 'auspicious', to Tongzhi, translated as 'restoring order together'. The leader of the eight-man council was beheaded, and two others were ordered to hang themselves with silk scarves. A Grand Council of the imperial court headed by Prince Gong was established for consultation. Four years later, in 1865, after the defeat of the Taiping rebellion, Gong's title of prince-regent was removed, although after pleading with the empresses, he was allowed to remain as head of the foreign ministry and member of the Grand Council.

While Empress Ci'an concentrated on family matters, Empress Cixi established direct control over the sprawling imperial bureaucracy, requiring that all officials above the level of provincial governor report directly to her. Together with powerful officials, notably the eight regional viceroys, she supported what came to be known as the 'learn from foreigners' and 'self-strengthening' movements, aimed at modernising the military. Arsenals were established in key ports such as Shanghai; administrators and engineers were recruited from the West; promising young boys were sent to the United States to study; a foreign language school was set up in Beijing; and military schools trained officers in modern warfare. Cixi's support for these measures was, however, cautious and often ambiguous. She ordered that steamships purchased from Britain be sent back because they were manned by British sailors, and she placed restrictions on the sending of Chinese boys to study abroad.

Empires, alliances, industry and competition

As Empress Cixi consolidated power in China, with the support of Empress Ci'an, great changes were underway in Europe. Colonial ambitions there continued to have a major impact on the Orient. In 1862, France under Napoléon III marked its influence in Indochina by signing the Treaty of Hue with Vietnam. British traders and missionaries were more active than ever throughout China and the rest of Asia. But the United States was mostly absent from the region as the American Civil War continued to tear the new nation apart. In 1865, the war was over at last, but Abraham Lincoln was assassinated in Washington after his second inauguration

In the same year, one of the earliest international institutions came into being, when the International Telegraph Union was founded in Paris. By then, economies were linked globally, and in 1866 a financial panic spread across the world from the city of London. Karl Marx and his supporters had formed the International Workingmen's Association, also known as the First International, in London in 1894 and they met again in a congress in Geneva in 1866. In 1867, Marx published volume one of *Das Kapital*. Some of those in power in Europe perceived the danger of Marx's revolutionary advocacy of class struggle, and they moved to support reforms such as recognition of the rights of workers: in Britain, a Royal Commission on trade unions stated that the establishment of such organisations was to the advantage of both employers and employees.

The nations of the West continued to compete for leadership in industrial progress. Napoléon III undertook major construction projects in the cities of Paris, Lyon and Marseilles, while his government extended the French railway system and expanded the merchant marine with steamships. Along with industrial advances came social reforms, including the right of workers to organise trade unions and the expansion of women's education. But Napoléon's Second Empire was marked by adventurism, as France pursued colonial ambitions in both the East and the West. Napoléon's intervention in Mexico was a failure, while closer to home he was challenged by the rise of a unified Germany under Prussia's chancellor, Otto von Bismarck.

The empires of Europe now co-existed with the emerging power of the republican United States of America, which purchased Alaska from Russia, while in central Europe the Habsburg dynasty declared the creation of the Austro-Hungarian Empire. Meanwhile in the Orient, the Tokugawa shogunate of Japan – after the shock of being forced by the United States to end the country's isolation – attempted reforms to its feudal system, but with little real change. In 1867, a new young emperor, Meiji, succeeded to the Chrysanthemum throne of Japan. By the next year, fifteen years after the arrival of Perry's 'black ships', a reform movement called the Meiji Restoration was launched to modernise Japan. Meiji declared: 'Knowledge shall be sought all over the world.'[7] There was a brief civil war as the last of the samurai made a stand in defence of their traditional way of life, but the reformists prevailed, and the shogunate handed over power peacefully to the modernisers of the imperial court. Japan moved quickly to integrate the modernising developments of the industrial revolution coming from the West, and with it such ideas as universal primary education and the election of a consultative Diet. Japanese emissaries were sent to study in Europe, where in clubs and meetings there were struggles over ideas of revolution and reform. By then, Marx and his revolutionary supporters had gained support for their tactics of confrontation at a meeting of the International in Brussels, while in Britain reformers founded the Trade Union Congress. The reformers advocated representation of working people in parliament, an eight-hour week, and free education. Thus, the Japanese modernisers gained more than technical expertise, as they were exposed to new ideas and ideological debates.

In China, there was a similar but more timid opening to the West. The Qing government decided to establish a translation bureau in Shanghai. The most prolific translator on the Chinese coast was John Fryer, son of an impoverished Anglican clergyman. Arriving in Hong Kong in 1861 at the age of twenty-two, Fryer quickly gave up being a missionary, became a teacher, then headmaster of the Anglo-Chinese school in Shanghai, and finally the head of the government's translation bureau. Over the next twenty-eight years, from 1868 until 1896, he translated well over a hundred English and French texts covering the sciences, medicine, manufacturing, law, and economics.

In 1861, President Lincoln of the United States had appointed an experienced diplomat named Anson Burlingame as Minister to China. Burlingame developed friendly and cooperative relations with the reformists in the Qing Court. When he retired from the US diplomatic service, these court officials invited him to accompany a Chinese delegation to the major Western capitals of Washington, London, Paris and Berlin, in 1868, the same year as the Meiji Restoration began in Japan. In Washington, he negotiated with his former superior, Secretary of State William Seward, a revision of the Treaty of Tianjin with respect to US-China relations. The Burlingame-Seward Treaty eased restrictions on Chinese immigration to the United States, enabled the appointment of Chinese consuls in US ports, accorded most-favoured nation status to China in trade, provided for reciprocal access to education for the citizens of each country when living in the other country and recognised Chinese sovereignty over local infrastructure projects. It was certainly more equitable than the 1858 Treaty of Tianjin.

In the wake of these openings to the West by Japan and China came the opening of the Suez Canal in November 1869. The passage by steamship between the West and the Orient was shortened dramatically. And as the conditions for global trade were enhanced, workers in the United States followed closely the actions of their counterparts in Britain by founding the first nationwide labour organisation, called the Knights of Labour. 1869 was also the year when Leo Tolstoy of Russia published *War and Peace* in its entirety. We shall see later that Tolstoy developed an intense interest in developments in China and India.

The changing face of Europe, America and the Orient
The 1870s were noteworthy for a stream of apparently unrelated events. The Franco-Prussian War ended the Second Empire in France, then the newly declared Third Republic repressed the revolutionary Paris commune with bloody fighting. Japan continued the determined pursuit of its industrial revolution. European and American interventions in the Orient increased emigration from a weakened China. Meanwhile,

revolutionary ideas spread from Europe to the Orient. By the end of the decade, all these strands came together, coalescing in epic struggles that would lead to the revolutions of the early twentieth century, in China then in Russia.

The Russian Empire was Eurasian, stretching from the Baltic Sea in Europe across Siberia and the north of Asia to the Chinese border. At the European end of these vast lands, on the banks of the Volga river southeast of Moscow, Vladimir Ilyich Ulyanov was born into the family of an inspector of schools in April 1870. Later, the world would know him as Lenin.

The United States sent an expedition to Korea in June 1871. US marines captured several ports, but the Koreans refused to negotiate. Then, in October of that year, opposition to Chinese immigration boiled over in Los Angeles, as a mob attacked Chinese immigrants. At the same time, Western influence was penetrating China through both merchants and missionaries. Christian missionaries had reached Japan with the Jesuits as far back as the 1540s, and Francis Xavier had died trying to reach China back then. Now, in the nineteenth century, as Western powers forced their way into China, Catholic and Protestant missionaries followed.

In 1872, the Tongzhi Emperor, who had been born as Cixi's son, Zaichun, reached the age of sixteen. Remember, his birth as the late emperor's only son was critical to the rise to power of his mother as one of the two dowager empresses. No longer a child, he now married and, in addition to a wife, took two concubines, as was customary. In the new year he officially took up his role as emperor. However, he clashed with his uncles, Princes Gong and Chun, over plans to rebuild the Summer Palace. He dismissed them, only to be overruled by his mother, Cixi, with the support of Ci'an. It was apparent that he was emperor in name only, and the two dowager empresses retained power. The young man abandoned his duties, frequented the brothels of the city disguised as a commoner, and died of smallpox in early 1875 at the age of eighteen, without a male heir.

Cixi took charge in resolving the succession crisis, choosing the second son of Prince Chun, Zaitian, aged four, who was also her nephew, since his mother was her younger sister. He was formally adopted as the son of the deceased emperor and named the Guang Xu Emperor, meaning 'glorious succession'. He was tutored by Weng Tonghe, who would later play an important role in introducing the young ruler to Kang You Wei. In the same year, on Cixi's orders, the government set up a State-supervised enterprise called the China Merchants Steam Navigation Company. In 1877, a State-run coal mine, the Kaiping mine, was opened north of Beijing in the Zhili region by the viceroy Li Hongzhang, a trusted advisor of Cixi and leader of the 'self-strengthening' movement.

In 1881, Empress Ci'an died suddenly, aged only forty-three. Although she was the senior of the two dowager empresses, she had occupied herself primarily with family matters, while affairs of State had been controlled by Cixi. Now, at the age of thirteen, the Guangxu Emperor began to conduct audiences alone, as Cixi, recovering from illness, communicated with officials only in writing. That year, Cixi approved the formation of the Imperial Telegraph Administration as a State-controlled corporation. For about a decade, China had been strengthening its four naval fleets, the strongest being the northern or Beiyang Fleet, with steamships purchased from Britain and Germany by the Viceroy Li Hongzhang. However, funding was cut for the fleet, as Weng Tonghe advised the boy emperor that Japan was unlikely to threaten China. Rebuilding of the Summer Palace continued.

Kang You Wei – the reformer

As Dowager Empress Cixi consolidated her power and supported some moves toward modernisation, Kang You Wei emerged from his period of meditation, believing himself to be a sage destined 'to set in order all under heaven'.[8] He began studying politics and government, while reading extensively about Buddhism. He visited Hong Kong in 1879, then Shanghai in 1882, and began seriously studying the West through the translations of John Fryer. Thus, while steeped in traditional Confucian education, and recognised among scholars as an accomplished calligrapher, Kang also plunged into the study of Western thought and technology. But access to the West beyond Hong Kong was becoming more difficult, as that year, 1882, the United States turned away from the Burlingame-Seward treaty signed back in 1868 and reacted to increasing Chinese immigration by adopting the Chinese Exclusion Acts.

Returning to his village briefly in 1883, Kang tried to abolish the ancient practice of foot-binding for women. By then he was married to the first of several wives. His second daughter, Kang Tong Bi, later to become a leading advocate for women's rights in China, was born during that time. Also in 1883, his younger countryman Sun Yat Sen, aged seventeen, returned to China after graduating from school in Honolulu, having received a prize for English from the King of Hawaii.

Kang pursued his study of national affairs, and in 1888 he wrote to the Qing court proposing an ambitious plan to save China from decline through institutional reforms. His paper was ignored, but his ideas were beginning to attract attention. Conservatives in the Qing hierarchy saw him as a dubious radical. By then he had attracted younger students. One of them, Liang Qi Chao, would be his life-long supporter. In February of the next year, 1889, Dowager Empress Cixi retired to the rebuilt Summer Palace and the Guangxu Emperor took formal power at the age of nineteen. Frequently, however, the new emperor would leave the Forbidden City with his retinue of courtiers to visit Cixi in the Summer Palace and seek her advice.

In 1890, Kang and Liang took the national examinations together in Peking for the equivalent of a Western doctorate. The examiners were determined to fail Kang because of his radical ideas. However, the exam papers were all presented anonymously. Singling out the most unorthodox paper, they assumed it had been written by Kang, and marked it for failure. The paper had been written in reality by Liang, while Kang disguised himself by writing a traditionalist essay. Kang passed and Liang failed. Back in their home city of Guangzhou, Kang founded a school dedicated to new learning and foreign affairs, with Liang as his star student. The following year they contested the establishment by publishing a book called *A Study of the Classics Forged during the Xin Dynasty*, which argued that the State cult of the Confucian classics was based on extensive rewriting earlier in China's dynastic history, and that Confucius was really a reformer. Although Kang was considered in ruling circles to be controversial, he won the interest and eventually the political support of Li Hong Zhang, the powerful viceroy of the region of Zhili in the north, which included the capital, Peking. As we saw, Li was a key adviser to Empress Cixi and was known as 'the great strengthener' because of his support for the 'self-strengthening' movement.

Sun Yat Sen, the revolutionary

While Kang pursued his personal odyssey as a scholar, challenging the mainstream of Confucian thought, Sun Yat Sen was studying medicine in Hong Kong. After a semester in college, Sun returned home. Influenced by Christian missionaries, he and a friend got into a conflict with local villagers by breaking the hand of a statue in a temple. They fled back across the river to Hong Kong, where Sun continued his English studies, and converted to Christianity. He studied medicine, graduating in 1892. By then he had married a fellow villager, Lu Muzhen. However, after practising medicine for only one year, he decided to devote himself to transforming China. At first, Sun Yat Sen aligned himself with the ideas of the reformists, including the ideas circulated by Kang You Wei and Liang Qi Chao.

As we have seen, after the defeats of the Opium Wars and the humiliations of the 'unequal treaties', influential figures within the imperial regime had called for a self-strengthening movement for China. Sun Yat Sen had the advantage that he had acquired fluency in English, so he immersed himself in books from the West. In 1894, a few years after Kang had sent his first letter to the imperial court, Sun Yat Sen also wrote a long letter to 'the great strengthener', Li Hong Zhang, setting out his own ideas for strengthening China through reform. Sun offered his services and requested an interview with the viceroy, but his request was refused. Because he had not studied the classics, the gentry did not accept him. From then on, Sun Yat Sen began to call for the abolition of the monarchy and the establishment of a republic.

This was also a time when radical ideas emerged in the outreaches of the British Empire. In 1893, universal suffrage for women as well as men was established in the Pacific colony of New Zealand. Another colony founded by free thinkers from England, Scotland and Wales, and also from Germany, that of South Australia, followed suit in 1894, going further by according women the right to be candidates for parliament.

War with Japan and defeat

During the years that followed the burning of the Summer Palace in Beijing in 1859 and the death of the Xian Feng Emperor in 1861, the Qing dynasty of the Manchus had undergone a series of succession crises. As co-regent from 1861 to 1881, then as sole regent, Dowager Empress Cixi was the real power in China. In line with the self-strengthening movement she had cautiously supported the modernisation of the Chinese army and navy, and an opening to Western technology.

However, the weakness of the Qing government became dramatically obvious with China's loss to Japan in the war that broke out in 1894 over control of the Korean Peninsula. In October of that year the Chinese suffered their first major defeats by Japanese land forces in Pyongyang and naval forces on the Yalu River. Within six months the Chinese were defeated by the superiority of Japan's modernised land and naval forces. Japan's modernisation had, in just twenty-five years, achieved a level of military and technological prowess with which China could not compete. It is worth noting that with the modernisation of Japan and the embrace of the industrial revolution coming from the West, ideas for social reform also began to emerge in Japan as they had in Europe and America.

The defeat of China by Japan was a defining moment for both Kang You Wei and Sun Yat Sen, and it marked a parting of the ways of these two advocates of Chinese modernisation. While they never met in person, they must have been aware of each other's proposals for institutional and political change. For Sun Yat Sen, the lesson to be drawn from the defeat was that the only way forward for China was the overthrow of the Qing dynasty, and its replacement by a republic. Returning to Hawaii he founded the Revive China Society (Hsing-Chung Hui) in November 1894. For Kang, on the other hand, China's loss highlighted his advocacy for reform of the government and the development of a constitutional monarchy.

After China's early defeats on the Korean Peninsula, Japanese forces invaded Manchuria, then Taiwan. In April 1895, the defeated Qing empire signed the Treaty of Shimonoseki. After the 'unequal treaties' imposed by Western powers, this treaty with Japan was a further humiliation. It recognised the independence of Korea, ceded the Liaodong Peninsula (south-eastern Manchuria) and Taiwan to Japan 'in perpetuity' and obliged China to pay war reparations of 200-million taels[9] of silver.[10] By defeating China and imposing such a treaty, Japan was now competing with the Western powers for influence on the Asian continent.

Five days after the signing of the humiliating treaty, Kang You Wei published a 'ten thousand words memorial', supported by the signatures of hundreds of candidates for the civil service examination, calling for rejection of the treaty and, most importantly, advocating wide ranging reform within China. Thousands of scholars and citizens demonstrated in Beijing in what was the first public manifestation in favour of reform in China. But the imperial court ignored both the petition and the protests, while maintaining official prohibition of any political groupings. Young scholars then formed 'study societies' (Hsueh-Hui), which they described as 'patriotic societies to save the country'. Their local branches spread over the provinces, urging the Qing government to reform, to translate more Western and Japanese books, and to declare Confucianism as a State religion.

Contestation from abroad, opposition within

As Kang You Wei mobilised young scholars within China to support reform, Sun Yat Sen worked to organise support for overthrow of the imperial dynasty, mainly through overseas Chinese communities. Sun returned briefly to China from Hawaii, then moved on to Japan. In Yokohama, he set up a branch of his Revive China Society. He then travelled extensively to seek political support and raise funds, then he crossed the Atlantic for the first time to London. There he was kidnapped by officials of the Chinese legation and there were fears for his life. After two weeks he was released through the intervention of his English teacher, following publicity in *The Times* newspaper. The following year he spent much time in the library of the British Museum (where Karl Marx wrote *Das Kapital*) studying European political thinking and developing the framework for his 'three principles of the people'. He visited Canada and established a military school in British Columbia, then returned to Yokohama. A branch of his Revive China Society was established in Taipei, Taiwan.

Meanwhile, a power struggle was underway within the imperial Qing court between conservatives and modernisers. During and after the Sino-Japanese War of 1894 and 1895, these court factions actually prepared two sets of memoranda on events, one for the emperor and another for the dowager empress. Following the empire's humiliating defeat, and the losses forced on China in 1895 by the Treaty of Shimonoseki, the emperor reportedly expressed his wish to abdicate, but his supporters prevailed on him to stay.

While the centre of power in the imperial court was weakened by internal factionalism, the humiliation of incursions by Western powers continued. In late 1897, Germany occupied Jiaozhou Bay and seized the trading post of Kiaochow, prompting a new scramble for concessions by other foreign powers. Russia had diplomatic support from Germany and France to oblige Japan to give up the Liaodong Peninsula. The Chinese government had engaged the German Krupp company to fortify the fishing village at the tip of the peninsula called Lushun, making it into a strategic seaport, which was then known by the English name of Port Arthur. But the Chinese were too weak to resist a Russian demand to lease the port, and Russia took it over, despite objections from Japan.

The Hundred Days' Reform

In 1898, Kang submitted a lengthy essay to the young emperor on the French Revolution of the previous century and the reasons for the overthrow of the Bourbon dynasty. In Kang's opinion, Louis XVI's government, under Jacques Necker, had been unable to carry out reforms in time, and had been overtaken by events.[11] He therefore recommended that reforms in China be implemented very quickly. Kang also warned that China was threatened with the same fate as Poland, which had been conquered and divided by foreign powers.[12] This essay showed the influence of events in Europe on the thinking of Kang and his fellow reformists in China. Kang suggested that there were two models for China to use as references. The first and principal one was Japan, modernised by the Meiji Restoration of 1868. The second model he presented, interestingly, was Russia. He saw Russia, another vast empire, as having much in common with China in its manners and customs.[13]

On 11 June 1898, the emperor responded decisively. He seized the political initiative by issuing his first reform decree, which called on the Chinese people to learn foreign knowledge. Reformers, with Kang in the lead, traced Japan's success to the modernisation that had begun thirty years earlier, under the young Emperor Meiji. Just as the reformists of the Meiji court had taken power away from the shoguns and had opened Japan to the technologies and the political ideas of the West, Kang and his followers sought their young emperor's support in modernising China. The emperor, now aged twenty-seven, shared Kang's belief that fundamental changes, including reforms of government institutions, were required to strengthen China's defences against the West. He accepted Kang's argument that reforms had to be implemented quickly if they were to succeed. He also accepted that reforms had to be far-reaching. He acknowledged Kang's argument that, while the dowager empress had cautiously supported the self-strengthening movement and acquisition of Western technology, including ships and weapons, the defeat by Japan showed that change had to go much further.

The reform movement called for a new educational structure to replace the traditional one, with its centuries-old 'eight-legged' examination system. The political system was also to be restructured. Kang sought a constitutional monarchy and a parliamentary government, along the lines adopted in many European nations after 1848. From June to September 1898, Kang and his followers prepared a host of edicts and decrees for the emperor to sign. Around 200 reform decrees were issued. They included the establishment of an imperial university with a medical school in Beijing; primary and secondary schools were to be established throughout the provinces for the study of both Chinese and Western subjects; and traditional private schools and Buddhist temple schools were to become public government schools. Government administration was also to be reformed with the abolition of sinecure posts, new recruiting of progressive officials, stricter discipline for civil servants, measures to check corruption, and the creation of twelve ministries to replace the old six boards. The military forces were to be modernised. Other important reform measures included the founding of banks, the promotion of industry and agriculture, the construction of railways and the encouragement of inventions. Officials were to be sent to visit foreign countries.

Kang's students were appointed to strategic posts in the administration to help ensure the implementation of all these reforms. But few were carried out, except in the southern province of Hunan. Elsewhere, the reform decrees met with passive non-cooperation or outright resistance. The reforms were ambitious, but they were too sweeping to win political support from the traditionally trained officials of the far-flung imperial regime. For the most part, they ignored the instructions from Kang's young and inexperienced supporters.

In Russia, the famous author Leo Tolstoy was following events in China, and began a friendship by correspondence with a traditional Confucian scholar, Gu Hong Ming, born in the Chinese community in Penang, Malaysia. Gu had studied literature at the University of Edinburgh, civil engineering in Leipzig, and law in Paris. With his command of Western languages, he was widely regarded outside China as an authority on Confucianism. Gu and Tolstoy agreed that Kang's reform ideas were foolish and would not succeed, because they were too radical, and tried to overthrow tradition. As we shall see in the next chapter on Russia, Tolstoy's arguments in favour of tradition in China were consistent with the position that he would take in opposition to reform in his own country. Interestingly, Tolstoy's arguments for a return to traditional ways of life would later influence a young Indian visionary named Mohandas Gandhi. In the case of China, Tolstoy's correspondent, Gu Hong Ming, gave intellectual support to conservatives opposed to Kang's ideas.

A visit to China by Itō Hirobumi of Japan, gave credence to claims by conservatives that the reforms would lead to foreign takeover. Itō was an important figure. In 1885, he had negotiated the Treaty of Tientsin with China's influential northern viceroy, Li Hong Zhang, and had then re-established Japan's diplomatic relations with China. Back in Japan, he proposed a cabinet system of government under the Meiji monarchy, and he then became Japan's first prime minister. A decade later, he was again prime minister when Japan defeated China in the Sino-Japanese War. Itō visited China on 11 September 1898, at the same time as a British missionary, Timothy Richard, who had been invited by Kang. Richard, apparently acting without any authority from the British government, persuaded Kang to support a plan for a federation of China with Japan, Britain and the United States. Kang sent the plan to the emperor on 18 September. It was politically naïve of Kang to support such a plan, which was bound to arouse fierce opposition from the conservatives who supported the more nationalistic policies of the dowager empress.

The following day Empress Cixi returned to Peking from the Summer Palace. At this point the young reformers made a major miscalculation. In the face of rumours that the empress planned to stage a coup and retake power, they planned a palace revolt and her capture. One of the reform leaders, Pan Si Tong, approached General Yuan Shi Kai, commander of the 'new army' established in 1895 after the defeat by the Japanese, to seek his support. However, Yuan Shi Kai told General Rong Ru – his counterpart in command of the Manchu troops who supported the empress – about the plan. Rong Ru's troops entered the Forbidden City in Beijing at dawn on 21 September and placed the emperor under house arrest, holding him in a palace by a lake. The empress gave orders to arrest the reformers. Six reform leaders known as 'the six gentlemen' were arrested and beheaded. They included Pan Si Tong and Kang You Wei's brother, Kang Guang Ren.

Kang You Wei and his long-time student and principal supporter, Liang Qi Chao, escaped to Japan. There, in exile, they continued to advocate for a constitutional monarchy in China. The emperor and Kang's young reformers had failed to emulate the success of the Meiji reforms in Japan thirty years earlier. The 100 Days' Reform (actually 103 days) was seen as being too fast and too far-reaching to win support. The reformers completely under-estimated the strength of resistance to their proposals.

Sun Yat Sen, also in exile in Japan, proclaimed that the failure of the 100 Days' Reform showed that the only path forward was revolution. Disputes between the revolutionaries and the reformists divided Chinese students and expatriates in Japan and elsewhere. The failure of the 100 Days' Reform gave great impetus to the revolutionary movement, both within China and among the overseas Chinese, where Sun Yat Sen was garnering much of his support.

Meanwhile, General Yuan Shi Kai was building his power base as commander of the modernised 'new army'. In a striking parallel with the rise to power of Louis Napoléon in France, the ambitious general would manoeuvre to become president of China, then try to become a new emperor.

The interactions between national societies at opposite ends of the globe increased dramatically through the nineteenth century. Economic penetration, military interventions and, above all, the circulation of ideas, meant that the destiny of China would be increasingly linked with the rest of the world.

Kang You Wei's travels

At the beginning of his exile in Japan, Kang stayed in hiding. The dowager empress and her generals had placed a price on his head, and there were repeated stories about assassins being sent to kill him, so he avoided the local Chinese communities. After failing to obtain assistance from the Japanese government, in 1899 he took a steamship from Yokohama across the Pacific to Victoria in Western Canada. As the ship docked, Kang was impatient to go ashore, intensely curious about the first Western city he could visit. But the Canadian immigration procedures imposed strict medical quarantine on all persons arriving from China, aimed particularly at combating typhoid and smallpox. As Kang waited for his quarantine to end, he attracted the attention of a local reporter, who wrote: 'He was on deck and everywhere asking questions, such as: what was Victoria's population, its manner of municipal government, its facilities for policing and protection against fires; its school and hospital arrangements?'[14]

Disembarking at last in Victoria, Kang met with reporters from the two local newspapers, and publicly requested British intervention in support of his Chinese reform movement. He was invited to visit the British Columbia Parliament building, and was so impressed that he told the minister accompanying him that he would build something similar in China once he gained power.[15] Meetings followed with the governor of the province and the mayor. He also approached the American Consul in Victoria to seek entry into the United States.[16] The US had adopted the Chinese Exclusion Acts in 1882, and Kang was required to produce certificates from the Chinese government but could not do so, as he was on the Qing regime's most wanted list. The US Consul tried unsuccessfully to get him an exemption.

In Victoria, Kang founded Bao Huang Hui, which was translated into English initially as the Protect the Emperor Society or as the Save the Emperor Society. For the first time, Kang made a public speech to an audience of overseas Chinese. As he concluded his speech, he cried out, 'Do you want China to strengthen itself? If so, please clap your hands. Do you hope for the restoration of the Guang Xu Emperor? If so, please clap your hands!' The audience responded with thunderous applause. Kang moved from Victoria Island to Vancouver, where a thousand people crammed into the City Hall to hear him. But again, he was in danger. A local reporter warned him after the meeting that an assassin was on his way from across the border in Seattle. On the request of the British colonial secretary in Ottawa, the Canadian government assigned him a red-coated Mountie policeman as a personal escort during the day. At night, Kang was protected by two bodyguards from the Chinese community.

The next month Kang, with his retinue from China and an interpreter born in Australia, took the Canadian Pacific Railway to the national capital, Ottawa. There he met Prime Minister Wilfred Laurier, and was received by the governor general at a ball with several hundred guests. He took steps with Chinese merchants to form a business corporation to raise resources for the reform movement. Still failing to obtain entry to the United States, he left for Montreal to take a steamer to London.

Kang's visit to London was a political failure and a financial disaster. He did not see the British Prime Minister, Lord Salisbury, or any high-ranking official. Salisbury opposed intervention in the internal affairs of China, despite support for Kang's reform movement in the British Parliament. Added to this, the lodgings of Kang and his retinue were burgled, and most of their travel funds were stolen. They had only enough cash left to return to Montreal, where they waited for funds to be sent by the Chinese community in Vancouver. Again, he had a Canadian Mountie assigned to him by day, and two Chinese bodyguards at night. Kang was again denied entry to the United States. He concentrated on building support for Bao Huang Hui which, while retaining its original name in Chinese, was renamed in English as the Chinese Empire Reform Association (CERA). Emissaries were sent across North America, Europe, Asia and Australia. At its height, the CERA would have chapters in 150 cities worldwide.

Sun Yat Sen also continued to travel. But there is no record that Sun and Kang ever met. In 1899 both Sun and Liang, Kang's main lieutenant, were in Canada where their paths crossed as they each sought support among the overseas Chinese diaspora. Liang visited Hawaii, then returned to Canada where he supported Kang in building the CERA. The turn of the century found Kang You Wei in Singapore. In February 1900, his host Lim Boon Keng wrote to the Governor of Singapore requesting the colonial government's protection and reminding him not to reveal Kang's presence to the outside world. Assassins sent by the Qing court were again on his heels, so the governor came up with a plan to throw them off the trail. Kang pretended to leave for Europe by sea, but returned secretly to Singapore, where he moved from house to house for the next six months.[17] From Singapore, Kang tried to start a rebellion in the southern city of Hangkou. After two weeks that rebellion failed, and Kang's reputation was diminished. Moreover, questions were raised among overseas Chinese over a lack of accountability in his handling of funds contributed to the CERA.

Rebellions

Liang Qi Chao embarked on a six-month tour of the Australian colonies as they formed the new national federation in January 1901, giving public lectures to both Chinese and Western audiences around the country. This was a time when Chinese and Pacific islander immigration had become a major issue in the colonies along the eastern seaboard of Australia, and the desire for a common policy – a restrictive one – was an important factor in the decision of all six colonies to form a national federation, the origin of the Australian nation. In Britain, the death of Queen Victoria brought an era of the great British Empire to an end.

Meanwhile, peasants across China suffered as crops withered in the grip of a severe drought. The reparations imposed by Japan after the war had left China bankrupt. Handicraft industries were destroyed by cheap imports, and the peasants were burdened with even higher taxation. Chinese emigrant communities were already established in many parts of the world – in Japan and in the Malay Peninsula and the trading ports of Singapore and Penang, in Hawaii, California, British Colombia and Mexico, in Australia and New Zealand, along the eastern coast of Africa and in South Africa, and in Europe. Often these early emigrants thrived, while maintaining family links with their homeland, and despite the restrictions in the US, Australia and elsewhere, they supported new migrants seeking escape from the grinding poverty of the Chinese countryside. They were also the main source of resources for the competing movements of the reformists and the revolutionaries.

Both Sun Yat Sen and Kang You Wei were involved in plots to foment rebellion at home in China. While a brilliant if utopian philosopher, Kang seemed susceptible to the influence of foreign adventurers. Just as his involvement with the Englishman Timothy Richard had left him open to the conservative counter-attack at the end of the 100 Days' Reform, now he accepted proposals from the Los Angeles chapter of the CERA to engage the services of an American adventurer named Homer Lea.

Homer Lea, the adventurer

From the time of the first gold rush of 1848, Chinese migrants had flocked to California. Homer Lea had moved from the midwest to California with his family as a young boy, and often visited Chinatown in Los Angeles. Physically handicapped with a hunchback, he was nevertheless an avid outdoorsman. At Stanford University, he became a skilful debater. In Chinatown he learnt Cantonese and established contacts with Bao Huang Hui.

Homer Lea and Kang You Wei did not meet for some time, but they exchanged messages through emissaries. On 22 June 1900, aged twenty-three, Lea boarded the steamship *China* in San Francisco. As he waved to friends on the dock he called, 'I've got business over there. You'll hear about it later.' The next day, articles appeared in the *San Francisco Call* and the *New York Herald* with his photo and a caption: 'Secret agent of Chinese Reform Society',[18] showing Lea with some of his Stanford University classmates. The ship *China* crossed the Pacific via Hawaii to the Philippines, then steamed north to Japan. In Yokohama, Lea met with the local Bao Huang Hui leader, Chen Lu Sheng, who gave him a letter of introduction for his meeting with Kang. Steaming south, the ship was delayed in Nagasaki by a typhoon. Unexpectedly he crossed paths with his Stanford University President, Dr Jordan, who was astonished to see him in Japan. Lea told Dr Jordan that he would intercede with the US representative in Japan 'to induce the powers of Europe to intervene on behalf of the lawful Emperor of China and against the dowager empress'.[19] In fact, Lea had no intention of travelling to Tokyo, and reboarded *China* to Hong Kong, where he met with the reformers: Crossing to Guangzhou, he met at last with Kang You Wei.

Kang was skeptical. 'Why have you come?' he asked. 'I have come to save China from the old tigress,' Lea replied. 'You are too young for that,' Kang said, to which Lea responded, 'I am the same age as Napoléon was at Rivoli.'[20] After further discussion, Kang agreed that Lea should go to China to lead a new uprising against the imperial court, aimed at restoring the reformist young emperor to power. Lea returned to Hong

Kong with the promise of the rank of general, and a plan to lead American mercenaries in an uprising. The Chinese government got wind of his plans, and the Chinese Consul General in San Francisco revealed details to the press. The British Governor of Hong Kong, Sir Henry Blake, followed the stories closely, and sent reports to the Foreign Office in London. Blake reported on a meeting in Hong Kong between Lea, a group of reformists, and supporters of Sun Yat Sen's revolutionary movement. Lea proposed a coalition, which the revolutionaries refused. This meeting was significant, for later Lea would lose patience with the reformers and join the revolutionaries. Meanwhile, the British and American governments were more preoccupied with the rebellion that had broken out in the north, around the capital Beijing. This would come to be known as the Boxer Rebellion.

The Boxer Rebellion

The 'Boxers' were so-called because of their origins in a martial arts cult, which perpetuated the idea that its fighters were endowed with supernatural protection against weapons. They were athletic young men of peasant origin from the northern provinces who had joined a secret society called the Yihequan, translated as 'Righteous and Harmonious Fists'. They resisted the growing activities of Western missionaries who they accused of encouraging Chinese converts to flout traditional ceremonies and family relations. In earlier times, the Boxers had opposed the Manchus of the Qing dynasty but by the late nineteenth century, after the failure of the 100 Days' Reform, they had become an active anti-foreigner movement, and began attacking Christian churches. In 1900, the Boxers mounted a rebellion aimed at expelling foreign powers. Empress Cixi hesitated to intervene, then ordered the Imperial Army to support the Boxers, another example of her readiness to change direction for tactical reasons. The Boxers killed the Japanese and German ambassadors. Manchu troops laid siege to the foreign Legation Quarter of the Chinese capital, where foreign citizens, diplomats and Chinese Christians took refuge, defended by a few foreign soldiers. Among those blocked in the city was a young American mining engineer named Herbert Hoover, a future President of the United States. The siege of the Legation Quarter lasted nearly two months, and as it wore on, an alliance of eight nations[21] was formed, and 45,000 troops were sent to China. The alliance defeated the Imperial Army and the Boxers, and by August had captured Beijing, ending the rebellion. Critically, Yuan Shi Kai, who had previously betrayed the reformers in 1898, now broke with Cixi and supported the foreign alliance with his Chinese 'new army' against the imperial Manchu troops. The imperial court evacuated the capital to the mountain city of Xian.

In the south, Kang You Wei's Bao Huang Hui formed a makeshift military force, with Homer Lea responsible for training rural volunteers. Lea arrived in Beijing with his ragtag army of poorly trained volunteers just as the alliance forces relieved the siege of the Legation Quarter, and he mounted a quixotic pursuit of the dowager empress as she fled with her court, before breaking off when confronted by the imperial guards protecting the empress and the court. Marching south to Hankou, his volunteers were defeated by the Imperial Army, and Lea escaped to Japan with a bounty on his head. From there he returned to California, where he established a network of military schools to train soldiers, with the aim of returning to China and helping restore the emperor to power.

The following year, in 1901, Viceroy Li Hong Zhang negotiated what came to be known as the Boxer Protocol with the eight-nation alliance. The protocol imposed reparations on the Chinese, prohibited the importation of arms or ammunition for two years, called for the trials of Boxers and government officials involved in the rebellion, and reserved the Legation Quarter for exclusive foreign use, to be defended by troops from the alliance. The emperor was required to send official regrets to the German and Japanese emperors over the killing of their ambassadors. An arch was to be erected in memory of the German ambassador, with inscriptions in Latin, German and Chinese. In return for these concessions, the alliance provided Li with assurances that there would be no more claims on Chinese territory and that the Qing dynasty under the rule of the dowager empress would be maintained. Uncharacteristically, Cixi issued a Decree of Self Reproach, assuming responsibility for the disaster of the Boxer Rebellion.

A birthday celebration

Festivals were and still are an integral part of Chinese life. They celebrate the changing of the seasons, the solstices, the equinoxes and, above all, the Lunar New Year. At the higher echelons of imperial society these were the occasions for displays of wealth, and festival gowns worn at the imperial court are today prized exhibits in museums around the world. In 1902, calm had returned to the capital after the Boxer Rebellion and the invasion by the alliance of foreign powers. In January, Empress Cixi decided that the time had come to provide a show of her status before the foreigners. Together with the emperor, who was still under house arrest, and the full imperial court, she made a ceremonious return to Beijing on a royal train of twenty-one carriages. By then Cixi had been the de facto ruler of China for forty years. She had acquired and maintained her power by shrewd manipulation, and throughout all those years had blown hot and cold on the modernisation of China. After the ignominy of the failed Boxer Rebellion and her Decree of Self Reproach, she decided to change strategy radically. Cixi gave orders to send top officials to Japan and Europe on fact-finding tours. They were instructed to research and draw up sweeping reforms, many modelled, like Kang's earlier proposals, on the Meiji Restoration in Japan. Cixi also changed her personal approach to governing, calculating that she had to accommodate the Western powers to ensure the survival of the Qing Manchu dynasty. The 'lady behind the curtain' now came out into the open and embarked on a charm offensive. She invited the wives of the foreign diplomats to tea in the Forbidden City. In summer, she held garden parties for the foreign community in the Summer Palace. She agreed to sit for a portrait by American artist Katharine Carl.

The governor of the capital, Zhang Zhi Dong, organised a lavish celebration of Cixi's sixty-seventh birthday, which exceeded anything seen before in China. The diplomatic corps and prominent members of the foreign community were invited. The purpose was to show that the imperial dynasty was still in place, despite the presence of a military garrison and the payment of reparations.[22] Metaphorically, the empress and her court were dancing before the storm. For that storm was brewing and would within a decade sweep away the imperial dynasty. The traditionalist Confucian scholar Gu Hong Ming – he who corresponded with Tolstoy in Russia – had been among the most fervent supporters of the Qing regime. Now he composed a song expressing his displeasure.[23] The traditionalist found the display of excess to be repugnant. For Sun Yat Sen and the revolutionaries, to parade such excess at a time of near national bankruptcy was sheer folly.

Kang You Wei in Asia

Although the policies now promoted by the dowager empress were similar to those advocated by Kang You Wei, he remained in exile in Japan. As the empress returned to the capital and celebrated her new openness to the West with afternoon teas and garden parties, Kang left for Penang in British Malaya, then for India. Although the British did not want to intervene in support of the Chinese reformers in exile, Kang's importance was now recognised and he had the benefit of British protection as he travelled through these colonies. In May 1902, he wrote to Liang from Darjeeling in India. The letter was a long essay on the fall of India to British colonialism. Kang argued that India's collapse as a sovereign country was due to the independence of its provinces, enabling the British to 'divide and rule'. For Kang, the Indian colonial experience was an example that China should take as a warning.[24]

In April 1903, General Rong Lu died in Beijing. He was the military strong man behind the dowager empress, and it was on his orders that assassins were sent to find Kang as he moved between Canada, Japan, Hong Kong and Singapore. The empress did not revoke the orders to find and kill him or remove the bounty on his head, but the death of Rong Lu took off the pressure. Kang now felt safe enough to leave British protection in India and visit the Chinese overseas communities in South-East Asia. He travelled to Burma, Java, Vietnam and Thailand, finally arriving back in Hong Kong in October of that year. This was the period when the CERA achieved its greatest strength in Chinese communities around the world, competing with Sun Yat Sen's more revolutionary Revive China Society.

Kang's grand tour of Europe

In Hong Kong, Kang You Wei began preparations for a grand tour of the West. Leaving Hong Kong in March 1904, he and his party travelled through Indochina and Burma to Penang in Malaysia. There he took a British ship to Ceylon. He then took passage on a large ocean liner through the Red Sea and the Suez Canal, reaching Italy in June. Touring

Naples, Rome, and Milan, he was impressed by the history but deeply disappointed by the poverty, banditry and begging he witnessed in the streets, which reminded him of Beijing. His perception was of two ancient centres of civilisation, linked centuries earlier by Marco Polo's visits to the Orient, now in decline and decay. Nevertheless, he noted the progress made in Italy since unification in 1871. From Italy, Kang crossed the Alps to Switzerland, visiting Geneva, Vienna, Budapest, Berlin, and Paris, then traversed the Channel to London and Edinburgh. Kang kept detailed notes of his eleven-nation tour which he published as an *Essay on national salvation through material construction.* Being popular in the overseas Chinese communities, he received substantial contributions to finance his travel.[25] No other Chinese person of his generation had toured the West so completely.

Kang was deeply worried by his rivals, led by Sun Yat Sen, within China and especially among the overseas Chinese. Their rivalry over reform and constitutional monarchy against revolution and a republic became fiercer than ever. Kang believed, accurately as it turned out, that revolution would be destructive, resulting in 'chaos and bloody turmoil'. While touring France that year, he wrote a new essay – *On the great French Revolution* – observing that France had rushed to emulate the American Revolution with disastrous consequences.[26] The key word in Kang's earlier essay was 'material', by which he meant that inventions and industrialisation were key to the success of modern nations. In particular, he noted the power of steamships. He wrote that back in 1831, just a short time after the building of the world's first ocean-going steamship, two British gunboats powered by steam had overwhelmed a fleet of Chinese junks in Guangdong.[27] Kang gave much attention in his writings to the importance of navies in the modern world, noting that the Chinese fleet had been almost totally destroyed during the Sino-Japanese War of 1894–95. In Europe, he observed the growing race to build warships to compete with Britain's domination.

Kang in America
From London, Kang crossed the Atlantic to Canada, and in late 1904 he took the train back to the familiar surroundings of Vancouver. The Chinese community on the west coast of Canada was his power base.

This was where he had made his first public speeches, five years earlier, and had founded the CERA, which had since won much support among the overseas Chinese in North America, not only because of its advocacy for reform in China, but also by supporting their concerns over discrimination against Chinese immigrants. The CERA's mobilisation of an anti-American boycott by Chinese businesses, calling for withdrawal of the exclusion laws, was effective.

Kang also took time to study English. In February 1905 he was at last able to enter the United States, travelling south from Vancouver to Los Angeles, visiting Bao Huang Hui chapters along the way. One of his students, Tom Leung, had founded the Los Angeles chapter, the largest in the US. Together Leung and Kang visited cities across America. In Washington, Kang met twice with President Theodore Roosevelt to discuss America's Chinese exclusion policy. The government was concerned about the threat of a protest boycott by the strong Chinese businesses in America, and Kang was seen as an influential figure.[28] He also visited leading American universities. As he travelled, Kang's entourage included interpreters and also Homer Lea, who was busy establishing a network of military schools to train young expatriates and American-born Chinese. Kang's daughter Tong Bi had been attending high school in Connecticut since 1903, and she was able to meet her father as he visited the state.

Kang also spent several months in Mexico, arriving in December 1905. The city of Torreon had a large Chinese community, and Kang made personal profit from land speculation. The CERA established a successful company there, with restaurants, a bank, an electric tramway, and its own building in the business centre.[29] Kang returned to Mexico in 1907, and met with President Porfirio Díaz, who as a general had successfully opposed Napoléon III of France back in 1867, and had since then established a dictatorship. But Mexican nationalism was on the rise, and Chinese businesses were attacked. The Mexican Revolution, beginning with the overthrow of Díaz, occurred just over five years later, at almost the same time as the Chinese Revolution.

Kang continued to fear assassination, but now the threat came more from Sun Yat Sen's revolutionaries, as tensions grew in the Chinese overseas communities between supporters of the two charismatic leaders. Debates between the constitutional monarchist reformers of Kang and the CERA and the revolutionary republicans following Sun Yat Sen became more and more vitriolic. Local Chinese newspapers in the overseas communities, notably in centres like Singapore and Penang, took one side or the other. Families with businesses were more likely to support the monarchist reformers and could contribute funds to support them, while students and indentured labourers were more receptive to the revolutionaries.

Sun Yat Sen had already been accused of having links with criminal triads operating in and around Hong Kong with a capacity to reach into overseas Chinese communities around the Pacific. The risk of conflicts between the groups becoming deadly was real. In Los Angeles, Kang and Tom Leung moved around wearing a form of traditional body armour made of paper and bamboo.[30] Kang had also founded a Bao Huang Hui commercial corporation, intended to generate resources to be used for the opening of Chinese schools in expatriate communities, for sending students abroad for study in the United States or Europe, and for the publishing of newspapers promoting the cause of constitutional monarchy in China. But the political missions and the commercial objectives ended up colliding, and there were accusations of mismanagement of funds, causing Kang and Leung to fall out later.

Competing for influence

After the Boxer Rebellion of 1900, Sun Yat Sen joined up with a radical Japanese intellectual named Tōten Miyazaki. The pair tried to enter Hong Kong, but they were refused entry. There were various groups jostling for influence. One was a secret society based in the lower Yangtze River called the 'Brothers and Elders'. This group formed a nationalist anti-Manchu 'Revive Han Association', which nominated Sun as its leader and formed an alliance with the Revive China Society. Sun's supporters staged an uprising in Huizhou, which failed after supplies of arms and ammunition they expected from Japan failed to arrive.

Sun Yat Sen continued organising the Revive China Society through visits to Vietnam, Japan, and Hawaii. He established a military academy near Tokyo. His alleged contacts through intermediaries with the infamous criminal triads in Hong Kong provided Kang You Wei's supporters with the argument they needed to have Sun Yat Sen expelled from Japan. Since the time of the Ming dynasty, secret societies (called Hung or Hong) had existed in China. Just as societies like the Freemasons had been important for figures like Franklin and Lafayette in eighteenth-century America and Europe, Chinese Hongs had a significant role in communities both within the mother country and in the overseas communities. Sun Yat Sen sought them out during his travels. He tried to enter Singapore with Tōten Miyazaki, but they were refused entry there as they had been in Hong Kong, and they were formally banned for five years. In 1904, Sun joined the Hung Men society in Hawaii, taking up a leadership position to strengthen links with his Revive China Society. He also established a Chinese newspaper in Hawaii, as his supporters had in Hong Kong and Penang. Throughout this period, Sun travelled continuously to raise funds for newspapers and military training, while forming alliances with any group that could support his goal of overthrowing the imperial dynasty. In 1904, Sun Yat Sen published an article in New York entitled: *The true solution of the Chinese question.*[31]

By 1905, the rivalry between Sun's revolutionaries and Kang's reformists had become more intense than ever, and Liang tried to take control of Sun's Revive China Society. Both groups tried to infiltrate the homeland and take action there. A revolutionary supporter tried to assassinate five high-ranking Qing officials at the Beijing railway station but was killed by his own bomb. Kang was rumoured to be associated with an obscure plot to assassinate Sun. To strengthen his political base, Sun worked to merge his Revive China Society with two other bodies to form the Federal Association of China (Tung Meng Hui) and was elected its president. This was the year when Sun Yat Sen published his famous essay in the journal *Min Bao*, entitled *Three Principles of the People.*

Like Kang You Wei, Sun Yat Sen referred to Confucius, writing in his essay that the term *kemin* or revolution, was first coined by the Chinese sage. He noted that revolutions had occurred repeatedly in Chinese history, as dynasties were replaced. But he also credited Abraham Lincoln's famous line in the Gettysburg address – 'Government of the people, by the people, for the people' – as an inspiration for his *Three Principles of the People.* Writing in the editorial of a newspaper in Tokyo, Sun described his three principles.[32]

The first was *minzu* meaning nationalism, immediately marking his difference with Kang. Sun's nationalism was about throwing off the yoke of the Manchus, who had ruled the majority Han Chinese for centuries under the Qing dynasty. Kang had a more universalist approach, advocating the restoration of China's great civilisation, which had always incorporated diversity. For Kang, the Manchu origin of the Qing dynasty was of little importance. What counted was education and culture. If the West had gained the upper hand through technology, the challenge was for China to learn from the West in order to re-emerge in the forefront of the civilised world.

Sun's second principle was *minquan*, meaning democracy or 'the people's power', which he asserted would require that the Qing dynasty be replaced by a republic. Here again, he marked his difference with Kang. He emphasised the importance of a constitution to underpin such a republic, with a three-fold separation of powers between the legislative, judicial and executive branches of government, as proposed firstly in France by Montesquieu and enshrined in the constitution of the United States. Sun and Kang both studied and drew lessons from the French and American revolutions, but they drew different conclusions. Like Jacques Necker and Germaine de Staël in the France of the late eighteenth and early nineteenth centuries, Kang remained a supporter of a constitutional monarchy, while from the United States he drew lessons of entrepreneurship, which he sought to apply through the commercial operations of the Bao Huang Hui. Sun was more influenced by the concepts of governance that the American founding fathers had drawn from the French thinkers of the Enlightenment, which reinforced his commitment to the idea of a republic.

Sun's third principle was *minsheng,* meaning welfare or livelihood. 'With the invention of modern machines, the phenomenon of uneven distribution in the West has become all the more marked,' he wrote, continuing, 'On my tour of Europe and America I saw with my own eyes the instability of their economic structures and the deep concern of their leaders.'[33] Again, Sun marked his difference with Kang. He asserted that it was not sufficient to restore China's greatness as Kang preached; China also had to address the grave inequalities of industrial society. Sun's prescriptions were strongly influenced by the ideas of American political economist and thinker Henry George. George's work *Progress and Poverty,*[34] published in 1879, sold millions of copies worldwide. George held that people should own the value of their own work, but that value derived from land and national resources should belong equally to all members of society. He, therefore, proposed taxation based essentially on land. We will see in the next chapter that the same ideas would be promoted at the same time by the author Leo Tolstoy in the debate over reform in Russia.

Kang continued his travels, while working on his book, *Datong Shu*. The title was taken from an utopian society imagined by Confucius, and literally means: 'The Book of Great Unity', which has also been translated as *The Great Society*.[35] Kang's utopian society would be free of political boundaries, end inequality between men and women, and end ethnic differences over time through the encouragement of inter-racial relations. Back in Japan, his twenty-year-old daughter Kang Tong Bi, met a young staffer at the Chinese Embassy and married. The young couple broke with tradition, as the match was not arranged by the families. Kang fully supported his daughter's decision.

Russia defeated in the East

As the reformists of Kang and the revolutionaries of Sun ramped up their increasingly bitter conflict, a major geo-political change was underway in east Asia. In 1902, Britain and Japan had signed an alliance, which while not mentioning Russia was intended to constrain the tsar's empire in the East. Japan's Itō Hirobumi tried to negotiate the withdrawal of some 100,000 Russian troops from Manchuria, where they had remained since the defeat of the Boxer Rebellion. After these negotiations reached an impasse, in early 1904, the Japanese imperial fleet attacked the Russian Far East fleet and captured Port Arthur, a strategic port on the tip of the Liaodong peninsula, occupied under a lease by Russia. The former Port Arthur is today named Lüshankou. The tsar sent reinforcements but, as we will see in the next chapter, the defeat of Russia by Japan, the first defeat of a European power by an Asian adversary, shook tsarist imperial power across the vast Russian Empire

Kang and Sun both remain in exile

Returning to Europe in 1906, Kang met his daughter Tong Bi, who was by then in Paris, then settled for a time in Sweden. He purchased an islet off the city of Saltsjöbaden and stayed there until 1908. It is not clear how he obtained the funds for this purchase, but there were rumblings about his use of the contributions made to the CERA from chapters spread around the world. He called the islet Shelter Island. His youngest daughter was born there. King Gustaf V of Sweden had a villa nearby and used to call in for tea and a chat.[36] Kang continued to write prolifically, analysing the findings of his extensive travels and continuing to propose solutions for China. His intellectual curiosity and his extensive travels led him to write that his objective was to 'sample different nations like herbs for developing a medicine to heal a sick China'.[37]

On the island he wrote *Swedish Diaries* and a series of essays on the historical evolution of France, Germany, Austria and Hungary.[38] His essay on France went further than his condemnation of revolution in his memorandum of 1898 to the emperor. Now he explored the nature of feudalism in France compared with that of China; he noted the oppression of the French people by the aristocracy and the clergy, and the philosophy of the Enlightenment. He argued that conditions were different in China, continuing to defend his concept of a modernising constitutional monarchy. But it was Germany that now attracted Kang's attention. He addressed the question of how Germany had overcome the weakness and disunity of its independent states. Kang wrote: 'In a short time the Germans became successful in extending their own culture and influence, while Great China, with its rich culture of five thousand years ... is forced to accept the instruction of others, bowing its head and lowering its eyes. There is no shame greater than this!'

While Kang settled in Sweden, Sun Yat Sen returned from visits to London, Brussels, Paris and Berlin, then Singapore, to re-establish his base in Japan. This is when he forged the alliance of his Revive China Society with two other groups to form the Tung Men Hu with himself as leader.[39] During the time that Kang spent writing in Sweden, his life-long supporter and fellow reformer, Liang Qi Chao, engaged in a great debate with Sun Yat Sen about nationalism and socialism.[40] Liang, like Kang and Sun, came from the south of China. He was born in Guangzhou (Canton) in 1873, so was fifteen years younger than Kang and seven years younger than Sun. Like Kang, Liang advocated *da minzu zhuyi* (broad nationalism), bringing diverse ethnic groups into a unified China. Sun disagreed. To him, the priority was to overthrow Manchu rule over the Han majority. For the reformers, nationalism based on ethnicity was an alien concept, as historically China had a concept of civilisation based on culture, tradition and learning, irrespective of ethnic origin.

In the nineteenth century, the Chinese had been shocked to see foreign barbarians using weapons they had never seen before to rip their ancient civilisation apart. They were humiliated by the Qing dynasty's acceptance of unequal treaties. In the early days of exile in Japan, Liang and Sun met with the idea of joining forces against the Qing court. But Liang supported Kang's campaign to protect the young emperor and bring about a modernising constitutional monarchy. Sun, on the other hand, believed that nothing short of the defeat of the entire Manchu imperial system could save China. They shared common ground in their desire to overthrow the control of the dowager empress, but they differed strongly on the system that should be put in place to govern the nation. Liang and Sun continued their debates in the journals of the Chinese overseas communities, notably between 1905 and 1907, debating the meaning of socialism and its application to China. Their writings drew strongly on the political and economic thinkers in the West, from Karl Marx in Europe to Henry George in the United States.[41]

Chinese students continued to move to Japan, many of them supporters of the nationalists and the revolutionaries. Sun Yat Sen established branches of his society in Malaysia. In late 1906 and early 1907, more rebellions broke out in China, this time in Jiangxi and Hunan provinces in the south, where a thirteen-year-old boy, the son of a wealthy farmer, witnessed first-hand the turmoil developing across his country. His name was Mao Tse Tung. In 1907, Sun Yat Sen established his revolutionary headquarters in Hanoi, Vietnam (French Indochina), and instigated more rebellions within China. In December, he took part in a revolt in Chengnan Kuan, which again failed. Retreating to Hanoi, he was declared persona non grata in 1908 by French colonial officials. He returned to Singapore and continued to call for rebellions in China, but each revolt failed. In all, Sun Yat Sen instigated at least eight rebellions during this period.

Deaths at the imperial court

In 1908, the Dowager Empress Cixi, having exercised power in China for forty-six years, was nearing the end of her life. In November, the thirty-seven-year-old Guangxu Emperor, who had been kept under house arrest since the end of the 100 Days' Reform, died suddenly. There was strong evidence that he had been poisoned with arsenic, found in abnormally high levels in his body.[42] The dowager empress named a two-year-old nephew, Puy Yi, as the new emperor and she died the following day. There was speculation that the emperor had been poisoned on her orders before her own death. Others believed that General Yuan Shi Kai ordered the murder, fearing that, because of his actions to end the 100 Days' Reform, he would be executed for treason if the emperor was restored to power after Empress Cixi's death.[43] As the dying Cixi named her nephew Puy Yi as boy emperor, she designated his natural father, the second Prince Chun (Zaifeng, son of the first Prince Chun, Yixuan) as regent and effective ruler of the empire. Immediately after the death of Cixi, the new regent summarily dismissed Yuan Shi Kai.

Although the Qing dynasty seemed to be in a period of terminal agony, two years of rebellion had failed to bring about a full revolution. By 1909, Sun Yat Sen left South-East Asia and travelled again to Europe and the United States to raise more funds.

Lea joins the revolutionaries

Kang You Wei's former general, the American adventurer Homer Lea, had been conspiring with a handful of businessmen, Chinese scholars and secret societies in the United States to form what was called the Red Dragons movement, with a network of military schools training young expatriates to fight for the Guang Xu Emperor to retake power in China. There were reports of these activities in American newspapers and investigations into infringements of US neutrality laws. After the deaths of the emperor and the dowager empress, Kang cut links with Lea. Lea lobbied US President Theodore Roosevelt and then his successor Howard Taft, seeking an appointment as US trade representative or ambassador to China. But these attempts were not taken seriously as Lea was perceived to be an erratic conspirator. When Sun Yat Sen arrived in America in late 1909, he was introduced to Lea by a common friend and persuaded him to support his goal of overthrowing the Manchu dynasty. Rebuffed by Kang, and by his own government, Lea saw Sun as opening for him a path to his dreams of greatness in China. Sun was taken with Lea's enthusiasm and apparent government connections – although Lea certainly overstated his influence – and took him on as a close advisor.

During the following two years, Sun Yat Sen spent most of his time in the United States and Canada, with a brief visit to Singapore. He continued to organise, publish, and instigate rebellions. In October 1911, the Wuchang uprising broke out. This time the revolution swept the country.

Conditions before the revolution

Prior to the industrial revolution in Europe, China had for centuries been the strongest economy in the world. In the Middle Ages, more steel was produced in China than in Britain.[44] Advances in metallurgy, movable type for printing, a silk-reeling machine invented centuries before the English spinning jenny, the invention of gunpowder, the magnetic compass, maritime exploration, astronomy and medicine, all dated from the Song dynasty in the twelfth and early thirteenth centuries. The Silk Road linked China with the Delhi sultanate in India and the Ottoman Empire, founded around that time in Turkey, and beyond them with Europe. Kublai Khan, founder of the Yuan dynasty later in the thirteenth century, welcomed the Polo family to Xanadu and sent a Christian monk of Turkic origin, Rabban Bar Sawma, as his ambassador to Europe, where he met the French king and several other monarchs, as well as the Pope in Rome.[45] In the fifteenth century, under the Ming dynasty, a fleet of great ships, under the Muslim admiral Zheng He, opened trading routes across the Indian Ocean as far as Africa. Until the end of the eighteenth century, China was well ahead of the West in innovations ranging from the production of paper to firearms and tools. At the time when the British were trying to put down the American Revolution, China had per capita income at the same level as that of Britain.

Conditions changed in China from the early nineteenth century onwards. The drivers of change were both internal and external. Internally the imperial system, supported by a nationwide civil service of scholar-bureaucrats called mandarins, failed to adapt. Externally, as European trade stretched around the globe, China became vulnerable. Defeats by

Benjamin Franklin in London, 1767: a man of influence.
Portrait by David Martin
Wikimedia Commons

King George III in 1771, portrayed in 1771, one year after the Boston massacre of 1770. Portrait by Johann Zoffany
Wikimedia Commons

Queen Charlotte, a year before the great ball of 1780. School of Joshua Reynolds, 1779
Wikimedia Commons

Lord Frederick North, British Prime Minister, 1770 to 1782. Portrait by Nathaniel Dance-Holland
Wikimedia Commons

Benjamin Franklin, John Adams and Thomas Jefferson drafting the
Declaration of Independence, 1776.
Wikimedia Commons

Alexander Hamilton, Benjamin Franklin and James Madison (seated) as
George Washington presides over the signing of the US Constitution, Philadelphia, 1787.
Tableau by Howard Chandler Christy
Wikimedia Commons

Jacques Necker, before his dismissal
on 11 July 1789.
Wikimedia Commons

Suzanne Necker, late 1780s.
Portrait by Joseph Duplessis
Wikimedia Commons

Germaine de Stael, circa 1800. Portrait by François Gérard
Wikimedia Commons

The women's march on Versailles, October 1789.
Wikimedia Commons

Lafayette takes the oath as Commander of the National Guard
on the first anniversary of the fall of the Bastille.
Serment de La Fayette à la Fête de la Fédération, le 14 juillet 1790 (anon.)
Wikimedia Commons

Lamartine declares the tricolour to be the flag of France, 1848.
Detail: Tableau by Félix Philippoteaux
Wikimedia Commons

The workers' uprising, rue Soufflot, 25 Paris,June 1848.
Painting by Horace Vernot
Wikimedia Commons

Napoléon III, on the 10th
anniversary of his proclamation as
emperor, 1862.
Portrait by Jean Hippolyte Flandrin
Wikimedia Commons

Wedding of Tsar Nicolas II and Princess Alix of Hesse, 1894.
Tableau by Laurits Tuxen
Wikimedia Commons

Kang You Wei in exile, circa 1900.
Wikimedia Commons

Dowager Empress Cixi, 1904.
Portrait by Katherine Carl, presented
to US President Theodore Roosevelt
Wikimedia Commons

Sun Yat Sen, first president
of the Republic of China.

Wikimedia Commons

Homer Lea, American adventurer in China,
circa 1909.

Wikimedia Commons

The battle of the Ta-Ping gate in Nanking, 1911.
Lithograph by T. Miyano
Wikimedia Commons

Bloody Sunday, Saint Petersburg, 1905;
Imperial soldiers fired on innocent petitioners outside the Winter Palace.
Artistic impression by Ivan Vladimirov
Wikimedia Commons

Pyotr Stolypin, Prime Minister of Russia, circa 1908.
Wikimedia Commons

Leo Tolstoy, Yasnaya Polyana, 1908.
Wikimedia Commons

Mohandas Gandhi, London, 1909.
Wikimedia Commons

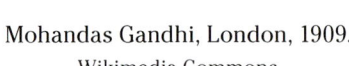

Lenin in action in the streets of Moscow, at Red Square.
Wikimedia Commons

First appearance of Lenin at a meeting in Smolny, the Petrograd Soviet, 25 October 1917.
Painting by Konstantin Yuon
WikiArt

Kofi Annan, Secretary-General of the United Nations
at the turn of the century.
Wikimedia Commons

Civil society challenges governments peacefully at the United Nations;
the International Labour Organization invites the Global March Against Child
Labour into its annual conference, Geneva, 2017.
United Nations

Violence in the streets; the 'yellow vests' protests in France, 2018.
Wikimedia Commons

The violent attempt to stop certification of the US presidential election;
the Capitol, Washington, 6 January 2021.
Photo by Tyler Merbler
Wikimedia Commons

Britain in the Opium Wars were followed by the series of imposed treaties, described by the Chinese and by most historians as 'unequal treaties'. There were internal uprisings, notably the Taiping Rebellion, which began in the south in 1850 and spread to other provinces over the next fourteen years. This was precisely the turbulent period when Kang You Wei and Sun Yat Sen were growing up.

At the pinnacle of their power, the Qing emperors were isolated from their vast empire. Living in the Forbidden City in the capital Beijing, their communications were essentially managed by the court eunuchs. The civil service of the mandarin class had eight ranks (with many sub-ranks), from the grand secretaries of the emperor, to governors of provinces, down to local tax collectors. The military had a similar structure. Parallel to the civil and military services were the merchants. China's merchant and trading class had a strong foundation from the time of the Ming dynasty. In the eighteenth and nineteenth centuries there was an effective banking system. Both government business and trade throughout China were conducted systematically in writing. The strong tradition of written memoranda and contracts meant that literacy and numeracy were valued and fostered at all levels of society. In the late Qing era literacy rates among males, including humble villagers, were estimated at between one third and one half of the population.[46] The literacy rate for females was much lower – estimated at two to ten per cent – and women were subjugated by such practices as foot-binding. But in general, literacy rates in China were significantly higher than those for pre-industrial Europe.

In the towns, artisans lived and worked, drawing upon centuries of tradition in manufacturing, ranging from textiles to tools. As in pre-industrial Europe, though, the population was predominantly rural. Across such a vast country, there were important regional differences in incomes, literacy, life expectancy, health, and infant mortality. In certain regions, such as the lower Yangtze River, which was the hub of domestic trading, people could aspire to progress. But from the mid-nineteenth century onwards, the migration of Chinese overseas increased dramatically. Most emigrants were labourers from the towns and villages in the southern coastal provinces of Fujian and Guangdong.

As we saw in the previous chapter, in the same year as the revolutions across Europe in 1848, the discovery of gold in California brought waves of Chinese migrants to the United States. In the following years, other migrants were attracted to Australia, where gold was discovered in the colony of Victoria. Others went to work as indentured labourers in South-East Asia, particularly in the tin mines and rubber plantations of Malaya. Some, like Sun Yat Sen's brother, crossed the Pacific to Hawaii, while others went as far as Africa. Chinese seafarers worked on ships, as trade expanded dramatically across the world's oceans in the latter half of the nineteenth century. As Singapore became a centre for free trade under the British, many Chinese migrated there as traders and labourers. After Japan's Meiji Restoration in 1868, large numbers of Chinese students went there to study. All these overseas communities provided support both for the reformist movement of Kang You Wei and for Sun Yat Sen's republican movement.

Within China, however, change was slow to come. Families continued to live and work as they had for generations, according to Confucian principles. In each house, a shrine was kept for offerings to ancestors. Inheritances were passed to the eldest sons. Daughters had to be given in marriage with a dowry, so were less valued. Growing insecurity caused by foreign incursions and repeated rebellions had a major impact on the everyday lives of villagers and labourers. This insecurity in turn fuelled the waves of emigration.

Corruption was endemic at all levels of government, as officials traded their influence for money, and formed cliques with businessmen and military leaders to protect themselves against investigations and punishment.[47] The imperial government was effectively bankrupted by the reparations and indemnities imposed by foreign powers, notably after the Sino-Japanese War and the Boxer Rebellion. Pressure to raise more taxes in the regions only increased support for more rebellions. Great infrastructure projects, such as the dikes or levees on the Yellow and Yangtze rivers, became degraded due to lack of maintenance. Railway development lagged behind that of Europe and Japan. The Chinese economy was caught in a vicious circle. Thus, conditions were in place for the series of rebellions that culminated in the overthrow of the Qing dynasty in 1911.

The Revolution

The chain of events leading to the first Chinese revolution began in April 1911, in the southern provinces. In Penang, Sun Yat Sen and other leaders of the Tong Meng Hui had planned for a decisive battle in the south. In April, the Tatar general in Guangzhou was assassinated.[48] A bomb attack was prepared on the viceroy's headquarters, but the authorities obtained information about the plot and arrested scores of revolutionaries, then summarily executed them. This uprising failed like the others instigated by Sun and his supporters.

Meanwhile, the imperial government, under the regency of Prince Chun, attempted to take over many of the provincially owned railroads that were just developing. The plan was to complete them with financing from foreign loans. Opposition was bitter in Guangdong province around Guangzhou and in neighbouring Sichuan. Across southern China, mass protests against the railroad takeovers continued and spread to the Yangtze Valley. Directly across the river from the great commercial city of Hangkou, in the city of Wuchang, the military mutinied and joined the rebellion. Wuchang was the capital of Hubei Province, and the military units were part of the modernised 'new army'. On 10 October 1911, the revolutionaries took control of Wuchang and declared an independent military government.

The revolt quickly spread to Hangkou and then to other cities. The Manchu government requested the recall of new army general Yuan Shi Kai, who had been dismissed by Prince Chun after the deaths of the Guangxu Emperor and Dowager Empress Cixi in 1908. Yuan Shi Kai at first refused. On 28 October, the flag of independence was hoisted over Canton. The Manchu garrison, which had repressed the uprising of April and executed the revolutionary plotters with great cruelty, now reached an amicable arrangement with the protestors. The secessionist movement spread from province to province. Troops mutinied and government officials were killed.

Sun Yat Sen was in America, in Denver, Colorado, to raise more funds when he received word that the long-awaited revolution was underway, and that he was to be president of the new Chinese provisional government. He immediately telegraphed Homer Lea to help arrange American and British support. Lea was in Wiesbaden, Germany, receiving medical treatment for his failing eyesight. Sun Yat Sen left Colorado, first by railway to New York, then by steamship to London. Sun Yat Sen and Homer Lea met in London, and approached the British government, but failed to win official support. They set off together on the long trip by steamship back to China, passed through the Suez Canal and made stops in India – taking about six weeks in all – to arrive in Shanghai on 25 December. Sun Yat Sen had announced en route that Lea would be chief of staff of China's republican army. But in Shanghai, Lea received notice from the State Department that under US law he could not aid a revolutionary movement. At the same time, the revolutionary leaders in China marginalised Lea, wary of his influence on Sun Yat Sen.

While Sun Yat Sen journeyed back to China, events proceeded apace across the country. Through October and November there was fierce fighting between revolutionaries and imperial forces, especially along the Yangtze River valley. The imperial forces recaptured Hanyang but lost Nanjing.

Yuan Shi Kai returned to the forefront of the political scene. Events moved quickly. On 1 November, he was recalled to Beijing by the imperial court and then accepted the positions of prime minister and generalissimo of the armed forces. He was mandated to form a reform government acceptable to both the revolutionaries and the mandarins of the imperial regime. Yuan Shi Kai had the loyalty of the northern army and tried to form a cabinet reconciling all parties. Negotiating with the leader of the Wuchang revolution, General Li Yuan, he tried to form a constitutional monarchy with the Manchu boy emperor, Puy Yi, as a figurehead. The senate was given forty-eight hours to draw up a constitution, which was adopted by an imperial edict of nineteen articles, on 3 November, replacing the imperial autocracy with a constitutional monarchy. But it was too little, too late. Revolutionaries of the Tong Meng Hui, led by a Sun Yat Sen ally named Chen Qimei, took over Shanghai with the support of local merchants and the police. By 5 November, the cities of Hangchow, Suchow and Shanghai had passed to the revolutionaries.

There was a divide between the northern provinces, which were traditionally more conservative and supportive of the Manchu monarchy, and the southern provinces where modernisation movements had combined with Han nationalists to oppose the northern Manchus. The notion of a constitutional monarchy was accepted by most of the northern provinces, but not by the southern provinces who now wanted an end to monarchy and its replacement by a republic. On 4 December, a truce of fifteen days was agreed, and Yuan Shi Kai called for a peace conference. On 6 December he gave an ultimatum to his nemesis, Prince Chun, and obtained Chun's abdication as regent, replacing him with Dowager Empress Longyu, consort of the late emperor. Two guardians were assigned to the boy emperor – one a Manchu and the other a Han Chinese – thereby signifying the end of Manchu exclusive control.

On 18 December the peace conference, also called the North-South Conference, was held in Hangchow, and the truce was extended. Six foreign powers – Britain, the United States, Russia, France, Germany, and Japan – were represented, and an agreement was hammered out. Yuan Shi Kai returned to Beijing, where he persuaded the imperial family to leave the city for its own safety, which it did on 28 December. On the following day, leaders from fourteen secessionist provinces met in Nanjing, and unanimously elected Sun Yat Sen as President of the Republic of China. On 1 January 1912, the new Republic of China was formally declared in Nanjing. Sun Yat Sen was inaugurated as president. He would go down in history as the founder of the republic.

Aftermath

The Republic of China was declared but the Qing dynasty was still formally in place. With the support of Yuan Shi Kai, pressure was exerted on the imperial family to abdicate. Two weeks later, on 17 January, Yuan was ambushed in a bomb attack in Beijing, organised by Tong Meng Hui revolutionaries. Ten of Yuan's guards were killed, but he was not seriously injured. Yuan sent a message to the revolutionaries pledging his loyalty to them. On the same day, a conference of princes was held at the palace to discuss the situation. On 22 January, Sun Yat Sen announced that he had agreed to resign the presidency in favour of Yuan Shi Kai if the general could secure the emperor's abdication. Yuan then told the imperial family that their lives would be saved if the emperor abdicated before the revolutionaries reached Beijing. The imperial family debated internally, then agreed. On 12 February 1912, the dowager empress formally announced the abdication of Puy Yi, the boy emperor, aged six, and the last of the Manchu dynasty. An official edict was published three days later, and the foreign legations were informed of the change of government.

One day after the abdication of the emperor and the end of the Manchu dynasty, Sun Yat Sen resigned as president of the new Republic of China. Yuan Shi Kai had emerged as the strong man of China. On 14 February 1912, he was elected president. On the same day, however, the provisional senate voted to make Beijing the capital rather than Nanjing. Sun Yat Sen immediately stated that one of the conditions of his deal with Yuan Shi Kai had been broken. Negotiations over the place of the capital led to a new agreement by Yuan Shi Kai to move to Nanjing. But riots and fire broke out across Beijing, allegedly started by an officer loyal to Yuan Shi Kai, who then argued he had to stay in Beijing, which was his power base, to prevent further unrest. On 10 March, he was inaugurated in Beijing as President of the Republic.

While in China, the American adventurer Homer Lea suffered a near-fatal stroke, which left him partially paralysed, and he returned to California, where he died.[49] Meanwhile, in the southern province of Hunan, the farmer's son named Mao Tse Tung, now a young man of eighteen, had joined the rebel army in the city of Changsha, capital of Hunan province. But when Yuan Shi Kai became president, Mao left the army and studied to be a teacher.

Sun Yat Sen's Tong Meng Hui was transformed into a political party, the Kuomintang (also known as the KMT or Chinese Nationalist Party), in order to contest the first elections for the new National Assembly. Sun Yat Sen appointed Song Jiao Ren, a young legal scholar and activist who had drafted the provisional constitution, as leader of the new party.[50] Only thirty years old, Song Jiao Ren proved to be a skilled political organiser. More than 300 parties competed in the elections in December 1912 and January 1913, but the Kuomintang won the most seats, just short of a majority in both the house of representatives and the senate.[51] Song campaigned across China to protect the powers and independence of the elected assemblies from the influence of the new president, and he openly and vehemently opposed the ambitions of Yuan Shi Kai. With the clear victory of the Kuomintang at the elections in early 1913, Song was certain to become prime minister.

However, on 20 March 1913, he was shot twice at close range at Shanghai railway station, and he died two days later. The trail of evidence led to the provisional premier of Yuan Shi Kai's government. The main conspirators investigated by authorities were either themselves assassinated or mysteriously disappeared.

With the assassination of Song Jiao Ren the political climate degenerated. Yuan Shi Kai ejected the Kuomintang from the elected assemblies. Sun Yat Sen tried unsuccessfully to organise a revolt against him. But with the failure of this new revolt in July 1913, Sun Yat Sen was again forced to seek asylum in Japan. Kang You Wei returned to China as Sun Yat Sen left, settling in Shanghai with his wives. He also joined the campaign to thwart the monarchical ambitions of the general. Yuan Shi Kai dissolved the assemblies in 1914 and declared himself emperor in 1915. By then, however, power in China was divided among regional warlords. The revolution had been betrayed. China was racked by civil war.

Yuan Shi Kai died of kidney failure in 1916 at the age of fifty-six. Sun Yat Sen returned to Guangzhou the following year and formed a military government in Guangdong province. Meanwhile Kang You Wei, in line with his idea of a constitutional monarchy, briefly supported an abortive attempt by some scholars to restore the Qing Emperor, to replace the usurper Yuan. Finally, he came to support the idea of a republic and even drafted a proposal for a constitution. But by then, none of the competing factions paid him attention. Kang Tong Bi, the American-educated daughter of Kang You Wei, returned to China soon after the revolution. She organised the various Shanghai women's groups into a united Shanghai Women's Association, which petitioned the nationalist government in Nanjing for a new constitution, with the slogan: 'Down with warlords and up with equality between men and women.'[52]

Sun Yat Sen continued as leader of the government in the south. Although he and Kang were now geographically close again, as they had been as young boys, there is no record that they ever met.

In 1919, student demonstrations broke out again in Beijing over terms of the Treaty of Versailles, ending World War I, which allowed Japan to take possession of Chinese territories previously occupied by German troops. Sun Yat Sen continued to strive for national unity, advocating military action from his base in the south while seeking negotiations with the warlords in the north. After travelling to Beijing in 1925 to hold peace talks with the northern regional leaders on the unification of China, he died there on 12 March, at the age of fifty-eight.

Kang You Wei continued to oppose both the warlords in the north and Sun Yat Sen's provisional government in the south. He called for the preservation of the best of China's heritage and the reform of Confucianism, publishing his last book *The Heavens*, before his death in Shandong two years after Sun Yat Sen, in 1927.

The next chapter in the story of China's revolution would be written in the epic struggle between Mao Tse Tung's communists and the Kuomintang nationalists of Chiang Kai Shek. Both would claim Sun Yat Sen as father of the nation. Both would claim their intellectual heritage from Kang You Wei. Meanwhile, Vladimir Ilych Lenin, by then living in the Polish province of Galicia, had been following the Chinese Revolution closely.

Chapter 5

The Russian Revolution

In November 1911, as Sun Yat Sen journeyed back to Shanghai and his destiny as first president of the Republic of China, there was great excitement within the imperial family of Russia. Grand Duchess Olga Nikolaevna, eldest daughter of Tsar Nicholas II, was about to turn sixteen. It was time for her debut into society. Already, high society buzzed with speculation about her marriage prospects, which could strengthen the links between the Romanovs of Russia and other royal families across Europe. A great ball was planned for her birthday in mid-November.

Violence at the opera

Yet, just a few weeks earlier, a violent event had revealed the deep tensions welling up within the vast Russian Empire, and Olga had witnessed it at first hand. On 14 September, she accompanied her father, the tsar, and her younger sister Tatiana, to the opera in Kiev. The imperial family had travelled to Kiev after the inauguration of their new Summer Palace in Yalta on the Crimean Peninsula. After the first intermission, as the tsar and his daughters returned to the imperial box in the front balcony of the opera house, a shot was fired among the people returning to their seats just below them. Pyotr Stolypin, the strong man of the Russian Empire, who had recently resigned as prime minister, and was considering a request by the tsar to return to power, was shot. There was tremendous commotion and confusion in the audience. Badly wounded, Stolypin was rushed to hospital. The next day, a distressed Tsar Nicholas knelt at his bedside, repeating over and over again: 'Forgive me.' Stolypin died three days later. Nicholas wrote to his mother, Dowager Empress Marie: 'Olga and Tatiana had followed me back to the box and saw everything that happened ... Tatiana cried a lot, and they both slept badly.'[1]

The assassination of Stolypin paved the way for the revolution that would sweep the Romanov dynasty from power. Like millions of their fellow Russians, they had only a few years to live. But in November 1911, even after the assassination of his most loyal political supporter, the tsar and his family remained oblivious to the fate awaiting them.

A new palace

Two years earlier, in 1909, the tsar and Tsarina Alexandra had gone to Italy, where they were captivated by the Renaissance palaces shown to them by Victor Emmanuel III. Returning to Russia, they engaged Yalta's most fashionable architect to design a brand new imperial palace. The tsar's personal diary recorded that the design was much discussed in the imperial family. The two palaces on the Yalta site, where Nicholas's father, Alexander III, had died were demolished to make way for a new palace, even though they had been built only a few decades earlier. While the construction of the new Livadia Palace was underway, Nicholas and Alexandra travelled to Potsdam, near Berlin, as guests of their cousin Wilhelm, the German Kaiser. The ball given in their honour in the flamboyant Sans Souci palace, built in the Rococo style, was said to rival those given by the tsar at the Winter Palace in St Petersburg. These balls were renowned among the great families of Europe for being 'unbelievably lavish, with as many as 3,000 aristocratic guests flaunting their wealth, dressed in colourful uniforms and magnificent gowns, sparkling with jewels and decorations'.[2] Such was the extravagance of the imperial families and aristocrats of Europe in the time before the storm clouds of war gathered over the continent.

Nicholas and Alexandra decided that the debut of their eldest daughter should be marked by a great ball in the new palace on 16 November, her sixteenth birthday. Olga wore a resplendent pink gown. Her hair was put up for the first time. Her parents gave her a diamond ring and a pearl necklace with diamonds as birthday presents, and as a symbol that she had become a young woman.[3]

The imperial family and their guests from the aristocracy danced away the night. Perhaps some of those present sensed that the recent assassination of the reformist Pyotr Stolypin was the harbinger of darker days to come. But nobody wanted to show their foreboding. So, they danced on.

Pyotr Stolypin

Pyotr (Peter) Stolypin was born in 1862 in Dresden, Germany, where his father served as Russian envoy. His forebears had served the tsars of Russia since the sixteenth century. One of his grandfathers had commanded the Kremlin Palace Guard, the other had commanded the Russian infantry during the Crimean War of 1853 to 1856 and was later governor-general of Warsaw in Poland. The Crimean War had to be seen in the context of what was described as the 'Great Game', a decades-long contest between the British and Russian empires for influence in Persia, Afghanistan, and the Middle East. As the Ottoman Empire weakened, the British wanted to stop further expansion of the Russians to the east and the south. The modernisers of Victorian Great Britain were intent on defending their interests in India and expanding trade, while the traditionalists of tsarist Russia saw opportunities to expand the Russian Empire. British and French commercial and strategic interests in the Middle East played an important part in the political calculations, and the powers were also influenced by disputes over the holy places in Palestine.

France under Napoléon III joined with Britain and Sardinia, forerunner of the kingdom of Italy, to oppose Russia, and all became bogged down in the Crimean Peninsula on the Black Sea. Out of this terrible war came legends such as the heroic work of Florence Nightingale, who pioneered modern nursing, and the charge of the Light Brigade. The latter popularised by the epic poem by Alfred Tennyson. The Treaty of Paris in 1856 brought the war to an end, with clauses requiring the Tsar of Russia and the Sultan of the Ottomans to refrain from establishing naval or military arsenals on the Black Sea Coast.

In the aftermath of the humiliation of this defeat, there were calls in the aristocratic circles of the Russian Empire to speed up the pace of modernisation. Five years earlier, a railway line had been opened from St Petersburg to Moscow, after ten years of construction and heavy loss of life among the serf labourers, and by the end of the Crimean War work was underway on a line to Warsaw. During the Springtime of the Peoples,

200,000 Russian cavalry troops had moved on horseback across Poland to Warsaw, then were loaded onto trains to Vienna, from where they helped the Habsburgs put down the Hungarian revolt of 1848.

The railway link to Western Europe was seen as having both military and economic importance. But efforts to catch up with the West were not straightforward. On the other side of the Atlantic, in the United States, railways had extended westwards beyond the Ohio River but had not yet reached the Rocky Mountains or the west coast. There was intense speculation in railway stock, and when the speculative bubble burst, the panic spread to Britain, then to continental Europe. The 1857 panic has been described as the world's first international financial crisis, and Russia was also affected. By 1862, the railroad from St Petersburg to Warsaw was finally completed. From that time, railways increasingly linked Russia to the rest of Europe, and in the following decades the Russian railway network would also extend all the way to the far east.

As Russia drew closer to Western Europe, there was increasing advocacy for liberal reforms. In March 1861, Tsar Alexander II issued his famous proclamation for the emancipation of the serfs. As prominent aristocrats in Russia, the Stolypin family owned vast estates, so their serfs were freed. But in practice little changed in the lives of the labourers on these and other estates. All this happened just before Pytor Stolyin's birth in 1862. A little later, in 1863, a workers' uprising broke out in Poland, where Pyotr's grandfather represented the tsar. Further to the west, there were rumblings among the labourers in the cities of Europe. Intellectuals in Russia and elsewhere questioned the established order. While Stolypin was just a young boy, developments across Europe began to sow the seeds of the revolution that he would try to forestall as Russia's prime minister several decades later.

Political developments in Europe up to 1870 have been described in Chapter 3, and Chapter 4 referred to the influence of these political debates on the young men sent from Asia to study in Europe, as Japan and China endeavoured to modernise; Japan doing so with greater success. In the early 1870s there were strikes in Russia but no recognised organisations of workers. In the West, however, an ideological struggle was underway between reformists who sought to organise labourers and influence parliaments, and revolutionaries who advocated overthrow of the entire economic system. By 1872, trade unions were legalised in Britain, and they developed in other industrialising countries, notably Germany and France. Much has been written about the tortuous ideological debates that were pursued through such bodies as the International Workingmen's Association, mentioned in the previous chapter, which became known as the First International. We will see in this chapter that the scene was being set for the emergence of Bolshevism. When the International met for the fifth time in 1872 in The Hague, it split into two factions, one led by Marxists, the other by anarchists.[4]

During these years, young Pyotr Stolypin grew up on his family's main estate near Moscow, then moved to Vilnius, now the capital of Lithuania, then to Oryol, where his teacher described him as 'standing out among his peers for his rationalism and character'.[5] At the age of nineteen, Stolypin went to St Petersburg to study agriculture at the capital's prestigious university under teachers such as the famous scientist Dmitri Mendeleev. Early that year, in April 1881, Tsar Alexander II was assassinated by an anarchist movement called the People's Will, almost exactly twenty years to the day after his signing of the emancipation decree. In a major setback for reforms, his son and successor, Alexander III, immediately cancelled his father's reforms and re-asserted autocratic rule. The recently created Russian secret police was strengthened, becoming the basis for the future Okhrana.

In 1884, while Pyotr Stolypin was still at university, events occurred that would reveal the character of this able young man. Stolypin's older brother, Mikhail, was killed in a duel. In those days the code of honour among aristocratic young Russian men could lead to duels with swords or pistols. Pyotr immediately challenged his brother's killer to another duel, with pistols. Pyotr survived but was shot in his right hand, which was paralysed from that time on. Mikhail had been engaged to a young woman, Olga, from a family of similar standing in the aristocracy. Pyotr proposed marriage to Olga, and they were married before he graduated, which was highly unusual in those times.

Graduating in 1885, Stolypin joined the civil service, like his father before him. An early assignment was in the Kovno region, now in Lithuania, and not far from the manor built by his father, which would remain Pyotr's favourite residence for the rest of his life. He was promoted rapidly, rising to the rank of state councillor in 1901. By then, he and Olga had four daughters.[6]

In 1902, after several years of a satisfying civil service career and happy family life, Stolypin was thrust into the centre of the political turbulence surging across the Russian Empire. He was appointed firstly as the youngest governor ever to the province of Grodno, and then, less than a year later, he was assigned to be governor of one of the poorest and most rebellious provinces in the country – the province of Saratov, on the Volga river.

Vladimir Ilyich Ulyanov (Lenin)

As Pyotr Stolypin rose through the civil service, another brilliant student was following a radically different path. Vladimir Ilyich Ulyanov (who would later be known to the world as Lenin) was born in 1870 to a wealthy middle-class family in the city of Simbirsk, on the banks of the Volga River, southeast of Moscow.[7] When Vladimir was sixteen, his father died of a stroke.[8] Four months later the young man experienced a defining moment that set him on his path as a revolutionary. His older brother was executed by the tsarist regime. Alexander Ulyanov, known as Sasha, had gone to St Petersburg to study natural sciences at the State University. There he engaged in illegal meetings and demonstrations with the most militant faction of the same People's Will movement that had killed Alexander II. In 1887, Sasha was a leader of an assassination attempt against the new tsar, Alexander III.[9] But the conspirators were infiltrated by agents of the secret police, and they were arrested before they could put their plan into action. Sasha was sent to trial, where he made a dramatic political speech. The tsar pardoned some of the conspirators, but Sasha and other leaders were executed by hanging. At the time, young Vladimir was taking his final school examinations. Despite the double trauma of his father's death and brother's execution, it was a sign of his determination and brilliance that he graduated with honours. The death of his older brother strengthened his commitment to revolution.

Vladimir enrolled at Kazan Imperial University, while living with his mother, Maria. Within months he was expelled for participating in protests against the tsarist regime, and he was sent back to the family estate. There he read voraciously. Through his mother's influence he was permitted to return to Kazan but joined a revolutionary circle where, like Sasha, he discovered the writings of Karl Marx. His mother had the resources to buy another estate in the hope of interesting her son in farm management. But Vladimir showed little interest in agriculture and they moved to the city of Samara, where he again joined a revolutionary circle. He translated *The Communist Manifesto* into Russian from the original German. Already, Vladimir could read and speak German, French and English, as well as his native Russian.

Again, through his mother's influence, he was allowed to take exams externally through the St Petersburg Imperial University, where he graduated with first class honours in law at the age of twenty. He began work as a legal clerk, firstly in Samara, before moving to St Petersburg in 1893. All the while, he continued his intense participation in revolutionary cells and discussion circles. In one such circle, Vladimir met his future wife, Nadezhda Krupskaya, the daughter of an impoverished military officer and nobleman. Her father had been decommissioned from the army and had found work in factories. Her mother, the daughter of landless nobles, had worked as a governess for noble families. The parents ensured that their daughter received the best possible education, sending her to Prince Obolensky's Female Gymnasium in St Petersburg, which provided a more liberal education than most. After her father's death, both Nadezhda, known as Nadya, and her mother gave lessons, their only source of income. She was particularly drawn to Leo Tolstoy's theories on education, and she studied many of his works.[10]

In October 1894, Tsar Alexander III died in Livadia, near Yalta. His son, aged twenty-six, was consecrated as Tsar Nicholas II with the title Emperor and Autocrat of all the Russias. Three weeks later, the young tsar married Princess Alix of Hesse and Rhine in Germany, a granddaughter of Queen Victoria of Britain. Converting from Lutheranism she was received into the Russian Orthodox Church as Tsarina Alexandra. At the very same time, Vladimir Ulyanov was leading a Marxist workers' circle in St Petersburg, carefully covering his tracks, as he knew that police spies were trying to infiltrate such groups. He authored a political tract and had 200 copies printed illegally.

Financed by his mother, Vladimir travelled to Switzerland. While there he met with Russian émigrés and fellow Marxists, including Georgi

Plekhanov and Pavel Axelrod. He went to Paris to meet Marx's son-in-law. He was keen to research the Paris Commune of 1871, which had governed the French capital for a time after the downfall of Louis Napoléon III and the declaration of the Third French Republic. As in 1848, the uprising of 1871 had been put down by republican forces with heavy casualties, but Ulyanov believed it provided an early prototype for a proletarian government. After staying at a Swiss health spa, he moved to Berlin, where he studied for six weeks at the state library and met other Marxists.

Returning to Russia with a case loaded with illegal revolutionary publications, he travelled to various cities distributing tracts to striking workers. Back in St Petersburg he produced a news sheet called *Rabochee Delo (Workers' Cause)*. In early 1896, along with forty other activists, he was arrested and charged with sedition. He was denied bail and held without trial. Shortly afterwards the formal coronation of Nicholas II – some eighteen months after his accession – was held in the Kremlin in Moscow. It was marked by tragedy. Some 100,000 citizens of Moscow were invited to a military training ground called Khodynka Field on the outskirts of the city for a festival with free beer and food in honour of the tsar. In a movement of panic, thousands fell into trenches and were trampled or crushed, leaving 1,400 people dead and as many injured. Informed of the tragedy, the tsar and tsarina nevertheless attended a gala ball given in their honour at the French Embassy. For Ulyanov and his fellow agitators, the tsar's decision to dance away the night as people were dying was further proof of the indifference of the imperial autocracy to the wellbeing of ordinary citizens. The parallel with the fireworks tragedy in Paris more than a century earlier, after the wedding of the future Louis XVI and Marie-Antoinette, was striking, for both monarchs would lose their lives after being overthrown by revolution.

Then it was the turn of Nadya to be arrested, in August 1896, for organising a strike. By February 1897, after a year in prison without trial, Vladimir learnt that he would be sentenced to three years of exile in Siberia. He managed to send a secret note to Nadya, delivered by her mother. His message was that she would be allowed to join him in Siberia if she told the authorities that she was his fiancée. A year later, permission for her to join Vladimir in Siberia was granted, on the condition that they would be married as soon as she arrived. Vladimir's mother and sisters were already with him in Siberia, and Nadya travelled with her mother. Vladimir and Nadya were married in the presence of their families in July 1898. The tsarist government considered the young couple to be only a minor threat, and Vladimir was able to correspond freely with other revolutionaries. Several of them visited him, and they could go on trips together to swim in the Yenisei River or to go duck-hunting. Meanwhile, the couple translated Marxist literature from English or German into Russian, and Vladimir wrote a book promoting a Marxist analysis of Russian economic development.

With the end of their exile in Siberia in 1900, Vladimir moved firstly to Pzoz near the Estonian border, then to Leipzig in Germany, then back to Switzerland, where in the village of Corsier alongside the lake in the canton of Geneva, he met other Russian Marxists. There he launched the newspaper *Iskra (Spark)*, the name of which was taken from a line by an earlier revolutionary poet, Alexander Odoevsky – 'one spark will start a flame'. He continued publishing *Iskra* as he moved to Munich, where Nadya joined him, working as his personal secretary Then, with the Bavarian police on their heels, the couple moved to London. Vladimir first used the pseudonym Lenin in December 1901, with the name thought to have been taken from the river Lena in Eastern Siberia. In 1902, under the name of Lenin, he published the political pamphlet *What is to be done?* which proposed a vanguard to lead the proletariat to revolution. It was his most influential publication to date and had a significant impact among revolutionary exiles.

Although the memoirs of Nadya later gave precious insights into the future Bolshevik leader's years of activism and exile, little was revealed about their personal lives. Nadya is believed to have suffered from Graves' disease, a thyroid condition that might have caused infertility, and the couple never had children. Their life-long relationship was driven by their shared political commitment. In her memoirs, Nadya wrote: 'With him, even such a job as translation was a labour of love.'[11]

In London Lenin met Leon Trotsky, who had changed his name from Lev Bronstein. Trotsky became one of the main writers for *Iskra*. With other Russian exiles, in 1903 they convened the second conference of the Russian Social Democratic Labour Party (RSDLP), which had been founded five years earlier in Minsk. At the conference there were fierce debates over party discipline and freedom of expression. Lenin had the majority with him, taking the Russian word for majority, *bolshevik,* as the name for his faction. Those in the minority, led by Julius Martov, a Jewish Marxist intellectual, were called the Mensheviks; they argued for alliance with liberal bourgeois reformers in Russia. Feelings ran high. Lenin angrily denounced the Mensheviks, calling them opportunists looking for ways to strike deals with the authorities. His opponents accused him of being a despot, citing his repeated calls for the enforcement of internal discipline in support of revolution.

To Lenin's surprise, Trotsky, and most of the other *Iskra* editors, sided with Martov and the Mensheviks, and Lenin lost his control of the paper's editorial board. Furious with Trotsky, Lenin called him a judas, a swine and a scoundrel. Returning to his writing desk, he quickly wrote a tract entitled *One step forward, two steps back*, attacking the Mensheviks. He became ill from stress and went hiking in the Swiss Alps to recover. Upon his return to London, his Bolshevik allies had succeeded in taking control of the RSDLP Central Committee and he launched a new newspaper with their support called *Vpered (Forward)*.

This was the scene among the exiled Russian activists by the end of 1904. It was not unlike the factional struggles going on around the same time among Chinese exiles. As we saw in the previous chapter, Kang You Wei finally entered the United States around this time and visited cities across the continent before heading south to Mexico to build support for his reform movement, while Sun Yat Sen and his allies continued to move around the Chinese overseas communities agitating for revolution.

By these early years of the twentieth century, political activists in exile, whether Russian or Chinese, could move across continents and oceans, organising their followers, printing pamphlets and newspapers, and raising funds. Ideas for change knew no boundaries, and there was no more striking example than the influence of the great Russian author, Leo Tolstoy, on the future father of Indian independence. For on the southern tip of the African continent, Mohandas Gandhi, a young London-trained lawyer in the Indian migrant community, established his first ashram, named Phoenix Settlement, based on his reading of Tolstoy's proposals for non-violent opposition to repression, with strategies for change that were diametrically opposed to those of Lenin and his Bolsheviks.

Bloody Sunday

Meanwhile, in Russia, an event that came to be known as Bloody Sunday shook the imperial dynasty. Discontent had been brewing across Russia among both the peasants and urban workers, when violence erupted in St Petersburg on 9 January 1905.[12] As we saw in the previous chapter, Russia by then was at war with Japan in the east. The war was increasingly unpopular. A wave of strikes had occurred, closing down most factories in the capital and cutting electricity. An organisation of workers, the Assembly of Russian Workingmen, authorised by the police, was set up by a priest of the Orthodox Church, Father Georgy Gapon. There were shadowy manoeuvres behind the scenes. It turned out later that Gapon was not only a police informer, but had also received funding for his organisation from a Japanese spymaster named Colonel Akashi Motojiro, based as a military attaché in Helsinki. In early January, on a day when the sun came out to shine on the snow-covered streets, Gapon organised a mass demonstration of workers and their families, followed by a march to the Winter Palace to present the tsar with a petition appealing for his support of working people. Some 200,000 workers and their families took part, dressed in their Sunday best clothes, and many carrying religious icons and portraits of the tsar to show their loyalty. The commander of the Palace Guard, an uncle to the tsar, tried to stop the peaceful demonstrators. Then, as Gapon and the other leaders defied his calls to halt the march, the commander ordered his police to fire into the crowd. As people recoiled in shock, he sent Cossack cavalry troops to ride repeatedly into the demonstrators, slashing with their swords. Gapon survived by quickly changing out of his priest's robes and taking refuge with the writer Maxim Gorky, a personal friend of Lenin. The number of deaths on Bloody Sunday was estimated to be up to a thousand, with many hundreds more wounded.

A young law school graduate had begun his professional career by giving free legal advice to poor urban workers in the capital. His name was Alexander Kerensky, and after the massacre of Bloody Sunday he joined a committee set up to aid the victims and their families. Kerensky was born in the same city as Lenin, Simbirsk, but was eleven years younger. The two men's families were friends. Vladimir's father was an inspector of schools and Alexander's father was principal of the high school attended by Vladimir. Kerensky senior taught the young Vladimir Ulyanov, and became an early mentor to the brilliant young student. In one of those twists of destiny that are to be found so often in the histories of the five revolutions, the student would one day overthrow the government of his former teacher's son.

The uprisings of 1905

The hardliners of the tsarist regime had badly miscalculated with their actions on Bloody Sunday, which became the catalyst for uprisings that shook the empire. Strikes swept the country, trains stopped running, banks closed, peasants revolted against their landlords, and industries were paralysed. Mutinies broke out in the armed forces, and universities closed as students staged walkouts. By April, liberal reformers had begun to organise themselves to confront the regime politically. Lawyers, doctors, engineers, teachers, and other middle-class professionals established the Union of Unions, and called on the Workingmen's Organisations to join them in a reform movement. Meeting together, they advocated the creation of a constituent assembly elected by universal suffrage. Meanwhile, local governments from across the country, called Demistovs, met in a National Congress, and supported the call for reform. In both bodies, there were fierce confrontations between radicals, who favoured revolution to overthrow the imperial regime, and liberals who argued for reform. The pattern of conflict between revolutionaries and reformers was essentially the same as we have seen in the lead up to each of the other revolutions – from the American through the French revolutions to the Springtime of the Peoples across Europe to the Chinese Revolution. In Russia, the revolutionaries agitated in support of the radicals within both the Union of Unions and the National Congress of Demistovs. In Moscow that August, secret meetings were held to found the All-Russian Peasant Union. In Tatarstan and other Muslim communities across the southern regions of Eurasia, demands grew for autonomy.

As peasant uprisings and workers' strikes spread across the empire, Pyotr Stolypin gained a reputation as the only governor able to keep a firm hand on his province. Stolypin believed that nobility of birth and sheer force of character would prevail against any protestors. Tall and handsome, his style was autocratic, even disdainful, always calm, and in control of every situation. His daughter, Maria, wrote: 'I have an amateur photo with my father riding his horse right into the crowd that moments earlier was in a frenzy and now everyone was on his knees. All the 10,000 dropped to their knees at the first words my father said.'[13]

Stolypin inspected rebellious areas unarmed and without bodyguards. During one of these inspections he experienced his first assassination attempt, when a bomb was dropped at his feet. Somehow, he survived unscathed. Behind this bravado, Stolypin had a method. Firstly, he cooperated closely with the local governments, the zemstva, listening carefully to grievances of the local peasants and their communities. Secondly, he was strict in preventing any form of corruption. Thirdly, he used what were then modern and innovative police techniques to detect and neutralise potential threats. It was said that he had a police file on every adult male in the province.[14] He would apply these same methods in his later attempts to reform the Russian economy.

Disaster in the East

As rebellion swept across the vast tsarist lands from Europe to Asia, disaster struck the Russian navy in the ongoing war with Japan at the eastern end of the empire in Asia. In 1902, Britain and Japan had signed an alliance which, while not mentioning Russia, was intended to constrain expansion of the tsar's empire in the east. Japan had never accepted having to give up the fortified Port Arthur, which was then leased by Russia, and objected to the tsar's railway projects on the peninsula. Japanese Prime Minister Itō Hirobumi tried to negotiate the withdrawal of some 100,000 Russian troops from Manchuria, where they had remained since the defeat of the Boxer Rebellion in China. In early 1904, these negotiations reached an impasse and diplomacy was over, replaced by the drumbeat of war. The Japanese imperial fleet attacked the Russian Far East fleet and captured Port Arthur. After the fall of the strategic port, the Japanese army moved northward in Manchuria. As winter ended, the Russian and Japanese land forces engaged each other at the Battle of Mukden. By March 1905, the Russians had lost 90,000 men.

Before the fall of Port Arthur the tsar had sent his Baltic fleet with orders to relieve the Russian garrison there. Denied access to the Suez Canal by the British, the Russian fleet took the long route around Africa.

The fleet of coal-fuelled steamers took seven months to travel halfway around the world via the Cape of Good Hope. In Madagascar off the Indian Ocean coast of Africa the Russian admiral learnt that Port Arthur had fallen. Steaming on with dwindling coal supplies, the fleet headed instead for the eastern Russian port of Vladivostok through the Tsushima Strait between Korea and Japan. There, it was intercepted by the Japanese navy and destroyed. The Russian defeat on sea and land was total. This was the first defeat of a European power by an Asian country. It sent shock waves through the circles of power on the old continent.

Back in European Russia, morale within the military was low, and revolutionary agents were at work. In June, sailors mutinied over rotten meat on the battleship Potemkin in the Black Sea: They killed their officers and sailed to Romania. The mutiny entered into Bolshevik revolutionary legend.

The imperial dynasties of Russia and China had both suffered humiliating defeats by Japan. As in China, Russia experienced a succession of political crises, interspersed with arson attacks and riots in cities. Faced with the defeat in the east and the unpopularity of the war, Tsar Nicholas decided to sue for peace. Accepting an offer of mediation by American President Theodore Roosevelt, he sent a delegation to negotiate with Japan in Portsmouth, New Hampshire, in the United States. His representative was Sergei Witte, who had overseen the extension of railways, including the Trans-Siberian Railway, under the tsar's father, Alexander III. He had also expanded education and had undertaken currency reform. He negotiated brilliantly in Portsmouth, such that Russia lost little in the final agreement, despite its defeat in the war. Russia accepted the Treaty of Portsmouth, ending the war with Japan in September 1905. Roosevelt was awarded the Nobel Peace Prize the following year for his efforts. Even while negotiating in Portsmouth, Witte was writing to the tsar, advocating political reform at home.

The tsar was still inclined to listen to those in his court who advocated maintaining the traditional autocracy of the tsar as 'father of the nation' by pulling down the rebellions with military force. But when Witte returned, he was able to convince most of the aristocrats around the reluctant tsar to pressure him to accept liberal reforms. Witte was mandated to draft a manifesto announcing an initial set of institutional reforms, prior to the drafting of a first constitution for the Russian Empire. This document, called formally the Manifesto on the Improvement of the State Order, was issued by the tsar in October, and became known as the October Manifesto. Witte was tasked with its implementation, and was appointed Chairman of the Council of Ministers, the equivalent of prime minister.

The manifesto announced the creation of an elected lower house of parliament, called a Duma, while retaining an Imperial State Council as the upper house. The term Duma came from the Russian word 'to consider' and had originally been conceived as only a consultative body. But for the first time in Russian history this new elected Duma would have legislative powers. Deputies to the Duma would be elected indirectly by male citizens over twenty-five years of age through a complex system of four electoral colleges, weighted in favour of property owners. Women and soldiers were excluded from voting. Kerensky, the young lawyer who had represented victims of Bloody Sunday, and would later take high office in Russia, wrote later in his memoirs of his feelings when the tsar announced his constitutional reform: 'I spent the rest of that night in a state of elation. The age-long bitter struggle of the people for freedom ... seemed to be over. A wave of warmth and gratitude went through my whole being, and my childhood adoration for the tsar revived.'[15]

The revolutionaries did not share Kerensky's relief, nor his optimism. Some revolutionaries, among them Trotsky, were able to return to Russia, where they established workers' councils, called soviets, in the big cities. Still aligned with the Mensheviks at this point, Trotsky became the leader of the most important soviet in the capital, St Petersburg. During the six-week period after the release of the manifesto, called the Days of Freedom, there were meetings everywhere and political declarations of all kinds. Some soviets went further and formed militias, while calling for the overthrow of the regime. In December, Trotsky and other leaders of the St Petersburg Soviet were arrested. Lenin, still in exile and fiercely advocating revolution, wrote: 'The uprising has begun ... rivers of blood are flowing, the civil war for freedom is blazing.'[16]

The tsar and the aristocrats around him who had opposed the liberal reforms were alarmed by the new protests and uprisings, and launched a new wave of repression. The loss of life was high. In Moscow, there were more than a thousand deaths and parts of the city were left in ruins. The army swept across Russia, crushing dissent. In Vladivostok, rebels declared the creation of a republic. They too were crushed. By the time of the elections for the first State Duma, in March 1906, calm was restored but at great cost. An estimated 14,000 people had been killed and 75,000 were imprisoned.[17] The elections were boycotted by the Socialist Revolutionary Party, itself split into pro- and anti-Bolshevik factions. About 500 deputies were elected, with the two main parties being the moderate constitutional democrats, known as the Kadets, and a workers' party, which disagreed with the boycott of the revolutionaries, called the Trudoviks.

Stolypin, the conservative reformer

In the week before the convening of the Duma in late April 1906, the tsar issued a new constitution, called the Fundamental Laws which, while conceding legislative powers to the Duma, limited those powers by retaining his right to veto laws, to appoint ministers, and to dissolve the Duma itself. The tsar was confirmed as absolute leader with control of the executive branch of government, and of foreign policy, the Church, and the armed forces. Over a century earlier, Louis XVI of France had unsuccessfully tried similar strategies to retain autocratic powers at the General Estates in Versailles, but Necker's boycott of the king's speech and subsequent dismissal had set the scene for the French Revolution. Tsar Nicholas II of Russia and his court thought they could avoid the same fate by calling on a strong man to keep order. That man was Pyotr Stolypin, who was appointed interior minister before the State Duma convened at the end of April 1906. With his reputation for keeping firm control as governor of the province of Saratov, the tsar tasked Stolypin with re-establishing law and order throughout the empire. The tsar gave the opening speech at the Duma, much as Louis XVI of France had done in Versailles, setting out his authority in relation to the new parliament. In response, the Duma pushed for amnesty for political prisoners, political freedoms and, especially, land reforms. Frustrated, the tsar said: 'Curse this Duma. It is all Witte's fault.' After ten weeks, the tsar accepted the resignation of the government, dissolved the Duma, and appointed Stolypin as prime minister, while retaining him as interior minister. The joining of the two posts gave Stolypin unprecedented powers. Later he would use those powers to pursue agrarian reform on a grand scale, but initially he used them for repression.

Terrorist groups were targeting senior officials. A month after his appointment as prime minister, Stolypin held a public reception at his dacha on an island. Three revolutionaries attempted to assassinate him with bombs, blowing much of the villa to pieces, and killing twenty-eight people – among them, one of Stolypin's daughters, aged fifteen, who was standing with her young brother on the balcony. The three-year-old boy was slightly wounded. Stolypin survived with a few scratches. The tsar offered the family money for medical treatment. Stolypin refused, replying: 'Your majesty, my children's blood is not for sale.' He accepted, however, to move with his family into the Winter Palace, where they could have better protection.

In response to the assassination attempt, the government created a special martial court, with powers to execute, imprison or exile political dissidents. More than 1,000 men were executed by hanging. Stolypin said: 'I have grabbed the revolution by the neck, and I will strangle it, if I remain alive.' A member of the Duma called the hangings 'Stolypin neckties'. When challenged by Stolypin to a duel, he retracted, but the label stuck. As we will see, Stolypin would later be remembered for his attempted reforms, notably agrarian reform. But, his early political career in the imperial system was marked by a forceful stance on law and order. His high-handed approach to governing was widely detested. During his years in power, there were ten assassination attempts against him, nine of which failed. The tenth, shortly after he retired as prime minister, succeeded.

In 1907, as part of Stolypin's attempts at controlled reform, elections for the Duma were held again. The two factions of the RSDLP, the Bolsheviks and Mensheviks, decided to abandon their previous policy of boycott and won many seats, outnumbering the centrist party, the Kadets. After three months, and accusations by Stolypin that the social democrats were preparing to overthrow the government, this second Duma was dissolved like the first by an imperial decree, called a *ukaz*. With the Bolsheviks and Mensheviks in the ascendancy in the Duma, the tsar, supported by Stolypin, was even less inclined than before to cede power to the legislature. Stolypin worked on a plan to change the electoral system, undoing the reforms of Witte, giving greater electoral value to the votes of landowners and property owners in the cities, and less value to the votes of the peasants and workers. With these electoral changes, a new election was held. This third Duma lasted a full five-year term, from November 1907 until 1912. Because of the emphasis on a property-holding electorate it became known as 'the Masters' Duma'. In this third Duma, Stolypin introduced his grand plan for agrarian land reform.

Lenin the agitator

When the first Duma convened in April 1906, Lenin returned to Russia after an absence of five years. He played an active role in the agitation that preceded the elections for the second Duma. But as Stolypin dissolved the Duma and ordered a crackdown on revolutionaries, Lenin joined other dissidents in Finland. As Stolypin's strategy of reform and control began to take effect, support for Lenin's hard line diminished among the dissidents. Lenin's tactics, including what he called 'expropriation', which meant robbing banks, were condemned by many as being criminal. Stolypin ordered the tsarist secret police, the Okhrana, to reach into Finland, which was a semi-autonomous duchy of the Russian Empire. Two years later, Lenin sailed for Western Europe, using banknotes stolen from a bank in Georgia by a group of Bolsheviks led by a man named Joseph Stalin. Lenin would not return to Russia for another ten years.

Back in Switzerland, Lenin changed some of the stolen banknotes from Georgia. From there he went to Paris, which he described as 'a foul hole', then to Italy, where he took a vacation at Maxim Gorky's villa on Capri, and on to London. In the British Library, where Marx had written *Das Kapital*, Lenin wrote another of his many tracts, this time attacking a competing faction within the Bolsheviks. The Russian secret service even sent a double agent, Roman Malinovsky, to support Lenin, perceiving him to be a useful source of division amongst the revolutionaries opposed to the tsar. Lenin was also active in the second International of Socialist and Labour parties, attending the eighth congress in Copenhagen in 1910, before meeting his mother and sisters in Stockholm. He then moved back to Paris with Nadya.

In Paris, Lenin met Inessa Armand, a French woman who had grown up with her aunt and grandmother, both teachers, in Moscow. Marrying early into a wealthy Russian family of textile manufacturers, she and her husband founded a school for peasant children, and she was active in a charity for destitute women. Inessa joined the RSDLP, was arrested for distributing illegal propaganda and, like many others, was sent into exile in Siberia. In 1908, she escaped to Paris and met Lenin for the first time. Over the next two years their relationship deepened. Armand had five children, four with her husband, then one with his younger brother. She spoke Russian, French, German and English, and could hold her own in factional debates in any of those languages. She became Lenin's closest ally. At some point they became lovers.

The Stolypin reforms

Russia had been well behind the rest of Europe in ending feudalism. The concept of feudalism had been characterised by French writers like Montesquieu in his work *De L'Esprit des Lois* in 1748[18] and by Adam Smith in *The Wealth of Nations*, published in 1776, to describe the medieval system where peasants were bound to the landowning aristocracy. While the French Revolution of 1789 declared an end to feudalism in that country, the Russian peasants, the serfs, were bound to landowners until 1861, the year when Alexander II proclaimed the emancipation of the serfs. In the decades that followed, the peasants were theoretically free, but in practice they remained dependent on the landowners for their livelihoods and housing. Often, they were indebted, with little prospect of achieving real independence. These were the conditions underlying the peasant revolts that broke out periodically across the Russian Empire.

As the industrial revolution extended eastwards during the latter half of the nineteenth century, an urban working class developed in Russia, as it had in Western Europe over the previous half century. Railways were built, telegraph lines were constructed, armies and navies were modernised, books and newspapers were printed. The uprisings of 1905 began in the cities, notably St Petersburg and Moscow. The peasants, who had been part of earlier protests and uprisings, then joined.

During the first Duma of 1906, Stolypin had listened carefully to the claims for liberal reform and he observed the balance of forces among the elected representatives. During the second Duma of early 1907, by which time he had been named prime minister, he developed his thinking about a way out of the conundrum that afflicted the autocracy of the Romanov dynasty. As an aristocrat, he remained dedicated to the tsar as 'father of the nation'. As a graduate in agriculture, and with a record of success as a young provincial governor, he had become interested in agrarian reform. He came to the conclusion that the way forward was to distribute land to the landless peasants, thereby building a class of small landholders. Convinced that the peasants were inherently conservative, he believed that giving land to them would lay the foundation for stability in the provinces. He believed it would break the link between peasant discontent and urban agitation. After the third Duma was elected later in 1907 with a more restricted electorate, and with political parties of landowners and businessmen more supportive of the government, Stolypin moved forward his agenda for agrarian reform.

In pursuit of the concept of individual land ownership, the Stolypin government opened up lands in Siberia, particularly along the Trans-Siberian Railway. Stolypin had the support of the tsar, who personally chaired the Trans-Siberian Railway committee. Before succeeding his father as tsar, young Nicholas had inaugurated construction of the eastern section of the line in Vladivostok in 1891, after visiting Japan as part of a world tour. This tour occurred well before the disastrous Russo-Japanese war of 1904. Later, as tsar, he travelled the railroad to Vladivostok in his specially built imperial train.

The aim of Stolypin's reform was to transform the traditional *obshchina* or collective form of Russian agriculture. After the dissolution of the second Duma, in late 1907, Stolypin had the tsar issue a *ukaz* abolishing the *obshchina* system, and introducing the right of individual ownership of land. With the election of the third Duma a year later, he was able to pursue his reforms with a broad range of measures, which encouraged the development of large individual farms, new methods of land improvement, agricultural education, cooperatives and affordable credit for peasants through a peasant land bank. These modernising reforms were intended to lay the groundwork for a market-based agricultural system, in which the Russian peasants would become landowners and have a stake in stability. They included resettlement benefits for peasants who moved to Siberia, with grants of land and other incentives. Between 1907 and 1915, more than 2 million peasants became individual landowners in their home regions, while even more migrated to take up land in Siberia. Stolypin stated: 'Give peace to the State for twenty years, inside and outside the country, and you will not recognise today's Russia.' Yet implementation was slow in the vast empire, with a population of over 130 million.

Stolypin also undertook other steps to modernise Russia and to reform policy on nationalities. Like the Austro-Hungarian and Chinese empires, the Russian Empire encompassed a diversity of national, ethnic and religious groups. In the case of Russia, the dominant faith was Orthodox Christian and the tsar was defender of the Orthodox faith. Stolypin sought to provide more scope for participation by minority groups in local decision-making. In particular, he tried to improve relations with Russia's Jewish minority. After the assassination of Alexander II in 1861, those looking for scapegoats – including his son and successor, Alexander III – had singled out Jews, and many were killed in pogroms, which the authorities did little or nothing to prevent. During the upheavals of 1905 another wave of pogroms swept through cities and towns in Russian-controlled Poland and Lithuania, killing thousands and pushing many others to emigrate to the new world. With his control of the police, Stolypin put a stop to further outbreaks of mob violence against minorities.

Tolstoy opposes reform

Arguably the greatest of Russian writers, and a towering figure of nineteenth-century literature, Count Leo Tolstoy clashed vehemently with Stolypin over his reforms. Tolstoy had served with Stolypin's father during the Crimean War in the 1850s, so there were strong historical links between the two aristocratic families. As Stolypin introduced his proposal for individual land ownership in the Duma in July 1907, Tolstoy wrote to him proposing instead the ideas of Henry George, the American political economist, whose thinking also influenced Sun Yat Sen. The main tenet of Georgism was that the economic rent derived from land should be owned in common, and should belong to communities rather than individual title-holders.[19] He argued that a single tax on land values would enable society to recapture the value of its common inheritance and eliminate the need for taxes on productive activity, such as sales or trade, or income tax. Stolypin replied three months later: 'I do not reject the teachings of George, and I think that the single tax will, in time, help in the struggle against very large ownership of property, but now I do not see any purpose here in Russia of driving off the land the more developed class of landholders; but, on the contrary, I see the undoubted necessity of relieving the peasant by giving him the legitimate opportunity to acquire the piece of land he needs and granting him full ownership of it.'[20]

Tolstoy replied that Stolypin was seeking 'to pacify the population by destroying the commune in order to form small land holdings', adding, 'This mistake was tremendous.' He continued: 'You sought to pacify them by means of seducing them with the base, old, outworn concept of the relation of man to land.' Fellow writer, Fyodor Dostoyevsky, had disagreed with Tolstoy. 'If you want to transform humanity for the better ... give them land,'[21] he had written in the late nineteenth century.

Stolypin faced opposition from many quarters. He worked towards increasing the power of local governments, but the zemstva (communal councils) often came into conflict with the provincial authorities. Tolstoy thought that Stolypin was too concerned with modernising Russia by simply emulating Western Europe. In one letter he wrote to Stolypin: 'Stop your horrible activity! Enough of looking up to Europe, it is high time Russia knew its own mind.'[22] Tolstoy's position was remarkably similar to that of opponents to Kang You Wei in China. This was no coincidence. As we saw in Chapter 4, Tolstoy corresponded with Chinese intellectual Gu Hong Ming, who opposed Kang's reforms, recommending that China remain an agrarian nation, and warning against modernising reforms like those of Japan under the Meiji Restoration.[23] During the Boxer Rebellion in China, Tolstoy praised the rebels, and harshly criticised the Russian and German troops for atrocities, naming Tsar Nicholas and Kaiser Wilhelm of Germany as being responsible. Yet, like Sun Yat Sen, Tolstoy was enthused by the economic thinking of the American economist, Henry George. He even wrote a preface to George's *Social Problems*, and he explored his thoughts on George's theories in his 1899 novel *Resurrection*. The common feature of Tolstoy's interest in the American economist and the views of Chinese traditionalists like Gu Hong Ming was the question of the ownership of land.

As we mentioned earlier, Tolstoy also attracted the interest of a young Indian lawyer named Mohandas Gandhi, who was inspired by

Tolstoy's book *The Kingdom of God is Within You* (1893). Writing later in his own book *An Autobiography*, Gandhi stated that Tolstoy's reflections on non-violent resistance 'left an abiding impression on me'. From his Phoenix Settlement in South Africa, Gandhi published a biographical sketch of Tolstoy. The story of the Russian nobleman, who had fought in the Crimean War, achieved fame as a writer, and then gave up his wealth to live as a peasant, resonated with the young activist. In September 1906, he started a 'passive resistance' struggle by Indians against racial discrimination in the Transvaal of South Africa. When imprisoned in Volksrust jail, he presented his warder with a copy of Tolstoy's book: *The Kingdom of God is Within You*.[24]

Returning to London in 1909, Gandhi came across a copy of Tolstoy's essay: *Letter to a Hindoo*, written in reply to an Indian who advocated violence to overthrow oppression. Gandhi then wrote to Tolstoy about his experience with passive resistance in the Transvaal, asking for permission to translate and print copies of the essay. Sent from London in October 1909, Gandhi's typewritten letter – signed in the English style of the day, 'I am, Sir, your most obedient servant, M.G. Gandhi' – reached Tolstoy at his estate outside Moscow in a matter of days. Tolstoy replied on 7 October, in his own hand, in perfect English.[25] Gandhi translated *Letter to a Hindoo* into Gujarati, and wrote a preface while on the ship back to South Africa in November. The correspondence between Tolstoy and Gandhi continued for another year, until just before Tolstoy's death in November 1910. Gandhi wrote, 'In India we would have described him as a Maharishi' (Great Seer). So it was that the great author, whose prolific writings and personal odyssey were set in the turbulent years before the Russian Revolution, also inspired the man who would lead the independence movement of India. The future father of India would set in motion the process of decolonisation nearly a half-century later. As Gandhi sought his destiny, he drew upon the writings and correspondence of Tolstoy, whose immense body of novels and essays reflected his lifelong search for understanding of human affairs.

Born to an aristocratic family in 1828, Tolstoy first achieved literary acclaim in his twenties with *Sevastopol Sketches*, which was based on his experiences in the Crimean War, and was published in 1855. As a young man of noble birth, it was natural to participate in the military action of the day, which happened to be the Crimean War, one of many military conflicts among the European powers, and one with heavy human loss. Like Lamartine in France forty years earlier, he did what young men of his rank were expected to do, and like Lamartine he quickly questioned the sense of it all. By 1855, a few short years after the revolutions that swept across Europe in 1848, but without much impact on Russia, the Third Empire of Napoléon III was firmly entrenched in France with an assertive foreign policy, inclined to military adventures abroad. Russia lost the Crimean War to an alliance of the French, the British, and the Ottoman Turks.

In 1860 and 1861, Tolstoy travelled across Europe, meeting Victor Hugo as the French author worked on *Les Misérables*, which was published the following year. He also met the French anarchist, Pierre-Joseph Proudhon, of whom Tolstoy said later, 'He was the only man who understood the significance of education and of the printing press in our time.' Returning to the family estate of Yasnaya Polyana, Tolstoy founded schools for the children of peasants who had just been emancipated from serfdom by Tsar Alexander II's decree in 1861. His schools were closed by the tsarist police, but can be claimed to be direct forerunners of A.S. Neill's Summerhill School in England, based on a concept of democratic education.

In the years that followed, Tolstoy produced his masterpiece *War and Peace*, with its 250 characters pursuing their lives on the vast canvas of the Napoléonic war with Russia. The novel was set sixty years before Tolstoy's day, but he had talked with people who lived through Napoléon's invasion of Russia in 1812. Tolstoy began writing the novel at Yasnaya Polyana at the age of thirty-eight, in the year when he married Sofia (known as Sonia to her family and friends), who was sixteen years his junior. The first draft was completed within a year, then published as a series in a Russian periodical, firstly under the title *1805*, taken from the year when the narrative began. By 1869, when the entire work was published as a book, Tolstoy had taken the title *War and Peace* from an essay written by his anarchist friend Pierre-Joseph Proudhon in Brussels.[26] Covering the period from 1805 to 1812, *War and Peace* addresses the aftermath of the French Revolution and the rise of Napoléon Bonaparte with his ambition to conquer Europe. This great novel describes the impact of historic events on the lives of people, whether from the nobility or from the rural countryside, both milieu that Tolstoy knew well. In his philosophical reflections, Tolstoy questioned the notion of the great man, the context for momentous events, and the impact of sheer chance on the outcomes of battles and diplomacy.

In 1869, within a year of the full publication of *War and Peace*, Bonaparte's nephew, Napoléon III, weakened by a military adventure in Mexico, had been defeated in Alsace by the German Kaiser and Bismarck, and had gone into exile in Victorian Britain. The map of Europe was changed yet again with the cession of Alsace and Lorraine to Germany. In 1878, Tolstoy published *Anna Karenina*, which placed him with Victor Hugo at the pinnacle of writers of realist fiction. Yet there was also in this novel the influence of the romanticists, from Germaine de Staël and Byron to Lamartine and Alfred Tennyson, his English contemporary. *Anna Karenina* portrayed powerfully the hypocrisies and obsessions of a ruling elite, with vivid portrayals of the intrigues played out wherever the elite gathered, in coffee shops and gambling houses, or when they were on show at great balls or at the opera or the ballet.

As he wrote *Anna Karenina*, Tolstoy wrestled with moral issues and spirituality, which he revealed in 1880 in his short non-fiction work *A Confession*. The similarity of his experience with that of Kang You Wei in China some time earlier is striking, although as he plunged into Confucian philosophy, he opposed Kang's modernising approach. In 1894, Tolstoy published *The Kingdom of God is Within You*. It was banned in Russia, so it was first published in Germany. This is the book that had a profound effect on Mohandas Gandhi, and later on Martin Luther King, as he led the civil rights movement in America, seeking the fulfilment of the ideals of the American Revolution and its Declaration of 1776 'that all men are created equal'.

With Sonia, Tolstoy had thirteen children.[27] She was his secretary and proofreader and managed the family finances. As his moral questioning evolved, however, and as his ideas became more radical – many said eccentric – Tolstoy and Sonia grew apart, becoming estranged in his later years when he wanted to give away his properties and even his author's royalties. This was the ageing, eccentric and brilliant man who challenged Pyotr Stolypin's strategy of agrarian reform, based on individual ownership of land.

It is remarkable that this same man, Tolstoy, wove together the threads of events before and during his lifetime, across Europe, but also reaching to the other extremities of the globe, in China, in America, in South Africa and India. He vehemently opposed exploitation, yet just as firmly opposed the whole idea of violent revolution. His writing drew upon and stimulated the intellectual ferment of the times, spanning across the continents, while he sounded vigorous warnings about the direction of his homeland. His entire body of work may be considered as an exemplary description of warnings against 'dancing before storms'. Yet the warnings of Tolstoy were perhaps too readily dismissed as being the thoughts of an eccentric. At the end of his life Tolstoy decided to leave Sonia and Yasnaya Polyana. On 20 November 1910, at the age of eighty-two, he died from pneumonia in an obscure railway station. It was said that during his last hours on the train he continued to preach non-violence and Georgism.

Stolypin was concerned about popular sentiment being aroused with the news of Tolstoy's death. Vladimir Lenin praised Tolstoy's lifelong struggle against exploitation but he articulated a diametrically opposite philosophy for change. He rejected Tolstoy's philosophy of non-violence. For Lenin, change could only come through violent revolution. By 1911, the scene was set for what would become the Russian Revolution.

Conditions in Russia

Tolstoy's writings and activism centred on the peasantry of Russia's vast rural expanses. But the industrial revolution, reaching Russia some decades after spreading from Britain across Western Europe, had major consequences for both the cities and the rural populations. As in the West, the movement of rural labourers off the estates after the emancipation of 1861 meant that an urban working class developed. At the same time, the extension of railways and the telegraph connected the rural expanses to the cities.

The paradox was that even as Russia modernised, archaic practices were maintained. In the rural areas, farming practices had changed little from the centuries-old era of serfdom. Human labour remained the basis for farming. There was a veritable explosion of railway construction. But water transportation continued to be used to move goods into the rural areas and to move grain out, and the barges were mostly hauled by men pulling them along from the banks of canals.

There were also slow moves towards political modernisation. After freeing the serfs in 1861, Alexander II created provincial councils – the zemstva. The nobles possessed seventy-four per cent of the land, and most peasants continued to work for their former masters.[28] At the beginning of the twentieth century, peasants made up eighty-eight per cent of the population, the remainder being urban labourers, artisans, middle-class industrialists and traders, the liberal professions, clergy and functionaries.[29] Taxes were levied according to different criteria, and families were required to supply recruits for the army according to their designated complements of able-bodied men.[30] Living conditions were basic. Bread was the main staple. Practically every peasant household had a cow to supply milk, and a sheep to be shorn for wool to make clothes. Yet a recent study suggests that inequality in Russia on the eve of the 1905 revolution was not as great as it is in Russia today, nor as it is in the United States or in China today![31]

That being said, there was clearly a major gap between the ostentatious lifestyles of the aristocracy and the grinding poverty of the peasants and urban workers. Somewhere between these two extremes were the bourgeoisie – business and professional families. Russia was a male-dominated society with women playing roles in support of their spouses. The Russian elite wanted to catch up with the rest of Europe, which they saw first-hand as the railways opened up travel across the continent. The tsar and tsarina travelled across Europe, spending time especially visiting the royal families of Italy and Germany. Aristocrats and the *nouveau riche* of the rising entrepreneurial and merchant classes also travelled widely. The paradox of the aristocracy was a fervent desire for the modernisation they could see during their travels, while maintaining a stubborn commitment to the traditions of an imperial court. The language of communication with the rest of Europe was French – the language of diplomacy – and all upper-class Russians were taught French from childhood. The Slavic tradition was maintained through the Orthodox Church, drawing on mystical ideas of the Russian soul.

The great drive for industrialisation that marked the final decades of the nineteenth century meant that the imperial government turned to international capital markets. The epic railway construction projects, notably the Trans-Siberian Railway, which was the personal priority of Nicholas, were not possible without such financing. Thus, growing volumes of Russian debt were floated abroad, exposing the nation to speculation in bond markets, which was rampant at the time. This speculation gave rise to 'bubbles' followed by 'busts', such as a financial panic in 1893 in the United States – linked like the earlier panic of 1857 to railroad construction, as well as speculation on properties in Argentina, Australia and South Africa – and then a later banking panic in 1907. Stability of the currency was perceived to be all-important, so Finance Minister Sergei Witte raised taxes to increase revenues. The taxes imposed on the rural sector were particularly harsh. They could only be paid by increasing exports of commodities like wheat, so Russia developed a trade surplus. By the end of the century, the rouble qualified for conversion to the gold standard, it was stable, and it had good standing on foreign capital markets. But this financial stability, while underpinning modernisation, came at the price of growing social unrest and protest. Modernisation also meant mobility and enhanced communications, so protests could spread rapidly from one end of the empire to the other.

Taxes imposed on the peasants were part of the story. Another part of the narrative leading to the ongoing movement of protest was the issue of military conscription. As in other empires – European or Asian – military service had been a key component of feudalism. The officers came from the nobility, and they raised army contingents in the service of the emperor. By the time of Alexander II, it had become necessary to meet military objectives by conscription. Under Alexander III, then Nicholas II, conscription of peasants and townspeople was based on a quota system based on population. Given that the Russian Empire was ethnically diverse, there were numerous exemptions for minorities, including the Finns in the west, and Muslims in the east. Families with only one son were also exempted. Actual service required was six years when the system was introduced in 1874, and by the outbreak of the Great War in 1914, it was reduced to three years for infantry and artillery, or four years for cavalry and engineers, followed by seven years in the reserves. Thus, a large pool of manpower was available for military action during the decades leading to the revolution.

Yet this extensive military reservoir of men[32] also contained the seeds of widespread discontent and protest. The government propagated the notion of an egalitarian and fraternal army raised uniformly across the empire. But strongly held grievances over poor food and the treatment of enlisted men by their officers provoked conscription riots. From 1912, the tsarist government tried to solve the problem by guaranteeing a basic ration (the *paek*) to the families of all serving soldiers. This was a kind of contract: the young men had a duty of military service and in return the State had a duty to support their families.[33]

Modernisation, industrialisation, foreign debt, and military conscription: all of these factors weighed mightily on the deep-rooted changes affecting the populations of the Russian Empire, those of the cities and towns, and those of the vast rural spaces. Linking all these factors together was the growing literacy of the people of Russia and hence their ability to read the many political tracts that were widely circulated. As Russia endeavoured to catch up with the modernity of Western Europe, and the rising powers of the United States and Japan, radical political literature captured the attention of activists. When the revolutions of 1848 swept across Western Europe, the empires of Russia and China were largely untouched. But the response to the industrial revolution that had been articulated from 1848 by writers like Karl Marx and Friedrich Engels, provided a powerful intellectual stimulus to the activists in exile. Among them was Lenin, the prolific political pamphleteer and newspaper editor, who was still considered by the tsar's secret police to be a minor figure.

In 1897, the overall literacy rate throughout the Russian Empire was estimated at twenty-four per cent, with the rural literacy rate just under twenty per cent. As elsewhere in Europe, schools in the dominant Christian regions were mostly administered by the Church, the emphasis being on Orthodox religious education. Few schools existed in rural areas. The local councils, the zemstva, sought to establish schools but without specific curricula or guidelines. The peasants were largely self-taught, and they were increasingly drawn to schools run by political dissidents. Tolstoy's schools became part of this movement.

As in China at that time, talented students from outside the aristocracy gained access to higher education. And, as in China, universities became hotbeds of intellectual debate, juxtaposing Slavonic and Orthodox traditions against the ideas coming out of Western Europe, and the huge changes flowing from the industrial revolution. As in China, dissent in Russia often meant active participation in political protests and uprisings, followed by exile and continued agitation from outside the country. In Russia, as in China, there was much intellectual wrestling over the interaction between tradition and modernity. In the case of Russia, we see this through the great novels and copious writings of Tolstoy, who himself changed his thinking radically over the course of his life. Earlier explorations of the clash of ideas could be found in the writings of Dostoevsky and other writers of the mid-nineteenth century, and the turbulence of that period had also been reflected in the emotional and explosive music of Pyotr Tchaikovsky.

Taking up national office in 1906 and observing these changes, as Witte had earlier, Stolypin believed that agrarian reform and industrial modernisation would bring into being a new Russia, but one that would continue to be governed by a paternalistic imperial dynasty. His attempt to build a bridge between tradition and modernity foundered with the obstruction of his move to extend the reforms to the western provinces of occupied Poland – once governed by his grandfather. Stolypin's political downfall in 1911 came over the issue of establishing local councils (zemstva) in Russian-controlled Poland. His government proposed the Western Zemstva Bill. Stolypin's opponents argued that the Polish aristocratic large landowners, threatened by this bill, were loyal to the tsar and should be protected. Stolypin had made many enemies during his years in power, not only by pressing for the redistribution of land to peasants, but also through his control of the police as interior minister. The police were mobilised to support the reforms. At the local level, they relentlessly prosecuted corruption, and at the same time, they were ruthless in suppressing dissent. The Western Zemstva Bill gave an opportunity, which Stolypin evidently underestimated, to those defending vested interests. The Bill failed to pass. On 5 March 1911, Stolypin tendered his resignation. At first the tsar refused to accept it, but on 20 March, it became official. It was a measure of Stolypin's stature that his resignation was reported around the world.[34]

As the summer of 1911 wore on, the political situation showed no improvement. The tsar desperately wanted Stolypin to return to the government. Meeting with his mother, Dowager Empress Maria, he was seen leaving with red eyes, as if he had been weeping. The Dowager Empress called Stolypin to tell him: 'My son believes you are the only one who can defend him.' It was agreed that the tsar would write personally to Stolypin proposing that he take up his posts again. This the tsar did. Stolypin's daughter Maria wrote that her father was deeply touched by the tsar's letter and was seriously considering acceptance of the proposal.

Even as Stolypin considered the tsar's request, the secret police knew of threats against the former prime minister. A special detachment was sent from St Petersburg to ensure his security. However, on that fateful evening at the opera in Kiev, Stolypin replaced his usual bodyguard, Police Lieutenant Dembash, who his wife disliked, with someone new, Captain Yessoulov. The chief of secret service police, General Alexander Spiridovich, wrote in his memoirs that Dembash was devoted to Stolypin 'body and soul' but Stolypin gave in to his wife's wishes.[35] Spiridovich was responsible for a huge detachment of uniformed mobile guards, backed up by secret service agents in plain clothes, all charged with protecting the tsar at the inauguration of a statue of his grandfather Alexander II, and other visits and ceremonies held in Kiev prior to the evening at the opera.

As the ceremonies came to an end, the secret police reported on the arrival in Kiev of a group of Bolsheviks. This information was relayed by a double agent named Dmitry Bogrov. Precautions to protect the tsar were strengthened, and alternative plans were put in place for the imperial convoy of automobiles carrying the tsar and his daughters. Stolypin was nervous, which was out of character for him. He was upset to be lodged in the governor-general's house instead of the imperial palace. He complained during a garden party that no place could be found for him on the boat taking the imperial family to the next stop on their tour. Upset by news of the arrival of Bolsheviks in the city, he was visibly shaken when the wife of a general pointed at a large red cross medal on his uniform and said: 'One might call it a funeral cross.' At this very moment, Bogrov, dressed impeccably as a gentleman, was standing and observing Stolypin, just a few steps from him in the garden.

Bogrov, the double agent, lived well from the payments he received from the Okhrana, the secret police. At the same time, he worried about how to keep his credibility with the Bolsheviks, who he had been betraying for years. Spiridovich had sent agents from his headquarters to check every detail of the Kiev Opera theatre, where a gala performance would conclude the tsar's official visit. They had lists of all the artists, musicians, and employees of the theatre. On the day of the gala performance, the theatre was searched from the basement to the rafters. In the evening, no-one was permitted into the theatre without an official invitation. Every member of the public with an invitation had been investigated.

After all these security precautions, on the night of the gala performance, the tsar entered the imperial box with his two eldest daughters, Olga and Tatiana, to a standing ovation from the hundreds of invited guests. In front of the imperial box were the governor-general and several police guards. In the next row forward, Stolypin was placed with two government ministers. His new bodyguard, Yessoulov, was just behind him.

The opera was Rimsky-Korsakov's *The Tale of Tsar Saltan,* based on the poem of the same name by Aleksandr Pushkin, an opera with rollicking music, and a great favourite with the imperial court and the general population. At the end of the first act, Spiridovich learnt that Bogrov had somehow come into the theatre on the pretext that he had new information about the Bolsheviks. Spiridovich ordered that Bogrov be sent away and confined to his apartment. As the second act began, the officer in charge of Stolypin's protection saw Bogrov and told him to leave. But he did not check that the man had actually done so.

Waiting impatiently as the second act ended with an intermission, and as the tsar and his children left the imperial box to take tea in a private room, Spiridovich went to Stolypin to tell him about Bogrov. 'What do you think we should do now?' asked Stolypin, adding 'You would do well to speak one more time to Kouliabka,' who was the head of Stolypin's security attachment. As Spiridovich moved away, he saw that the bodyguard Yessoulov was no longer with Stolypin. He had gone outside to smoke.

Bogrov, elegantly dressed, calmly approached Stolypin as he talked with the two ministers, his back to the stage. Bogrov fired three shots. One hit Stolypin in the arm, another in the chest; someone in the orchestra shouted. Stolypin put his hand to his chest. 'I am wounded,' he said, then took off his coat, looked down at the blood pouring out, and fell into his seat. He turned towards the imperial box. Seeing the tsar, he made a gesture with both hands for the tsar to go back. Tatiana had time to look out and see the wounded Stolypin slumped in his seat. The orchestra began playing *God Save the Tsar*. Bogrov was tackled. Hearing the shots Spiridovich drew his sabre, but could not push his way through the crowd. Jumping from seat to seat, he saw the assassin's face and recognised Bogrov. 'Shall I finish him off,' cried the chief of the escort, drawing his sword. 'No, he must be arrested,' replied Spiridovich. Then, convinced that other terrorists were in the theatre, with the word 'treason' ringing in his ears, he planted himself in front of the imperial box. 'Get the emperor out,' he ordered. The tsar and his children were evacuated. Once done, Spiridovich demanded: 'Who let Bogrov pass?' It was Kouliabka, the head of Stolypin's security.

Stolypin died three days later, with the weeping tsar at his bedside. An inquiry was held, with a detailed report from Spiridovich. Bogrov was hastily executed ten days later, and the judicial investigation was halted by order of the tsar. To this day, historians debate whether the assassination of Stolypin was the work of a lone double agent, or whether there was a wider conspiracy involving the Okhrana, the secret police, and conservatives who feared the political return of Stolypin, the reformer. These events in 1911, and the unresolved debate, would eerily foreshadow another assassination some fifty-two years later, in Dallas in the United States.

Stolypin's reforms were stopped definitively by his assassination. Lenin wrote: 'Stolypin tried to pour new wine into old bottles, to reshape the old autocracy into a bourgeois monarchy; and the failure of Stolypin's policy is the failure of tsarism on this last, the last conceivable, road for tsarism.'[36]

At Lenin's request, Inessa Armand went back to Russia after the assassination of Stolypin, while he moved with Nadya to Krakow in Galicia, at that time the northernmost province of the Austro-Hungarian Empire. Armand was arrested again, then with her first husband's support she was given bail. Breaking her bail she fled to Krakow, where she lived with Lenin and Nadya.

The Great War

Another political assassination, that of the heir to the Austro-Hungarian Empire in Sarajevo in July 1914, was the spark that lit a great war between the powers of Europe, and their colonial empire. When the First World War broke out in 1914, Lenin was briefly arrested by the German authorities, then released when he explained his opposition to the tsarist regime. Accompanied by Armand, Lenin and Nadya returned to Bern in Switzerland, where Nadya had surgery for a goitre. At congresses of the Socialist International, Lenin attacked the German Social Democrats for supporting the German war effort. According to him, they had betrayed the 1907 Stuttgart resolution opposing militarism.[37] Armand joined Lenin in distributing tracts that urged troops to turn their rifles against their officers and support a socialist revolution across Europe. In Germany, a minority of the Social Democratic Party (SPD), including Rosa Luxemburg and Hugo Eberlein, supported the anti-war position.[38]

Allied by the triple entente with Britain and France against Germany, tsarist Russia had initial successes in Galicia and penetrated into Eastern Prussia. But by 1915, the Russians were forced back, and Tsar Nicholas took personal control of the armies. While Britain and France became bogged down in a war of attrition on the Western Front, Russia was confronted on the Eastern Front along the entire frontier with the Austro-Hungarian and Ottoman empires, as well as Bulgaria. Casualties were enormous, with more than a million-and-a-half killed by the summer of 1915, many wounded and nearly a million taken prisoner.

The end of the Romanov dynasty

Saint Petersburg was renamed Petrograd, a name with a Slavic rather than a Germanic connotation. With Tsar Nicholas away from the capital with the troops, domestic issues and affairs were governed by Tsarina Alexandra. She was widely criticised because of her German origin and the influence of the mystical monk named Grigori Rasputin. One account by a man named Vecchi, the owner of a leading French restaurant in the capital, conveyed a sense of the times. Vecchi described how Rasputin came to his restaurant to enjoy good food, wine, and the company of ladies of the Russian aristocracy. A party was organised by a princess and continued until 3.30 in the morning. An extract from Vecchi's account follows:

'Throughout the evening the behaviour of Rasputin was intolerable. Remember that he was an adventurer, possessed of undoubted powers of personal magnetism, a skilled psychologist, and was the secret power behind the Russian Court. Many of the ladies present had favours to beg from the Court which Rasputin was in a position to influence. Though his supporters vowed that he was a man of ascetic life, he was, nevertheless, a man entirely without principle ... and he was surrounded by some of the loveliest and youngest women in Russia, only too anxious to court his favours. Such a compliment might go to any man's head, and it certainly went to Rasputin's. Strive as I will, I can find no words to mitigate or excuse his disgusting behaviour.'[39]

In December 1916, a group of nobles, including a cousin of the tsar, murdered Rasputin. The dynasty was crumbling. By the beginning of 1917, the army had taken 15 million men from farms, and food prices soared. Eggs and butter increased in price five-fold from the pre-war era. The winter was severe and had an impact on the railways; almost half of the 20,000 locomotives were out of service, and many wagons were immobilised. Supplies of flour and fuel were scarce in the capital.

Riots broke out in Petrograd[40] and from 800 kilometres away at the front, the tsar gave orders that firm steps be taken against the demonstrators. Some 200 were killed, but several regiments refused to fire on the crowds. On 8 March 1917 (of the Western calendar, 24 February of the Russian calendar[41]), the protesters were joined by women marking International Women's Day, which had been so designated by activists in America and Europe since 1910. By 12 March 1917, most of the regiments had mutinied and joined the rebellion.[42] Members of the Duma, with Alexander Kerensky, the son of Lenin's former teacher, playing a key role, formed a committee, which allied with the Petrograd Soviet – holding de facto power over much of the city – to form a provisional government. This temporary power-sharing arrangement between Duma deputies and the Soviet – the workers' committee in the capital – was described as the period of dual power. Together, they demanded the abdication of the tsar. Nicholas was exhausted and suffered a minor heart attack. The generals with him advised that they could not continue to support him. The tsar tried to return to the capital, but his train was blocked. With his family held under orders of the provisional government, he had no choice but to submit. Three days later, on 15 March, Tsar Nicholas II abdicated and named his younger brother, Grand Duke Michael, to succeed him. But Michael refused to accept the throne without the consent of the people, stating that he would wait for a Constituent Assembly to be formed with power to decide on whether Russia should continue to have a monarchy or adopt a new constitution as a republic. With the abdication of Nicholas, and the effective refusal of Michael to take the crown, three centuries of absolute rule by the Romanov dynasty came to an end.

The Finland Station

Lenin celebrated the news of the tsar's abdication with other dissidents in exile in Switzerland, then tried to return to Russia. He negotiated a plan for some thirty dissidents to cross Germany by train. The German government agreed, seeking to weaken their adversary, and calculating that these dissidents would cause problems for the incoming Russian government. Lenin's group travelled by a special sealed carriage, from Zurich northwards across Germany to Sassnitz, a Baltic seaside port. From there they took a ferry to Trelleborg in Sweden, and from there they sailed to Helsinki, Finland. Finally arriving at Petrograd's Finland station, Lenin made a powerful speech condemning the provisional government, calling again for a revolution of workers – the proletariat – across Europe. He also lambasted the Mensheviks and the Socialists in the Petrograd Soviet for supporting the provisional government.

The initial task of the provisional government was to organise elections to a Constituent Assembly, which would draw up a new constitution. The leader was Prince Georgy Lvov from the centrist Kadet coalition – drawn from the aristocracy, landowners and businessmen. They were joined by a small socialist coalition, called the Socialist Revolutionary Party, led by Alexander Kerensky, who was named minister of war. Kerensky was an eloquent orator and an independent political thinker. In many ways he resembled Lamartine, who had led the provisional government after the downfall of King Louis-Philippe in France in 1848.

The provisional government in Russia had a tenuous hold on power. In the cities, workers and soldiers set up more soviets to act as local governments. A national council of soviets was established. Kerensky was both a member of the provisional government and a delegate to this council of soviets, and for a time served as the main liaison between the two centres of power. But confrontation between the provisional government and the soviets was inevitable. And all these political upheavals occurred against the backdrop of the most extensive and deadly war the world had known. The provisional government continued to support the Russian war effort, while the soviets took up Lenin's slogan of 'Bread, Land and Peace'.

In the July Days of 1917, Bolsheviks led demonstrations and armed uprisings in the streets. Lenin was recovering from ill health in a Finnish village and avoiding the police, who were under orders from the provisional government to arrest him. Leon Trotsky had reunited with Lenin and the Bolsheviks, and he was arrested. Lenin returned to Petrograd and appealed for calm but the provisional government labelled him a German agent provocateur, and he went back into hiding outside the capital. Then he found his way, by train and on foot, back to Finland.

Kerensky replaced Prince Lvov as minister-president (prime minister). Launching an offensive to try to retake Galicia from the Germans, he went personally to the front, trying to boost the morale of the troops with speech after speech. But the Kerensky offensive failed, with the loss of 200,000 lives among the Russian troops. The failed offensive cost him dearly in political support. Soldiers mutinied and anti-war sentiment increased.

Growing calls for public order and discipline came from the officers and business circles. In August 1917, the commander-in-chief of the armed forces, General Lavr Kornilov, attempted a coup d'état. The putsch failed, Kornilov was dismissed and arrested, and Kerensky became commander-in-chief as well as prime minister. Trotsky was elected president of the Petrograd Soviet, and with the soviet's consolidation of power, the situation was safe for Lenin to return to the capital. This time he made no calls for calm. As he had at the Finland station, Lenin called for the Bolsheviks to lead an armed insurrection against the government. The Petrograd Soviet met at the palatial Smolny Institute, Russia's first educational establishment for women, which became the centre for Bolshevik activity. John Reed's book *Ten Days that Shook the World* gives vivid descriptions of the debates and the atmosphere at the Smolny Institute and elsewhere on the streets of Petrograd. Kerensky was everywhere. He was prime minister and commander-in-chief of the armies, he was vice-president of the Petrograd Soviet, and he was also in attendance at debates at the Smolny Institute. He headed a five-person directorate. Like Lamartine in France in 1848, he tried to get ahead of events by declaring Russia to be a republic in September 1917, without waiting for the convening of the Constituent Assembly. He issued declarations on the right to vote for all men and women, and the right to freedom of speech, while at the same time, he sought to maintain Russia's war against Germany.

Kerensky put out statements branding Lenin as a criminal, while Lenin was vitriolic towards Kerensky and the provisional government. Tracts were churned out calling workers, soldiers, and peasants to take part in insurrection. Lenin initiated the formation of a military revolutionary committee, elected from representatives of the soviets, factory and soldier committees, and the Bolshevik Red Guards. This committee became the instrument for the revolution. On 25–26 October of the old calendar (6–7 November of the new calendar),[43] the Bolsheviks took over the government, taking control, without bloodshed, of the ministries, key transport and communication centres, printers, and utilities. The only shots were fired by sailors on the ship *Aurora,* aimed at the Winter Palace where the provisional government met. The Red Guards overcame the only resistance, from a women's battalion, and arrested the government ministers. Kerensky fled, probably using a car provided by the American Embassy, with an American flag helping him to pass through the Bolshevik patrols.[44]

The Bolsheviks declared the formation of a new government. Lenin wrote: 'To All Workers, Soldiers and Peasants. The Soviet authority will at once propose a democratic peace to all nations and an immediate armistice on all fronts. It will safeguard the transfer without compensation of all land – landlord, imperial, and monastery – to the peasants' committees; it will defend the soldiers' rights, introducing a complete democratisation of the army; it will establish workers' control over industry; it will ensure the convocation of the Constituent Assembly on the date set; it will supply the cities with bread and the villages with articles of first necessity; and it will secure to all nationalities inhabiting Russia the right of self-determination ... Long live the revolution!'[45]

In November, the Bolsheviks declared a general right to self-determination for the peoples of the Russian Empire. On the same day, Finnish leaders formed a Senate that shortly afterwards proclaimed the independence of Finland, recognised rapidly by neighbouring Sweden and Western powers, then by the Soviet government. Similar declarations were made in Ukraine, Lithuania, Latvia, Poland, and Transcaucasia, although these states would later be integrated into a new Union of Soviet Socialist Republics.

Aftermath

Lenin initially proposed that Leon Trotsky be named as chairman of the new Council of People's Commissars, before agreeing to take the position himself. Elections were held for a Constituent Assembly. The Bolsheviks won only a quarter of the votes. Under Lenin's impulse, the Council of People's Commissars forcibly disbanded the assembly. The RSDLP was renamed the Russian Communist Party. In January 1918 there were two attempts to assassinate Lenin. During 1918 and 1919 the government expelled Mensheviks and socialist revolutionaries from the soviets. Russia became a one-party state, governed by the Council of Soviets, called the Sovnarkom. The government relocated to Moscow and established quarters in the Kremlin, where Lenin lived in an apartment with his wife and sister, next to the Sovnarkom meeting room. In August, there was another assassination attempt by a Russian Jewish woman named Fanny Kaplan, who believed that Lenin had betrayed the February revolution, and this time he was seriously injured. Lenin moved to the estate of Gorki, outside Moscow, to recuperate. He continued to issue decrees through the Sovnarkom. His decree on peace proposed a three-month armistice, which was accepted by Germany. Trotsky led the Russian delegation to negotiations in Brest-Litovsk. The treaty signed in March 1918 would have resulted in massive losses for Russia, including Poland, Ukraine, and the Baltic States – a quarter of the former empire's population. By November, however, the German Kaiser had abdicated, and the Sovnarkom declared the Brest-Litovsk treaty to be devoid of meaning.

On the domestic front, Lenin issued decrees on land redistribution and the press, closing down newspapers deemed to be counter-revolutionary. Other sweeping changes included abolition of the courts, election of commanders in the military, popular education and a mass literacy campaign, the eight-hour day, equality between the sexes, and separation of Church and State. In economics, banks were nationalised, foreign debts were cancelled without payment of interest, utilities were nationalised, and workers' committees were established in factories.

By August 1918, Russia's cities faced famine. Lenin blamed the wealthier peasants (*kulaks*) and black-market speculators. He gave orders for the hanging of *kulaks* and the shooting of speculators. He emphasised the need for violence to overthrow the old order and to ensure the success of the revolution. He established a political police force called the Cheka,[46] which carried out executions across Russia. Lenin wrote: '[The bourgeoisie] practised terror against the workers, soldiers and peasants in the interests of a small group of landowners and bankers, whereas the Soviet regime applies decisive measures against landowners, plunderers and their accomplices in the interests of the workers, soldiers and peasants.'[47] From 1919 onwards the Cheka built concentration camps, to be administered by a new government agency, the Gulag. Intellectuals deemed to oppose the Bolsheviks were sent to a gulag (forced labour camp) or deported. A later decree called for the execution of anti-Bolshevik priests. As opposition grew to the Bolsheviks, Russia sank into civil war. Trotsky established the workers' and peasants' Red Army, opposed by the White Army formed by former tsarist officers. Nicholas and his family had been evacuated by Kerensky in August 1917 to Tobolsk in the Ural Mountains. But in July 1918, as White Army forces advanced in the region, the imperial family was executed by firing squad in a remote village.

In June 1919, Germany signed the Treaty of Versailles with the allied powers. The treaty included the covenant of the League of Nations and the establishment of the International Labour Organization. This new tripartite organisation, with the powers of governments, employers' and workers' organisations, was an institutional response to the enormous social and political changes of the industrial revolution, and in particular the shock of the two revolutions in Russia.

Meanwhile, the allied nations sent support to the White Army. By 1921 the country was afflicted by famine, resulting in an estimated 5 million deaths. Inessa Armand visited Lenin often at the Kremlin. As she was in poor health,

Lenin sent her to a sanatorium in the North Caucasus, but she died there that September of cholera. Grief-stricken, Lenin arranged a national funeral. By late 1921, Lenin's own health had declined seriously. Profiting from Lenin's frequent absences, Stalin consolidated his power. In January 1923, Lenin dictated his testament, calling for Trotsky to succeed him.

Lenin wrote: 'Stalin is too crude and this defect, which is entirely acceptable in our milieu and in relationships among us as communists, has become unacceptable in the position of general secretary. I therefore propose to comrades that they should devise a means of removing him from this job and should appoint to this job someone else who is distinguished from comrade Stalin in all other respects only by the single superior aspect that he should be more tolerant, more polite and more attentive towards comrades, less capricious, etc.'[48]

Lenin suffered a series of strokes. He died in Gorki in January 1924. By then, the Union of Soviet Socialist Republics, the USSR, had come into being. Despite Lenin's political 'testament', he was succeeded by Stalin, whose conflict with Trotsky deepened. By 1927 Stalin had prevailed, and Trotsky went into exile. He was killed in Mexico on Stalin's orders in 1940.

Hugo Eberlein, the young German dissident who had supported Lenin and Inessa Armand in their campaign against the war in 1914, returned to Germany. There he participated in the creation of the German Communist Party, which he represented at the creation of the Communist International in 1919, after the war. As Hitler and the Nazis rose to power in Germany, Eberlein went into exile in France, and was arrested in Strasbourg in 1935. Fleeing to Switzerland, he went to the Soviet Union in 1936, but was arrested the following year and deported to a gulag, where he died. Nadya continued her political activity after the death of Lenin, becoming deputy to the People's Commissar of Education. She died in 1939 at the age of seventy. There were rumours that she was poisoned on the orders of Stalin as she celebrated her birthday.

It was said that Vladimir Lenin and Inessa Armand had a daughter, who married Hugo Eberlein. If this was so, nobody knows what became of her. Vladimir Lenin, the brilliant, obsessive, and cruel man who changed the course of the twentieth century, also had a human side, in his love for Inessa. But any descendant from that expression of his humanity simply disappeared into the sands of time.

Alexander Kerensky, the progressive republican reformer, went to London where his two sons studied and became renowned engineers. After divorce and the death of his second wife, an Australian journalist, he moved to the United States to give lectures and to write his memoirs. When he died in New York in 1970, he was refused a Russian Orthodox burial and ignored by the Soviet authorities. His sons had him buried in Putney Green, near Wimbledon in London.

Pyotr Stolypin's beloved wife and their children joined the flight of Russian emigres to Western Europe. His daughter, Maria von Bock, wrote the most widely cited memoir of her father, an autocratic and once powerful conservative who had a vision for reforming and modernising the Russian Empire.[49] On the 150th anniversary of his birth, President Vladimir Putin approved the construction of a monument to Pyotr Stolypin, which was inaugurated in December 2012 near the White House, the seat of Russian government.

Part IV:
A new world
1920 to 2020

After Europe and Asia were ravaged by a second World War, the United Nations was founded in 1945. In that year, a young boy in the city of Kumasi in the Ashanti region of western Africa, now Ghana, was in primary school. By the turn of the century, that boy, Kofi Annan, would be the seventh Secretary-General of the United Nations. In that position he would confront the complexity of the issues facing a global community of nations. As he completed his second term in 2006, he warned of storms yet to come.

Chapter 6

One hundred years later

Just over 100 years have passed since the last of the five revolutions that changed the world. Those revolutions have defined the political contours of the past century. What a century it was – a great depression, a second World War, discoveries of nuclear fission and fusion, decolonisation in Africa, Asia and Latin America, the division of Europe by an iron curtain, the Cold War then the collapse of the Soviet Union, the creation and expansion of the European Union, genocides, and long drawn-out wars in Africa, Asia and the Middle East, global supply chains, financial turbulence, and the internet. Then came the new millennium, a global financial crisis, the challenge of climate change, and a global pandemic. In early 2021, came a riotous invasion of the legislature of the nation born of the first of the five revolutions in our narrative, the United States, as it convened to certify the results of a presidential election.

A question arises inevitably from the story of the five revolutions: Are the conditions ripe for a new earth-shaking revolution? The answer to that question is, quite simply: Yes!

Yes, the world is primed for a new revolution, or revolutions, that will upset the existing order, just as the late eighteenth-century American and French revolutions did, just as the mid-nineteenth-century revolutions that swept Europe did, and just as the early twentieth-century Chinese and Russian revolutions did …

Answering that question in the affirmative does not tell us how and when such a revolution might occur. But we *can* say that the conditions are ripe for it.

Twentieth century wars

The five revolutions – from the American of 1776 to the Russian of 1917 – set the scene for the dramatic changes and conflicts of the next 100 years. The United States of America grew spectacularly during the nineteenth century, to reach from the Atlantic to the Pacific, then entered the twentieth century as a rising economic power. To mark the centenary of the revolution of 1789, France built the Eiffel Tower for the World Exposition in 1889, and enthusiastically pursued the industrial revolution. Europe modernised and trade expanded. The quest for modernity was a driver of the revolutions of 1911 and 1917 in the dynastic empires of China and Russia. Then, the industrial revolution created the technological conditions for the most devastating war in human history up to that time – the Great War of 1914–18, later called World War I.

The formal end of the Great War came in November 1918, one year after the Russian Revolution. By then, four empires had crumbled – the Russian, the German, the Austro-Hungarian, and the Ottoman. The war's victors attempted to build institutions for lasting peace into the Treaty of Versailles, which was signed in 1919. Under the treaty, the new League of Nations was formed with headquarters in neutral Switzerland, but without the United States, the nation that proposed it. The League failed, however, to achieve its lofty objectives of preventing war and assuring world peace. One durable outcome of the treaty was the creation of a new institution in response to the social and political consequences of the industrial revolution: the tripartite International Labour Organization.

The revolutions of the early twentieth century in China and Russia had set the scene for devastating civil wars in each of those countries. In the case of Russia, the civil war was resolved brutally. Lenin's successor, Josef Stalin, ruthlessly consolidated the Union of Soviet Socialist Republics (USSR) as the successor to the empire of the tsars. In the case of China, the civil war continued for decades until Mao Tse Tung prevailed and established the People's Republic of China in 1949.

The combination of the great economic depression of the 1930s and the ethnic patchwork of Europe – the result of centuries of wars and conquests – provided fertile ground for the rise of new movements, notably the fascists in Mussolini's Italy and the nazis in Hitler's Germany. In Asia, Japan invaded Manchuria and set up a puppet government under the last Chinese Emperor, Pu Yi, then left the League of Nations in 1933. That same year, Germany left the League over attempts by other nations to restrain its rearmament. Italy and Spain left in 1937. There was appeasement in Munich and a secret deal between Hitler's Germany and Stalin's USSR to carve up Poland, while the latter settled border conflicts with Japan in the East. In 1939, Europe was plunged again into devastating war. Again, that war became a world war. The Soviet Union invaded Finland and was expelled from the League of Nations – the League's last significant act before its demise.

Nazi Germany used modern military technology to overrun Europe, extending its axis with fascist Italy to include imperial Japan, which pursued its conquests in a weakened China and across South-East Asia and the Pacific. Again, there was immense loss of life, especially in the main theatres of war in Europe and Asia. There were appalling atrocities. The genocidal scheme of the nazi Holocaust to eliminate Jews from Europe increased emigration by those who escaped to the United States, and resulted in political support for the creation of a Jewish state in the biblical lands of the Middle East. With the conclusion of World War II – in Europe in May of 1945 and in Asia in August of the same year – the world changed even more dramatically. For with the atomic bombing of Hiroshima and Nagasaki in Japan, the end of this second great war marked the dawn of the nuclear age.

By then, the victorious allied powers had set about creating an improved successor to the League of Nations – the United Nations. But with the end of war, they had also created the conditions for a new era of strategic competition, starting with the division of Europe into West and East. Israel was recognised by the Western powers, while Arab nations supported the Palestinians who became refugees.

Decolonisation
The end of the war gave impetus to the decolonisation movement, notably with the independence of Kofi Annan's Ashanti and the Gold Coast to form Ghana in March of 1947. This was followed in August of the same year by the independence of British India and its partition into India and Pakistan, despite the efforts of Mohandas Gandhi to avoid conflict between Hindus and Muslims.

East-West competition extended to the 'Third World' – so named with a nod to the Third Estate of the French Revolution – comprising the newly emerging countries in Asia, Africa, and Latin America. A non-aligned movement emerged in 1955, including among its leaders Ghana's Kwame N'Krumah and India's Jawaharlal Nehru, and it was formalised into the Non-Aligned Movement forum in 1961, with membership of some 120 Third World countries. This alliance was a partial response to East-West geopolitical competition. During these years, young Kofi Annan, a bright student and by now aged sixteen, left the local school in Kumasi to live and study at the Mfantsipim Methodist boarding school on the coast.[1]

In this post-war period, an ideological battle took hold between liberal capitalism seeking order while pursuing commerce, Marxist socialism promoting revolution, and social democrat or centrist movements advocating social justice through reform. That struggle played out across many national societies, notably in political parties, trade unions and independence movements. As technology continued to develop dramatically, the East-West contest was pursued in the space race. Overshadowing everything was the nuclear arms race.

In 1957, the Soviet Union launched the first satellite – Sputnik – to circle the earth in near space. As a boy, the writer remembers watching that small point of light blinking across the southern hemisphere sky. The Soviets followed with an unmanned moon landing and four years later, the first man to orbit the earth – Yuri Gagarin. Then came the Cuban Missile Crisis of October 1962, and the whole world held its breath as the threat of nuclear catastrophe became all too real.

By then, Kofi Annan had graduated from the Kumasi College of Science and Technology, he had been awarded a Ford Foundation grant to study in St Paul, Minnesota, in the United States, and he had completed a diploma at the Graduate Institute of International Studies in Geneva, where he learnt French. He began working in 1962 as a budget officer at the Geneva-based World Health Organisation.

Before the Cuban Missile Crisis, President John F. Kennedy had announced the intention of the United States to send a man to the moon. Technology and the politics of armament came together, for the rockets that could send a man to the moon used the same technology as the missiles that could deliver multiple hydrogen bomb warheads, numerous enough to wipe out human civilisation. And the satellites that followed Sputnik made almost-instantaneous worldwide communication possible. In 1969, the drama of the first moon landing was marked not only by the remarkable technological and human exploit, but also by the fact that, for the first time in human history, a fifth of the world's people watched a momentous event on television as it happened.

Within a few decades, microchip technology developed from the space race had enabled personal computers and mobile phones to reach every corner of the planet. The infrastructure of satellites and a vast network of undersea cables enabled the communication revolution of the twenty-first century.

There were major geo-political shifts, too. Henry Kissinger, a student of nineteenth-century Realpolitik, orchestrated a visit by United States President Richard Nixon to China in February 1972. After the death of Stalin in 1956, there was a split between his successors and Mao Tse Tung's China. With echoes of the nineteenth century 'Great Game' in Europe and the Middle East against tsarist Russia, Kissinger sought to exploit this Sino-Soviet split to the advantage of the West, while seeking a path out of the war in Vietnam, where China was a key player. Although China remained in the grip of its cultural revolution until after Mao's death four years later, the visit laid the groundwork for China's subsequent opening to the global market economy. In 1978, China's new paramount leader, Deng Xiaoping, initiated *Boluan Fanzheng*, a term he used to mean ending chaos and returning to normal.

By the 1980s, the competitive but relatively stable world order of the Cold War, which had emerged after World War II, reached its peak. The superpowers of the United States and the Soviet Union had each been weakened internally by their engagement in protracted foreign wars – in Vietnam for the United States, in Afghanistan for the Soviet Union. In 1985, a new man – Mikhail Gorbachev – rose to power as general secretary of the Communist Party of the Soviet Union and de facto head of government. Then came an explosion at the nuclear power station at Chernobyl in Ukraine in 1986. Despite attempts by the Soviet authorities to cover up the accident, the news was soon out, as a radioactive cloud spread across Europe. Communication had become global, and the story swept around the world. News like this could no longer be contained. Gorbachev knew that the Soviet system had become sclerotic. He announced reforms using the terms *perestroika* (restructuring) and *glasnost* (openness).

Ten months that changed the world

In May 1989, Gorbachev made a visit to China, the first by a leader of the Soviet Union in thirty years. During the weeks prior to his visit, students had held large-scale protests calling for democracy, centred on Tiananmen Square in Beijing. The historic summit between Gorbachev and Deng in the Great Hall of the People was held against a backdrop of protestors occupying Tiananmen Square. Several top Chinese leaders favoured conciliation and dialogue with the students. But as soon as Gorbachev left the country, Deng ordered martial law, and troops moved with tanks into the square and repressed the protest. To this day the number of deaths is unknown.

The following month, June 1989, the national trade union in Poland, called Solidarity, supported by the Catholic Church, ended communist rule there. Gorbachev made it clear that, unlike his predecessors, he would not order Soviet military interventions in Central and Eastern Europe. Communications, especially Western television broadcasts that could be picked up in Eastern Europe, also played a critical role in the opening of the borders and the fall of the Iron Curtain across Europe. One after the other, the single-party regimes of Eastern Bloc countries were replaced by multiparty democracies; the most iconic event being the fall of the Berlin Wall in East Germany during November of 1989.

The repercussions were felt around the world. In February 1990, two months after the fall of the Berlin Wall, Nelson Mandela in South Africa walked free after twenty-seven years in prison, and began discussions with President F.W. de Klerk on an end to apartheid and transition to one person, one vote democracy. De Klerk had already signalled his intentions for reform, taking into account protests and sanctions against the apartheid regime, but the fall of the Berlin Wall convinced him that with the end of the Cold War there was no longer any place for the argument often used by nationalist politicians that apartheid provided a bastion against communism.[2] In the ten months between May 1989 and February 1990, the world had changed.

By the end of 1991, following a failed coup attempt in Moscow quashed by the President of the Russian Federation, Boris Yeltsin, Russia declared its independence and Gorbachev was obliged to sign the end of the Soviet Union. In 1992, American writer Francis Fukuyama published the bestseller *The End of History and the Last Man*,[3] arguing that liberalism had prevailed over collectivism and that this was 'the end-point of mankind's ideological evolution'. But, as Fukuyama himself later recognised, history had not ended – far from it. For the technological revolutions that had driven so many of the economic and political upheavals of the late twentieth century also set the scene for changes far beyond the cleavage between liberalism and collectivism that had underpinned the ideological debates of the Cold War era.

The new millennium

After the end of the Cold War, in the year of the publication of Fukuyama's book, the United Nations began to convene a series of major summits with the aim of bringing together world leaders to address global challenges. The series began with a summit in Rio de Janeiro in June 1992, called the United Nations Conference on Environment and Development, which became known as the Earth Summit. An important feature of this meeting of heads of government was the engagement of organisations of civil society, and the recognition by participating governments, at least in their official declarations, of the potential role of non-government actors in helping to tackle the big issues of the day.

Three years later, in 1995, the United Nations convened a Social Summit in Copenhagen, with representatives of the world's governments and civil society organisations from north and south, east, and west. The president of the UN General Assembly and Social Summit Chair, Juan Somavía, declared: 'We do not have to accept that the poor will always be with us. Poverty can be eliminated.'[4] Among the national leaders, President François Mitterrand of France gave a stirring speech, proclaiming: 'If we do not act, we mock the world and generations to come.'[5] The mood was determined, ambitious and hopeful. Out of the Social Summit, came a set of targets for the world to achieve in order to overcome poverty.[6]

In the two decades since the Cuban Missile Crisis, Kofi Annan had obtained a master's degree in management at the Massachusetts Institute of Technology (MIT) and he had pursued his career as a management expert in the United Nations system, becoming assistant secretary-general for programme planning, budget, finance and control. In 1993, he was appointed as under-secretary-general for peacekeeping operations. Having built a reputation as a management expert, Annan now took on a quite different task, which was central to the UN's role in the mediation of international conflicts. Immediately he faced tough decisions. Ethnic conflict in Rwanda led to genocide, with an estimated 1 million Rwandans killed, but the UN peacekeeping mission there had a limited mandate and did not intervene. Ten years later, Annan regretted that he had not acted more strongly.[7] The next year, Annan acted decisively, backed by a UN Security Council mandate calling on NATO forces to protect civilians, as well as the UN's own peacekeeping forces, in Bosnia. In doing so he impressed the US administration of President Bill Clinton, as it worked to achieve the Dayton peace accords ending the civil war in the former Yugoslavia.

In 1996, the United States vetoed a second term as UN Secretary-General for Egypt's Boutros Boutros-Ghali, who they blamed for UN ineffectiveness in Somalia, Rwanda, and the former Yugoslavia. Boutros-Ghali was supported by the other fourteen members of the fifteen-nation Security Council, but the US refused to lift its veto, putting forward instead the name of another candidate from the African region – Kofi Annan. Boutros-Ghali was strongly supported by France, which in turn vetoed Annan's candidacy four times. Finally, France relented, lifted its veto by abstaining, and Kofi Annan was elected the seventh Secretary-General of the United Nations. He was the first person to rise to the post, often described as 'the most impossible job in the world', from within the ranks of the UN staff. He took up office on 1 January 1997.

Very quickly Annan released two reports on UN management reform. Then he took up the outcomes of the Copenhagen Social Summit. He proposed a Millennium Summit in the year 2000, with the aim of committing governments world-wide to real action on poverty. His report to prepare the summit called on governments to 'put people at the centre of everything we do'. He continued: 'No calling is more noble, and no responsibility greater, than that of enabling men, women and children, in cities and villages around the world, to make their lives better.'[8]

Annan also mobilised support from the private sector. In an address to the World Economic Forum (WEF) – the premier gathering of corporate and political leaders from around the world – meeting in Davos, Switzerland, in January 1999, Annan proposed 'a global compact of shared values and principles', which, he said, would give a human face to the global market'.[9] In July 2000, the Global Compact was officially launched to support broader UN goals around ten core principles related to human rights, development, labour standards, the environment, and anti-corruption.

In September 2000, 150 national leaders, with 8,000 other participants, met for three days at UN Headquarters in New York, at the largest world gathering of leaders in history, to adopt the Millenium Declaration. Subsequently, all 191 member states and twenty-two international organisations committed to achieving eight measurable Millenium Development Goals (MDGs) by the year 2015. The Millenium Declaration was nothing short of a new vision for a world with greater equity and justice. It reflected a widely shared spirit of optimism, determination, and hope.

The following year, 2001, Annan issued a five-point 'Call to Action' to tackle the HIV/AIDS global epidemic, leading to the establishment of the Global Fund to fight AIDS, tuberculosis, and malaria. In June of 2001 the UN General Assembly approved Annan's appointment for a further five-year term. That year the Nobel Peace Prize was awarded to both the United Nations and to Kofi Annan personally.

9/11 and its aftermath

As the UN's ambitious global programmes were being put in place to tackle poverty and disease, and to keep peace, out of a clear day on 11 September 2001, came the most destructive attack on the United States homeland in its history. Downtown from the UN Headquarters on the East River in Manhattan, the twin towers of the World Trade Centre, which dominated the skyline of the financial district around Wall Street, were hit and destroyed by two hijacked airliners. Another airline crashed into the Pentagon, the seat of US military power in Washington, while a fourth aimed at Washington, targeting either the White House or the Capitol building, was brought down in a field in Pennsylvania as passengers fought with hijackers.

The suicide attacks resulted in 3,000 deaths. The psychological impact on the United States was dramatic. Decisions taken by the United States and its allies in response to the attacks of 9/11 continue to have grave consequences to this day. Four weeks after the attacks, US and British aerial forces targeted camps of Al Qaeda – the terrorist group responsible for the attacks – and their Taliban protectors in the mountains of Afghanistan. By November, US and NATO ground forces had taken Kabul, and Al Qaeda and Taliban leaders retreated into the high mountains on the porous border with Pakistan. In December, the UN Security Council established an International Security Assistance Force, with troops from eighteen nations, to hold the area around Kabul.

The ambitions of the 2000 Millennium Summit were maintained. But the optimism of global solidarity, aimed at building a better world for billions affected by poverty and disease, was now overshadowed. The United States under President George W. Bush began preparing to go beyond Afghanistan and planned to invade Iraq. There were strong disagreements among Western allies, with the UK under Prime Minister Tony Blair supporting the US position,[10] while France and Germany adamantly opposed military intervention. The differences were played out at a dramatic meeting of the UN Security Council in February 2003. Without the endorsement of the UN Security Council, the US and UK went ahead with the invasion of Iraq, with the support of several other countries. The power play undermined the principles of the UN Charter of 1945 and weakened the United Nations.

Later that year, reports emerged of terrible ethnic cleansing in the Darfur region of western Sudan, and Annan worked with the African Union to send in a peacekeeping mission. The Arab–Israeli conflict continued to be intractable. Mid-way through his second five-year term, a documentary film on the role of the UN Secretary-General was produced, entitled aptly *Kofi Annan: Center of the Storm*.[11] In his final year in office, Annan visited Iran to negotiate inspection of uranium enrichment facilities. While there, he disagreed publicly with the Iranian president over the latter's denial of the World War II Holocaust. In his farewell address to world leaders gathered for the UN General Assembly in September 2006, he outlined the major problems of 'an unjust world economy, world disorder, and widespread contempt for human rights and the rule of law'.[12]

The Global Financial Crisis

As Kofi Annan spoke these words to political leaders, in the wealthier countries there continued to be a mood of general complacency about the state of the world economy. The financial pages of respected economic journals regularly ran articles suggesting that a new era of steady growth was underway in the industrial economies. An interconnected financial system had passed seamlessly into the new century.[13] It had survived the shock of the 9/11 suicide attacks on the financial capital of the world five years earlier. Back then, in what was stated to be a gesture of solidarity, the World Economic Forum had moved its annual meeting in January 2002 from the winter snows of the Swiss resort of Davos to New York.[14] The stock markets recovered, WEF moved back to Davos in 2003, and business resumed as before. Financial markets appeared to have shaken off these shocks and they continued their upward trajectories.

From the 1980s, the opening of China to a market economy had provided the global economy with a massive new source of cheap labour.[15] Russia, having privatised much of its industry under President Boris Yeltsin and his prime minister and successor, Vladimir Putin, in the 1990s, experienced robust economic growth after 2000, buoyed by the export of oil and gas. Indicators suggested that the emerging economies in Asia, Latin America and Africa were getting stronger. But there was relatively little progress in those countries towards the attainment of MDG targets related to hunger, food security and sanitation. There were, however, some bright spots, as access to primary schools increased for many children, especially girls, and some health statistics improved.

Despite all the positive signs and upbeat commentaries, some shakiness began to appear in financial markets in 2007. Then the entire world was buffeted in 2008 by the Global Financial Crisis. The Great Recession that followed seemed to be a defining moment for the global economy, just as the Great Depression had been in the 1930s.

Home prices in the US had peaked in mid-2006, then declined steeply. Millions of mortgage securities described as 'subprime mortgages' had been sliced and bundled as triple-A-rated securities. Few perceived the underlying risks of complex financial instruments that were supposed to minimise risk, but were in reality ready to collapse, like a house of cards. In July 2007, a New York-based global investment bank and brokerage firm, Bear Stearns, announced that it was closing two hedge funds because of losses on subprime mortgages. Only six months earlier, in January 2007, Bear Stearns had announced record profits, and was a darling of Wall Street. Strain began to appear in two major US government-sponsored mortgage enterprises – Fannie Mae (founded in 1938 as a response to the Great Depression) and Freddie Mac (established in 1970). In August 2007, the French bank BNP Paribas froze three of its investment funds, acknowledging that the bank had no way of assessing the value of complex assets such as packages of subprime loans. In September 2007, British bank Northern Rock had to borrow heavily to meet mortgage debt payments. As news got out, there was a run on the bank as people queued in the streets around the bank's London headquarters, trying to withdraw their money.

Still, most financial commentators sought to reassure the world. In December 2007, the writer attended a meeting of the Organisation for Economic Co-operation and Development (OECD) in Paris – an annual meeting between the OECD's top officials, ambassadors from the thirty-four member countries at that time, and the 'social partners', trade unions and employer organisations.[16] OECD Secretary-General Ángel Gurría reported from a meeting of central bankers he had attended in Basel, Switzerland, the previous week. The heads of central banks were considered to be among the most objective and sophisticated actors in the global economy. They prided themselves on being independent of politics. They and their national boards worked with an array of data-based economic analysis, which they used to make decisions on interest rates and monetary supply, aimed at maintaining economic and financial stability. Their pronouncements were scrutinised closely by financial experts and commentators for clues as to the direction of economic policies. The decisions of their boards were eagerly anticipated by financial markets. When they met at the Bank of International Settlements in Basel, the intellectual firepower of the world's economy was gathered in one room.

Ángel Gurría had just attended this gathering as the first signs were emerging of the subprime mortgage crisis. Gurría summed it up like this: 'We looked at each other around the table, put our hands on the table, touched wood, and said: "We *think* we've got it under control."' The writer remembers turning to a colleague and saying: 'That doesn't sound very reassuring!' A few months later, on 6 May 2008, the US Treasury Secretary told *The Wall Street Journal*, 'I do believe that the worst is behind us.'[17]

But by September of 2008, it had become clear that the measures taken by central banks to contain the emerging crisis had failed. On 7 September, the US government bailed out the two government-sponsored enterprises, Fannie Mae and Freddie Mac, which had combined losses of US$15 billion on mortgages in the US market.[18] Then on Monday 15 September, one of the giant US-based trading and investment banks, Lehman Brothers, filed for bankruptcy. The impact on worldwide financial markets was dramatic.

As the next day dawned in the Pacific, the Australian stock exchange suspended trading in Lehman Brothers stock. By the end of the day in New York, the Dow Jones had plunged by the largest one-day loss in history, then rebounded by the largest one-day point gain in history! This extreme volatility signalled that no one knew really what was happening. The chairman of the US Federal Reserve, Ben Bernanke, one of those participants in the Basel meeting the previous December, who thought 'we've got it under control', rushed to Congress with Treasury Secretary Henry Paulson and told House Speaker Nancy Pelosi: 'If we don't do this today we won't have an economy on Monday.'[19] 'This' was a proposal to create a 700-billion-dollar fund to buy toxic mortgages, which would amount to a massive bailout for US banks. The US Federal Reserve took emergency steps over that weekend to allow credit markets to keep operating. As turmoil continued, President George W. Bush addressed the nation saying, 'Congress must act', and an emergency bill with the 700-billion-dollar bailout was approved. Panic continued to spread through the world's financial markets. On 11 October, the International Monetary Fund (IMF) warned that the world financial system was teetering on the 'brink of systemic meltdown'.[20] Iceland, with a small domestic market, had engaged heavily in international finance, lending to Britain, the Netherlands and elsewhere, and all three major banks in the country collapsed. Local banks collapsed in the US. Around the world, banks were bailed out by governments or were sold to competitors in so-called 'fire sales'. The Swiss banking giants, UBS and Credit Suisse, were supported by their federal government. The US economy slid into recession. By November, 200,000 jobs had been lost in the US alone.

World trade plummeted. Europe was hit badly. Spain, Portugal, Italy, and Greece, in particular, suffered huge increases in unemployment, as the recession hit all of the Euro-zone countries. Riots broke out in Greece. Losses on the value of homes in the US were estimated at more than US$4 trillion. As people defaulted on their mortgage payments, millions of homes were repossessed, and the crisis spread to the wider economy.[21] In December, the US Congress extended emergency assistance to major automobile manufacturers.

French President Nicolas Sarkozy, chairing the European Union (EU) at the time, and British Prime Minister Gordon Brown proposed a summit of leaders from the twenty largest economies. This group, the G20, had previously held meetings of finance ministers. Now, for the first time, heads of government of the G20 countries met in a summit hosted by President Bush in Washington in November 2008. The G20 had the advantage of broadening international consultation beyond the G8 countries to include emerging economies such as China, Brazil, India, Indonesia, Turkey, Argentina, Mexico and South Africa, and significant second-tier economies such as Australia, South Korea, and Saudi Arabia. Out of the Washington and subsequent summits emerged a degree of coordination on financial policies, and stimulus policies were implemented in most G20 countries.

In late January of 2009, Barack Obama took office as US President and quickly signed a new economic stimulus bill. The IMF projected huge losses by banks of over US$4 trillion.[22] But as the banking and financial sectors emerged from the crisis, different approaches to macro-economic policy became evident, notably at the G20 summit in Toronto in 2010. By then, in contrast to the position of the US administration,[23] several European governments and Canada were calling for austerity measures, which would in turn severely affect resources for public services. Fiscal austerity was supposed to be compensated by monetary stimulus, described as quantitative easing. This meant that central banks bought large amounts of government bonds and other securities, so as to inject money into national economies.

Then a strange thing happened. Financial sectors grew strongly again. The financial pages of major newspapers ran articles pointing to the disconnect between Wall Street and Main Street. 'Wall Street' meant the world of finance, and 'Main Street' meant the real economy, which continued to be in major trouble, with high levels of unemployment. What happened was that quantitative easing released a flood of money, and in a world of financial mobility, that supply of money was sloshing around the planet. It was like printing money, except that the increase in money supply was no longer seen in big piles of banknotes, as in inflationary European economies before the Great Depression of the 1930s, but in the computerised records of banks and other financial institutions. This big increase in money supply provided opportunities for savvy investment fund managers to speculate on equity and commodity markets and new financial instruments. The clever ones made huge profits, with little or no government regulation, and they often paid minimal or no taxes. One might legitimately ask why the increase in money supply was not used for badly needed infrastructure projects or for improving public services. That simply did not happen.

The quantitative easing policies and the pouring of trillions of US dollars into global markets made it possible for many of the hyper-rich to become even wealthier. Here is the key point: even though financial markets were saved, and investors made a great deal of money in the process, the great majority of people received little benefit from the very big increase in the supply of money.

By 2009, the hopes and aspirations of billions of people, of families around the planet, had been dashed, as they lost jobs, savings, and homes. Middle-class revenues stagnated or declined. In the United States, inequalities deepened significantly, and many were unable to afford medical care, causing an increase in health issues across swathes of the poorer urban and rural areas. In Japan, then the world's second biggest economy, there was a major shift from life-long employment to precarious work. The debt crisis was devastating across southern European countries like Greece, Italy, Spain, and Portugal, as well as in Ireland, and the crisis threatened the common currency – the Euro – shared by more than 300 million people in nineteen countries. Urban dwellers in many developing countries experienced a reversal of improvements in their living conditions, and rural areas were hit even harder, so more people migrated from rural areas to cities, adding to those living in urban slums. Crime increased dramatically in countries like Mexico and Brazil, and across Central America, and Southern Africa. Refugees and desperate illegal migrants – often paying their life savings to people traffickers – reached record numbers, as they fled poverty, crime and ongoing wars in Africa and the Middle East. Public service budgets for education, health and security were cut everywhere. The inequality gap between the wealthiest one per cent of the world's population and the remaining ninety-nine per cent increased even more dramatically.

We saw from the story of five revolutions that, historically, growing inequality and the dashing of aspirations for the majority of people, combined with serial scandals, generally created pre-conditions for revolution. Add to this mix today the impact of wars and of ongoing intractable conflicts, and we have social and political conditions of great volatility. By 2009, there was every sign that such a period of volatility was upon us again. Yet, as in the past, those who benefited the most from tectonic changes in the planet's social and economic substrata mostly turned their eyes away from any signs of disequilibrium. As their predecessors did in the eighteenth, nineteenth, and early twentieth centuries, they continued to dance before the impending storms.

The revival of Queen Charlotte's Ball

Our description of the original Queen Charlotte's Ball during the London Season of 1780 was a metaphor for the way in which the 200 families who ran the British Empire danced before the storm of their empire's defeat in the American Revolution. Was it just coincidence that in the year following the 2008 Global Financial Crisis, Queen Charlotte's Ball was revived? From 1780, the tradition of presenting debutantes to the queen had been maintained, until Queen Elizabeth II hosted the last of these balls at Buckingham Palace in 1958. By this time, the pretensions of the wealthy had fallen out of step with social change and this high society ritual was seen as antiquated. With his usual candour, the queen's husband, Prince Philip, described the event as 'bloody daft'. Then, in 2009, Queen Charlotte's Ball was given new life, with a trademark registered by the non-profit London Season organisation. Each year since then, young women aged from sixteen to twenty have been presented as debutantes at the new Queen Charlotte's Ball, bowing not to the queen but to a multi-layered birthday cake, in prestigious London locations, such as Kensington Palace (2015) and Lancaster House (2016 and 2019). The Sunday newspapers have shown the young women in white designer gowns, taking photos of each other with their smartphones. The ball is the pinnacle event of a year-long introduction to etiquette in high society. The London Season's mission statement: 'to continue British traditions and promote global protocol in today's multicultural society',[24] conveys nostalgia with modernity. Debutantes are selected through an interview process. The cost of participation is high, so the young women come from wealthy families. No longer exclusively from the British ruling class, they include the daughters of billionaires from America, Europe, Russia, and China – from the very same countries in which revolutions overturned the established orders of a bygone era and forged the main centres of power and wealth of the new millennium. Queen Charlotte's Ball and other events attract corporate sponsorship. Benefits are donated to a range of charities.

The question as to why the resuscitated version of this elite event re-emerged in the wake of the 2008 financial crash is pertinent. As we have just seen, in the years since the Great Recession of 2008, the fortunes of the ultra-wealthy increased at a greater pace than ever. The liberal British newspaper *The Guardian* published an opinion piece in 2013, with the comment: 'It's no wonder people are agog over pictures of the debutantes' ball – the gap between poshness and poverty has never been wider' and the paper posed the question: 'So why are people falling in love with debutante culture again?'[25] *The Guardian*'s writer concluded with this thought: 'The trouble is that social mobility is stuck. The inequality gap is widening ... but our fetishisation of poshness is a sure sign that we're frustrated and dreaming of something better.' The 'debutante culture' of the twenty-first century's London Season and Queen Charlotte's Ball is but a symbol – touching in its relative innocence. More to the point are the substantive facts about commerce in luxury on a global scale. The luxury trade in items ranging from real estate to mega-yachts and private jets, to art collections, jewellery, horlogerie, sporting teams or racehorses, fashion, and vacations, flourished on an unprecedented scale in the decade after the Global Financial Crisis.

How the wealth gap became a chasm

Le Monde of France published a study in June 2016 showing that private wealth increased by 5.2 per cent over 2014, following an annual increase of 7.5 per cent from 2013 to 2014.[26] These increases were largely superior to growth rates in GDP, both worldwide and in each region. The Boston Consulting Group study, cited in *Le Monde*, estimated that US$10 trillion was kept in fiscal paradises – see below for more on those exposed by the Panama Papers. The American business magazine *Forbes* publishes an annual ranking of the world's billionaires.[27] Forbes showed that their net worth increased from less than US$1 trillion in the year 2000 to more than US$7 trillion by the year 2015. That was a seven-fold increase in just fifteen years after the turn of the century. These figures do not include royal families and their households, or heads of state and their families, many of whom also have immense wealth. By 2020 the figure increased to US$8 trillion.

While private levels of luxury reached the stratosphere for a small percentage of the population, the resources used to house, educate, and nourish the majority of people in the world stagnated. In January 2020, at the WEF annual meeting in Davos, the charity Oxfam released its latest report on inequality, showing that the 2,153 billionaires named by *Forbes* in the previous year had more wealth than 4.6 billion people in the world.[28] The richest one per cent had more than twice as much wealth as 6.9 billion people.[29]

In a global economy much wealth is held by transnational corporations. These companies also often use fiscal paradises, and much of their revenue is stored and moved around in ways that legally minimise taxation in the countries where they operate.[30] We have seen that the major efforts made by governments and monetary authorities to mitigate the Global Financial Crisis of 2008–9, with techniques such as quantitative easing, resulted in floods of money. Little of this money was invested in areas of social need, such as education or health. Much of it provided yet more opportunities for speculation – and for the rich to get richer.

The dramatic increase in inequality worldwide was documented in a 2013 bestselling book by French economist Thomas Piketty, called *Le capital au XXIème siècle* (*Capital in the 21st Century*). Based on analysis of great quantities of data from a range of countries stretching back 250 years to the beginning of the industrial revolution, Piketty showed how levels of inequality had fluctuated over times of war and peace. Taking the examples of France and the United States, he showed that in both countries, inequality increased significantly, even explosively in the case of the US, since the 1980s, with the gaps widening after the turn of the century.[31] Piketty's book was heavy on statistics and graphs, but for many people the issues underlying all those statistics – issues of unfairness in the midst of inequality – were brought into stark relief by news headlines in April 2016.

The Panama Papers
After the 2008 crash, a series of financial scandals hit the headlines including, at the end of that year, the exposure of large-scale fraud by the Wall Street firm Bernard L. Madoff Investment Securities. Then several years later, in April 2016, the biggest leak in history revealed just how the super-rich hid their wealth. During the previous nine months, a consortium of investigative journalists from 106 newspapers in seventy-six countries had pored through terabytes of information obtained from the database of the legal firm Mossack Fonseca, based in Panama – one of several major firms specialising in the creation of offshore companies.

As the articles rolled out in newspapers around the world, political figures, sports celebrities, businesspeople, and heirs to family fortunes were named, in country after country, as having taken advantage of offshore arrangements. Over a fifteen-year period, more than 200,000 offshore companies had been used to hide wealth, evade taxes, avoid United Nations sanctions, and conceal sources of income. No region, country, political system, or political party seemed untouched by the scandal. These revelations showed that elites in major powers, irrespective of their political systems, had more in common with each other than they had with the great majority of people in each of their national societies.

The offshore companies created by Mossack Fonseca and similar legal firms continue to serve the barely legal tax 'optimisation' not only of wealthy individuals, but also of immensely wealthy companies, especially those that operate in the global economy of the twenty-first century. The captains of finance and industry of the modern era, with wealth built on surging stock values, are the modern-day equivalents of the aristocrats of feudal times before the industrial revolution. The parallels are all there – the spending on modern-day palaces, the acquisition of rare collections, the competitive splurging on lavish parties and celebrations, the avoidance of taxation, the use of philanthropy to demonstrate social conscience, the sense of entitlement, and the scandals. One can only be struck by the parallels between the situation today and those that preceded each of the five revolutions in this narrative.

Uncivil society

Kofi Annan coined the term 'uncivil society' to describe the 'terrorists, criminals, drug dealers, traffickers ... and others who undo the good works of civil society [taking] ... advantage of open borders, free markets and technological advances'.[32] Vast sums of money are transmitted internationally as a result of these illegal activities. In the past, the slave trade and the opium trade generated huge profits for the perpetrators. The modern-day equivalents of those now discredited and dehumanising practices wreak havoc in communities around the world. They include people trafficking for sex or forced labour. They include trade in narcotics like heroin and cocaine derived from cultivations in poor countries, and newer synthetic drugs fabricated in clandestine laboratories. In the colonial era, archaeological treasures were pillaged, and exotic animals hunted. Today, we continue to see large-scale trafficking of all kinds, including armaments, 'blood diamonds' from conflict zones, ivory or rhinoceros horns, and wild animals.

The profits of these illegal activities also circulate internationally. Those profits, driving criminality and gang warfare, are huge but difficult to trace and record. They are not included in the documented rankings of *Forbes* or *Bloomberg*. Banking regulations have been tightened across the world to combat money laundering, but there is a continuous game of cat and mouse. It is certain that a high proportion of illegal money transits through or is kept in the same tax havens as those used to shelter money accumulated from legal activities. The boundaries between legal and illegal are ambiguous, to say the least.

Corruption

There is nothing new about the prevalence of corrupt behaviour in human affairs. It is best constrained by the rule of law and by a robust consensus in society about appropriate and ethical behaviour. But when those responsible for law and order engage in corruption themselves, and their actions are exposed, the consensus that keeps societies together inevitably becomes fragile. Whenever exposures bring corrupt behaviour into the light of day and they become a prevalent feature of political life, the conditions for revolution begin to fall into place. Not only do people find these behaviours to be deeply reprehensible, they lose their basic trust in the political systems, which are supposed to respond to their needs and to protect their rights. Those who feel their exploitation most intensely no longer accept rules for the maintenance of order in society, for they perceive those rules as designed to maintain dominance by an elite, and to be stacked against them. So they challenge, protest and confront. Anger rises until a boiling point is reached. When confrontation begins, the space for cool and rational debate is lost. Either the confrontation will lead to the overthrow of the prevailing order, or it will be repressed. And if it is repressed, anger deepens, only to explode again some months or years later.

Equality, equity and excess

The American Declaration of Independence stated: 'all men are created equal' and defined 'unalienable rights' for everyone. 'Liberty, Equality, Fraternity' was the slogan of the French Revolution. The call for equality was proclaimed in the Chinese and Russian revolutions. As we have seen in the story of all five revolutions, these aspirations responded each time to a sense of great injustice.

Inequity is to be distinguished from inequality. 'Inequity is about the deep structure of inequality ... Inequity is about disparities that are both great and manifestly unjust,' stated Piketty in 2013.[33] Our narrative suggests that aspirations for economic equality are utopian, for the proclamation of such aspirations in the slogans of the French, Russian and Chinese revolutions was followed each time by immense suffering, while in the United States those of African or native origin were excluded. The key issue is equity, which is about justice, about fair opportunity.

Equitable access to education, for example, was recognised in the twentieth century as the basis of equality of opportunity.

Piketty noted that there had always been intense debate about the distribution of wealth. That debate, he wrote, had often been conveyed through literature, noting that: 'Nineteenth century novels, especially, are full of detailed information about the relative wealth and living standards of different social groups ... the novels of Jane Austen and Honoré de Balzac paint striking portraits of the distribution of wealth in Britain and France between 1700 and 1830 ... and its ... implication for the lives of men and women, including their marital strategies and personal hopes and disappointments.'[34] Here we find the echoes of our stories about the times leading up to those early revolutions.

The balance between equity and excess has waxed and waned throughout history. In 1953, Simon Kuznets published a detailed study of US federal income tax returns over a thirty-five-year period from 1913 to 1948.[35] This study showed a long-term trend towards greater equality in the United States, despite the deprivation of the depression of the 1930s and the impact of two world wars. It became the basis for economic theories and the notion that: 'Growth is a rising tide that lifts all boats.'[36] Piketty noted that the trend towards reducing inequalities continued in the industrialised countries of Europe and Asia until around 1975.[37] During the same period, many newly independent developing countries experienced rapid growth, so the idea set in that sustained growth would naturally lead to greater equality.

But then, almost imperceptibly, the balance began to change, and it changed as national economies became more interlinked. By the time of the American bicentenary in 1976 there was a growing awareness of global interdependence. A world gathering of teacher leaders in Washington DC adopted a 'Declaration of interdependence: Education in a global community'.[38] Major reports on development and growth were produced by agencies such as the World Bank and UNESCO.[39]

By the last two decades of the twentieth century, there were major changes in global trade, investment and financial flows. There was also a huge shift from mainly local or national production and distribution of goods and services towards the globalisation of supply chains. Similarly, investments and financial flows were more international than ever – less constrained by national borders, these shifts towards globalisation of economic activity were greatly boosted by new technologies. Advocates of a liberal economic order saw such shifts as being widely beneficial. But the benefits were enjoyed only by some. The post-World War II trend towards greater equality was reversed.

Deeper and stronger forces were changing the entire picture. Piketty wrote: 'In a way, we are in the same position at the beginning of the twenty-first century as our forebears were in the early nineteenth century: we are witnessing impressive changes in economies around the world, and it is very difficult to know how extensive they will turn out to be or what the global distribution of wealth, both between and within countries, will look like several decades from now.'[40] Piketty noted that 'the resurgence of inequality after 1980 is largely due to the political shifts of the past several decades, especially in regard to taxation and finance'.[41]

In an earlier era of inherited wealth – the period covered by our five revolutions – the great leveller had been education. Piketty wrote: 'Over a long period of time, the main force in favour of greater equality had been the diffusion of knowledge and skills.'[42] But, he added: 'This potent force can nevertheless be thwarted and overwhelmed by powerful forces pushing in the opposite direction, towards greater inequality.'[43]

Piketty suggested two main reasons for this accelerating divergence. Firstly, 'top earners can quickly separate themselves from the rest by a wide margin'. Witness huge increases in the revenues of top managers, even as employees are laid off, and salaries are pegged. Secondly, 'growth is weak and return on capital is high'.[44] In other words, financial speculation produces much greater wealth than the real economy.

Here we come to the nub of the question. Today we see greater and accelerating divergence in incomes and wealth, and of outright excess, than ever before. This is no longer a phenomenon occurring in one or two countries, or across a region. It is global. The gap is widening *within* countries, and *between* national economies, while the numbers of people thrown into poverty by wars, creeping desertification, or national dysfunction have increased dramatically.

At the dawn of the new millennium, there was hope: international solidarity began to grow, but with the onset of the Global Financial Crisis, that hope diminished. The consequences of that loss of hope in the decade from 2009 included the movement of refugees and migrants, legal or illegal, at levels never seen before, even during the great movements of the nineteenth and twentieth centuries. Anyone following political debates over the past decade or more can recognise the often divisive impact of these movements on national and regional politics. National politics has been impacted, whether in the United States, or across Europe, including over Brexit, in relations with the Middle East, around the Mediterranean or in the Pacific. The impact has been felt in South Asia – India and Sri Lanka; in South-East Asia – Myanmar and Bangladesh; across Africa – South Africa and Sudan; and in South and Central America – Colombia, Honduras, and Mexico – to cite just some examples. The consequences are inescapably global.

Piketty wrote that disruption arises not only because of growing inequality, but even more out of a deepening feeling of injustice, of inequity, of unfairness. Add a resurgence of terror attacks and we have the makings of a 'perfect storm' of conditions for revolutions across the planet, just as they existed across Europe in the mid-nineteenth century, as we described in Chapter 3.

Democracy and equality of rights

As the first industrial revolution rolled across the planet, societies emerged from feudalism and autocracy in fits and starts and with a great deal of strife and upheaval. The five revolutions of our narrative were defining political events. Ideas of equality were in opposition to the feudal order. They were debated and disseminated from early in the eighteenth century, in the movement of ideas that preceded the early industrial revolution. This movement became known as the Enlightenment. Among the powerful ideas of the Enlightenment was the notion that all men had equal rights, regardless of wealth, property, or position. The foundations were laid for the concept of governance based on equality of civil rights. The thinkers of the Enlightenment did not make a case for economic equality, but rather for equity in the pursuit of happiness. Debates raged between defenders of the existing order, reformers, and revolutionaries. Democratic systems of government evolved from the notion of linking the right to vote with property ownership to respect for the egalitarian principle of one person, one vote. Even then, the principle applied at first only to men. Full attainment of the 'one person, one vote' principle was only approached later when women won the right to vote in most countries early in the twentieth century. In the United States, the Constitutional Convention of 1787 left to one side the question of slavery. It took Abraham Lincoln's emancipation declaration of 1862, and the civil rights movement a century later in the 1960s, to tackle the removal of barriers to African American voting rights. Today, however, the 'one person, one vote' principle is in peril in liberal democracies, including the United States, as elections are distorted by massive campaign spending and marred by tactics to suppress the voting rights of the least privileged.

In any democratic society, the framework for political debate and electoral contests is set firstly by its constitution. Detailed rules are set out in legislation adopted by elected representatives, which may then be subject to interpretation by an independent judiciary. Among the liberal democracies, there are many different electoral practices codified in their constitutions and legislation. They all have advantages and disadvantages; each nation will have debated them intensely and the debates over the 'rules of the game' often re-emerge at election time. Whatever the system, the key to keeping a society together is confidence in electoral processes, in free and fair elections. The constitutional framework and the way it is applied and interpreted must be accepted by a broad consensus of citizens.

Today, throughout the liberal democracies, there is an increasing sense of disillusion with political processes and institutions. Combine disillusion with increasing inequity and we have conditions ripe for revolution.

The heaving pyramid

Think of the distribution of wealth as a great pyramid. At the pinnacle are the hyper-rich – those with the greatest capacity for excess. At the base are those living in absolute poverty – about 1.5 billion globally. Between these extremes is a gradation of wealth. Many hundreds of millions of people are somewhere just below the top of the pyramid, and they have relatively affluent lifestyles. Most are in the industrialised economies, but there are also many in emerging and developing economies. In the vast middle of the pyramid is to be found the bulk of the 7.8 billion individuals who inhabit the earth – people and families who are neither affluent nor absolutely poor. To over-simplify, it is within these middle levels of the pyramid, composed of several billions of people, that the conditions for revolution are most likely to develop, for these are the people who see the excesses, and who feel most intensely a sense of injustice.

But the pyramid is a limited metaphor, for a classical pyramid is symmetrical and static. The reality of the distribution of wealth is that the pyramid is far from symmetrical and it is constantly changing. Our metaphorical pyramid is distorted, bulging at one level, and retracting at another. At the turn of this century, there was a base of absolute poverty that began to shrink, and there was a levelling out of wealth in the middle levels. The numbers at the pinnacle increased, too, as new technology billionaires were joined by Russian oligarchs after the breakdown of the Soviet Union, and wealthy entrepreneurs in China, as well as in other emerging economies, such as India, Mexico, and Brazil. So, the pyramid was misshapen – getting smaller at the base, bigger at the top, and expanding in the middle.

Then came the Global Financial Crisis. In the years that followed, growth of wealth at the top increased, and the movement to reduce then eliminate absolute poverty at the base came to a shuddering halt. There were still many people living in affluence. But there were many millions more who found themselves sliding backwards. Both globally and within nations, equity decreased while excess increased. This was precisely the imbalance that preceded each of the five revolutions in our narrative.

Perceptions of injustice

Let us take another look at the perceptions of injustice that preceded each of the five revolutions. In the eighteenth century, for a British officer or functionary from the ruling class, time in the American colonies was an opportunity to make a fortune, often by unscrupulous means, before returning to high society in the mother country. It was part of the paradox of the American Revolution that some of the patriots had themselves made fortunes based upon the inequities of the plantation system and slave labour. They were among those who proclaimed most sharply the injustice of taxation without representation.

In the case of eighteenth-century France, inequity was based on a class system derived from the ancient feudal separation between the aristocracy and the remainder of the people. At the apex was the court of the king, whose extravagance almost defied belief. The court of aristocratic nobles lay just below, controlling the country estates and the towns. But as those who claimed to speak for the Third Estate developed the capacity to organise, they were able to challenge the pre-existing order in the name of the people, who were ready to revolt against their traditional rulers.

Six decades later, after the revolution, the Napoléonic Empire, the restoration of the Bourbons, and then the constitutional monarchy of the Citizen King, inequity still prevailed in France and throughout Europe. Merchants and entrepreneurs had by then obtained access to the upper levels of power and wealth. But the pyramid of inequity remained. The Campaign of Banquets was a liberal protest movement, reacting to the scandals of the day, yet excluding the working class and the peasantry. When the liberal protestors toppled the monarchy, Lamartine proclaimed his determination to avoid the catastrophe of the first revolution. His declaration of the Second Republic called for a government based on justice and equity. But labourers excluded by underlying inequity rose up when the Party of Order tried to turn back the clock. Paris was again the scene for massacres as the June 1848 uprising was suppressed. This time revolutions swept across Western Europe. In France, Lamartine was discredited. Louis Napoléon manipulated his way to power and to the Second Empire. Inequity remained.

In China, as in Europe, inequity was part of the structure of society. The Qing dynasty, while inheriting the greatest of all civilisations prior to the European voyages of discovery, reigned over a vast population that was essentially agrarian. The great majority of people were peasants eking out a subsistence existence. So it was in Russia, where the emancipation of the serfs in 1861 had done little to reduce the huge disparity between the landed aristocracy and those who laboured in the fields. This inequity was exposed by Tolstoy in his prolific writing, in his attempts to establish schools for peasants, and ultimately in his personal odyssey to renounce the privileges of his origin.

Information wars

In the pre-revolutionary periods we describe, scandals, rumours and conspiracy theories spread rapidly, partly by word of mouth and more widely by the written word. In feudal societies, literacy was largely reserved for nobles and merchants. Way back in 1440, the invention of the printing press in Europe had gradually opened opportunities for people to read. By the time the industrial revolution began, ordinary working people in Europe and settlers in the colonies were reading newspapers. While literacy rates were greater for men than for women, the power of the written word was apparent more and more in political debate. The lead up to each revolution was the scene for information wars, in which newspapers and pamphlets played key roles in propagating news and views. During the decades leading to the American Revolution, newspapers in the colonies reported abuses of power by British representatives and reflected the growing discontent of the people. Benjamin Franklin was himself the leading publisher of the American colonies. But his reputation came under attack from rival media, which fired up a mob that set siege to his Philadelphia home. He turned the tables with the distribution across the colonies of pamphlets containing his famous testimony to the British Parliament. Leaks of the Hutchinson letters to the press in Massachusetts helped instigate the Boston Tea Party. Franklin's humiliation over those leaks, when he was pilloried before the British Privy Council, was instrumental in his decision to join the American patriots.

As battles raged along the eastern coast of America, Jacques Necker's publication in France of his *Report to the King* was intended as a warning. But it helped to lay the groundwork for the French Revolution several years later. And as conditions worsened, so the rumours of plots and British spies became more prevalent. Prior to the revolution, pamphlets distributed in the streets attacked excesses in the lifestyles of Queen Marie-Antoinette and the king's brothers. But then Necker himself became a target. After his return to Paris, he was attacked in virulent screeds penned by Paul Marais.

Sixty years later, after Alphonse de Lamartine charged in his speech in the storm in Mâcon that corruption was rife in France, the Campaign of Banquets of 1847 was covered extensively in the newspapers of the day, including reports by none other than Friedrich Engels, and his close friend and co-author Karl Marx. Lamartine had analysed with insight and articulated with eloquence the experience of the first French revolution, and he strove to map a way forward for non-violent change in the second revolution. But his efforts to avoid violence and dictatorship failed, as his attempts to reform were attacked scathingly on the right by newspapers aligned with the Party of Order, and on the left by those carrying the reports of Engels and like-minded writers.

Later in the nineteenth century, the battle for influence between Kang You Wei and Sun Yat Sen among overseas Chinese communities was waged largely through their competing newspapers. After repeated cycles of uprising and repression in China, the revolution was sparked in Wuchang by reporting on an attempt by the imperial government to take over the construction of railways.

In Europe, the exiled Lenin was first and foremost a publisher of revolutionary newspapers, using his talents as a writer to build opposition to the tsarist empire. Within Russia, Stolypin saw the danger posed by reports of corruption reaching Russia through clandestine pamphlets. In response, as interior minister, he installed a code of conduct for the police, who became his front-line forces to crackdown on corruption across the empire. Leading up to the revolution, nobles were concerned by reports of Rasputin's influence on the tsarina. After the tsar abdicated, Reed's book *Ten Days That Shook the World* gave a vivid account of the ebb and flow of rumour and information, false or true, leading up to the Bolshevik Revolution of 1917.

Fast forward to the twenty-first century and we have precisely the same phenomenon, but now amplified exponentially through social media based on the internet. In today's interconnected society, information wars are pursued as they always have been, but they are amplified immeasurably by new means of communication. Gossip no longer stays in the village – it speeds around the world. Accusations and counter-accusations of 'fake news' can be amplified millions of times over Twitter, Facebook, YouTube and Instagram. The same is true for the dissemination of conspiracy theories. Even images, still or moving, can be edited and altered.

In the twentieth century, the instruments for communication were the mass media, firstly print media and radio, then television. By the twenty-first century, social media had become the new vector. This interconnectivity can be very democratic, in the sense that anyone can disseminate information or videos filmed on a smartphone, and abuses of authority can be quickly and widely exposed. But social media can also amplify the human tendency to spread rumour and gossip, and so add greatly to the volatility of political discourse. Today, the wildest stories can have planetary reach and there are always people ready to believe them. Of increasing concern is the use of social media taken to extremes in justifying violence. It is striking to see the power of conspiracy theories among all classes of society.

The internet and the development of algorithms have enabled platforms for people to find reinforcement for their biases. Important debates have become necessary over issues such as freedom of expression versus the regulation of hate speech and the dissemination of lies, the right to privacy versus the need to identify potential terror plots and, more generally, the power of data harvesting, as the potential for manipulation of consumers or electors is dramatically increased. Fact-based analysis of complicated issues is all too easily replaced by tweets of no more than 280 characters. Yet, even if the social media of today enables a dramatic acceleration of the circulation of accusations and counter-accusations, true or false, the essence of human behavior has not changed so much. One cannot help but be struck by the parallels between the virulence conveyed in today's social media, and that expressed in the newspapers and pamphlets that circulated prior to each of the five revolutions of 1776 to 1917.

Education is not necessarily the moderator or the filter that one would hope for and expect. Educated elites are as prone to the dissemination of conspiracy theories as anyone. Their embrace of such theories was seen among the British elite of the 1770s and 1780s, among the French elite of the same era, among the European elites of the mid-nineteenth century, and in the Chinese and Russian elites of the late nineteenth and early twentieth centuries. We see the same phenomenon today. Conspiracy theories are generally self-serving. One notorious example in recent times was the so-called 'birther movement' in the United States, which promoted the idea that Barack Obama, the forty-fourth President of the United States and first African American to be elected to that position, was not born on US soil and was therefore ineligible to be president.[45]

Active promotion of that unfounded conspiracy theory helped his successor, Donald Trump, to launch his political career. We will conclude with the aftermath of this movement, playing out in the United States as this book is completed.

In their hubris, the elites who propagate these stories generally manage to convince themselves of their validity. They lock themselves into denial about the risks of growing imbalances in society. Denial explains why they continue dancing before storms.

The yellow vests

By the year 2016, major upheavals were altering the nature of politics not only in the United States but across virtually all the liberal democracies that had grown out of the revolutions of the eighteenth and nineteenth centuries. The European Union (EU) had developed through a series of treaties that sought to heal the battle scars of the past and pursue peace across the old continent. The Union had grown dramatically since it was formed in 1993, more than doubling in area and population after the collapse of the USSR. Then the EU faced the exit of one of its strongest economies, that of Britain; the exit being consummated at the end of 2020. Across Europe and beyond, more authoritarian, less liberal ideas and practices of governance attracted increasing popular support, especially in eastern European countries such as Hungary and Poland, previously controlled by communist governments.

In May 2017, France seemed to buck the trend with a resounding defeat of the National Front and the emergence of a new centrist political movement under Emmanuel Macron, a young former minister of the economy with a reformist and modernising agenda. But in 2018, a decade after the Global Financial Crisis, the *gilets jaunes* (yellow vests) protest movement seemed to come out of nowhere. Violence erupted on successive weekends across major cities and towns, and symbols of the republic were desecrated. To begin with, the yellow vest protests were compared by some commentators to the student protests of May 1968, which had shaken the fifth French republic and its founder, Charles de Gaulle, to the core. This comparison was probably a natural reflex since those events of the late 1960s had also marked a memorable challenge to the system in France.

But a more relevant historical comparison came from 1848 – the year of the Springtime of the Peoples revolutions. As we saw in Chapter 3, an independent candidate, Alphonse de Lamartine – poet, historian and academic, stating that he was neither of the left nor the right – came to power in France. Macron's rise to the presidency at the head of his *En Marche* movement harked back to that time, when Lamartine introduced a series of modernising reforms and became, for a moment, the most popular politician in France. The revolution of 1848 and the rise of Lamartine had their roots in the profound changes in society brought about by the first industrial revolution. But the Lamartine reforms were overrun by the Party of Order, and then the populism of Louis Napoléon. The parallels between the events of 2018–19 and those of 1848 are striking, for in each of those two eras the rise of a new centrist, reformist and modernising political leader had its roots in profound changes in society. The paradox that confronted Macron was in fact similar to the one that confronted Lamartine. For the profound changes that propelled him to power, which we will discuss next, were also at the root of resistance to the reforms that he sought to push forward.

An underlying theme of this narrative has been that the five revolutions that shaped the political contours of the modern world were strongly influenced by the underlying and continuous beat of the initial industrial revolution. As we fast forward to the present time, let us look at the changes in economy and society that have been underway in the past 100 years. A useful way to do that is to take up the idea of a series of industrial revolutions.

A series of industrial revolutions

In 2016, the founder of the World Economic Forum, Klaus Schwab, put forward the notion of a series of industrial revolutions.[46] The **first industrial revolution**, starting around 1760, in the age of Benjamin Franklin and the merry band of innovators of the Lunar Society, replaced muscles with machines. This early industrial revolution dramatically disrupted manufacturing, trade, and warfare, firstly with coal-fired steam power. Schwab stated that this first revolution spanned from about 1760 to around 1840.[47] This may have been so for Western Europe and North America, but it reached Asia later in the century, with the Meiji

Restoration of Japan in 1868, and the attempted modernisation of China over the next thirty years, leading up to the failed reform movement at the end of the century.

Stating that he was 'mindful of the various definitions used to describe the first three industrial revolutions', Schwab placed the advent of electricity in the second one. But it is arguable that the harnessing of electricity proceeded through a continuum from Benjamin Franklin's famous experiment of 1752 to Michael Faraday's early development of DC motors in the 1820s, the invention of the incandescent light bulb in 1870, of Thomas Edison's generators in 1878, and Nikola Tesla's invention of the AC motor in the 1880s. The early internal combustion motors powered by fuel refined from oil in the late nineteenth century, the first motor vehicles, and the beginning of aviation in the early twentieth century, were all developed in the continuity of the first industrial revolution. This first disruptive industrial revolution rolled across the planet from West to East. It drove and underpinned the momentous social and political transformations that emerged painfully from the five historical political revolutions of this narrative.

If the word 'revolution' connotes major disruption, the **second industrial revolution** really began in 1913, on the eve of World War I, as Henry Ford in the United States pioneered mass production. This second revolution led to a consumer society. Ford was also a pioneer in mass advertising, paving the way for the emergence of mass media. This second industrial revolution, the revolution of mass consumption, lasted about fifty-five years in the industrialised countries of Europe, North America, Japan and Australasia. In 1968, the protests of students and intellectuals in France, at almost the same time as civil rights and anti-war protests in the US, challenged the established social and economic orders of consumer societies, which had underpinned economic growth during the two decades following World War II.

Just as the established orders of the post-World War II era were being challenged, a **third industrial revolution** began to take shape. 1969 was a key year in this new transformation, epitomised by three apparently disparate events. In that eventful year, a man first set foot on the moon, and a worldwide television audience watched as Neil Armstrong said the now-famous words – 'One small step for [a] man, one giant leap for mankind.' That step was significant, not only because of the technological and heroic exploit of man reaching the moon, but also because the age of global media had arrived.

In that same year, the Toyota motor company in Japan invented the concept of just-in-time production management, so that companies could keep stocks close to zero and rely instead on mobility to ensure the rapid 'in-time' delivery of components. And in the same year, the Boeing aircraft company in the United States flew the first jumbo jet, the 747, lowering air-travel costs and opening the way to mobility for the masses. Jumbo jets quickly replaced ships for low-income earners to migrate or travel for work and tourism. Then, in the early 1970s, the first microprocessors for computers were developed, opening a new mass market in information technologies. It was this combination of industrial and personal mobility, with global means of communication, that heralded the third industrial revolution.

This new revolution built mobile production and supply lines across continents and oceans, it promoted mobility of employment, and it enabled mobility of people and mobility of finance. All these mobilities became the basis for the world's market economy, and for globalisation.

The mobility of production and supply chains altered economic paradigms. China, along with other Asian economies, reaped the benefits. Container ships crisscrossed the oceans, while overnight air-freighters and millions of long-distance trucks delivered fresh products and spare parts just-in-time. Mobility was promoted politically and academically, and through such bodies as the OECD.[48] But by the second decade of the twenty-first century, the third industrial revolution of mobility ran up against two immense challenges – one from mother nature, the other from ordinary people.

The first challenge – that of mother nature – was the impact on the environment. The fossil fuels powering this mobility are warming the planet, increasing the climatic impact of the first and second industrial revolutions. The countries of the world met at summits in Rio de Janeiro, in Kyoto, then in Paris, to negotiate agreements to slow down this warming process. But in the suburbs, in the countryside, for thirty or forty years, people had been obliged to become more mobile in their daily lives. They had to travel to get to work, to go shopping, for health services, for the education of their children, for their leisure. All of this has had a collective cost, in terms of pollution, health and, more generally, through the impact on climate change. Meanwhile, the industrialisation of food production accelerated deforestation of land and the depletion of fish stocks, once thought to be inexhaustible.

The second challenge – that of the people – was a rise in inequality. From around 1980, the conventional wisdom driving economic policy in liberal democracies was that greater flexibility in labour markets would boost growth for the benefit of all.[49] The reality, however, for many hundreds of millions of working people was that greater flexibility meant greater insecurity in their jobs and lives. As companies chased lower labour costs and relocated production to emerging economies – China among others – hundreds of millions more people left rural communities to work in cities, or to find jobs as migrant workers in other countries, living in poor conditions away from families, and sending remittances back home. Precarity ended up increasing in both the emerging nations *and* the developed market economies. Certainly, some millions of people were able to boost their opportunities and join the growing middle class, while entrepreneurs and investors made fortunes. But another outcome of flexibility, and of the mobility of production chains and the mobility of workers, has been the dramatic widening of the gap between rich and poor over the past thirty to forty years. The policies of the central banks, instigated to help recovery from the financial crisis of 2008, made this gap wider. Wealth at the top of the pyramid exploded; incomes at the base and in the middle layers of the pyramid stagnated. These inequalities were no longer mitigated by progressive forms of taxation as they had been in the post-World War II period, as national anti-tax movements had succeeded in cutting upper tax rates. And increasingly, national taxes could be circumvented by the wealthy as the economy had become global and finance had become mobile.

The yellow vest protesters in France reflected the limits of the third industrial revolution, that of mobility. Since the 1970s, mobility and flexibility had been touted by economic opinion leaders as keys to growth. In practice that meant people had to travel further and further from home to find work, and often they had to change jobs or seek retraining. Mobility replaced proximity, even for shopping and children's schooling.

Mass transport in and between urban centres was unable to keep up with demand, and vehicles carrying people and goods clogged the roads. When the government in France announced an increase in the tax levied on fuel, that technically rational decision unleashed a wave of protest, for it was perceived by a large slice of the population, somewhere in the middle to lower reaches of the economic pyramid, as the last straw. The fuel tax hike became a proxy for a deeper level of frustration, and the protestors cried out: 'You want to save the planet; we want to pay our bills at the end of the month.'

The yellow vest protests in France were a harbinger, a warning. Our story of five revolutions describes how there were often harbingers of that kind before full political revolutions occurred.

A fourth industrial revolution is already on its way. The third revolution of mobility has run its course over a period of about fifty years. Now, leaders of industry state that the world is on the threshold of a fourth industrial revolution. It has been on the table for discussion among industrial and political leaders at the World Economic Forum in Davos since Schwab published his book in 2016. This fourth revolution of artificial intelligence, robotics, virtual reality, blockchains and biotechnology, is approaching fast. We might call it the cyber revolution. We are grappling with the social and political consequences of the third industrial revolution, while the fourth one is already on the horizon. Each industrial revolution has disrupted the existing order. The potential for social disruption will be greater than ever as we cross the threshold of the fourth industrial revolution, because it is highly probable that these changes will further increase inequalities. In his book, Schwab recognises the 'structural shifts which have contributed to rising inequality – and which may be further exacerbated as the fourth industrial revolution unfolds'.[50] He notes that: 'rising inequality is more than an economic phenomenon. It is a major challenge for societies,' and he warns that 'unequal societies tend to be more violent'. He also suggests that while citizens would receive more direct information via social media, paradoxically they would increasingly feel themselves to be excluded from decision-making processes. The growing prevalence of online conspiracy theories, their exploitation for political ends in the United States and Europe, and in countries like Brazil and India, and more seriously their role in inciting violence by those feeling rightly or wrongly that elections have been stolen, suggests that Schwab was prescient in identifying this consequence of the rise of Twitter, Facebook, YouTube and other platforms.[51]

Politics and democracy in a new era

In the United States, the antiquated electoral college system, dating from the nation's origin as a union of thirteen states, has increasingly distorted the principle of one person one vote. As we saw in Chapter 1, the Electoral College was the product of a difficult compromise, for which Benjamin Franklin pleaded with almost his last words, in order to save the new union. Twice in the twenty-first century – in 2000 and again in 2016 – this system produced a presidential election result at odds with nationwide voter tallies, the latter with a disparity of some 2.8 million votes.[52]

Our narrative has shown how the concept of representative democracy emerged amidst social changes wrought by the first industrial revolution and the political upheavals that overthrew old empires. That concept is now challenged by the disruptions of social media. Those in power and those who contest power can use social media to manipulate the spread of information to their own ends. An example was the Cambridge Analytica scandal. In 2018, multiple media broke news of the misuse of the personal data of up to 87 million Facebook users for targeted messages in support of conservative causes and candidates in the 2014 US midterm elections, in the 2016 US presidential election, in support of Brexit in the UK, and in some 200 elections in sixty-eight countries. Along with the widespread use of social media to promote extremist views and causes, there is a deeply worrying re-emergence of extremism in the politics of liberal democracies, and outbreaks of violence. There is a renewed danger that electoral processes will be captured by demagogues, just as after the Great Depression of the 1930s. The precursors of revolution are all there.

The response to risk

Denial is one form of response to risk. But there are many among the wealthy today who do recognise the risks inherent in a society that is fundamentally out of balance. Some of them are adopting a fortress mentality. Home security is one of the most rapidly growing industries worldwide. For the hyper-wealthy, security can be taken to extremes, with the setting up of bunkers equipped to military and governmental standards. The founder of SAFE (Strategically Armored & Fortified Environments) was quoted in a 2013 article estimating that 'families could survive in the best planned of these luxurious strongholds for up to three generations'.[53]

Others seek to engage directly with society in order to achieve a better balance. Some of the wealthiest individuals on the planet are contributing a portion of their immense wealth to programmes aimed at improving the lives of those living in great poverty. The Bill and Melinda Gates Foundation, the largest private foundation in the world, proclaims: 'All lives have equal value.' Joining the two founders as trustee is Warren Buffett, who has pledged his own massive fortune to the foundation's work. With a current endowment of some 45 billion US dollars, potentially to be increased under the testament arrangements of the trustees, the foundation has more resources than many national governments. Globally, many of its resources go into ambitious health programmes. The foundation seems to be driven by both a laudable moral commitment and by a belief that business methods can be applied to difficult problems in the public domain.[54] The trustees have also played a significant role in encouraging other wealthy individuals to commit to redistribution through philanthropy. But the Gates Foundation has also been the target of wild conspiracy theories, for example by anti-vaccine militants. The Open Society Foundation founded by George Soros – who made his billions by speculating on global financial markets – supports civil society groups in some thirty-seven countries, with a stated aim of advancing justice, education, public health, and independent media.[55] Soros has been in turn the target of vehement attacks from populist political leaders in Europe and in the United States.

Back in the time of Napoléon III and the Second French Empire, a businessman from Geneva, Henri Dunant, witnessed the aftermath of the battle of Solferino in 1857 between French and Austrian troops, where some 23,000 soldiers were left to agonise on the battlefield with no care. He used his fortune to create a neutral organisation to provide care for wounded soldiers, and the International Committee of the Red Cross came into being in 1863. This was an example of philanthropy in terms of its original meaning – the desire to provide welfare for others. In 1901, Dunant was awarded the first ever Nobel Peace Prize.

But the term 'philanthropy' should be used with caution. It is a generic term that is often used to describe gifts to universities that perpetuate the donors' names for posterity. The founding of art galleries seems to serve a similar purpose. Two of the wealthiest men in France made their fortunes in luxury goods – a market that did not suffer from the Global Financial Crisis, but indeed flourished. When these two men each decided to construct a gallery of contemporary art in Paris, we were witness to a clash of egos more than an ethical desire to do good in the world. Bernard Arnault of LVMH built his museum in 2019, while François-Henri Pinault of Kering opened his museum in May 2021. It reminds us of the monarchs of old competing to build the most extravagant palaces.

The philanthropy of Dunant as founder of the Red Cross,[56] or of Gates and Buffett aimed at improving health and opportunities for the world's poorest, or of Soros promoting civil rights, is of a different nature. The question remains as to the legitimacy of such private philanthropy for social purposes as distinct from investment in quality public services supported by adequate taxation revenues. This is a large question – probably the subject of another book.

Returning to the focus of our narrative, the key point is that some of the wealthiest people on the planet recognise that a system that is fundamentally unbalanced cannot be sustained. Prominent members of the global elite, people at the very top of the wealth pyramid, present a compelling case for redistribution of wealth. They present a counterpoint to those who continue to deny the need for change.

The lessons of history

'Those who cannot remember the past are condemned to repeat it,' wrote Harvard philosopher George Santayana. Or as American sports star Kareem Abdul-Jabbar put it: 'That simple concept of not drinking from the same carton of sour milk twice is the foundation of civilisation.'[57]

When common patterns emerge from the narrative of several momentous events, each of which changed the course of history, there is a case for learning the lessons. Those historical lessons will never predict the future. Rather they ring warning bells. The question then is whether the warnings will be heeded. In *The March of Folly*, historian Barbara Tuchman showed how such warnings were often ignored throughout history.[58] There are several lessons to be learnt from the story of five revolutions, and each has relevance today.

Lesson 1: The most fundamental lesson is the most obvious one. This is that **when imbalances develop in a society** – at any level, local, national, or global – **a point will be reached when that society will become unstable**. The consensus that keeps society together will crumble. At some point, the structures and conventions that provide order will be overturned. The term 'tipping point' has been used to describe, as one author put it, 'the moment of critical mass, the threshold, the boiling point'.[59] That description fits rather well the point at which major social upheavals and revolutions occur. In 2015, the WEF identified twenty-one potential tipping points when technological shifts would hit mainstream society – from artificial intelligence to tax collection by block-chains.[60]

Lesson 2: The next lesson from the story of five revolutions is that **no one can predict when and how a tipping point will occur**. In each of the revolutions described, conditions had been building for decades. Then, at some point, the revolution was underway. In the case of China, the father of the revolution, Sun Yat Sen, had tried to incite rebellion many times without success, and when the revolution finally occurred, he was taken by surprise. All we can say is that when there is underlying disequilibrium, sooner or later, some event will set the revolution in motion. A quotation attributed to Aristotle in the time of the ancient Greeks states: 'Revolutions are not about trifles, but spring from trifles.' Mao Tse Tung captured the same idea when he wrote: 'A single spark can start a prairie fire.'[61] We have described the various conditions that set the scene for our five revolutions. When these conditions coincide, the probability of revolution being set off by a spark is high. Such is the situation in the world today.

Lesson 3: A further lesson from history is that **not every uprising becomes a fully-fledged revolution straight away**. The revolt in the American colonies against the Stamp Tax died down as the British Government made concessions, but the colonists learnt to mobilise and prepared for another day. In Britain, the Gordon Riots of 1780 were stamped out ruthlessly by the government, and a potential revolution was averted. In Russia, peasant revolts broke out frequently, but were put down. In China, local uprisings were common, but the imperial dynasty thought it had the situation under control. In more recent times, the Prague Spring of 1968 was put down, as was most of the Arab Spring of 2011. But, often, an apparently unsuccessful uprising was a harbinger of greater upheaval to come.

Lesson 4: **When revolutions became more than uprisings, when the structures of societies were overturned, the consequences were rarely predictable, but always far-reaching**. The rebels who launched the American Revolution declared their aspiration to build a society based on the right of all men to life, liberty, and the pursuit of happiness. Yet they could hardly have imagined the dark course of American history, leading to a civil war of epic proportions in the nineteenth century.[62]

Even less could the revolutionaries of France have anticipated the course of their rebellion. From the call for 'Liberty, Equality and Fraternity', the tortuous path of the revolution would lead to the Terror, the dictatorship of Napoléon Bonaparte, war across Europe, and then the restoration of the Bourbon dynasty. Six decades later, Lamartine articulated with keen perception and eloquence the lessons to be learnt from the outcomes of the first revolution. He anticipated the risks of conflict between the traditionalists and the emerging socialists, and he thought that it would be possible to navigate a middle way between extremes. Yet this second revolution, like the first, degenerated into violence, and a new Napoléonic dictatorship emerged.

Another sixty years later, neither Kang You Wei nor Sun Yat Sen in China could do better than Lamartine in France. After the failure of reform, then the revolution that Sun had sought so relentlessly for decades, he was thrust aside within weeks of taking office as the first President of the Chinese Republic. Yuan Shi Kai tried, like Louis Napoléon in France, to establish a new dynasty. The country plunged into a civil war that lasted for decades, until Mao Tse Tung drove out the Japanese and declared a People's Republic in 1949. Nor could those supporting the Russian Revolution early in 1917 have anticipated the course of events, from the October Revolution of the Bolsheviks just ten months later, to the civil war, the establishment of Stalin's dictatorship and the Gulag.

Revolutions born out of the desire of people to rise up against injustice have led too often to immense suffering and loss of life. No one can predict the path or the consequences of such seismic events. More often than not, revolutions that began with the ideals of achieving justice for all have instead brought about massive suffering. This was certainly the case with the first French revolution, and the Chinese and Russian revolutions. We have noted that in the case of the American Revolution, the colonists of European descent prospered, but those descended from African slaves and Native Americans suffered. In the European revolutions of 1848, the regimes of feudal times were replaced by modernisers and a somewhat benevolent dictatorship in France. But the seeds were sown for the great tragedies of the twentieth century.

Signs of the times

In today's global society, all the signs for revolution are there: decreasing equity and increasing excess; the rising discontent of the middle levels of the heaving, distorted pyramid. Protests by those who feel ignored and disenfranchised by ruling authorities are rising: protests ranging from Podemos in Spain to Occupy Wall Street in America, to the yellow vests in France and farmers in India. These protests are usually sparked by a single event or announcement. A young street vendor sets himself alight after being harassed by police in Tunisia; an increase in fuel taxes is announced in France; subway fares are hiked in Chile; a fee on WhatsApp messaging is imposed in Lebanon; a change to extradition laws is announced in Hong Kong; a change to citizenship laws is adopted in India.

Added to this already potent cocktail of dissatisfaction are anti-immigration movements reacting against the mobility of peoples – the very mobility that has been at the heart of the third and current industrial revolution – often with tacit or explicit xenophobic undertones. On top of all this, just as anarchists sowed fear and reaction in the late nineteenth and early twentieth centuries, desperate young men and women have been attracted by fundamentalists in not just one but several of the world's major religions. They enrol in terrorist ventures, driven by nihilist ideologies of destruction and medieval rhetoric, while being influenced by the dark corners of the internet, and using the communication tools of the twenty-first century to plan their attacks.

What does all this mean in today's interconnected world? The truth is that nobody knows for sure. All we know is that underlying conditions – like those that preceded five revolutions over a 140-year period of history – are developing not just in one country, but globally. Technologies have evolved dramatically. The impact of technological change is now many times greater than that of the industrial revolution that began our narrative. The impact of worldwide travel, of media, the internet and instantaneous communication is still being played out.

So, too, is the highly significant impact of technological change on our collective capacity for destruction, from nuclear weapons to remotely controlled drones, to space weapons. We should not forget that each of our five revolutions occurred in the context of international conflicts. The American Revolution came after the Seven Years' War between Britain and France; the course of the French Revolution was influenced by conflict between the empires of France and Austria; the European revolutions of 1848 interacted with conflicts in Poland and Hungary; the Chinese Revolution came in the wake of numerous European interventions and the war between Russia and Japan; and most obvious of all, the Russian Revolution came after three devastating years of World War I.

Jump forward from 1918 to World War II. As that war concluded, with the dropping of the first atomic bombs in Hiroshima and Nagasaki in 1945, humankind developed the capacity for its own destruction. The fundamentally significant lesson of history is that the course of each revolution is unpredictable, as are its consequences, both within national borders and beyond them. Can anyone predict the consequences of revolutions in the nuclear age? Those consequences, while unpredictable, are almost certain to be devastating for humanity.

With that dire warning in mind, we return to the first lesson of history identified in this narrative, which is that imbalances in society are unsustainable. To deny this lesson is to continue dancing before storms.

The challenges we face

The human capacity for denial is remarkably powerful. Specific interests tend to prevail over collective interests, unless and until consensus develops that gives priority to the public good. And human societies do not have a record of success in anticipatory learning. What can be done to redress the imbalance – to move back closer to some form of equilibrium that would enable societies to avoid disaster and, rather, to evolve healthily?

The story of five revolutions shows that each time there were people in key positions of influence, who saw the writing on the wall and tried to reform the existing system. Each time, their warnings were minimised or ignored. Their attempts at reform were swept aside. Revolutions followed. Does this mean that attempts to reform are always doomed to fail? Not necessarily, as another study might show examples of evolutionary rather than revolutionary change. Examples that come to mind are Britain during the Victorian era, Japan after the Meiji Restoration, or Switzerland, one of the world's earliest democracies and one based on a culture of consensus (although one of the last to recognise the right of women to vote). But the lesson of this narrative is that the road to peaceful change is paved with obstacles. Overcoming vested interests and the natural propensity of people to deny the writing on the wall can make the task of rational reform extraordinarily difficult. So is the challenge of navigating between extremes, which so often fuel reactions from opposite ends of the spectrum and thereby undercut or sabotage intelligent solutions to issues affecting everyone.

By the new millennium, as in the past, people who could be actors for positive change emerged again. Kofi Annan was one. He knew the world's premier global organisation – the United Nations – from the inside, firstly as a management expert then as head of UN peacekeeping operations. Elected as secretary-general, he had the support of world leaders for an ambitious programme to improve living conditions for billions of people. But his second term was over-shadowed by the rise of terrorism and responses to that threat by powerful nations that side-stepped the UN. After he completed his second term, Annan continued his work through a foundation he created, and as chair of The Elders, a group of eminent leaders founded by Nelson Mandela, which could offer often discreet counsel to those in power.

Nelson Mandela and Kofi Annan have died, but they have successors. They are eminent scholars, national leaders, and heads of international organisations. Do they have enough influence to encourage rational decision-making by those who wield military and economic power? Can they inspire a sense of common purpose at a time when the political temptation of nationalism is resurgent? In many liberal democracies, political candidates use slogans and sound-bites to promote deceptively simple 'solutions' to complex problems. These methods are often used by those described as populists. Perhaps the greater the complexity of the problem, the greater is the tendency to turn to simplifiers, which may help to explain the new ascendancy of populist movements.

Even the most powerful national governments cannot simply dictate greater equity in their nations or in the world. Nor can a balanced society be achieved solely by legislation. It is wishful thinking to believe that the solution is to be found in political processes alone. Elections can change leaders and representatives, they help to define policy options, and importantly they can define a sense of direction. But elections cannot of themselves provide the solutions. The power of special interest groups is simply too overwhelming, and the potential for gridlock is too great, for electorally driven politics to address the overarching trends that affect the balance between equity and excess.

An example is tax law, almost always a major issue in elections. A report published by the Council of Global Unions in 2011 pinpointed the reality that national laws are inadequate to address the issue of fair and reasonable taxation in a global economy.[63] The issues raised in that report, showing how major global corporations can legally minimise taxation, have since been placed on the agenda of the OECD, the European Union, and G20 summits, and have been debated by national legislatures. In 2016, *Newsweek* described in detail how the Amazon corporation had pursued 'aggressive tax minimisation policies which entailed a complex web of companies, and moving its European retail headquarters to Luxembourg in 2004'.[64]

Another example is labour law, which is inherently national or local. The global economy of the twenty-first century has been largely built on asymmetry between the costs of labour in different countries – and consequently trade policy has become a major issue in national elections. National governments and legislatures try to address the implications of the global economy through trade agreements. Global agreements have become so complex that the work of the World Trade Organization is effectively gridlocked. Emphasis has been placed instead on regionally and bilaterally negotiated agreements, and respect for labour and environmental standards has become a major issue in these tortuous negotiations. Trade agreements may also affect the shifting shape of the distorted pyramid of distribution of wealth. But they do not, any more than national legislation, provide the answer to the overarching question: how can a global human society achieve a reasonable balance between equity and excess?

The United Nations continues to convene high-level summits. In 2015, the General Assembly approved the renewal and extension of the Millennium Development Goals. A series of summits on climate change culminated in the 2016 Paris Agreement. Meanwhile, the UN's specialised agencies do important work to ensure the basic functioning of a global society in telecommunications, meteorology, intellectual property, health, education, human rights, transport, food and agriculture, employment, science, culture, and support for refugees. But even the technical agencies have been the subject of controversies, often driven by national politics and competition between member states. The International Monetary Fund has strained to maintain financial stability. The World Bank, its sister organisation born of the post-World War II Bretton Woods Agreement, has striven to foster equity through development. Both institutions have been too often at the mercy of larger forces, such as global financial trends and crises. If we count all the regional and local wars that have afflicted nations since World War II, some of them protracted over decades, the United Nations has not been very successful in fulfilling the mandate of its charter to keep peace between nations. National interests have almost always prevailed over collective interests. So, the institutions of our global society, important as they are, do not provide the solution either.

Given the cumbersome nature of global institutions, with the United Nations having 193 sovereign states as members, the concept of the G20, as it emerged from the financial crisis, seemed to be more manageable. The G20 communiqués have recognised many of the issues that underlie this book. But recognition is not action – and effective action is proving slow to take shape. As in the periods leading up to the five revolutions, agreements from the G20 summits have had the air of 'too little, too late'. It is impractical to think that either international or regional political institutions or their economic and technical partners can resolve the fundamental conundrum of imbalance. They are no more likely to succeed than the reformers of the dynasties of the eighteenth to twentieth centuries. So where else can we look?

The involvement of civil society, in its broad sense, is critically important. Organisations that grew out of the wrenching experiences of the industrial revolution – notably trade unions – developed the concept of representative civil society, giving a voice to diverse interests. It has been 100 years since the role of trade unions and employer organisations – now described as 'social partners' – was recognised in the Treaty of Versailles by the creation of the tripartite International Labour Organization (ILO). This was an institutional response to the first industrial revolution, its social consequences, and the impact of the Bolshevik Revolution in Russia. But, as the third industrial revolution of mobility advanced, labour organisations declined in membership, and thus their ability to advocate for employees was diminished. Often, they were portrayed as barriers to flexibility. They have to reinvent themselves, as they can and should play a vital role in providing checks and balances in the global economy of the twenty-first century. Bodies like these are joined by employers' organisations and chambers of commerce, and membership associations. These range from volunteer organisations like Rotary to religious-based groups like the World Council of Churches, Pax Romana, the World Jewish Congress, the Muslim World League, or the Buddhist Soka Gakkai, to many secular bodies, all seeking to do good in the world. Representative civil society organisations with defined criteria for membership provide opportunities for advocacy and activism, and they can exercise influence on political processes. But that is not enough to address the issue of inequity and excess that underlies the conditions for revolution.

In the late twentieth century, new and less-structured civil society groups developed. Rather than having defined memberships, they are movements driven by support for causes, just as those striving to abolish slavery did in earlier times. Activists in these movements engage in development, combating poverty, human rights, saving the planet, and much more. Examples are Médecins Sans Frontières (Doctors Without Borders), Oxfam, Amnesty International, Greenpeace, the Global March against Child Labour, the Youth Strike for Climate – the list goes on. There are thousands of such groups – some better known than others, some more structured than others, all engaging citizens in practical work and advocacy for causes. Using the possibilities offered by new technologies, these organisations have engaged younger generations. They have overlapped with political activists and movements. They have joined representative civil society organisations in parallel events at UN summits, or around G8 or G20 summits. They have established environmental, human rights and safety standards to be applied to the supply lines of the global economy. Making use of social media, the highly diverse memberships of these open civil society organisations has been effective in advocacy and mobilisation.

But still, these movements are merely knocking at the doors of the holders of economic and political power. Some of them knock politely, others do so vehemently, or stage spectacular stunts to attract attention And there are often anarchist movements, such as those using 'black bloc' tactics, who seek to disrupt with violence any gathering of leaders, such as the G20, capturing the media headlines and overshadowing the peaceful advocacy of civil society organisations. As we have reiterated in this chapter, anarchist and violent movements almost always set back, and do not advance, progress – and they have all too often provided justification for reaction and repression.

Neither political institutions nor civil society organisations are able to fundamentally shift the balance between rich and poor, because none of them controls the levers of financial and economic power. The controllers of financial and economic power are far from a monolithic group. They include major manufacturing corporations with a century or more of history; huge trading groups and giants of logistics on land, sea and in the air in the era of mobility; the traditional banking sector and powerful new financial actors such as private equity and hedge funds; the print, radio and television media and the new actors of the internet age, who have accumulated immense wealth, and are now challenged about the power they wield in societies. Nor should we overlook the economic clout of state-owned or -sponsored corporations and, of course, the defence and armament industries that intertwine economic and political power. The interests of all these actors in the economy are inevitably diverse, and it is in their very nature to pursue specific interests rather than some form of common interest. Institutional business groups have rarely risen to the challenge of looking beyond the interests of their sectors to the overarching questions of equity in society, and they are not prone to express much concern about visible forms of excess.

One business-oriented organisation, which has pursued a more searching quest for answers in a global economy, is the Swiss-based World Economic Forum, with its slogan 'Committed to improving the state of the world.' In July 2016, its website published an article *Globalization for the 99%: can we make it work for all?*[65] Composed of the heads of major corporations, WEF has developed a successful formula to enable interaction between its corporate membership and political leaders, while inviting input from civil society groups, including militant environmental and development movements, trade unions, and also academic researchers who challenge the conventional wisdom. The Forum prides itself on being open to fresh thinking, and does not hesitate to debate questions such as climate change and equity, although it tiptoes around human rights and other issues that might jeopardise what it describes as its 'convening power' – its ability to attract the participation of key leaders and major players on the world stage. Another sensitive issue is taxation policy. As the Forum grew from its initial modest origins in the Swiss Alps, it rather successfully reinvented itself from a small gathering of company heads into the world's premier networking venue for business and political leaders, with extensive media coverage for its major events. But its readiness to reinvent should include being prepared to enlarge topics for debate, including those that directly affect its corporate constituency. This means being prepared to address the seemingly taboo 'T' word – taxation – in a rational way, with readiness to eschew sloganeering and rhetoric on any side of the debate. Otherwise, the position of the Forum would be analogous to that of the French aristocracy at the General Estates in Versailles in 1789, that is to say, a readiness to debate everything except taxation on themselves and, of course, their control of the economy.

So, we have national governments and legislatures, international and regional inter-governmental organisations, representative civil society organisations and movements, and networking venues for the holders of economic and political power. Not to be overlooked, we also have the 'fourth estate' – the media – and, of course, social media. Yet, out of all these means for communication, we do not readily see a coherent response to the essential question: 'What is to be done about the challenge of equity?'

Just as the masters of finance felt that they had matters under control in 2007, so political leaders like to convey that they are on top of the changes shaking society. But they are not. Rather, taking the example of Mikhail Gorbachev, the last President of the Soviet Union, they are like surfers, doing their best to keep on top of the waves. They do not control the waves. The best they can hope to do is to ride them.[66] We return to the thesis of Tolstoy in *War and Peace*. Writing about Napoléon Bonaparte, Tolstoy challenged the notion of a great man able to forge the destiny of an entire continent. That notion is too simplistic. The course of history is far more complex. This narrative of five historical revolutions provides a glimpse of that underlying complexity.

The conclusion of this narrative is that today there is convincing evidence that conditions are in place for a new revolution, or a series of revolutions. Today's global economy is undergoing an uneven but inexorable transition from the third industrial revolution, that of mobility, into a fourth industrial or cyber revolution driven by technological change. Yet, whatever the era, and the impact of technological disruptions, society must deal with the age-old debate between the common good and private interests. Underlying that debate is the fundamental issue of equity and justice. When societies have tried but failed to address these matters, they have moved out of the shaky equilibrium required for survival, and they have set themselves on the road to revolution.

In the meantime, events are overtaking the writing of a conclusion to this story. Before we advance some more thoughts about what might be done, let us consider what is happening as the entire world grapples with a global threat to human health and well-being, on a scale not seen since the narrative of the last of our five revolutions ended, some 100 years ago.

Pandemic

As the final chapter of this book is written, the pandemic of COVID-19, by definition a global epidemic, has hit the world. Most of humanity has experienced lockdowns, while air, sea and land travel have ground almost to a halt. Nations are battling to contain waves of infection and mortality. Governments have taken extraordinary measures, trying not only to control the pandemic but also to stave off the risk of an economic recession deeper and longer lasting than the one following the Global Financial Crisis of 2007–2009. Our societies face economic and social transformations. There will undoubtedly be winners and losers. The relevance of this book has been dramatically brought into focus.

By early 2021, after about eighteen months of the pandemic, recorded infections passed 200 million, while recorded deaths passed the tragic mark of 4 million. Mutations of more contagious strains prolonged the challenge, even as vaccines became available. We are experiencing the greatest disruption to life since the Second World War.

An earlier pandemic swept the globe just over 100 years ago, as World War I ended. In 1918, a pandemic of a virulent strain of influenza caused by an H1N1 virus spread like wildfire around the world. In successive waves over the next two years, it was estimated to have infected 500 million people, or one third of the world's population at that time, and to have been responsible for at least 50 million deaths. The pandemic of a century ago spread with the movement of troops, refugees, and migrants in the age of steamships and railways. Further back in history, waves of the bubonic plague were spread by traders in the age of sail. The word 'quarantine' comes from the old word in Venetian dialect, *quarantina*, for the forty days that sailing ships, returning to Venice from China, were obliged to wait offshore before docking in the harbour. Now, in the twenty-first century, in the age of air travel and cruise ships, the rate of global transmission of a new virus and its mutations has accelerated dramatically.

The spread

The rapid spread of COVID-19 was exacerbated by the extraordinary and unprecedented worldwide mobility of people in the twenty-first century. This mobility has accelerated over the past fifty years. From the time when the first wide body 'jumbo jet' took to the skies in 1969, air travel has expanded exponentially, whether for business, tourism, migration, work, education or family reasons. Despite earlier, more limited, coronavirus outbreaks – SARS and MERS – in Asia and the Middle East, airport border controls have remained ill-equipped to screen for health risks. For a new and poorly understood virus, air-travel borders are quite simply porous, and land borders are even more so. By the time controls slammed down on borders between the twenty-six European countries joined by the Schengen treaty for free movement of peoples (reflecting again the third industrial revolution of mobility) the coronavirus had already crossed them. Far away, in New Zealand, in Australia, and in Taiwan, the early implementation of strict border controls, along with strict shutdown measures, initially brought success in almost eliminating the virus locally. As for travel by sea: cruise-ships, the icons of an industry which had grown by leaps and bounds in previous decades, proved to be floating 'petri-dishes' for the virus.

The consequences

In March and April of 2020, about 50 years after the mobility revolution began, human mobility came to a sudden halt. Travel slowed almost to a standstill, as countries went into isolation. The people of most Western nations were forbidden or discouraged from travelling during the Easter vacation, and Muslim pilgrimages to Mecca were cancelled. Israel was already in strict quarantine. With Italy being an early epicentre in Europe, the Pope conducted Easter ceremonies in an empty Saint Peter's Square in Rome, after musing in an interview that possibly 'this is nature's hour of reckoning with us'.[67] Military forces were called out in many countries to strengthen the enforcement of confinement and provide logistical support to hospital and medical services. The most visible symbols of military power – nuclear-powered aircraft carriers – also proved vulnerable to the virus: two of them – American and French – were forced to dock for quarantine and disinfection.

By mid-April 2020, governments began to release figures revealing dramatic slowdowns in economic activity for the first three months of the year, with predictions of worse to come. The OECD in Paris and the IMF in Washington released early estimates of the economic impact across the globe. In Geneva, the WTO released estimates for a dramatic drop in worldwide trade, while the ILO warned that 1.25 billion workers would see their livelihoods threatened – with the highest rates of unemployment expected since the Great Depression of 1930 to 1939 – far more than during the more recent Global Financial Crisis. The United Nations Conference on

Trade and Development in Geneva, the Food and Agriculture Organisation of the UN in Rome, and the World Bank in Washington all warned of the high risk for populations in developing countries with poorly equipped health systems, as did the Gates Foundation in the US and the Global Fund in Geneva, with their experience of combating epidemics of typhoid, malaria and HIV/AIDS. In Brussels, Education International, a major civil society organisation, highlighted the impact of lockdowns on billions of students in schools, colleges, and universities around the world. It presented proposals for the maintenance of education for the younger generations, who will face the challenge of rebuilding their societies once, hopefully, the crisis passes.

Some governments recognised the risk and moved quickly to 'flatten the curve' of the rate of propagation of the virus. But authorities, in most countries scrambled to tackle the need for adequate medical facilities, in races against time to save lives and test vulnerable populations. Medical research was ramped up worldwide to find effective treatments and vaccines. While doing so, frontline medical personnel paid a heavy price, with many becoming infected.

Governments rushed out economic rescue packages, acknowledging that they were playing for time. A total of 8 trillion US dollars was pledged to American and European private companies in loans and tax breaks[68] and most commentators observed that it was just the beginning. A new stimulus package aimed at providing relief for families and boosting consumption was prepared by the incoming Biden administration in the United States. Even in the best-case scenarios, these rescue packages could impose a burden on future generations, who will have to manage the economic fallout, including debt. A trade union leader and economist, who over three decades has engaged directly in consultations with government leaders as they prepared for G7, G8 and G20 summits, wrote that the global economy was in uncharted waters, and was facing 'an economic crisis like no other'.[69]

Already by April, the political strains on existing institutions were beginning to show. The United States government accused the World Health Organization (WHO) of being too accommodating – some politicians said complicit – with the authorities in China, where the outbreak originated. As the United States engaged in a trade war with

China, the latter imposed tough trade restrictions on Australia after it called for a WHO investigation into the outbreak of the virus.

Features of the third industrial revolution – the internet, teleconferencing and smartphones – have helped people, businesses, and public services to cope with confinement. From schooling to international summit meetings, online sessions have become a part of life. A key feature of the fourth industrial revolution or the cyber revolution – artificial intelligence – is being put to work for contact tracing. Already, before the pandemic, issues were emerging around the use of such tools by authoritarian regimes, their impact on privacy, and their potential for manipulation in market economies, ranging from consumption patterns to electoral processes. These privacy issues are more pertinent than ever, as authorities consider vaccination passports as requirements for travel or employment.

In some countries, there were protests against lockdowns and other restrictions, and against the wearing of masks. As second and third waves and mutations prolonged the pandemic into the new year, medical researchers were engaged in a race between the variants and the vaccines. Authorities faced challenges of vaccine supply and distribution, while conspiracy theories about the vaccines circulated on social media. The challenge of reaching most of the world's population with vaccines again brought into sharp focus questions of national interest versus global solidarity and, most of all, the fundamental question of equity, within countries and among countries, in access to health.

The global health crisis ... the global economic crisis. Will political crisis follow?

On 20 March 2020, the journal *Foreign Policy* stated that 'like the fall of the Berlin Wall or the collapse of Lehman Brothers, the coronavirus pandemic is a world-shattering event – whose far-ranging consequences we can only begin to imagine today. This much is certain: Just as this disease has shattered lives, disrupted markets and exposed the competence (or lack thereof) of governments, it will lead to permanent shifts in political and economic power in ways that will become apparent only later.'[70]

Writing in *The Wall Street Journal* on 3 April 2020, former US Secretary of State Henry Kissinger harked back to the Enlightenment thinkers, who provided the intellectual underpinning for the American and French revolutions, writing: 'Enlightenment thinkers (argued) that the purpose of the legitimate state is to provide for the fundamental needs of the people: security, order, economic well-being, and justice. Individuals cannot secure these things on their own. The pandemic has prompted an anachronism, a revival of the walled city in an age when prosperity depends on global trade and movement of people.' Kissinger continued: 'The world's democracies need to defend and sustain their Enlightenment values. A global retreat from balancing power with legitimacy will cause the social contract to disintegrate both domestically and internationally.'[71] Kissinger's reference to 'the social contract' recalls the 1762 book of that title by Jean-Jacques Rousseau, which presented the case that the whole population constituted 'the sovereign', not a monarch who ruled by divine right – a seminal work in developing the concept of republicanism at that time.

Five years earlier, in 2015, Kissinger wrote in the conclusion to his book *World Order*: 'The political and the economic organizations of the world are at variance with each other. The international economic system has become global, while the political structure of the world has remained based on the nation-state.' He went on ... 'In these conditions, the challenge becomes governance itself.'[72] Kissinger presented the same analysis as the editors of the Global Unions report of 2011 referenced above. The simplistic rhetoric of nationalism must confront the complex yet undeniable reality of interdependence.

It would be hard to find two writers more diametrically opposed in their analyses of politics than Henry Kissinger and Thomas Piketty. Yet, in recent years, both have highlighted the instability of the economic and political constructions of today's world.[73] As in the example of the central bankers who on the eve of the Global Financial Crisis looked at each other, touched wood, and said 'We think we've got it under control,' there is a natural human tendency in the face of uncertainty to hope for the best. Now, as the third industrial revolution of mobility comes to a grinding halt because of the spread of a highly contagious virus, there is an assumption expressed by many political and business leaders that, once the health crisis is over, trade, travel and economic activity will simply be kick-started, and the world will get back to business as usual. But neither Kissinger, nor Piketty, nor any of the writers who contributed to the edition of *Foreign Policy* on 20 March 2020, cited above, shared that assumption.

And here is another lesson from history: the Great Depression of the 1930s set the conditions for the rise of nationalism, and a second devastating world war. It will not be so easy to get back to business as usual. Disruption and dramatic political changes are more probable.

Black Lives Matter

Seven weeks after Kissinger's warning of the risk of social disintegration appeared in *The Wall Street Journal* in April, a 17-year-old girl was witness to an awful scene outside a local store in Minneapolis. A black man was pinned to the ground gasping for breath as a white policeman knelt fatally on his neck. With her smartphone she filmed the whole scene, and the videoclip went viral on the internet. Protests under the banner Black Lives Matter erupted across the United States. Polls indicated that upwards of 20 million people participated in them during the following days and weeks. Curfews were declared in 200 cities and 96,000 national and state guard troops were called out – the largest military mobilisation in the US since the Second World War. Peaceful demonstrations turned violent in some cases, resulting in riots and looting, and in confrontations provoked by white supremacist extremists. The Black Lives Matter movement had developed earlier, in 2013 and 2014, following other killings of black men – one by a vigilante, two by police – and other cases of deaths in custody. In 2020, the protests went global, with demonstrations against racial discrimination and calls for reform of policing and criminal justice in the US, Britain, Germany, France, Denmark, Canada, Australia, New Zealand and Japan.[74] Here was yet another example of a single event sparking upheavals worldwide.

Two blocks of K Street north of Lafayette Park, named for the French statesman and hero of the American Revolution, and located in President's Park opposite the White House, were officially renamed Black Lives Matter Plaza. Even as the coronavirus pandemic continued to spread, the movement played into the 2020 US presidential election, and especially the intensive campaigns of the competing parties to mobilise voter turnout.

In the United States, the democratic principle of 'one person, one vote' was historically denied to many African Americans and, even after the passing of the Civil Rights Act of 1964, the suppression of opportunities for voter registration among minorities continued. Myriad laws adopted by state legislatures and interpreted by various courts provided fertile ground for manipulation, as contending parties and candidates sought electoral advantage.

By mid-2020 it was apparent that minorities concentrated in poorer neighbourhoods in the US were significantly more impacted by the pandemic than affluent Americans.[75] Underlying inequalities, racial divisions and the pandemic all came together as factors in the get-out-the-vote strategies of the competing parties and their candidates at multiple levels – in the presidential and vice-presidential election itself, but also in congressional, senate and many state elections, and ballots on issues, including some twenty related to voting rights and the police. Ahead of the November election, the incumbent, Donald Trump, and the Republican Party mounted systematic attacks, through everything from social media to TV advertising and mass rallies, against mail-in voting, which would help millions of those most affected by the pandemic to vote. This was especially the case in the electoral counties of cities with concentrations of African Americans and other minorities at the lower end of the socio-economic scale. Trump had launched his political campaign for the US presidency with a racist conspiracy theory – the birther movement. He protested the end of his presidency with another racist conspiracy theory – that the election was stolen by massive fraud in cities with a majority of African Americans. This was the latest iteration of a long history of voter suppression. Despite 250 years of progress, issues of race were still haunting democracy in the land of the free. These issues, as we saw in Chapter 1, dated from the drafting and adoption of the Declaration of Independence in 1776 and the Constitution in 1783, and then the civil war of the nineteenth century, and the civil rights movement of the twentieth century.

It is also pertinent to make a comparison with at least two other pre-revolutionary periods in our narrative. The first example, also from Chapter 1, was the control of parliament exerted in eighteenth-century Britain by the landed gentry, the resulting corruption decried so strongly by Benjamin Franklin, and the way in which that blinded the British elite to the concerns and demands for voting rights of the American colonists. The second comparison, from Chapter 5, was the insistence of the Russian reformist, Pyotr Stolypin, from 1905 onwards, on the restriction of voting rights in order to privilege property holders. The lesson surely to be drawn from each of these examples is that the denial or suppression of the voting rights of those people most subject to inequalities, based on race or socio-economic status, or both, will end badly. Think again of Henry Kissinger's recent warning of the risks of disintegration of the social contract.

For hope that, as Martin Luther King said, the arc of history bends towards justice,[76] look again at our account in Chapter 3 of Alphonse de Lamartine's achievement of universal male suffrage in France. And reflect again on Abraham Lincoln's address at Gettysburg, 'government of the people, by the people, for the people', which in turn inspired Sun Yat Sen in China, as we saw in Chapter 4.

The US election; the storming of the Capitol

Our story of five revolutions began in a storm over Philadelphia in 1752 and continued with the Declaration of Independence in 1776. In 2021 we return to the nation that was founded during those times and not only gave rise to the biggest economy and the strongest military of the twentieth century, but also held as a central tenet of political discourse the conviction that the US was the leading democracy, and leader of the free world.

After four turbulent years of the Trump presidency, once all the votes were counted and certified, former Vice President Joe Biden and his running mate Kamala Harris had a nationwide lead of more than 7 million votes, and in the Electoral College a clear majority of 306 to 232 votes. Trump refused to concede, claiming that the election had been stolen, launched numerous court challenges, all of which were rejected, and pressured officials in key states to change their certifications. On 6 January, as Congress met in joint session to certify the votes of the Electoral College, Trump held a large rally in the park behind the White House and urged his supporters to march to the Capitol to 'fight'.

So they did. Thousands of supporters streamed along the Washington

Mall to the Capitol, burst through police lines, climbed stairs and walls, smashed windows and doors, entered the main hall and the Senate chamber as members of Congress were hastily evacuated, and sacked offices. Trump's vice president, Mike Pence, was taken to safety with seconds to spare, and he, not Trump, called for reinforcements from the National Guard. After the mob was cleared from the building several hours later, the joint session of Congress, chaired by Pence, resumed to complete the counting of the certified Electoral College votes. At 3.40 the following morning, Pence declared Biden and Harris elected, to take office, in accordance with the constitution, on 20 January. The following week, the House of Representatives voted to impeach Trump for incitement of insurrection.

Briefings given by the FBI to members of Congress and the media highlighted serious and continuing threats to the inauguration and also to state legislatures. By the weekend before inauguration day, 25,000 National Guard troops were deployed into central Washington to guard a heavily fortified Capitol. Other troops were deployed to guard state capitols throughout the country. Investigations of social media by the FBI and other law enforcement agencies indicated that extremist white supremacist groups were coalescing around plans to continue armed opposition to the transition of power and beyond.

On 6 January 2021, after nearly 245 years, the American Revolution completed a full circle. In the many video clips taken by the media and others during these events, the rioters were heard to repeat the rhetoric of Trump and his supporters that they were patriots fighting to take back America, just like the patriots who took up arms back in 1776. Ironically, they used the American Revolution to justify their violence. But they swept aside the principles set forth in the Declaration of Independence, and they sought to override by force the electoral provisions of their own constitution.

As a new administration took its place in the seat of power, there was hope that the United States would overcome this crisis as it had others. Time will tell. Meanwhile, the underlying issues of injustice and imbalances and governance present challenges to all nations on a scale that far exceeds even the challenges faced by the reformers recounted in our story of five revolutions.

Conclusion

We return to the question posed at the beginning of this chapter. What is the probability of a new revolution that will upend the world as we know it? Before March 2020, conditions were already taking us towards a new revolution – or series of revolutions.

The global pandemic has significantly increased the odds that earth-shaking upheavals are still to come. Black Lives Matter protests and the storming of the US Capitol by a mob carried along by white extremists reveal how the social fabric has been shredded in the country born out of the revolution of 1776. As the rioters at the Capitol were filmed and seen by millions in many countries, their actions were harbingers of the potential for disastrous breakdowns of national societies, not only in the United States but around the world.[77]

Revolutions are driven by the rejection of old orders and the aspiration for new ones. If history is any guide – and again, each situation is unique – the advocates of revolution will proclaim a utopian vision for a new order. But the dilemma has always been that to aspire to utopia is to invite disillusion. Moreover, revolutions do not follow rational paths, and when irrationality prevails, the consequences are usually catastrophic. Calls justifying violence will surely emerge, and the risk of violence may be greater as societies grapple with the economic fall-out from the global pandemic.

Already, protests around the world have been symptomatic of a growing sense of injustice within many societies. The economic consequences of the pandemic, which can only be imagined at this time, will almost certainly add to that profound sense of injustice. Such fundamentally important issues as access to quality healthcare and quality education must come to the fore. Once viable therapies to treat COVID-19 are found, and the recently developed vaccines that prevent It are produced at scale, there will be enormously challenging issues of priorities in distribution and access. Tragedy on a vast scale cannot be ruled out.

And it has to be said – the shadow of the threat of nuclear war has never gone away. For seventy-five years, since the bombing of Hiroshima and Nagasaki, the use of nuclear weapons has been avoided. It cannot be assumed that avoidance of their use will be maintained in a time of unpredictable upheaval.

The opposite of utopia is dystopia. In popular fiction and cinema there has long been a theme of the courageous hero confronting a dystopian world – as though deep down we always felt that the risk of the catastrophic failure of civilisation was never too far away. Frustration of the governed over the dysfunction of governmental systems is entirely understandable. The temptation to heed the siren calls of deceptively simple solutions is great.

Even before the pandemic, the concept of representative democracy was in crisis, not only in the United States, but in many countries in Europe and across the developing world. Democracy – the notion of government by the people, of the people, for the people – requires more than institutions. It requires a culture of trust between the governors and the governed; this confers legitimacy on institutions with their rules and their customs. That culture of trust and of shared purpose is all too absent in the politics of today's turbulent world.

Models of representative democracy, with competing parties and freedom of expression, are today juxtaposed with models of centrally controlled political systems that insist on discipline over the contest of ideas. Those committed to the former describe the latter as authoritarian and riding roughshod over human rights. Those in the latter category riposte that they observe dysfunction and disillusion in the governance of the societies that reproach them. Incoming US President Biden referred to a contest between autocracy and democracy. That is an important debate to be played out as a political – hopefully not military – contest. But there is more to it than that. As the immense wealth of elites in countries like China and Russia shows, centrally controlled systems do not deliver greater equity for the people. There is a case to be made that the elites of nations, whatever their model of governance, have more in common with fellow elites than they have with the majority of the people in their respective nations. The point is that the injustice of inequity is terribly pervasive in today's world.

These five revolutions sound, above all, a warning. There is nothing to say that a revolution or revolutions cannot happen again. Any reasonable assessment would conclude a high degree of probability that humanity will be taken down the unpredictable and uncharted path of major revolution again.

Business as usual is the riskiest of options, for a continuing imbalance between equity and excess will only increase the probability of radical revolution. The vast misshapen pyramid of wealth distribution will bulge and contract and heave until something bursts. The fallout from the pandemic will most likely heighten that risk.

Somehow, amid the discord of political debate and contestation, a search for common cause must be found. The initiative for that search might come from political leadership, but it is most likely to come from civil movements outside of the institutions of government. These movements have the capacity to make links between local communities and the global imperatives that affect everyone.

The challenge before all is to recognise the risk of inaction. Ways must be found for people to embark on the enterprise of forging new layers of consensus and trust in their societies – locally, nationally, and globally – about what is required to guarantee survival with decency and justice. Against the drumbeats of revolution and war must be opposed the simple human desire for peace and happiness.

Otherwise, we will go on dancing before the greatest of all storms.

Notes

Chapter 1 - The American Revolution

1   Fleming, T. (2014) *Franklin* New York: New World City, Book 2, Chapter 2. The house at Craven Street is today the Benjamin Franklin museum.
2   *ibid.*
3   The Lunar Society, Number 1726, available at http://www.uh.edu/engines/epi1726. htm. Retrieved 3 May 2020.
4   Gibbon, E. *The History of the Decline and Fall of the Roman Empire* was published in seven volumes between 1776 and 1789.
5   *Poor Richard's Almanack* (sometimes *Almanac*) was a yearly almanack published by Benjamin Franklin. It appeared continually from 1732 to 1758.
6   Deborah Franklin's letter to Benjamin, 22 September 1765. Franklin's papers, vol. 12, p. 270. Deborah wrote with a form of phonetic spelling.
7   Check www.bartleby.com *The World's Famous Orations* at https://www.bartleby. com/268. Retrieved 3 May 2020. 'The examination of Doctor Franklin', 15 February 1766 first published in London by J. Almon in 1766. Check also 'Examination before the Committee of the Whole of the House of Commons', 13 February 1766,' *Founders Online*, National Archives, last modified 5 October 2016, http://founders.archives. gov/documents/Franklin/01-13-02-0035 [Original source: *The Papers of Benjamin Franklin*, vol. 13, *January 1 through December 31, 1766*, ed. Leonard W. Labaree (1969) New Haven and London: Yale University Press, pp. 124–162.] Among those who asked questions were Grenville, Townshend, North and Burke.
8   *ibid.*
9   Tuchman, B. (1984) *The March of Folly: From Troy to Vietnam* New York: Random House, p. 201.
10 Priestley, J. (1767) *The History and Present State of Electricity, with original experiments* London: Printed for J. Dodsley, J. Johnson and T. Cadell.
11 Tuchman, B. *The March of Folly: From Troy to Vietnam*, p. 201
12 The Acts would impose direct revenue duties, payable at colonial ports, on lead, glass, paper, paint, and tea. See *Encyclopedia Britannica* available at https://www. britannica.com/event/Townshend-Acts. Retrieved 5 January 2015.
13 Fleming, T. *Franklin*, Book four, Chapter 15.
14 Skousen, M. (2005) *The Compleated Autobiography of Benjamin Franklin* Washington, DC: Regnery History.
15 Isaacson, W. (2003) *Benjamin Franklin: An American Life* New York: Simon & Schuster.

16   Fleming, *Franklin*, Book four, Chapter 15.

17   Tuchman, B. *The March of Folly: From Troy to Vietnam*, p. 241.

18   'Rules by Which a Great Empire May Be Reduced to a Small One, 11 September 1773,' *Founders Online*, National Archives, last modified 5 October 2016, available at http://founders.archives.gov/documents/Franklin/01-20-02-0213. Retrieved 2 April 2020. [Original source: *The Papers of Benjamin Franklin*, vol. 20, *January 1 through December 31, 1773*, ed. William B. Willcox (1976) New Haven and London: Yale University Press, pp. 389–399.]

19   'An Edict by the King of Prussia, 22 September 1773', *Founders Online*, National Archives, last modified 5 October 2016, available at http://founders.archives. gov/documents/Franklin/01-20-02-0223. Retrieved 3 April 2020 [Original source: *The Papers of Benjamin Franklin*, Vol. 20, *January 1 through December 31, 1773*, ed. William B. Willcox (1976) New Haven and London: Yale University Press, pp. 413–418].

20   Francis Dashwood, the 11th Baron le Despencer, had a salacious reputation as an early member of the Hellfire Club, known for drunkenness and debauchery. He later became a prominent politician and succeeded Charles Townshend as Treasurer of the Chamber in the royal household.

21   Benjamin Franklin, letter to William Franklin 6 October 1773, autobiography and other writings, pp. 291–292.

22   Tuchman, B. *The March of Folly: From Troy to Vietnam*, p. 2.

23   *ibid.* p. 193.

24   Fleming, T. (2014) *Franklin* New York: New World City, Book four, Chapter 27.

25   *ibid.* Book four, Chapter 28.

26   Sparks, J. (1856) *The Life of Benjamin Franklin: Containing the Autobiography, with Notes and a Continuation* Boston: Whittemore, Niles and Hall, p. 408.

27   Title of a lecture by Ian Hayward, Gresham College, London, 11 March 2013, taken from the words of the poet, William Cooper: 'a metropolis in flames and a nation in ruins'.

28   Sir George Saville, Lord Sandwich, and Lord Mansfield, whose house in Leicester Square burnt so intensely it 'lit up the night sky'.

29   Babington, A. (1990) *Military intervention in Britain: from the Gordon riots to the Gibraltar incident* London: Routledge, p. 27.

30   More than two centuries later, the Gordon Riots were evoked again in commentary on the British riots of August 2011. See Jones, J. (2011) 'London burning: history just went sci-fi' in *The Guardian* available at https://www.theguardian.com/ artanddesign/jonathanjonesblog/2011/aug/08/london-riots-sci-fi-dystopian. Retrieved 2 August 2020.

31   Rudé, G. (1974) 'The Gordon Riots', in *Paris and London in the Eighteenth Century* London: Fontana/Collins.

32   Mahon, Lord (1858) *History of England, from the Peace of Utrecht to the Peace of Versailles, 1713-1783*, vol. 7, appendix, pp. xiii–xv. The original letter from Necker to North was offered at auction by Christies of London in June 2012.

33   Fortescue, Sir J. (1928) *Correspondence of King George III*, vol. V pp. 162–163.

34   Tuchman, B. *The March of Folly: From Troy to Vietnam*, p. 283.

35   Mason Locke Weems (1835) *The life of Benjamin Franklin* Philadelphia: Uriah Hunt.

36   McCullough, D. (2011) *John Adams* New York: Simon & Schuster.

37   Fleming, T. *Franklin*, Book seven, Chapter 2.

38   *ibid.* Book seven, Chapter 3.

39   Lambert, T. 'Life in 18th Century England' available at www.localhistories.org. Retrieved 26 April 2020.

40 Floud, R. and McKloskey, D. (1981), *The Economic History of Britain since 1700*, vol. 1, 1700–1860, pp. 24–26.

41 Harris, R. (2012) *The Foundling Hospital*, BBC History available at http://www.bbc.co.uk/history/british/victorians/foundling_01.shtml. Retrieved 3 April 2020.

42 Lambert, T. 'Life in 18th century England'.

43 Razzell, P. and Spence, C. (2005) 'Social capital and the history of mortality in Britain' in *International Journal of Epidemiology*, vol. 34, Issue 5, October 2005, pp. 1163–1164, https://doi.org/10.1093/ije/dyi132.

44 Lambert, T. 'Life in 18th century England'.

45 For this section and more information on the topic see Matthew White in the British Library on Georgian Britain available at https://www.bl.uk/georgian-britain/articles?authors_sorted=matthew%2awhite. Retrieved 2 August 2020.

46 Tuchman, B. *The March of Folly: From Troy to Vietnam*.

Chapter 2 – The French Revolution

1 An alliance between France and Austria was established with the first Treaty of Versailles, signed in 1756 at the outset of the Seven Years' War.

2 Hardman, J. (2000) *Louis XVI, The Silent King* New York: Oxford University Press, pp. 37–39.

3 Womersley, D. (2002) Gibbon and the *'Watchmen of the Holy City'; the Historian and His Reputations, 1776–1815* New York: Oxford University Press, as cited by G.M. Bowersock in *The New York Review of Books*, 25 November 2010, p. 56).

4 De Diesbach, G. (1978) *Necker ou la Faillite de la Vertu* Paris: Perrin, p. 108.

5 See https://en.wikipedia.org/wiki/Jean-Baptiste_Greuze#Legacy. Retrieved 3 August 2020.

6 De Diesbach, G. *Necker ou la Faillite de la Vertu*, p. 107.

7 Tuchman, B. (1984) *The March of Folly: From Troy to Vietnam* New York: Random House.

8 *Lettres de Cachet* (Letters of the Signet) were sealed orders signed by the king, against which there could be no appeal. For Mirabeau, they were prime examples of the absolutism of the *ancien régime*.

9 De Diesbach, G. *Necker ou la Faillite de la Vertu*, p. 154.

10 Benjamin Franklin's autobiography.

11 De Diesbach, G. *Necker ou la Faillite de la Vertu*, p. 223.

12 ibid., p. 226–227.

13 See https://www.christies.com/lotfinder/Lot/necker-jacques-1732-1804-lettersigned-necker-to-5573333-details.aspx. Retrieved 3 August 2020.

14 De Diesbach, G. *ibid.*, p. 232.

15 *ibid.*, p. 234.

16 Doyle, W. (1989) *The Oxford History of the French Revolution* New York: Oxford University Press.

17 Both brothers became Kings of France after the Restoration of 1815, respectively as Louis XVIII and Charles X.

18 De Diesbach, G. *Necker ou la Faillite de la Vertu*, p. 249.

19 *ibid.*, p. 252.

20 *ibid.*, p. 268, citing D'Haussonville, P.G. (1880) *Le Salon de Mme Necker*, p. 183.

21 *ibid.*, p. 269.

22 The island was called Gustavia, after the king, and operated as a free port. In 1888, following a referendum, Sweden returned the island to France.

23   *Défense de m. Necker, contre m. le comte de Mirabeau: Précédée de quelques observations sur les mémoires dont Paris est inondé* (1787) London: Elibron Classics.

24   De Diesbach, G. *Necker ou la Faillite de la Vertu*, pp. 318–321.

25   The livre was the currency used under the *ancien régime* in France, and in much of Europe. It was based on a measure of weight in silver. By the time of the General Estates, prior to the revolution, its value had diminished significantly compared with the era of Louis XIV.

26   Mirabeau, Honoré Gabriel Riqueti (1901) *Memoirs and Secret Chronicles of the Court of Berlin*. Preface by Oliver H.G. Leigh. Ohio: St. Dunstan Society. Doyle, W. (2002) *The Oxford History of the French Revolution* Oxford, UK: Oxford University Press. p. 97.

27   Harris, R.D. (1986) *Necker and the Revolution of 1789*, Lanham MD, University Press of America, pp. 433–434.

28   Herold, J.C. (1958) *Mistress to an Age: a life of Madame de Staël* New York: Grove Press.

29   De Diesbach, *ibid.*, pp. 367–369.

30   De Staël, G. (1818) *Considérations sur la Révolution Française*.

31   The *sans-culottes* referred to the workers and servants who wore simple striped pants and skirts instead of the elaborate costumes with stockings of the nobility and bourgeoisie. Already, Benjamin Franklin had popularised a simpler form of dress during his years as an American minister and ambassador.

32   The palace had been purchased by the Duc de Crillon in 1788, but was confiscated as the revolution advanced. Talleyrand later made it his home.

33   Gross Domestic Product.

34   Bairoch, P. (1989) 'L'économie Française dans le contexte européen à la fin du XVIIIème siècle' in *Revue* économique, no. 6, november 1989, pp. 939–964.

35   Hibbert, C. (1980) *The French Revolution* London: Penguin.

36   Delforge, F. (1985) *Les Petites Ecoles de Port-Royal* Paris: Cerf.

37   Shampa,S. (1982) *Citizens: a chronicle of the French Revolution* New York: Vintage Books, p. 180.

38   Rolf Reichardt with Eberhard Schmitt (1980) 'The French Revolution – Change or Continuity?' in *Journal for Historical Research*, vol. 7, pp. 257–320 (contribution to the Bamberg International Colloquium on the French Revolution, June 1979).

39   'Napoleon in conversation' (1817), quoted in Herold, J.C. (1955) *The Mind of Napoleon* New York: Columbia University Press, p. 14.

40   De Diesbach, G. (1978) *Necker ou la Faillite de la Vertu* Paris: Perrin, p. 328–332.

41   *ibid.*

42   *ibid.*, p. 333.

Chapter 3 - The European revolution of 1848

1   The sons of Louis XVI had died. The elder of the two died of tuberculosis one month before the revolution; his brother, Louis Charles, who died in prison in 1895 at the age of ten, was known to royalists as Louis XVII, hence his uncle was designated Louis XVIII.

2   de Lamartine, A. (1870) *Mémoires inédites de Lamartine 1790–1815* Paris: Hachette, p. 223.

3   *ibid.*

4   18 June 1815.

5   From November 1814 to June 1815.

6   Franklin had also witnessed the first unmanned flight a few months earlier.

Notes

7   Toesca, M. (1969) *Lamartine ou l'Amour de sa vie* Paris: Editions Albin Michel, p. 128.

8   A fictional account of their first meeting described Lamartine rescuing Julie from a storm on the lake, but this account has no basis in fact.

9   *Correspondance d'Alphonse Lamartine*, 2ème série (1807–1829) vol. II. Paris: Honoré Champion.

10 Toesca, M. *ibid.*, p. 197.

11 Jackson had won the popular vote and had more votes in the Electoral College, but fell short of a majority in the latter – there were four candidates. The one with the least votes was eliminated, leaving a three-way contest in the House. Jackson defeated Adams four years later, and Adams refused to attend Jackson's inauguration.

12 Hearder, H. (1988) *Europe in the nineteenth century* London: Routledge.

13 Furet, F. (2002, ed.), *La Révolution 1770–1880* Paris: Hachette, p. 238.

14 de Lamartine, A. (1849) *Histoire de la Révolution de 1848* Paris: Hachette.

15 Kelly, G.A. (1987) 'Alphonse De Lamartine: The Poet in Politics'; *Daedalus* vol. 116, No. 2, 1987, pp. 157–180; Boston: MIT Press.

16 The 'infernal machine' can be seen in the Police Museum in Paris.

17 The title of the head of government was 'President of the Council'.

18 De Toqueville, A. (1893) *Souvenirs* Paris: Calmann Levy, p. 8.

19 As minister for public instruction, Guizot had greatly increased the number of primary schools in France.

20 See for example, Victor Hugo's *Choses Vues: 1830–1846*.

21 de Lamartine, A. *Histoire de la Révolution de 1848*, pp. 12–20.

22 *ibid.*, p. 26.

23 *La Revue indépendante* (1841–1848), 10 juillet 1847.

24 de Lamartine, A. *Histoire de la Révolution de 1848*, pp. 33–40.

25 *ibid.*

26 *ibid.*

27 Lalouette, J. (2001) 'Les femmes et les banquets publics de France (vers 1848)' in *Festins de Femmes*, No 14, Paris: Editions Belin, pp. 71–91.

28 de Lamartine, A. *Histoire de la Révolution de 1848*, pp. 48–49.

29 Coutant, A. (2008) *Tocqueville et la Constitution Démocratique: Souveraineté du peuple et libertés. Essai.* Paris: Mare et Martin.

30 De Toqueville, A. *Souvenirs*, p. 16.

31 *ibid.*, p. 26.

32 de Lamartine, A. *Histoire de la Révolution of 1848*, p. 63.

33 *ibid.*

34 *ibid.*, p. 84.

35 Duc De Castries (1983) *Monsieur Thiers* Paris: Librairie Académique Perrin, p. 190.

36 de Lamartine, A. *Histoire de la Révolution de 1848*, pp. 88–89.

37 *ibid.*, p. 144.

38 Hugo, V (1862) *Les Misérables* 'First Edition A' Brussels: Lacroix, Verboeckhoven & Cie.

39 de Lamartine, A. *Histoire de la Révolution de 1848*, p. 259.

40 *ibid.*, p. 273.

41 *ibid.*, p. 306.

42 *ibid.*, p. 442.

43 d'Orléans, P. *Histoire de la Guerre Civile en Amérique* by Michel Lévy Frères (1874) Paris, translated into English and published by Porter and Coates, Philadelphia, in 1886.

44 Samuel Morie had developed Franklin's earlier work on electricity to invent the electric telegraph in 1837, while two English inventors succeeded independently in the same year.

45 Engel's report of Marx's expulsion was published in *Northern Star* on 25 March 1848.

46 Wordsworth, W. (1888) 'XLII. Steamboats, viaducts and railways', in *Complete Works* London: Macmillan.

47 de Lamartine, A. (1870) *Mémoires inédites de Lamartine 1790–1815* Paris: Hachette, Tome II, p. 6.

48 *ibid.*

49 *ibid.*, p. 9.

50 *ibid.*, p. 11.

51 *ibid.*, p. 27.

52 *ibid.*, p. 29.

53 *ibid.*, p. 30.

54 *ibid.*, pp. 33–38.

55 *ibid.*, p. 41.

56 *ibid.*, pp. 96–97.

57 *ibid.*

58 *ibid.*

59 Wright, G. (1958) 'A Poet in Politics: Lamartine and the Revolution of 1848' in *History Today Vol. 8*, issue 9, September 1958, available at https://www.historytoday.com/archive/poet-politics-lamartine-and-revolution-1848. Retrieved 2 June 2020. 60 The law of 1794 under the First Republic had decreed the end of slavery in the French colonies but it had not been applied in many of them.

61 Full account available at Herodote.net at https://www.herodote.net/almanachjour-0623.php. Retrieved 17 August 2020.

62 Hugo, V. *Les Misérables.*

63 Engels, F. (1898) in *Neue Rheinische Zeitung*, 28 June 1898, No 28, pp. 1–2.

64 Séguin, P. (1990), *Louis Napoléon Le Grand* Paris: Bernard Grasset, pp. 61–62.

Chapter 4 - The Chinese Revolution

1 Now named Guangzhou.

2 *The Encyclopedia of China* (2009): Berkshire Publishing Group.

3 See www.encyclopedia.com The encyclopedia of world biography: Kang Yu-Wei. Retrieved 6 May 2020.

4 Grieder, J. (1983) *Intellectuals and the State in Modern China* New York: Simon & Schuster, p. 88.

5 'Death by a thousand cuts'.

6 Victor Hugo to Captain Butler on 25 November 1861, https://www.napoleon.org/en/ history-of-the-two-empires/articles/the-chinese-expedition-victor-hugo-on-thesack-of-the-summer-palace. Retrieved 8 March 2020.

7 Beasley, William G. (1972) *The Meiji Restoration* Stanford: Stanford University Press.

8 See https://www.newworldencyclopedia.org/entry/Kang_Yu-wei. Retrieved 6 March 2020.

9 A 'tael' was a silver piece weighing about forty grams.

Notes

10   Estimated as six times the annual revenue of the Japanese government. The 'triple intervention' of Germany, France and Russia obliged Japan to give up the Manchurian cession for another 30 million taels of silver, but sowed the seeds for the Japan-Russia war ten years later.

11   Felber, R. (1997) 'The use of analogy by Kang You Wei in his writing on European history' in *Oriens Extremus*, vol. 40, No. 1 Berlin: Harrassowitz Verlag, pp. 64–77.

12   *ibid.*

13   *ibid.*

14   *Daily Colonist*, Victoria BC, 8 April 1899.

15   *Daily Times*, Victoria BC, 10 April 1899.

16   Based on: Zhongpin, C. (2014) 'Kang You Wei activities in Canada and the Reformist movement among the global Chinese diaspora, 1899–1909' *Twentieth-Century China*, 39:1, 3–23.

17   Boon Keng Lim (2012) *The Chinese Crisis from Within* Charleston: Nabu Press.

18   Kaplan, L. (2010) *Homer Lea: American Soldier of Fortune* Lexington, Kentucky: University Press of Kentucky, p. 39–40.

19   *ibid.*, p. 43–44.

20   Soodalter, R. (2019) 'How an American helped the Chinese Revolution', *MHQ – The Quarterly Journal of Military History*, Autumn 2019, Vol. 32, No. 1. Check www.historynet.com/soldier-of-misfortune. Retrieved 4 May 2020.

21   Japan, Russia, the British Empire, France, the United States, Germany, Italy and Austria-Hungary. Most of the troops were from Japan and Russia.

22   Conditions of the 'Boxer Protocol'.

23   Khoon Lee Choy (2005) *Pioneers of modern China* New Jersey: World Scientific, p. 10.

24   Liu, Xi, Kang You Wei's Journey to India. Chinese discourse on India during the late Qing and Republican periods; *China Report*, July 2012.

25   Young-Tsu Wong (2008) 'The search for material civilization: Kang You Wei's journey to the West' *Taiwan Journal of East Asian Studies* vol. 5, No. 1, June 2008 available at http://tjeas.ciss.ntnu.edu.tw/en-us/shared/redirect/85?folder=journals &file=5-1-2.pdf. Retrieved 17 August 2020.

26   *ibid.*, p. 40, Kang 'Travel Notes' pp. 378–426.

27   *ibid.*, p. 42.

28   Leung Larson, J. (2020) 'An Association to Save China, the Baohung Hui: A documentary account' *China Heritage Quarterly*, Australian National University, No 27, September 2020.

29   *ibid.*

30   *ibid.*

31   National Sun Yat Sen Memorial Hall, Taipei, check https://www.yatsen.gov.tw/en. Retrieved 17 August 2020.

32   See http://college.cengage.com/history/primary-sources. Retrieved 4 May 2020.

33   See https://www.oikonomia.it/index.php/en/2016/57-2001/giugno-2001/191-threeprinciples-of-the-people-sun-yat-sen-1866-1925. Retrieved 8 May 2020.

34   George, H. (1879) *Progress and Poverty: An Inquiry into the Cause of Industrial Depressions and of Increase of Want with Increase of Wealth: The Remedy* New York: Appleton.

35   Other translations include: 'The Great Commonwealth', or the 'The Great Unity'.

36   Lily Xiao Hong Lee & AD Stefanowska, eds (2008) *A Biographical Dictionary of Chinese Women* New York & London: Sharpe, p. 273.

37   Evans Chan, Interview in *China Heritage Quarterly*, No 27, September 2011 available at http://www.chinaheritagequarterly.org/articles.php?searchterm=027_datong. inc&issue=027. Retrieved 24 August 2020.

38   Published in the 1970s by Goran Malmouth and released in English in Hong Kong in 2007.

39   Felber, R. (1997) 'The use of analogy by Kang You Wei in his writing on European history' in *Oriens Extremus*, vol. 40, No. 1 Berlin: Harrassowitz Verlag, pp. 64–77.

40   Jia, S: Sun Yat Sen, Liang Qi Chao: Friends, Foes and Nationalism, available at http:// history.emory.edu/home/documents/endeavors/volume4/Jia.pdf. Retrieved 24 August 2020.

41   Cheng-chung, L. and Trescott, P.B. (2005) 'Liang Qichao, Sun Yat-sen, and the 1905–1907 debate on socialism' in *International Journal of Social Economics*, vol. 32, No. 12, 1 December 2005.

42   The symptoms of arsenic poisoning noted at the time of his death were confirmed by forensic tests conducted 100 years later, in November 2008. (Mu, Eric. 'Reformist Emperor Guangxu was Poisoned, Study Confirms' *Danwei*. 3 November 2008; 'Arsenic killed Chinese emperor, reports say.' *CNN*, 4 November 2008.)

43   This version was favoured by Pu Yi, who stated in his autobiography that he had heard it from a court eunuch Pu Yi, H (2010) [1967]. *The Last Manchu: The Autobiography of Henry Pu Yi, Last Emperor of China*: Skyhorse Publishing, edited by Kramer, P. (translation).

44   Petras, J. (2012) 'China: Rise, Fall and Re-Emergence as a Global Power: Some Lessons from the Past' *Global Research* 7 March 2012, available at https:// canadiandimension.com/articles/view/china-rise-fall-and-re-emergence-as-aglobal-power. Retrieved 17 August 2020.

45   Rabban Bar Sawma, a monk of Turkic origin (from the Uyghur or possibly Ongud lands in the west), wrote an account of his travels at about the same time as Marco Polo. His student Rabban Markos was later named Patriarch of the Church of the East as Yahballaha III.

46   Rawski, T.A. (2011) *The Rise of China's Economy Foreign Policy Research Institute Newsletter*, June 2011, available at https://www.fpri.org/docs/media/1606.201106. rawski.chineseeconomy.pdf. Retrieved 17 August 2020.

47   Cuska, A. (2016) 'Long history of corruption in China', available at https://gbtimes. com/long-history-corruption-china. Retrieved 17 August 2020.

48   Tatars, of Turkic origin from the west of China, were among the ethnic groups integrated into the Manchu Imperial Army. Many Russian noble families also had Tatar ancestry.

49   Homer Lea died in California in October 1912.

50   The 'Republic of China Interim Government Organization Act'.

51   See https:en.wikipedia.org/wiki/1912_Republic_of_China_National_Assembly_ election. Retrieved 21 August 2020.

52   See https://en.wikipedia.org/wiki/Kang_Tongbi. Retrieved 21 August 2020.

Chapter 5 – The Russian Revolution

1   See https://www.newworldencyclopedia.org/entry/Pyotr_Stolypin

2   McDonald, D. and Dronfiled, J. (2016) *A very dangerous woman: The lives, loves and lies of Russia's most seductive spy* Oxford: Oneworld Publications.

3   In 1945, the Livadia Palace would be the site for the Yalta Conference, where the division of Europe after World War II was decided. The US President, Franklin Roosevelt, and his delegation, stayed in the private apartments.

4   It is somewhat intriguing that the Marxists decided to relocate the general council of the International to New York in the US. The American Federation of Labor

was founded in 1886, and the next year, French syndicates formed the Bourse du Travail, forerunner of the General Confederation of Labour.

5   Fedorovo, G.G. (1971) *I believe in Russia: biography of Peter Stolypin*, translated into English, Limbus Press, 2002.

6   His daughter Maria would later write a book quoted by several historians with accounts of Stolypin's life: Von Bock, M. (1970) *Reminiscences of my father, Peter N. Stolypin* (Translation by Margaret Datoski).

7   The city was renamed Ulyanovsk after the death of Lenin.

8   Fischer, L. (1964) *The Life of Lenin* New York: Harper and Row.

9   The attempt was to be made on the sixth anniversary of the assassination of Alexander II, the tsar's father.

10 Nadya Krupskaya was Deputy Minister of Education of the Soviet Union from 1929 until 1939.

11 See www.marxists.org/archive/krupskaya. Retrieved 18 August 2020.

12 The Julian calendar was used by Russia until after the revolution of 1917 when the Bolsheviks changed to the Gregorian calendar used by the rest of Europe. So, 9 January in Russia was 22 January elsewhere in Europe.

13 Von Bock, M. *Reminiscences of my father, Peter N. Stolypin*.

14 Figes, O. (1996) *A people's tragedy; the Russian Revolution, 1891–1924* London: Jonathan Cape, p. 223.

15 Whitman, A. (1970) 'Alexander Kerensky Dies Here at 89' in *New York Times*, 12 June 1970, available at https://www.nytimes.com/1970/06/12/archives/alexanderkerensky-dies-here-at-89-alexander-kerensky-who-led-first.html. Retrieved 18 August 2020; Kerensky, A. (1965) *Russia and History's Turning Point* New York: Duell, Sloan and Pearce.

16 Available at sparknotes.com: Vladimir Lenin: 'The 1905 Revolution and its aftermath'. Retrieved 18 August 2020.

17 Thatcher, I. 'The First State Duma, 1906: the view from the contemporary pamphlet and monograph literature', *Canadian Journal of History*, 22 December 2011.

18 In English: *The Spirit of the Laws*.

19 George, H. (1879) *Progress and Poverty: An Inquiry into the Cause of Industrial Depressions and of Increase of Want with Increase of Wealth: The Remedy* New York: Appleton.

20 Pyotr Stolypin to Leo Tolstoy, 23 October 1907.

21 World Bank Group (1996) *Groundswell Policy Paper*, March–April 1996, p. 2.

22 *ibid.*

23 Chunmei D. (2019) *Gu Hongming's Eccentric Chinese Odyssey* Philadelphia: University of Pennsylvania Press

24 Gandhi applied Tolstoy's ideas of passive resistance in the Transvaal from 1906 onwards, negotiated a settlement with General Smuts in 1913, and returned to India in 1915.

25 See https://www.openculture.com/2015/09/tolstoy-and-gandhi-exchange-letters. Retrieved 29 August 2020.

26 The paradox of friendship between an anarchist and a conservative traditionalist is worth noting.

27 He also had a son, with a serf of his estate, which he revealed to Sonia on the eve of their marriage.

28 Ascher, A. (2014) *The Russian Revolution: A Beginner's Guide* Oxford: Oneworld Publications.

29 Mironov, B. (2012) *The standard of living and revolutions in Russia 1700–1917* New York: Routledge, p. 49.

30   *ibid.*

31   Nafzinger, S. and Lindert, P. (2012) 'Russian Inequality on the Eve of Revolution' in National Bureau of Economic Research, Working Paper, 13 March 2011.

32   By 1917, there were also some military units of women – see Reed, J. (1919) *Ten days that shook the world* New York: Boni & Liveright.

33   After the revolution, the new Soviet government of Lenin developed this policy in order to maintain troops in the civil war.

34   *New York Times*, 20 March 1911, 'Stolypin resigns as Russian Premier. Made a personal issue of split on Bill granting self-government to Western Provinces', available at https://www.nytimes.com/1911/03/21/archives/stolypin-resigns-as-russianpremier-made-a-personal-issue-of-split.html. Retrieved 18 August 2020.

35   This account of Stolypin's assassination is from a translation of the memoirs of Alexander Spiridovich, by Mosheim, R. (2004). https://www.alexanderpalace.org/palace/stolypin-murder-1911-kiev.php. The original text was published in Russian and French in 1829 as: *Les Dernieres Annees de la Cour de Tzarskoe Selo* (the imperial village) Paris: Payot.

36   Lenin, V.I. (1974) 'Stolypin and the revolution'. *Lenin Collected Works*, vol. 17, pages 247–256. Moscow: Progress Publishers, available at https://www.marxists.org/archive/lenin/works/1911/oct/18.htm. Retrieved 18 August 2020.

37   The 1907 Stuttgart Congress was attended by more than 900 delegates from around the globe. It adopted resolutions on militarism, colonialism and women's suffrage.

38   In 1917, they were expelled from the SPD. Rosa Luxemburg founded the Spartacus League and played a leading role in the Socialist International.

39   See http://www.alexanderpalace.org/palace/rasputin-restaurant-joseph-vecchi. Retrieved 2 May 2020.

40   Renamed in August 1914, as Saint Petersburg was considered to be 'too Germanic'.

41   Orthodox Russia still used the Julian calendar at that time. Protestant Britain adopted the Gregorian calendar in 1570, as did Catholic countries in Europe from 1582. Historical accounts of the Russian revolutions often include both Julian (Old Style or OS) and Gregorian (New Style or NS) dates.

42   This was 27 February OS, and it was therefore called the February Revolution.

43   This second revolution was called the October Revolution. The new government changed to the Gregorian calendar used in most of the rest of the world in early 1918.

44   Kerensky denied this account in his memoirs, claiming that he used his own vehicle, but the role of the US Embassy has been accorded some historical credibility.

45   'Lenin's political programme', October 1917. Rice, C. (1990). *Lenin: Portrait of a Professional Revolutionary* London: Cassell.

46   Emergency Commission for Combating Counter-Revolution and Sabotages.

47   See https://alphahistory.com/russianrevolution/lenins-hanging-order-kulaks-1918. Retrieved 18 August 2020.

48   Lenin, 4 January 1923. See https://en.wikipedia.org/wiki/Lenin%27s_Testament. Retrieved 18 August 2020.

49   Von Bock, M.P. *Reminiscences of my father Peter A. Stolypin.*

Chapter 6 – One hundred years later

1   Kofi Annan's early school years were described to the writer by Tom Bediako, then a young primary school teacher in Kumasi. Tom would later make his mark by refusing, as a matter of principle and at the risk of his life, to join a Presidential

Notes

Commission after a military coup in Ghana, and then as a leading advocate for education and development throughout Africa.

2   This account of de Klerk's reasoning is based on a conversation in July 2011 in Cape Town with the then Premier of Western Cape Province, national opposition leader and anti-apartheid activist Helen Zille.

3   Fukuyama, F. (1992) *The End of History and the Last Man* New York: Free Press.

4   Juan Somavía later became Director-General of the International Labour Organization.

5   The writer's notes on the Summit.

6   The concept of measurable objectives, as distinct from general statements of intent, can be attributed to Julian Disney, then President of the International Council on Social Service, and advisor to the Australian delegation in Copenhagen.

7   Annan, K. (2013) *Interventions: A Life in War and Peace* London: Penguin Books.

8   Annan, K. (2014) *We the peoples – the role of the United Nations in the 21st century* London: Routledge.

9   'Secretary-General proposes global compact on human rights, labour, environment in an address to World Economic Forum in Davos', 1 February 1999, available at https://www.un.org/press/en/1999/19990201.sgsm6881.html. Retrieved 21 June 2020.

10   A close ally of Tony Blair, now a member of the British House of Lords, told the writer privately at this time that the planned intervention in Iraq was 'all about oil'. Blair's decision to support the US over Iraq hastened the end of his years in office as British Prime Minister, after three consecutive electoral victories and ten years in the position.

11   Grubin, D. (2003) *Kofi Annan: Center of the Storm* PBS Documentary.

12   Annan, K. '10 years after – a farewell statement to the General Assembly' 16 September 2006, available at https://www.un.org/sg/en/content/sg/speeches/2006-09-19/10-years-after-%E2%80%93-farewell-statement-general-assembly. Retrieved 4 June 2020.

13   As the twentieth century came to an end, much media attention was given to the risk of a 'millennium bug' linked to the change of dates from 1999 to 2000, particularly in computerised banking and other financial systems. It was a sign of the interconnected age, affecting most sectors of activity, especially finance. But the old millennium rolled over to the new one, and global computerised systems did not crash. There was also an abundance of more esoteric and superstitious theories about the millennial change.

14   This move also helped the WEF president to resolve a difference with the Swiss Federal Government about the cost of security arrangements for the high-profile annual meeting in Davos.

15   Chinese leader Deng Xiaoping introduced market reforms in the late 1970s and early 1980s. The private sector's share of GDP in China increased from 1% in 1978 to 70% in 2005.

16   The 'Liaison Committee' brought together senior OECD officials and ambassadors representing member states, with the Trade Union and Business and Industry Advisory Committees, TUAC and BIAC.

17   'Paulson Says Markets Emerging From Crunch: WSJ' Reuters, 6 May 2008, available at https://web.archive.org/web/20140421060146/http://www.cnbc.com/id/24493133/Paulson_Says_Markets_Emerging_From_Crunch_WSJ . Retrieved 3 June 2020.

18   Paulson, Henry M., Jr (7 September 2008). 'Statement by Secretary Henry M. Paulson, Jr. on Treasury and Federal Housing Finance Agency Action to Protect Financial Markets and Taxpayers' (press release). United States Department of the Treasury, available at https://www.treasury.gov/press-center/press-releases/Pages/ hp1129.aspx. Retrieved 6 June 2020.

19 See, for instance, *Los Angeles Times* 'Op-Ed: The bank bailout of 2008 was unnecessary. Fed Chairman Ben Bernanke scared Congress into it', available at https://www.latimes.com/opinion/op-ed/la-oe-baker-bailout-20180914-story.html. Retrieved 14 August 2020.
20 Wroughton, L. and Murphy, F. (11 October 2008). 'IMF warns of financial meltdown' Reuters. Available at https://www.reuters.com/article/us-financial3-idUSTRE49A36O20081011
21 See, for instance, Baily, M.N., Litan, R.E., and Johnson M.S. (2008) 'The Origins of the Financial Crisis, Initiative on Business and Public Policy at Brookings', Fixing Finance Series, Paper 3, November 2008, available at https://www.brookings.edu/wp-content/uploads/2016/06/11_origins_crisis_baily_litan.pdf. Retrieved 15 July 2020.
22 See https://www.nytimes.com/2009/04/22/business/global/22fund.html. Retrieved 3 March 2020.
23 As the writer participated in a pre-summit consultation with the Canadian Prime Minister, Stephen Harper, as host of the Toronto summit, he and other participants received a copy of US President Obama's letter to the Canadian Prime Minister setting out the US position. The final summit communique, however, downplayed the policy difference, which was tantamount to accepting that each country would follow its own path, marking an effective end to coordinated fiscal stimulus measures. A subsequent meeting of OECD ambassadors in Paris turned its attention to a winding down of these fiscal measures, with much talk about 'green shoots', which were claimed to signal recovery from the recession.
24 See https://thelondonseason.org. Retrieved 3 March 2020.
25 Buchanan, D. (2013) 'Prince Philip called debutante balls "bloody daft" – yet posh is the new pop' *The Guardian* available at https://www.theguardian.com/commentisfree/2013/oct/30/posh-pop-debutante-ball-inequality. Retrieved 3 March 2020.
26 *Le Monde*, 8 June 2016.
27 See www.forbes.com/billionaires. Retrieved 3 March 2020.
28 Oxfam, press release, 20 January 2020 'World's billionaires have more wealth than 4.6 billion people' available at https://www.oxfam.org/en/press-releases/worlds-billionaires-have-morewealth-46-billion-people. Retrieved 30 June 2020.
29 Oxfam (2020) 'Time to care'. Full report available at https://www.oxfam.org/en/research/time-care. Retrieved 30 June 2020.
30 Harris, B. and Figazzolo, L., eds (2011) *Global Corporate Taxation and Resources for Quality Public Services* Brussels: Education International Research Institute.
31 Piketty, T. (2013) *Le capital au XXIème siècle* Paris: Seuil. English version: *Capital in the 21st Century* (2014): Cambridge, Mass, & London, Belknap/Harvard University Press. He describes the history of inequality as 'chaotic' (pp. 274–276 English version), and then discusses the experiences of France and the United States since the 1980s (pp. 290–296).
32 Annan, K. 'Address to the signing conference of the UN Convention against transnational organized crime', Palermo, Italy, 12 December 2000. Available at UNODC http://www.unodc.org/unodc/en/about-unodc/speeches/speech_2000-12-12_1.html. Retrieved 4 July 2020.
33 Piketty, T. *Le capital au XXIème siècle*
34 Piketty, T. *Capital in the Twenty-First Century*, p. 2.
35 Kuznets, S. and Jenks, E. (1953) *Shares of upper income groups in income and savings* Cambridge (USA): National Bureau of Economic Research.
36 Piketty, T. *Capital in the Twenty-First Century*, p. 11.
37 *ibid.*, p. 15.

38   World Confederation of Organisations of the Teaching Profession (WCOTP) World Assembly of Delegations, hosted by the National Education Association of the United States in Washington DC. As a young staff member of WCOTP from Asia and the Pacific, the writer had a role in the drafting of this 'Declaration of Interdependence'.

39   See Coombs, P.H. (1985) *The world crisis in education: the view from the Eighties* Oxford: Oxford University Press, and other works by Coombs.

40   Piketty, T. *Capital in the Twenty-First Century*, p. 16.

41   *ibid.*, p. 20.

42   *ibid.*, p. 22.

43   *ibid.*

44   *ibid.*, p. 23. Piketty illustrates the points about the change from decreasing inequality to rapidly increasing inequality with 'U-shaped' graphs.

45   Check for instance CNN Politics on 16 September 2016 https://edition.cnn.com/2016/09/09/politics/donald-trump-birther/index.html. Retrieved 9 July 2020.

46   See WEF website, *The Fourth Industrial Revolution* by Klaus Schwab available at https://www.weforum.org/about/the-fourth-industrial-revolution-by-klaus-schwab. Retrieved 30 June 2020.

47   Schwab, K. (2017) *The Fourth Industrial Revolution*, p. 6. New York: Penguin Random House Portfolio.

48   OECD: Organisation for Economic Co-operation and Development, grouping market economies, the OECD grew out of the Marshall Plan of trans-Atlantic economic cooperation to relaunch economies after World War II.

49   See, for example, the conclusions of OECD Employment Ministers' meeting in Venice, Italy, 17–18 April 2008, available at http://www.oecd.org/fr/presse/moreflexibilityinlabourmarketpolicymanagementwouldboostgrowthsaysoecd.htm. Retrieved 15 June 2020.

50   Schwab, K. *The Fourth Industrial Revolution*, p. 92.

51   *ibid.*, pp. 93–95.

52   State legislatures in the United States send representatives to the Electoral College according to the voting results in each state. But at a time of national crisis over the coronavirus pandemic, and a breakdown of national consensus about the functioning of democracy, this process was contested by the defeated US president and a large proportion of his party, culminating in the events of 6 January 2021 at the US Capitol.

53   Brennan, M. (2013) 'Billionaire Bunkers: Beyond the Panic Room, Home Security Goes Sci-Fi' 27 November 2013 available at https://www.forbes.com/sites/ morganbrennan/2013/11/27/billionaire-bunkers-beyond-the-panic-room-homesecurity-goes-sci-fi/#c7af04e463d7. Retrieved 15 June 2020.

54   This promotion of a data-driven business model in funding projects to reform public service has placed the Gates Foundation at odds with education unions within the United States.

55   Open Society Foundation mission and values, Soros, 6 September 2012 available at https://www.opensocietyfoundations.org/who-we-are. Retrieved 1 August 2020.

56   Today, the Geneva-based Federation of Red Cross and Red Crescent Societies represents national humanitarian organisations around the world.

57   Kareem Abdul-Jabbar, 13 July 2016 'There is terror on both sides of the badge', available at https://kareemabduljabbar.com/time-there-is-terror-on-both-sides-ofthe-badge. Retrieved 1 August 2020.

58   Tuchman, B. (1984) *The March of Folly: From Troy to Vietnam* New York: Random House.

59   See 'The Three Rules of Epidemics' https://archive.nytimes.com/www.nytimes.com/books/first/g/gladwell-tipping.html; 2000.

60   Schwab, K. *The Fourth Industrial Revolution*, pp. 25–26

61   Letter written by Mao Tse Tung to his supporters in July 1930, citing an ancient Chinese saying.

62   'Four-Score Years and Seven', from Abraham Lincoln's Gettysburg address, available at http://www.abrahamlincolnonline.org/lincoln/speeches/gettysburg.htm. Retrieved 1 August 2020.

63   Harris, B. and Figazzolo, L., eds (2011) *Global Corporate Taxation and Resources for Quality Public Services* Brussels: Education International Research Institute.

64   Marks, S. 'How Amazon saved billions in taxes' *Newsweek*, 2 March 2016.

65   By Stéphanie Thomson, 6 July 2016 available at https://www.weforum.org/agenda/2016/07/globalization-for-the-99-can-we-make-it-work-for-all. Retrieved 15 July 2020.

66   For a nice story about Gorbachev's invitation to San Francisco by then mayor, now Senator Diane Feinstein, see 'The Gorbachev Surfboard' by George Orbelia, available at https://georgeorbelian.org/surfing/gorbachev-surfboard. Retrieved 16 June 2020.

67   See https://edition.cnn.com/2020/04/08/europe/pope-francis-coronavirus-natureresponse-intl/index.html. Retrieved 4 November 2020.

68   *Economist*, 4 April 2020.

69   Evans, John (2020) 'Economic Impact of the Covid-19 Crisis', 17 April 2020, available at TUAC https://tuac.org/news/economic-impact-of-the-covid-19-crisis-by-johnevans. Retrieved 24 July 2020.

70   *Foreign Policy* 'How the world will look after the Coronavirus pandemic', 20 March 2020, available at https://foreignpolicy.com/2020/03/20/world-order-aftercoroanvirus-pandemic. Retrieved 15 July 2020.

71   Kissinger, H. (2020) 'The coronavirus pandemic will forever alter the world order', *The Wall Street Journal* 3 April 2020 available at https://www.wsj.com/articles/the-coronavirus-pandemic-will-forever-alter-the-world-order-11585953005. Retrieved 1 August 2020.

72   Kissinger, H. (2015) World Order New York: Penguin Books, pp. 368–369.

73   Following his 2013 bestseller, *Capital in the Twenty-first Century*, Piketty came out with a new book, which canvassed how, throughout history, elites have justified inequality: Piketty T. (2019) *Capital et Idéologie* Paris: Seuil.

74   See https://en.wikipedia.org/wiki/Black_Lives_Matter. Retrieved 15 January 2021.

75   See statement by Joe Biden, US President-elect, 15 January 2021; https://edition.cnn.com/2021/01/14/politics/biden-economic-rescue-package-coronavirusstimulus/index.html. Retrieved 15 January 2021.

76   'We shall overcome because the arc of the moral universe is long, but it bends toward justice.' Dr Martin Luther King Jr, 'Remaining Awake Through a Great Revolution'. Speech given at the National Cathedral, 31 March 1968.

77   We could add farmers' protests in India, riots in Barcelona, and others.

The People

During this express ride through 160 years of modern history, the narrative refers to many people. The reader will no doubt recognise quite a few names, and there are many others.

This annex – The People – is included to help the reader to place those names in their context. It is organised according to the chapters – some names come up in two or more chapters as we follow the thread of history. For each chapter, the main personality is noted with those closest to him, then for the first five chapters, the names are arranged according to nationalities, with brief notes to recall what each person was known for as the story unwound. The main personalities and others who played significant roles in the five revolutions are highlighted in **bold type**. For the final chapter, leaping from the last of the five revolutions to today, the names that appear are simply arranged according to the roles that people played.

CHAPTER ONE

THE FRANKLINS
Benjamin Franklin, scientist, inventor, publisher, diplomat, Founding Father of the United States of America (also Chapter 2)
James, his brother
William, his son, Royal Governor of New Jersey
Deborah, his wife
Sally, his daughter
William Temple and Benny Bache, his grandsons

THE BRITISH
King George III (also Chapter 2)
Queen Charlotte
Lord George Grenville, prime minister
Lord Frederick North, prime minister (also Chapter 2)
William Pitt the Elder, Lord Chatham, former prime minister
Margaret Stevenson and her daughter Polly Stevenson, provided
  lodgings for Franklin in London
James Hargreaves, inventor of the spinning jenny
James Watt, inventor
Matthew Boulton, industrialist
Joseph Priestley, scientist
Jonathan Shipley, bishop
Edward Gibbon, historian and Suzanne Necker's former fiancé
Lord Hillsborough, secretary of state for America
Lord Dartmouth, secretary of state for America
Baron le Despencer, postmaster general
Paul Whitehead, poet
Governor Hutchinson of Massachusetts
Alexander Wedderburn, solicitor-general
Thomas Paine, writer (see also The Americans, Chapter 2)
Edmund Burke, member of parliament
Sir William Howe, army general
Lord Richard Howe, admiral of the fleet
Lord Stormont, ambassador to France
Lord George Gordon, Protestant leader
Lord Cornwallis, army general
Henry Clinton, army general
William Pitt the Younger, prime minister (also Chapter 2)

THE AMERICANS
Thomas Jefferson, Founding Father, ambassador, 3rd president (also
  Chapter 2)
Paul Revere, express rider, who gave the alert
Joseph Galloway, Continental Congress delegate
John Hancock, Continental Congress chair

George Washington, general, Founding Father, 1st president
John Adams, 2nd president
Silas Deane, Continental Congress delegate to France
Arthur Lee, Continental Congress delegate to France
John Jay, delegate, Paris Peace talks
Henry Laurens, delegate, Paris Peace talks

THE FRENCH
King Louis XV (also Chapter 2)
King Louis XVI (see Chapter 2)
Queen Marie-Antoinette (see Chapter 2)
Jacques Necker, director of the Royal Treasury (see Chapter 2)
Suzanne Necker, his wife, and Anne-Louise Germaine Necker, their
    daughter (see Chapter 2)
Comte Vergennes, foreign minister (also Chapter 2)
Comte Honoré Mirabeau, author, member of the Constituent Assembly
    (also Chapter 2)
Marquis de Lafayette, captain in the Royal Dragoons; major general in
    the American continental army (also Chapters 2 and 3)
Duc Charles-François de Broglie, military commander
Comte de Rochambeau, army marshall
Comte de Grasse, admiral of the French fleet
Jacques Charles, inventor, and builder of the first manned hydrogen
    balloon
Voltaire, real name François-Marie Arouet, philosopher and author (also
    Chapter 2)
Jean-Jacques Rousseau, philosopher (see also Chapter 2)

CHAPTER TWO

THE NECKERS
Jacques Necker, banker, industrialist, author, director of the Royal
    Treasury, then finance minister of France.
Suzanne Necker (née Curchod), his wife
Anne-Louise Germaine Necker, their daughter, later Madame de Staël
    (also Chapter 3)

Louis Necker, brother of Jacques

Albertine de Staël, daughter of Germaine, later wife of the Duc Victor de Broglie

THE FRENCH

King Louis XV

Louis-Auguste de Bourbon, later King Louis XVI

Marie-Antoinette von Hapsburg of Austria, later Queen of France

Madame de Vermenoux, a widow once courted by Jacques Necker

Jean-Baptiste Greuze, portrait artist

Abbé Terray, minister of finance

Anne-Robert Turgot, minister of finance

Chrétien de Malesherbes, minister of the royal household and the police

Comte Honoré Mirabeau, author, revolutionary leader

Sophie de Monnier, wife of the Marquis de Monnier, Mirabeau's lover

Marquis de Sade, philosopher and author

Comte de Vergennes, foreign minister

Antoine de Sartine, secretary of state of the navy

Comte Jean-Frédéric de Maurepas, first minister of state

Jean-Étienne-Marie Portalis, lawyer, later an author of the Napoléonic Code

Charles Alexandre de Calonne, finance minister

Archbishop Étienne Charles de Brienne, finance minister

Charles-Maurice de Talleyrand-Périgord, bishop, revolutionary leader, ambassador, grand chamberlain, prince, president of the Senate, prime minister and foreign minister (also Chapter 3)

Pierre-Victor Malouet, leader of the Constitutional Party

Camille Desmoulins, revolutionary

Duc d'Orléans, later Philippe l'Egalité

Louis-Philippe d'Orléans, his son, later king

Voltaire, real name François-Marie Arouet, philosopher and author

Baron Charles-Louis Montesquieu, philosopher

Denis Diderot, founder of l'Encyclopédie

Marquis de Lafayette, commander of the revolutionary National Guard (also Chapter 3)

George Washington Lafayette, his son

Saint-Léon, messenger

Jean-Paul Marat, journalist

Comte Louis Marie de Narbonne, minister of war

Maximilian Robespierre, revolutionary leader, president of the National
  Convention

Napoléon Bonaparte, general, first consul, then emperor
  (also Chapter 3)

Lucien and Joseph Bonaparte, his brothers

Joséphine, wife of Napoléon, later empress

Delphine, widow, whose name inspired Germaine de Staël's first novel

Jacques Charles, scientist and inventor (also Chapter 3)

Julie Charles, his wife (also Chapter 3)

Stanislas de Bourbon, later King Louis XVIII (see Chapter 3)

Duc Victor de Broglie, member of the Chamber of Peers, later prime
  minister (see Chapter 3)

THE BRITISH

King George III

Lord Frederick North, prime minister

William Pitt the Elder, Lord Chatham, former prime minister

Edward Gibbon, historian, later member of parliament

William Pitt the Younger, prime minister

Adam Smith, economist

David Hume, philosopher

Lord Horatio Nelson, admiral, commander of the British fleet

Edmund Burke, member of parliament and author

Duke of Wellington, military commander, politician,
  twice prime minister

Lord Byron, poet and politician

THE AUSTRIANS

Empress Maria-Theresa of the Hapsburg dynasty, mother of
  Marie-Antoinette

Emperor Joseph II, her son, brother of Queen Marie-Antoinette

Emperor Leopold II, brother and successor of Joseph II

THE AMERICANS

Benjamin Franklin, representative of the American Continental
Congress, 1st ambassador to France

Thomas Paine, essayist

Thomas Jefferson, 2nd ambassador to France, secretary of state,
3rd president

Alexander Hamilton, secretary of the treasury

Aaron Burr, vice-president

John Adams, 2nd President

THE SWISS

Jean-Jacques Rousseau, philosopher and author

Peter Thellusson, banker

Baron Pierre Victor Besenval, commander of the Swiss Guards in France

Benjamin Constant, politician and companion of Germaine de Staël

Albert Jean de Rocca, second husband of Germaine de Staël

THE SWEDES

King Gustav III

Baron Erik Magnus de Staël von Holstein, ambassador to France, first
husband of Germaine de Staël

THE GERMANS

Johann Wolfgang von Goethe, writer, playwright, acting chancellor of
Weimar Republic

Friedrich Schiller, playwright, poet, philosopher

THE RUSSIANS

Count Fyodor Rostopchin, Governor of Moscow

Alexander I, tsar

Mikhail Kutuzov, commander of the army

COLONIAL INDEPENDENCE LEADERS

Toussaint L'Ouverture, leader of the Haitian fight for independence

Simón Bolívar, leader of the Spanish American fight for independence

CHAPTER THREE

LAMARTINE, HIS FAMILY AND JULIE
Alphonse de Lamartine, poet, historian, member of the Académie
  Française, provisional leader of the Second French Republic, minister
  for foreign affairs
Julie Charles, his lover
Marianne Elisa Lamartine (née Birch), his wife
Alphonse de Lamartine, his son, died in infancy
Julia de Lamartine, his daughter, died at the age of ten
Baron de Vasserot, host to Lamartine in Switzerland

THE FRENCH
Napoléon Bonaparte, emperor
Charles-Maurice de Talleyrand-Perigord, foreign minister and chief
  negotiator at the Congress of Vienna
King Louis XVIII
Germaine de Staël, romantic author and opponent of Napoléon
  Bonaparte
Jacques Charles, inventor, president of the Academy of Science
King Charles X, last of the Bourbon brothers
Marquis de Lafayette, now elder statesman, restored as commander
  of the National Guard
George Washington Lafayette, his son
Victor Hugo, writer, playwright, essayist, politician (also Chapter 4)
Duc Victor de Broglie, member of the chamber of peers,
  later prime minister
François Guizot, education minister, ambassador, foreign minister,
  prime minister (also Chapter 4)
King Louis-Philippe, previously Duc d'Orléans, alias Monsieur Chabaud,
  the 'Citizen King' (also Chapter 4)
Queen Maria Amalia of Naples and Sicily, his wife
Prince Louis, Duc de Nemours, their second son
Prince Philippe d'Orléans, Louis-Philippe's grandson and heir, later
  captain in the Union Army during the American Civil War, and
  historian

Prince Robert d'Orléans, brother of Philippe

François Furet, historian

Édouard Mortier, marshall, ambassador, minister of war, prime minister

Guiseppe Fieschi, assassin

Alexis de Tocqueville, author, conservative politician, director of the
 Académie Française

Countess Marie d'Agoult, author (as Daniel Stern) and historian, and
 partner of Franz Liszt, pianist

Jean-Baptiste Testé, minister for public works

Odilon Barrot, constitutional monarchist, prime minister

Adolphe Thiers, political leader, later president of the Third Republic

Thomas Bugeaud, marshall, army commander

Louis Blanc, pamphleteer, historian, leader of the Socialist Party

Jacques-Charles Dupont de l'Eure, first head of state of the
 Second Republic

Alexandre Ledru-Rollin and François Arago, members of the
 provisional republican government

Louis-Napoléon Bonaparte, nephew of Napoléon I, elected president of
 the Second Republic, prince-president, then Emperor Napoléon III

James Mayer de Rothschild, banker

Aurore Dupin, author known as Georges Sand

Louis-Eugène Cavaignac, general, Governor-General of Algeria,
 then minister of war

Denis-Auguste Affre, Archbishop of Paris

THE BRITISH

Duke of Wellington, soldier, statesman and, later, prime minister

Prince Edward, Duke of Kent, army commander of Upper and Lower
 Canada, father of Queen Victoria

Lord Henry Palmerston, prime minister

Queen Victoria (also Chapter 4)

Prince Albert, royal consort (also Chapter 4)

William Wordsworth, poet

Benjamin Disraeli, prime minister

Charles Dickens, author

THE AMERICANS
James Monroe, 5th president
James Madison, 4th president
Thomas Jefferson, 3rd president
John Quincy Adams, 6th president
Andrew Jackson, army general, 7th president
Abraham Lincoln, 16th president

THE AUSTRIANS
Prince Klemens von Metternich, foreign minister, chancellor

THE GERMANS
Karl Marx, political theorist, and revolutionary (also Chapters 4 and 5)
Friedrich Engels, journalist, friend and co-author with Marx
Otto von Bismarck, minister, President of Prussia, first Chancellor of
  Germany (also Chapter 4)
Wilhelm I, King of Prussia, first Kaiser of the German Reich

THE RUSSIANS
Tsar Alexander II, father of Alexander III (also Chapter 5)
Vladimir Ilyich Lenin, revolutionary (see Chapter 5)
Leo Tolstoy, essayist, author (see Chapters 4 and 5)
THE ITALIANS
Guiseppe Garibaldi, independence leader in Uruguay with his wife,
  Anita (Ribeiro da Silva), then unifier of Italy
Victor Emmanuel of Savoy, first King of Italy

CHAPTER FOUR

THE KANGS
Kang You Wei, Confucian scholar, calligrapher, reform leader, founder
  of the Chinese Empire Reform Association
Kang Tong Bi, his daughter, feminist leader
Chu Tz'u Chi, his tutor
Kang Guang Ren, his brother

THE CHINESE

Sun Yat Sen, medical doctor, revolutionary leader, first President of the
  Republic of China

Sun Mei, his brother, merchant in Hawaii

Lu Muzhen, Sun Yat Sen's first wife

Xian Feng, 9th emperor of the Qing dynasty

Dowager Empress Ci'an, first consort of Xian Feng

Dowager Empress Cixi, second consort of Xian Feng, mother of
  Zaichun, who became Tongzhi, 10th emperor of the Qing dynasty

Prince Gong, brother of Xian Feng, Prince-regent to the child-emperor
  Tongzhi, then head of the foreign ministry

Prince Yixuan Chun, brother of Xian Feng, father of Zaitan, who became
  Guangxu, 11th emperor of the Qing dynasty

Weng Tonghe, tutor to the Guangxu Emperor

Li Hongzhang, viceroy of the Zhili region, leader of the
  self-strengthening movement

Liang Qi Chao, student and supporter of Kang You Wei

Gu Hong Ming, Confucian scholar, educated in Scotland,
  Germany and France

Yuan Shi Kai, general, commander of the New Army, 2nd President of
  the Republic of China, later declared himself to be a new emperor

Rong Ru, commander of the Manchukuo Imperial Manchu Guards

Pan Si Tong, reform leader

Chen Lu Sheng, CERA leader in Yokohama, Japan

Zhang Zhi Dong, Governor of Peking

Tom Leung, CERA leader in Los Angeles, USA

Mao Tse Tung, teacher, later founder of the People's Republic of China

Puy Yi, last Emperor of China

Prince Zaifeng Chun, father of Puy Yi and regent

Li Yuan, general, leader of the Wuchang uprising

Chen Qimei, ally of Sun Yat Sen in Shanghai

Dowager Empress Longyu, consort of the Guangxu Emperor, last regent

Song Jiao Ren, leader of the Kuomintang (Chinese Nationalist Party)
  founded by Sun Yat Sen

Chiang Kai Shek, leader of the Kuomintang and, for a time, leader of
  China, before losing power to Mao Tse Tung and retreating to Taiwan.

The People

HISTORICAL FIGURES
Marco Polo, Venetian adventurer and writer
Kublai Khan, grandson of Genghis Khan and founder of the
  Yuan dynasty
Francis Xavier, Jesuit missionary
Rabban Bar Sawma, Kublai Khan's ambassador to Europe
Zheng He, admiral of the fleet during the Ming dynasty

THE BRITISH
Queen Victoria
Prince Albert, royal consort
Lord James Elgin, Viceroy of India, then high commissioner to
  China and the Far East
John Fryer, head of the translation bureau in Shanghai
Timothy Richard, missionary
Lord Salisbury, prime minister
Lim Boon Keng, physician, educational and social reformer in Singapore,
  host to Kang You Wei
Sir Henry Blake, Governor of Hong Kong

THE FRENCH
King Louis-Philippe
François Guizot, foreign minister
Emperor Napoléon III
Empress Eugénie, his wife
Victor Hugo, author and politician (also Chapter 5)

THE AMERICANS
Matthew Perry, Commodore of the Navy
Abraham Lincoln, 16th president
Anson Burlingame, minister to China
William Seward, secretary of state
Homer Lea, adventurer, military advisor to Kang You Wei, then to
  Sun Yat Sen
David Jordan, founding president of Stanford University, later president
  of the National Education Association (NEA)

Herbert Hoover, mining engineer, later US president
Katharine Carl, portraitist of Empress Cixi
Theodore Roosevelt, 32nd president

THE GERMANS
Karl Marx, political theorist, revolutionary (also Chapter 5)
Otto von Bismarck, chancellor

THE RUSSIANS
Tsar Alexander II (also Chapter 5)
Tsar Alexander III (also Chapter 5)
Vladimir Ilyich Lenin, revolutionary (see Chapter 5)
Leo Tolstoy, essayist and author (see Chapter 5)

THE JAPANESE
Meiji, 122nd emperor of Japan
Itō Hirobumi, first prime minister in the Meiji era
Tōten Miyazaki, philosopher, host to Sun Yat Sen

OTHER NATIONAL LEADERS
Wilfred Laurier, Prime Minister of Canada
Porfirio Díaz, President of Mexico
Gustaf V, King of Sweden
Guiseppe Garibaldi, unifier of Italy
Victor Emmanuel II of Savoy, first King of Italy
Mohandas Gandhi, leader of India's independence movement
  (see Chapters 5 and 6)

CHAPTER FIVE

THE STOLYPINS
Pytor Stolypin, regional governor, minister of internal affairs,
  prime minister
Mikhail Stolypin, his brother
Olga Stolypin, his wife
Maria von Bock (née Stolypin), his daughter and biographer

The People

THE RUSSIANS

Tsar Alexander II

Tsar Alexander III

Tsar Nicholas II, House of Romanov, last tsar and autocrat of
all the Russias

Tsarina Alexandra, his wife

Olga Nikolaevna, their eldest daughter

Tatiana, their second daughter

Dowager Empress Maria (Princess Dagmar of Denmark),
mother of Nicholas II

Dmitri Mendeleev, scientist, teacher of Stolypin

Vladimir Ilyich Ulyanov, later Lenin, leader of the Bolshevik Revolution

Alexander Ulyanov, his brother, executed by order of the tsar

Maria Ulyanov, his mother

Nadezhda Krupskaya (Nadya), his wife, later deputy commissar
for education

Leo Tolstoy, author and essayist

Sonia Tolstoy, his wife

Georgi Plekhanov and Pavel Axelrod, Russian Marxists in Paris

Alexander Odoevsky, poet

Leon Trotsky (Lev Bronstein), leader of the Saint Petersburg Soviet

Julius Martov, Russian Marxist in London

Georgy Gapon, priest and trade union organiser

Alexander Kerensky, lawyer, later prime minister in the
provisional government

Sergei Witte, minister of finance, prime minister

Joseph Stalin, revolutionary leader, later successor to Lenin

Roman Malinovsky, double agent

Inessa Armand, revolutionary, Lenin's lover

Fyodor Dostoyevsky, author

Pyotr Tchaikovsky, composer

Alexander Spiridovich, police general in the Imperial Guard, historian

Dembash, lieutenant, and Yessoulov, captain, Stolypin's bodyguards

Dmitry Bogrov, double agent, assassin of Stolypin

Kouliabka, head of Stolypin's security

Grigori Rasputin, mystical monk

Grand Duke Michael, brother to Tsar Nicholas
Prince Georgy Lvov, leader of the Kadet Party, prime minister
Lavr Kornilov, general
Fanny Kaplan, revolutionary who attempted to assassinate Lenin

THE JAPANESE
Akashi Motojiro, colonel, intelligence officer, later
  Governor-General of Taiwan
Itō Hirobumi, prime minister

THE CHINESE
Kang You Wei, philosopher, leader of the reform movement
Sun Yat Sen, first president of the Republic
Gu Hong Ming, philosopher

THE AMERICANS
Theodore Roosevelt, 32nd president
Henry George, political economist
John Reed, journalist and author

THE GERMANS
Kaiser Wilhelm II
Karl Marx, political theorist, revolutionary
Rosa Luxemburg, Marxist economist and revolutionary
Hugo Eberlein, Communist Party leader

THE FRENCH
Victor Hugo, author and politician
Pierre-Joseph Proudhon, philosopher, politician, and anarchist
Napoléon III

THE BRITISH
Florence Nightingale, nurse, social reformer and founder of
  modern nursing
Alfred Lord Tennyson, poet

OTHER NATIONAL LEADERS
Mohandas Gandhi, leader of India's independence movement
  (also Chapter 6)
King Victor Emmanuel III

CHAPTER SIX
Kofi Annan, seventh Secretary-General of the United Nations,
  Nobel Peace Prize laureate, later chairman of The Elders

HISTORICAL FIGURES OF TWENTIETH-CENTURY CONFLICTS
Joseph Stalin of the Soviet Union
Adolf Hitler of Germany
Benito Mussolini of Italy
Mao Tse Tung of China

INDEPENDENCE LEADERS
Mohandas Gandhi of India
Jawaharlal Nehru of India
Kwame N'Krumah of Ghana
Mao Tse Tung of China

NATIONAL POLITICAL LEADERS
John F. Kennedy, 35th US president
Charles de Gaulle, 1st president of the 5th Republic of France
Richard Nixon, 37th US president
Henry Kissinger, US secretary of state and author
Mikhail Gorbachev, last president of the USSR
Deng Xiaoping, paramount leader of the People's Republic of China
Boris Yeltsin, 1st president of Russia
F.W. de Klerk, last president of South Africa under apartheid
Nelson Mandela, 1st democratically elected President of South Africa
Bill Clinton, 42nd US president
François Mitterrand, 4th president of the 5th Republic of France
Vladimir Putin, 2nd president of Russia
George W. Bush, 43rd US president
Tony Blair, Prime Minister of Britain

Gordon Brown, chancellor of the exchequer,
 later Prime Minister of Britain
Nicolas Sarkozy, 6th president of the 5th Republic of France
Ben Bernanke, chairman of the US Federal Reserve
Henry Paulsen, US secretary of the treasury
Nancy Pelosi, speaker of the US House of Representatives
Emmanuel Macron, 8th president of the 5th Republic of France
Barack Obama, 44th US president
Donald Trump, 45th US president
Mike Pence, US vice-president
Joe Biden, 46th US president

LEADERS OF INTERNATIONAL ORGANISATIONS
Boutros Boutros-Ghali, 6th Secretary-General of the United Nations
Juan Somovia, president of the United Nations General Assembly,
 later director-general of the International Labour Organisation
Àngel Gurría, secretary-general of the Organisation for Economic
 Cooperation and Development (OECD)

AUTHORS
Simon Kuznets and E. Jenks (1953): *Shares of Upper Income Groups in
 Income and savings*
Barbara Tuchman (1984): *The March of Folly*
Francis Fukuyama (1992): *The End of History and the Last Man*
Thomas Piketty (2013/14): *Capital in the 21st Century*
Henry Kissinger (2015): *World Order*
Klaus Schwab (2017): *The Fourth Industrial Revolution*

BUSINESS LEADERS, PHILANTHROPISTS, INFLUENCERS
Henri Dunant, founder of the Red Cross
Klaus Schwab, founder of the World Economic Forum
Bill Gates and Melinda French Gates,
 founders of the Bill and Melinda Gates Foundation
William Buffett, financier,
 major supporter of the Bill and Melinda Gates Foundation
George Soros, financier, founder of the Open Society Foundations

Bernard Arnault and François-Henri Pinault, entrepreneurs,
founders of museums of contemporary art in Paris

OTHER PERSONALITIES

Michael Faraday, scientist renowned for his discoveries of
electricity and magnetism

Thomas Edison, inventor, and entrepreneur, developed electric
power and electric light utilities and motion pictures

Nikola Tesla, inventor, developer of alternating current (AC) motors

Henry Ford, entrepreneur, developer of mass production and
mass consumer advertising

Yuri Gagarin, cosmonaut, first man in space

Neil Armstrong, astronaut, first man on the moon

Queen Elizabeth II of the United Kingdom of Britain and
Northern Ireland, and her consort, Prince Philip

Martin Luther King, civil rights leader

Index

Index

Index

Necker Hospital for Sick Children 5, 57
Nehru, Jawaharlal 240
Neill, Alexander 216
Nelson, Admiral Horatio 85, 90, 242, 280
Nemesis 147–148
Nemours Duc de 119–120
Newsweek 281
Nicholas I, Tsar 137
Nicholas, II, Tsar 6, 193–194, 199–200, 206, 208, 212, 214, 220, 226–228, 232
Nightingale, Florence 195
Nixon, Richard 241
N'Krumah, Kwame 240
Nobel Peace Prize 206, 245, 275
Non-Aligned Movement 240
North, Lord Frederick 12–13, 19–20, 23, 26–27, 30, 36–38, 44, 46, 51, 56, 58, 63
Northern Rock Bank 248

O

Obama, Barack 250, 266
Obolensky's Female Gymnasium 199
Okhrana 197, 210, 223, 225
Olga, Duchess Nikolaevna 193–194, 197–198, 224
On Germany 90
Open Society Foundation 274
Opium War 109, 149, 151
Opium Wars 147, 150, 160, 185
Organisation for Economic Co-operation and Development (OECD) 248, 270, 281, 288
Orléanists 106
Orléans, Duc de (Philippe Egalité) 69, 81,
Orléans, Duc Louis-Philippe (King Louis-Philippe) 102–103, 107–110, 112, 119–120, 124, 136

P

Paine, Thomas, 26, 28, 48, 71
Palmerston, Lord Henry 110, 112
Pan Si Tong 166
Panama Papers 254–255
Party of Order 118, 123, 130–131, 133, 263, 265, 268
Paulson, Henry 249

Paxton Boys 14
Pearl River 145–148
Pelosi, Nancy 249
Pence, Mike 295
Penn, William 13–14
Pennsylvania Gazette 12, 14, 17, 26
Perestroika 242
Perry, Commodore Matthew 149, 155
Philippe, Prince (Comte de Paris) 120, 124
Philip, Prince (Duke of Edinburgh) 252
Phoenix Settlement 202, 215
Piketty, Thomas 254–255, 257–260, 291–292
Pitt, William (the Elder), Lord Chatham 14, 19–20, 48,
Pitt, William (the Younger), 38, 62–63, 81
Place de la Concorde 50
Plekhanov, Georgi 200
Polo, Marco 146, 175, 184
Poor Richard's Almanack 12, 18
Port Arthur 163, 180, 205, 206
Portalis, Jean-Étienne-Marie 62, 66
Potemkin 206
Priestley, Joseph 15, 19, 45
Progress and Poverty 179
Proudhon, Pierre-Joseph 216
Putin, Vladimir 234, 247
Puy Yi, Emperor 183, 188–189, 239

Q

Qing (Dynasty) 146–148, 150, 152, 155–156, 159–162, 167–168, 171–173, 178–179, 182–183, 185–186, 189, 191, 263
Quakers 108
Quantitative easing 250–251, 254
Quebec 109
Queen Charlotte's Ball 33–34, 61, 252–253
Quincy Adams, John 102

R

Rabban Bar Sawma 184
Railways 4, 125, 128–129, 134, 140, 154 ,164, 168, 178, 186–187, 190, 195–196, 205–206, 218, 220, 227, 265, 287
Rasputin, Grigori 226–227, 265
Realpolitik 241
Red Army 232

Index

OCHRE AND RUST

Artefacts and encounters on Australian frontiers

Philip Jones

Ochre and Rust takes nine Aboriginal and colonial artefacts from their museum shelves, and positions them at the centre of these gripping, poignant tales set in the heart of Australia's frontier zone. Philip Jones is a curator and historian, based at the South Australian Museum.

Winner of the 2008 Prime Minister's Literary Award for Non-Fiction

Shortlisted for the 2007 Queensland Premier's Literary Awards

Praise for *Ochre and Rust*:

'This is a beautiful book ... Wakefield Press's overall design, high quality paper, appealing lay-out, plus the numerous, well-reproduced and integrated illustrations and attractive cover, make for an experience that is aesthetic as well as intellectual. This befits the topic: a study of artefacts and encounters on a variety of Australian frontiers. ... This book contains some finely realised prose and elegantly told stories ...'
– Ann McGrath, *Aboriginal History*

Philip Jones is an author and historian based at the South Australian Museum, where he undertakes research on Aboriginal art, history and material culture, and on anthropological, photographic and expeditionary history. He has undertaken fieldwork with Aboriginal people in the Simpson Desert region and, more recently, with Warlpiri people of Yuendumu. He has an abiding interest in unlocking the histories of objects and their collectors.

For more information visit www.wakefieldpress.com.au

FOUR YEARS IN A RED COAT

The Loveday Internment Camp diary of Miyakatsu Koike

Miyakatsu Koike, Hiroko Cockerill, Peter Monteath, and Yuriko Nagata

Before the Japanese Imperial Navy Air Service staged its surprise strike on Pearl Harbor, Miyakatsu Koike lived the privileged life of a Japanese expatriate in the Dutch East Indies. Through the working week he was a conscientious employee of the Yokohama Specie Bank in Surabaya. The rest of his time he could devote to playing golf and tennis, to indulging his hobby photography, and to exploring Java with his wife Fumiko. When his countrymen committed themselves to the 'Greater East Asia War', however, that world came to an abrupt and painful end.

Four Years in a Red Coat presents for the first time in English translation Miyakatsu Koike's wartime diary. It is a keenly observed record of his arrest, his hellish voyage to distant South Australia, his endurance of years in the Loveday Internment Camp, and his return ultimately to a war-ravaged homeland. More than that, it is a testament to one man's calmly stoic triumph over sustained adversity. The scars of his war are indelible, yet Koike emerges from it with his humanity not just intact but enhanced.

Miyakatsu Koike worked in 1941 for a Japanese bank in Indonesia (at the time known as the Dutch East Indies). When Japan entered World War II, he was arrested by Dutch authorities and, eventually, transferred to Australia's Loveday – the largest World War II internment camp in the country. Koike remained in Loveday until February 1946, and wrote a diary of his experiences during the war.

Hiroko Cockerill is an honorary research fellow at the University of Queensland, specialising in translation studies.

Peter Monteath is Professor of History at Flinders University in Adelaide.

Dr Yuriko Nagata is an Honorary Senior Research Fellow with the School of Languages and Cultures of the University of Queensland..

For more information visit www.wakefieldpress.com.au

Wakefield Press is an independent publishing and
distribution company based in Adelaide, South Australia.
We love good stories and publish beautiful books.
To see our full range of books, please visit our website at
www.wakefieldpress.com.au
where all titles are available for purchase.
To keep up with our latest releases, news and events,
subscribe to our monthly newsletter.

Find us!

Facebook: www.facebook.com/wakefield.press
Twitter: www.twitter.com/wakefieldpress
Instagram: www.instagram.com/wakefieldpress